Uncrewed Vessels and International Law

Maritime Cooperation in East Asia

Series Editors

Seokwoo Lee (*Inha University Law School*)
Keyuan Zou (*University of Central Lancashire*)

VOLUME 14

The titles published in this series are listed at *brill.com/mcea*

Uncrewed Vessels and International Law

Edited by

Haiwen Zhang
Yao Huang
Lijuan Xing

BRILL | NIJHOFF

LEIDEN | BOSTON

Library of Congress Cataloging-in-Publication Data

Names: Zhang, Haiwen, editor. | Huang, Yao, 1964- editor. | Xing, Lijuan, editor.
Title: Uncrewed vessels and international law / edited by Haiwen Zhang, Yao Huang, Lijuan Xing.
Description: Leiden ; Boston : Brill/Nijhoff, 2024. | Series: Maritime cooperation in East Asia, 2405-934X ; volume 14 | Includes bibliographical references and index.
Identifiers: LCCN 2024017864 | ISBN 9789004706262 (hardback) | ISBN 9789004706279 (ebook)
Subjects: LCSH: Automatic pilot (Ships) | Ships–Automation. | Shipbuilding industry–Technological innovations–Law and legislation. | War, Maritime (International law) | Remote submersibles. | Navigation–Automation. | Shipment of goods–Law and legislation. | Law of the sea. | Vehicles, Remotely piloted.
Classification: LCC K4176.A98 U57 2024 | DDC 343.09/62–dc23/eng/20240511
LC record available at https://lccn.loc.gov/2024017864

Typeface for the Latin, Greek, and Cyrillic scripts: "Brill". See and download: brill.com/brill-typeface.

ISSN 2405-934X
ISBN 978-90-04-70626-2 (hardback)
ISBN 978-90-04-70627-9 (e-book)
DOI 10.1163/9789004706279

This book is printed on acid-free paper and produced in a sustainable manner.

Contents

Figures, Table and Maps

Figures

Tables

Maps

Notes on Editors and Contributors

Editors

Yao Huang
Lead Expert in the Innovation Team of Marine Strategy and Law, Southern Marine Science and Engineering Guangdong Laboratory (Zhuhai); Professor at Sun Yat-sen University School of Law, where she served as the Dean from 2015 to 2020. She is the founding Director of the Center for Ocean Law Studies of Sun Yat-sen University and founding Editor-in-Chief of Local Legislation Journal. She has degrees of LL.B. & LL.M. from Sun Yat-sen University and Ph.D. in international law from Peking University, China. She was a visiting scholar at Washington University in St. Louis and a visiting fellow at the Lauterpacht Centre for International Law, University of Cambridge. Dr. Huang specializes in public international law, particularly international legal theory, law of the sea, use of force, dispute settlement. She has published widely on these fields.

Lijuan Xing
Associate Professor at Sun Yat-sen University School of Law and research fellow of the Southern Marine Science and Engineering Guangdong Laboratory (Zhuhai), concentrating in International and Comparative Law, with specialization in International Economic Law, Public International Law, Maritime Law, and International Trade Law. She earned her LL.B. and LL.M. degrees from Dalian Maritime University School of Law and her Ph.D. in Economics from Dongbei University of Finance and Economics in China before undertaking advanced US legal studies at the University of Kansas, USA, where she earned her S.J.D. degree in 2012. Her principal recent books include: *The Essentials of Chinese Maritime Law* (2017), *Behind the Multilateral Trading System: Legal Indigenization and the WTO in Comparative Perspective* (2014), *Legal Transparency in Dynastic China: The Legalist-Confucianist Debate and Good Governance in Chinese Tradition* (2013), and *Asian Development Bank: International Encyclopaedia of Law—Intergovernmental Organizations* (3rd edition 2014; 4th edition 2018), which were published in the United States, the Netherlands, and Hong Kong SAR. Dr. Xing has also presented and published book chapters and law journal articles in the United States, the United Kingdom, Canada, the Netherlands, Australia, Korea, Hong Kong SAR, and the mainland China.

Haiwen Zhang
Ph.D. in International Law; Lead Expert, Innovation Team of Marine Strategy and Law, Southern Marine Science and Engineering Guangdong Laboratory

(Zhuhai); Director-General, Senior research fellow, China Institute for Marine Affairs (CIMA), Ministry of Natural Resources (PRC). She serves as an Adjunct Professor, in the Institute of International Law of Wuhan University, the South China Sea Institute of Xiamen University and the Ocean College of Zhejiang University. Professor Zhang has participated in several bilateral negotiations on maritime issues between China and its maritime neighbors, and multilateral negotiations including the BBNJ negotiation organized by the United Nations. She has been engaged in research on the law of the sea and maritime policy for 30 years and had managed more than 200 research projects. She published more than ten books. She received her doctorate in international law in Peking University in 1995. She has served as Director-General, the Department of International Cooperation (2013–2017) and Director-General, Legal and Policy Office (1997–2003) of the former State Oceanic Administration (SOA) and a Judge of the Intermediate People's Court of Jianyang District, Fujian Province, PRC (1984–1989).

Contributors

Haibo Chen
Associate Professor at Ningbo University Law School. She obtained her master's and doctorate degrees in law from Dalian Maritime University and Xiamen University respectively. Since 1997, she has been involved in teaching and conducting research in maritime law, law of the sea, and WTO law, and has published many articles. One notable contribution is titled 'Competent International Organizations and the Development of International Legal System for Marine Scientific Research' (SJTU Law Review 1 (2023)), reprinted by International Law of Information Center for Social Sciences, RUC. She has also co-authored and co-translated many books and textbooks.

Roman Dremliuga
Professor of law at the Far Eastern Federal University, Vladivostok, Russia. He currently works at the Department of International Public and Private Law, Far Eastern Federal University. Roman does research in Cyber Law, Cybercrime Law, and the Law of the Sea. His current project is 'AI and Law'.

Junming Gong
Master's student at the Wuhan University China Institute of Boundary and Ocean Studies and the Leiden University Law School. His research areas are the law of the sea, maritime law, environmental law, intelligent ship, green shipping decarbonization, African ocean economy, and south-east Asia international studies.

Ping Guo

Research Fellow of Southern Marine Science and Engineering Guangdong Laboratory (Zhuhai); Professor in Maritime Law and Ocean Environmental Law, School of law of Sun Yat-sen University (SYSU); Executive Director of The Supreme People's Court Fourth Civil Judicial Division Research Centre for International Maritime and Ocean Law (SYSU), China. Arbitrator of Several arbitration Committees, such as CMAC, SCIA, GCIA, DAC, etc. Doctor of Law (2006) and Master of Law (1998) in Dalian Maritime University (DMU). Being Lecturer (1995–1999), Associate Professor (1999–2003), Professor (2003–2018) in law school of DMU, Professor (2018-now) in law school of SYSU. Visiting Research Scholar in Institute of Maritime Law of Law School of University of Southampton of UK (2000–2001), Fulbright Scholar in Maritime Law Center of Tulane University of USA (2007–2008).

Yao Huang

Lead Expert in the Innovation Team of Marine Strategy and Law, Southern Marine Science and Engineering Guangdong Laboratory (Zhuhai); Professor at Sun Yat-sen University School of Law, where she served as the Dean from 2015 to 2020. She is the founding Director of the Center for Ocean Law Studies of Sun Yat-sen University and founding Editor-in-Chief of Local Legislation Journal. She has degrees of LL.B. & LL.M. from Sun Yat-sen University and Ph.D. in international law from Peking University, China. She was a visiting scholar at Washington University in St. Louis and a visiting fellow at the Lauterpacht Centre for International Law, University of Cambridge. Dr. Huang specializes in public international law, particularly international legal theory, law of the sea, use of force, dispute settlement. She has published widely on these fields.

Valentin Koshkin

Ph.D., a scholar and researcher specializing in Public International Law, the Law of the Sea, and Russian Civil Law. He earned his Ph.D. in International Law from Sun Yat-sen University. Dr. Koshkin's research primarily revolves around the delimitation of the continental shelf beyond 200 nautical miles and the regulatory aspects of autonomous vessels. His scholarly contributions have been featured in prestigious journals like the "Arctic Review on Law and Politics." Presently, Dr. Koshkin serves as an international lecturer at the School of Law of Jilin University.

Chenhong Liu

Ph.D., Associate Professor of Dalian Maritime University. Her main research fields are international law theory, law of the sea and maritime law. She has published five English articles in SSCI journals, more than ten Chinese papers in authoritative journals such as CSSCI. She presided over two Subtopics of the National Social Science Foundation Major Project and four provincial and ministerial level projects, and won the title of 'the first batch of Young Talents in Philosophy and Social Sciences of Liaoning Province'.

Dan Liu
Associate Research Professor with the Center for Polar and Deep Ocean Development, KoGuan Law School, Shanghai Jiao Tong University. Her research areas include public international law, the law of the sea and polar law. She has published four monographies on international law. Her publications in English and Chinese have appeared in more than 40 journals, such as Marine Policy, Ocean & Coastal Management, the Yearbook of Polar law, the Arctic Yearbook and Chinese Yearbook of International Law. She has been principal organizer of almost 20 research projects regarding International Law. She served as visiting fellow at the Stefansson Arctic Institute of Iceland, the East Asian Institute of the National University of Singapore and the Albany Law School of the U.S. As one of the Chinese delegations, she has actively participated in various rounds of track-II dialogues on the issues of the law of the sea and the Arctic.

Zhaoran Lin
Postdoctoral fellow both of Institute of Ocean Research and School of Law, Peking University. He was selected in a state-funded continuous master-doctor program in 2017 and obtained his doctoral degree of law in School of Law, Sun Yat-sen University. He was also a visiting scholar in the Max Planck Institute of Comparative Public Law and International Law, Heidelberg, Germany in 2021–2022. His research interests and publications include: law of the sea, law of war, law of territorial acquisition, history and theory of international law.

Song Pan
Born in Dalian, Liaoning, China, studied Law (Maritime Law Direction) at the Law School of Dalian Maritime University for undergraduate degree. He obtained a Bachelor's degree in Law in 2019 and is currently a Master's degree graduate student in Law (Marine Rule of Law Direction) at the National Institute of Marine Governance and Development of Dalian Maritime University. His research focuses on ocean law and international law.

Dhiana Puspitawati
Assoc. Prof. Dr. Dhiana Puspitawati is a lecturer at Faculty of Law, Universitas Brawijaya, Indonesia. She obtained her PhD from University of Queensland, Australia. Her area of research interest is law of the sea and maritime policy.

Mohd Hazmi Mohd Rusli

Lecturer at the Faculty of Syariah and Law, Universiti Sains Islam Malaysia (USIM). He obtained his PhD from University of Wollongong, Australia in 2012. He was appointed as visiting professor/research fellow at universities worldwide namely Far Eastern Federal University, Vladivostok, Russia (2014, 2015, 2017 & 2018), Xiamen University, China (2019), Universitas Brawijaya, Indonesia (2018, 2021 & 2023) and the Australian National University, Canberra (2022). He has written numerous articles published in high-impact journals and popular magazines/newspapers on the law of the sea and public international law.

Wei Wu

Ph.D., Associate Professor in China Institute of Boundary and Ocean Studies, Wuhan University. Dr. Wei Wu was an Erasmus Mundus Programmes Scholar, a Visiting Scholar to Deusto Univeristy, Law School in Spain. Co-teaching and giving lectures about Chinese Legal System, and she was also a Visiting Scholar in Lauterpacht Centre of Internaional Law in Cambridge University and in Law school in Edinburgh University. Her research area is the Law of the Sea, Maritime Law, Artificial island building, fishery law and enforcement, Smart ship and Green shipping decarbonization. And She makes publications on these issues, which covers three books and more than 30 papers.

Bo Yu

Graduate student at Harbin Engineering University, studying for a master's degree in law. Her main research interests are legal issues on maritime autonomous surface ship and the Arctic legal governance.

Xue Yuan

Professor in Law at Department of Law, School of Humanities and Social Sciences, Harbin Engineering University. She graduated from Law School Jilin University with Doctor degree of Law. She has been a visiting scholar in Law School of University of California, Berkeley 2007–2008. At present, her research fields focus on Arctic legal governance, legal issues on maritime autonomous surface ship, legal governance of international maritime emission reduction, legal issues on BBNJ, etc.

Shuning Zhang

Ph.D. candidate in international law at the Law School of Sun Yat-sen University. She holds an LLB from South China University of Technology and an LL.M. from Sun Yat-sen University. Her fields of interest include law of the sea, law of armed conflict, etc.

Introduction: Charting the Course on the Autonomous Ocean

*Haiwen Zhang**, *Yao Huang***, *and Lijuan Xing****

Whereas uncrewed vessels have the least connection to international law, they have the most connection to international law. This seemingly paradoxical statement depicts the complex and ambiguous relationship between uncrewed vessels and international law.

1 Contours

A key feature of this nascent era of autonomy is taking place on the world's oceans.[1] Uncrewed vessels are deemed as 'an exciting technological development and have the potential to revolutionize the maritime world'.[2] Most agree that autonomous technology will serve a multitude of beneficial uses—military, administration, civil, commercial, recreational, etc.[3] Uncrewed

* Haiwen Zhang, Lead Expert, Innovation Team of Marine Strategy and Law, Southern Marine Science and Engineering Guangdong Laboratory (Zhuhai); Director-General, Senior research fellow, China Institute for Marine Affairs (CIMA), Ministry of Natural Resources (PRC).

** Yao Huang, Professor at Sun Yat-sen University School of Law; Lead Expert, Innovation Team of Marine Strategy and Law, Southern Marine Science and Engineering Guangdong Laboratory (Zhuhai).

*** Lijuan Xing, Associate Professor at Sun Yat-sen University School of Law; research fellow, Innovation Team of Marine Strategy and Law, Southern Marine Science and Engineering Guangdong Laboratory (Zhuhai).

1 *See* Joel Coito, 'Maritime Autonomous Surface Ships: New Possibilities—and Challenges—in Ocean Law and Policy' (2021) 97 Intl L Studies 259, 260; Paul Dean & Henry Clack, 'Autonomous Shipping and Maritime Law, in New Technologies' in Baris Soyer & Andrew Tettenborn (eds), *Artificial Intelligence and Shipping Law in the 21st Century* (Informa Law from Routledge 2020) 67, 67; Stephanie Guerra, 'Ready About, Here Comes AI: Potential Maritime Law Challenges for Autonomous Shipping' (2017–2018) 30 USF Maritime LJ 69, 73.

2 Paul W Pritchett, 'Ghost Ships: Why the Law Should Embrace Unmanned Vessel Technology' (2015) 40 Tulane Maritime LJ 197, 225.

3 *See* Craig H Allen, 'Determining the Legal Status of Unmanned Maritime Vehicles: Formalism vs Functionalism' (2018) 49 JMLC 477, 512; Coito (n 1) 261–64; Samantha Jordan, 'Captain, My Captain: A Look at Autonomous Ships and How They Should Operate under

 | DOI:10.1163/9789004706279_002

vessels can rapidly expand human possibilities on the ocean, shattering many of the practical and economic limitations that have constrained maritime operations for centuries.[4] Though the concept of uncrewed vessel is a relatively recent development, estimates indicate that such ships may set sail sooner than expected,[5] with little room left for objection in their wake.[6] The impact on the shipping industry of the replacement within the proximate future of the hard work of masters, ships' officers and crews by computer programs, artificial intelligence, or assistance from shore-based controllers has the potential to change the social and economic parameters of the shipping industry as much as the introduction of steel construction and steam propulsion did in the nineteenth century.[7]

That reality carries with it the promise of a more capable global regime for autonomous operations on the ocean.[8] Both advantages (mainly including the prospect of enhanced economic efficiency and safety and better protection of the environment) and risks (such as those in legal, ethical, labor, human rights, and cybersecurity fields) have been extensively discussed in the existing literature.[9] While uncrewed vessels may be the future of navigation and shipping and provide global benefits, current international regulations must change to accommodate the evolving technology that those vessels represent. Autonomous technology at sea has been a perennial topic in jurisprudence, with focal issues of (i) concept, categorization, and legal status of an uncrewed vessel; (ii) applicability of the prevalent international regulatory framework thereto; (iii) maintaining, changing, or creating specific rules therefor; as well as (iv) perceived or recommended courses of actions at the domestic, regional, and multilateral levels.

Admiralty Law' (2020) 30 Indiana Intl & Com L Rev 283, 284–87; Annie Brett, 'Regulating the Autonomous Ocean' (2022) 88 Brooklyn L Rev 1, 1–4; Eric Van Hooydonk, 'The Law of Unmanned Merchant Shipping—An Exploration' (2014) 20 JIML 403, 404.

4 Brett (n 3) 1.

5 Michal Chwedczuk, 'Analysis of the Legal Status of Unmanned Commercial Vessels in U.S. Admiralty and Maritime Law' (2016) 47 JMLC 123, 125.

6 Guerra (n 1) 90.

7 Van Hooydonk (n 3) 423.

8 Coito (n 1) 306.

9 *See* Danielle Gabay, Roee Furman & Dov Greenbaum, 'Autonomous Ships: Engines of Environmental Protection' (2023) 47 Tulane Maritime LJ 403; Johan Schelin, 'The Responsibility for Unmanned Ships—Shipmaster's Position' (*Maritime Law Library*, April 2020) <https://www.maritimelawlibrary.se/wp-content/uploads/2020/04/Responsibility-for-Unmanned-Ships.pdf> assessed 7 January 2024; Guerra (n 1); Gershon Hasin, 'Ocean Governance in the 21st Century: A "New Package-Deal"' (2023) 48 Yale J Intl L 223; Van Hooydonk (n 3); Lindsay I. McCarl, 'Untethering UMVs From Vessels: Why the United States Should Construct a New Environmental Legal Scheme for Unmanned Maritime Vehicles' (2023) 127 Dickinson L Rev 469.

This volume expects to offer some insights in legal implications of the advent and use of uncrewed vessels for the evolution of international law from a perspective that has not been found in the extant literature—that is, a perspective both international and comparative, both normative and functional, and with an accentuation of eastern views which should not have been absent from the current jurisprudence that has witnessed a flourish of western ones. This Introduction discusses such cross-cutting issues in this volume as terminology, fundamental assumptions of our analysis, source of doubts about the prevalent research methodology, and the aims and structure of this volume, with a view to navigating the reader through a variety of topics covered hereby.

2 Terminology

Terminology in this field is complex, inconsistent, and sometimes contradictory.[10] A wide range of terms have been used when uncrewed vessels are discussed.[11] Basically, control of uncrewed vessels is performed in essentially two ways—by remote control or by autonomous control.[12] Further classification thereof has been made in accordance with interrelated but differentiated standards such as 'level of human intervention', 'locations of human operators', 'sophistication of onboard decision-making processes', or 'degree of autonomy'.[13]

In effect, the dichotomy between crewed and uncrewed vessels may have represented an over-simplification of the reality.[14] For one thing, the existing categories of levels of autonomy may be criticized for not reflecting fully and

10 Gabay, Furman & Greenbaum (n 9) 415.

11 Some commonly used ones are unmanned vehicle (UV), marine unmanned vehicle (MUV), unmanned surface vehicle (USV), unmanned aerial vehicle (UAV), unmanned underwater (or undersea) vehicle (UUV), unmanned combat underwater vehicle (UCUV), unmanned combat surface vehicle (UCSV), unmanned combat vehicle (UCV), remotely operated vehicle (ROV), Maritime Autonomous Surface Ship (MASS), unmanned maritime vehicle (UMV), unmanned maritime system (UMS), unmanned ground vehicle (UGV), autonomous vehicles (AV). *See* Natalie Klein, 'Maritime Autonomous Vehicles within the International Law Framework to Enhance Maritime Security' (2019) 95 Intl L Studies 244, 248; Van Hooydonk (n 3) 403–4.

12 Robert Veal & Henrik Ringbom, 'Unmanned Ships and the International Regulatory Framework' (*UiO-DUO*, January 2017) <https://www.duo.uio.no/bitstream/handle/10852/61634/Unmanned-Ships-and-the-International-Regulatory-Framework-JIML-01-06-17-RV.pdf?sequence=5&isAllowed=y> accessed 29 December 2023.

13 Guerra (n 1) 72; Chwedczuk (n 5) 128; Klein (n 11) 248; Jordan (n 3) 288; IMO's four levels: IMO, 'Autonomous Shipping" (*IMO*) <https://www.imo.org/en/MediaCentre/HotTopics/Pages/Autonomous-shipping.aspx> assessed 6 January 2024.

14 Schelin (n 9) 40.

properly the entire picture of technological development in this field, partially because most uncrewed vessels are 'somewhere in the middle of the spectrum, making them difficult to categorize.'[15] In addition, rather than discussing different types of uncrewed vessels, the level of autonomy forms a sliding scale where the same ship can during a certain period of time be operated manually and during other periods be fully autonomous.[16]

By referring to 'uncrewed' in the title of this volume, we intend to elide all degrees of autonomy that exist in relation to vessels, and do not intend to indicate or limit any type of control (remote or autonomous), any extent of human intervention (reduced or none), any purpose a vessel is employed for (such as navy, war, scientific research, commercial shipping, recreation, and law enforcement), or any location (blow, on, or above the surface of the waters). The term 'uncrewed' is used to gloss over all those distinctions and to encompass the varying degrees of autonomy. Concurring with the observation that the relevant level of autonomy will impact profoundly on legal questions,[17] the contributors of this volume refer to those different classifications individually in the following chapters, where a distinction needs to be drawn.

We also note that significant discussion has emerged around the word 'vessel' or 'ship',[18] particularly given the divergent definitions thereof which are provided in varied international instruments.[19] The legal definitions of 'ship' and 'vessel' differ greatly from one international maritime convention to another, because they are 'very much a function of the subject matter concerned'.[20] Those maritime conventions dealing with specific topics apply their own definitions tailored to the matter at hand, either public or private law in nature.[21] National maritime laws give an equally heterogeneous picture.[22]

The ship-vessel debate remains pertinent in the international regulation of autonomous navigation and shipping settings. The heterogeneity of definitions of ship or vessel reflects in international conventions the diverse ways autonomous technology is currently being used in the marine realm.[23] The legal status of uncrewed vessels, accordingly, will depend on a contextual

---

15 Brett (n 3) 6.
16 Schelin (n 9) 40.
17 Veal & Ringbom (n 12) 18–20.
18 Klein (n 11) 250.
19 ibid; Allen (n 3) 480.
20 Van Hooydonk (n 3) 406.
21 ibid.
22 ibid 408.
23 Brett (n 3) 6.

analysis when considering ordinary meaning of vessel and ship. For the purposes of this volume, we use the term 'vessel' to embrace all the possible structures that may fall within the scope of any of the two, except where a distinction is drawn.

3 Assumptions

The first assumption, as is posited at the beginning of this Introduction, that uncrewed vessels have hardly any connection to international law stems from the unanimous observation that none of the prevalent international legal instruments had considered modern autonomous technology at sea when entering into force. After all, when those treaties were written, the standards of minimum and proper manning did not contemplate an unmanned vessel.[24] In other words, autonomous technology is being caught in laws that were never meant to apply to it.[25] Some international rules, such as those in the Convention on the International Regulation for Preventing Collisions at Sea (COLREGS) and the International Convention for the Safety of Life at Sea (SOLAS), are not a mere framework or constitutive treaty—they are prescriptive regulations,[26] presupposing human crews and at times demanding uniquely human judgments.[27]

An unforeseeable application of the existing rules to uncrewed vessels can thus theoretically and intrinsically refute the applicability thereof to those vessels,[28] in that those vessels are not encompassed by the ordinary meaning to be given to ship or vessel in the context of the treaty containing the same and in the light of the object and purpose of that treaty.[29] Also, there is insufficient State practice to have established, at minimum, a new norm in this field.[30] Based on this line of normative analysis, uncrewed vessels have the

24 Nanci K. Carr, 'As the Role of the Driver Changes with Autonomous Vehicle Technology, So, Too, Must the Law Change' (2020) 51 Saint Mary's LJ 811, 835.

25 Pritchett (n 2) 225; Malgorzata Materna, 'Adjusting the Aperture: The International Law Case for Qualifying Unmanned Vessels as Warships' (2023) 100 Intl L Studies 452, 476–77.

26 Allen (n 3) 505.

27 Coito (n 1) 306.

28 *See*, e.g., Materna (n 25) 476–80.

29 Vienna Convention on the Law of Treaties (adopted 23 May 1969, entered into force 27 January 1980) 1155 UNTS 331, art 31.

30 Materna (n 25) 476.

least connection to the prevalent international regulatory framework, and a new framework that specifically applies to uncrewed vessels must be drafted.[31]

The second assumption that uncrewed vessels and international law are closely interrelated is posited based on the fact that, the active building, testing, and deployment of uncrewed vessels by naval, administrative and industrial stakeholders keep the questions as to the effectiveness of existing rules raised to international law. The rights and obligations of different stakeholders—such as States (including flag, coastal, port, small-island, land-locked, and geographically-disadvantages States), international organizations (e.g., the United Nations, the institutions under the United Nations Convention on the Law of the Sea (UNCLOS), and non-governmental organizations, military forces, administrative agencies (especially those with law enforcement functions), commercial parties (like shipowners, financial institutions, insurers, brokers and agencies, as well as investors), and workforce (such as masters, seafarers, pilots, tugmasters, traffic controllers, and stevedores)[32]—need to be revisited on a large scale, against the backdrop of an enlarged international fleet consisting of both crewed and uncrewed vessels.

The most affected legal areas by the advent and use of uncrewed vessels are the *lex maritima* which embraces 'a wide range of laws, conventions, and other legal sources that regulate ships and their operations,'[33] and the law of the sea which deals with the rights and obligations of States over the sea,[34] despite possible overlaps between these two areas in both conceptual and regulatory proximity. One commentator categorizes the greatly influenced international rules into three groups: one for state jurisdiction; one for safety and environmental concerns at sea, along with training and watchkeeping standards; and one adopted to address private law issues.[35]

In the public law arena, the pertinent conventions include typically UNCLOS,[36] the SOLAS,[37] the International Convention for the Prevention of

31 ibid.

32 Van Hooydonk (n 3) 411–18.

33 Jordan (n 3) 295.

34 Veal & Ringbom (n 12).

35 Jordan (n 3) 295.

36 United Nations Convention on the Law of the Sea (adopted 10 December 1982, entered into force 1 November 1994) 1833 UNTS 397.

37 International Convention for the Safety of Life at Sea (adopted 1 November 1974, entered into force 25 May 1980) 1184 UNTS 2.

Pollution from Ships (MARPOL),[38] the COLREGS,[39] the International Convention on Standards of Training, Certification and Watchkeeping for Seafarers (STCW),[40] and the Maritime Labor Convention (MLC).[41] Under those conventions, frequently-revisited topics include right of innocent passage;[42] right of hot pursuit;[43] right of visit;[44] law enforcement regimes at sea (including those against drug trafficking, terrorism, migrant smuggling, search and rescue, etc.);[45] criminal activities by a non-State actor;[46] scientific research activities and intelligence gathering for security purposes;[47] freedom of navigation on the high seas, the exclusive economic zones and the areas above the continental shelf;[48] ship registration; state immunity;[49] jurisdiction, rights, and obligations of flag, coastal, and port States;[50] etc.

In the private law field, almost all those addressing shipping activities and operations have been re-examined through the lens of autonomous technology, such as the International Convention for the Unification of Certain Rules of Law relating to Bills of Lading (the Hague Rules),[51] United Nations Convention for the International Carriage of Goods Wholly or Partly by Sea (the Rotterdam Rules),[52] the Athens Convention Relating to the Carriage of Passengers and Their Luggage by Sea,[53] the Convention on Limitation of Liability

38 International Convention for the Prevention of Pollution from Ships (adopted 2 November 1973, entered into force 2 October 1983) 1340 UNTS 61.

39 Convention on the International Regulation for Preventing Collisions at Sea (adopted 20 October 1972, entered into force 15 July 1977) 1050 UNTS 16.

40 International Convention on Standards of Training, Certification and Watchkeeping for Seafarers (adopted 7 July 1978, entered into force 28 April 1984) 1361 UNTS 2.

41 Maritime Labour Convention (adopted 23 February 2006, entered into force 20 August 2013) 2952 UNTS 3.

42 Klein (n 11) 252.

43 ibid 253.

44 ibid 256.

45 ibid 253.

46 ibid.

47 *See* generally, ibid.

48 Van Hooydonk (n 3) 409.

49 ibid 425–27.

50 Guerra (n 1) 71.

51 International Convention for the Unification of Certain Rules of Law relating to Bills of Lading (The Hague Rules) (adopted 28 August 1924, entered into force 2 June 1931) 1938 AJIL 121.

52 United Nations Convention for the International Carriage of Goods Wholly or Partly by Sea (The Rotterdam Rules) (adopted 11 December 2008 UNGA A/RES/63/122).

53 Athens Convention Relating to the Carriage of Passengers and Their Luggage by Sea (adopted 13 December 1974, entered into force 28 April 1987) 1463 UNTS 19.

for Maritime Claims (LLMC),[54] the International Convention on Civil Liability for Oil Pollution Damage (CLC),[55] the York-Antwerp Rules (YAR),[56] and the International Convention on Salvage.[57] The revisited topics comprise various concepts and regimes—such as unseaworthiness, manning, welfare of crewmen and operators, personal injuries, salvage, insurance, collision, general average, ship building, marine pollution, scope of liable parties, allocation of liabilities, personification of ships, pilotage, and Captain's law.[58]

The following excerpt offers a brief explanation as to why the legality of many activities at sea will be inevitably affected by the involvement of an uncrewed vessel:

> [W]hen a challenge to the legality of certain actions arises, the preliminary questions remain: where is it happening and what is happening? It is in the latter setting that we start asking whether [an uncrewed vessel] is a ship or a vessel in relation to the activities being undertaken. Who is on board may become relevant once we start articulating the rights and duties that adhere to different actors depending on where something is happening and what is happening.[59]

Apart from the *lex maritima* and the law of the sea, such areas in international law as the law of war, law of armed conflicts, international humanitarian law (*jus in bello*), and international environmental law, are being seriously challenged by the use of uncrewed vessels as well. The past decade has also witnessed a surge of discussions from those perspectives.[60]

54 Convention on Limitation of Liability for Maritime Claims (adopted 19 November 1976, entered into force 1 December 1986) 1456 UNTS 221.

55 International Convention on Civil Liability for Oil Pollution Damage (adopted 29 November 1969, entered into force 19 June 1975) 973 UNTS 3.

56 York-Antwerp Rules (latest version adopted by Comité Maritime International Assembly on 6 May 2016) <https://comitemaritime.org/work/york-antwerp-rules-yar/> assessed 17 January 2024.

57 International Convention on Salvage (adopted 28 April 1989, entered into force 14 July 1996) 1953 UNTS 165.

58 Guerra (n 1) 141–56; Jordan (n 3) 295; Chwedczuk (n 5) 128; Henry H. Perritt, Jr. 'Who Pays When Drones Crash?' (2017) 21 UCLA J L & Technology 1, 12–13; Gabay, Furman & Greenbaum (n 9) 420–28; Sean T Pribyl, 'Autonomous Transport Claims' 52 Brief 46, 49. *See* also, generally, Schelin (n 9); Eliseo Sierra-Noguero, 'The Work and Legal Liability of Classification Societies in the Certification of Autonomous Vessels' (2023) Tulane Maritime LJ 387.

59 Klein (n 11) 251.

60 ibid 246; *see* generally Remus Titiriga, 'Autonomy of Military Robots: Assessing the Technical and Legal ("jus in bello") Thresholds' (2016) 32 John Marshall J Information Technology & Privacy L 57.

As one observer detects, in response to such a wide range of intersections between uncrewed vessels and international law, some scholars, arguing that autonomous technology is already here and therefore must be accommodated by international law, have displayed 'symptoms of confirmation bias' in their analysis on the applicability of existing international rules to uncrewed vessels.[61] Those who have embraced such a bias, though also acknowledging that what should not be missing from the applicability discussions 'are the established principles of treaty interpretation and, when appropriate, assessment of customary law rules', do not concede the conclusive effect of the foreseeability test in treaty interpretation.[62] For instance, as to whether UNCLOS applies to uncrewed vessels, one scholar views that the foreseeability test contravenes the predictability of UNCLOS, as is expressed in the following text:

> UNCLOS … generally avoids the need to formulate more precise obligations of flag states by referring to an abstract, and continuously changing, set of international rules to be developed elsewhere. In this way it avoids 'freezing' the requirements at a given point in time or at a given technical level, while still preserving the international character of the rules in question.[63]

Similarly, it has been held that a restrictive reading of the warship definition would be inconsistent with the historical context and purpose of the international conventions that gave rise to that definition.[64] Holding that a lack of onboard crew does not fundamentally change the nature of a ship,[65] some authorities defy the non-applicability of current law to uncrewed vessels just based on manning conditions, as is explained below:

> While existing legal regimes may not have been drafted in anticipation of the development of vessels capable of independent navigation, this condition alone does not preclude the application of those principles to vessels incorporating these technological advancements. The legal frameworks themselves do not need to be changed; rather, we must

61 Allen (n 3) 491.

62 ibid 491–92.

63 Veal & Ringbom (n 12).

64 Materna (n 25) 482.

65 Simon McKenzie, 'When Is a Ship a Ship? Use by State Armed Forces of Uncrewed Maritime Vehicles and the United Nations Convention on the Law of the Sea' (2020) 21 Melbourne J Intl L 373, 401.

> become accustomed to simply applying them to the maritime systems of today—and tomorrow.[66]

One commentator observes that, if foreseeability serves as the basis of assessment alone, the need for a definition which was integrated into international law at a later stage, such as 'warship', would itself seem to come into question when considering today's naval warfare activities and the eradicated practice of privateering.[67] According thereto, the mere fact that unmanned vessels may not have been foreseen at the time of the drafting of the definition of a warship does not preclude the application of the existing legal framework to this novel development in the maritime arena.[68] It is further held that, strict readings of this type of new concepts would have necessitated new rules for a variety of technological advancements in naval warfare or challenges of interpretation where no directly applicable precedent exists, and this is not the first such instance challenging the traditional understanding of the elements of the warship definition.[69]

The risk of applying the foreseeability test, according to that commentator, lies in that 'armed, unmanned vessels will remain outside any [international] framework at all—including any potential accountability mechanism for flag States.'[70] Accompanying that scenario will be an increasing difficulty in getting States to agree on new rules, as is stated below:

> State practice is already evolving in this area and is likely to continue at an increasingly rapid pace. It would be imprudent to assume that the very States investing heavily in unmanned maritime capabilities will agree to new rules or a new legal framework that has the potential to slow or limit those technological advancements.[71]

Those rejecting the foreseeability test in treaty interpretation have demonstrated a strong inclination toward the continued application of current law, as is recapped in the following text:

> [W]e may need to become more satisfied with the application of current law to developing technologies and consider how they may be used

66 Materna (n 25) 482.
67 ibid 477.
68 ibid.
69 ibid.
70 ibid 480.
71 ibid 481.

> in compliance with those legal principles. It is a much more straightforward task to require new systems to fit established paradigms than it is to attempt to enforce compliance with a novel framework of legal principles that are unlikely to receive broad consensus in the international community.[72]

To encapsulate the opinions reviewed above, what the policymakers and legislators should do is not to rely on the mistaken premise that the rapidly advancing new technology can be outlawed outright, but to consider the application of longstanding legal principles to the use of the ever-growing number of technological advancements, with a view to avoiding failures to appropriately place the burden on States to employ new means and methods of navigation and shipping in compliance with international law, especially the current era of competition involving autonomy.[73]

Once having circumvented the foreseeability test, those scholars usually examine first the inclusion of an uncrewed vessel by the pertinent concept of ship or vessel under a given international instrument. Some contend that 'for the purposes of the law of the sea unmanned vessels must be regarded as ships.'[74] It is argued both that UNCLOS references to 'vessel' or 'ship' apply *mutatis mutandis* to unmanned maritime systems,[75] and that the meaning of 'vessel' or 'ship' in UNCLOS is broad enough to include uncrewed vessels.[76] Such opinion is exemplified as follows:

> There is no reason why unmanned ships ought not to be regarded as 'ships' so as to fall within the ambit of UNCLOS and why, therefore, the rights and obligations of flag and coastal states ought not to apply to them, *mutatis mutandis*. This is the case even though UNCLOS as not drafted with unmanned ships in mind.[77]

Following the analysis of legal status of uncrewed vessels under a particular instrument is normally an examination of the practicability or appropriateness of an uncrewed vessel to comply with a specific rule in that instrument. For instance, to some analysts, the limitations on freedom of uncrewed vessels

72 ibid 480.
73 ibid 481.
74 Van Hoodydonk (n 3) 406; J Kraska 'The Law of Unmanned Naval Systems in War and Peace' [2010] J Ocean Technology 44–53; Andrew H Henderson, 'Murky Waters: The Legal Status of Unmanned Undersea Vehicles' [2006] Naval L Rev 55–72.
75 Allen (n 3) 511.
76 ibid.
77 Veal & Ringbom (n 12).

to be imposed by flag, coastal, or port State under the law of the sea 'are by no means unique' compared with those on crewed vessels.[78]

According to some commentators, unmanned vessels must initially learn to adapt rather than expect the law to accommodate to artificial intelligence.[79] It is further argued that the absence of a crew 'does not in itself obviate' the duties consigned to vessels by UNCLOS, such as the duty to provide assistance to the extent necessary and reasonable to persons in danger or distress according to Article 98(1) thereof.[80] In sum, 'unmanned ships would be covered by the great majority of the existing regulatory definitions and it would appear that the existing conventions and national laws would in principle continue to be functional'.[81] Not surprisingly, extensive assessments have revealed that many current rules need to be changed or replaced in order to accommodate autonomous technology, while some others may still continue to operate as what they currently are.[82]

We have been reminded, nonetheless, that the above lines of thought may be not compatible with a justifiable method of treaty interpretation—a method which aligns with the position of the International Court of Justice that any treaty must be 'interpreted and applied within the framework of the entire legal system prevailing at the time of the interpretation.'[83] Concerns arise from the perception that, '[a] too-casual approach to treaty interpretation in the rush to accommodate [uncrewed vessels] will diminish respect for the rule-based order.'[84] Adverse impacts of a quick decision to apply or not apply certain rules to uncrewed vessels are illustrated in the below excerpt:

> The framework must be mindful of the consequences of including or excluding [Unmanned Marine Vehicles (UMV)] from a given rule set applicable to 'vessels,' and of the fact that any relaxation of regulatory requirements for [Maritime Autonomous Surface Ships (MASS)] will likely be seized on by operators of manned vessels to reduce manning.

78 ibid.

79 Guerra (n 1) 90.

80 Veal & Ringbom (n 12).

81 Van Hooydonk (n 3) 409.

82 *See*, e.g., ibid 418–19. The fields that do not need innovations include, *inter alia*, chartering, ship management, carriage of goods by sea, liability of stevedores and terminal operators, the liability of the passenger carrier, collision law, liability for pollution damage, arrest of ships, rules of liens and mortgages, etc. ibid 410.

83 Klein (n 11) 247.

84 Allen (n 3) 513.

> Some regulators have expressed concerns that UMV might be classified as a vessel under one rule set, but not another.[85]

Some scholars admit that possible interpretation of international law applicable in different scenarios involving the use of uncrewed vessels may help address, but not fully resolve, the legal questions.[86] For instance, as the task of a shore-based vessel controller is not entirely similar to that of a ship's master, one cannot escape the feeling that an interpretation to the effect of including a remotely-controlled vessel into the definition of a ship is too extensive and slips into interpretation *per analogiam*, something that tends to be frowned upon in international law.[87]

4 Source of Doubts

In addition to a surge of jurisprudence on the relationship between uncrewed vessels and international law, the past decade has also witnessed numerous debates between those advocating one of the above two assumptions, with a pending outcome in both the academic community and the international organizations. It is worth noting that those that appear to insist on the applicability of current legal framework have often expressed such opinion in a betwixt-and-between tone of voice. For instance, in discussions on the application of the law of armed conflict to maritime autonomous vehicles (MAVs), commentators observe that MAVs will 'potentially' fit within the definition of warships under Article 29 of UNCLOS.[88] Similarly, in arguing that unmanned ships are subject to the same rules of the law of the sea as any ordinarily manned ship, the commentators underscore that such an argument is made '[f]rom the *assumption* that unmanned ships are "ships" and "vessels" within the meaning of UNCLOS'.[89]

It appears that treaty interpretation which has been conducted in a manner that is preferred by those rejecting the foreseeability test still have not help establish a one hundred percent certainty, on their part, regarding the applicability of current laws. This legal uncertainty has noticeably impeded substantive steps that should have been taken by the international regulatory

85 ibid.
86 *See*, e.g., Klein (n 11) 247.
87 Van Hooydonk (n 3) 410.
88 Klein (n 11) 252.
89 Veal & Ringbom (n 12).

framework. Investment and development in the autonomous navigation and shipping sector is undermined by that regulatory uncertainty, whereas numerous uncrewed vessels are already in use around the world, operating in regulatory gray areas as operators await clarity from national and international regulatory bodies.[90] Meanwhile, stability for environmental, safety, workforce, surveillance, and other critical maritime areas will be dependent on updating global regulation to include autonomous vessels.[91] It is undeniable that uncrewed vessel regulation is outpaced by technological innovation.[92] One analyst even contends that the apparent shortcomings that exist in the international legal framework for maritime security are not obviated by the operation of uncrewed vessels, but rather the utility of the technology continues to be hampered by the operation of the law.[93] It seems that legal scholars have attempted to fit UMVs into current legal schemes in a piecemeal manner that uncrewed vessels practically and realistically cannot comply with.[94]

Hence, there naturally arises a question out of this reality of lasting legal uncertainty: Is the primary problem faced by international law truly a problem of treaty interpretation? As has been correctly pointed out by one scholar, '[t]he problem of interpretation appears when a rule is obscure and has various meanings.'[95] Accordingly, in the cases involving uncrewed vessels, a problem of interpretation may arise only when the treaty concerned itself contains such obscurity or flexibility.[96] More specifically, only when (i) one cannot tell, at the time a treaty was written, whether the term 'ship' or 'vessel' embraces an uncrewed vessel (i.e., the case of obscurity) , or (ii) one is certain, at that time, one of all the possible meanings of the term 'ship' or 'vessel' includes an uncrewed vessel (i.e., the case of flexibility), will a problem of treaty interpretation arise. Given the unanimous observation that no prevalent treaty contains such obscurity or flexibility, it is evident that the primary problem faced by international law is *not* a problem of treaty interpretation.

We further note that all speculation about the applicability of international law to uncrewed vessels begins from the supposition that regulating uncrewed vessels falls within the legitimacy of international law. This raises a question as to what determines the legitimacy of international law, which might have been an even more potent source of confusion in the theories of international

90 Brett (n 3) 55.
91 ibid.
92 ibid 33.
93 Klein (n 11) 247–48.
94 *See* generally McCarl (n 9).
95 Titiriga (n 60) 79.
96 Allen (n 3) 513–14.

law. Despite continuous challenges and skepticism, state consent has been widely accepted as necessary for a norm or rule to be legally valid in the international legal system. Belief in the necessary existence of the legally unlimited sovereign prejudges a question as to the legitimacy of domestic law or that of international law. The question for domestic law is: what is the extent of the supreme legislative authority recognized in this system? For international law it is: what is the maximum area of autonomy which the rules allow to States?[97]

It is true that 'modern international law is very largely treaty law, and elaborate attempts have been made to show that rules which appear to be binding on States without their prior consent do in fact rest on consent, though this may have been given only "tacitly" or has to be "inferred".'[98] The doubt which legal scholars commonly raise is often expressed in the opening parts of their analysis on uncrewed vessels in the form of the question 'Is an uncrewed vessel a vessel under international law?'[99] Yet there is something very confusing in this favorite form of question; and before we can deal with it, we must face, as is enlisted by the consent theory, a prior question to which the answer is not clear so forth. This prior question is: Do States consent to authorize international law to regulate uncrewed vessels?

Evidently, the question 'Do States consent to authorize international law to regulate uncrewed vessels?' and those 'Is an uncrewed vessel a vessel under international law?' and 'Can current rules be applied to uncrewed vessels?' are questions addressing different legal concerns. While the latter two express a doubt about the applicability of international law, the first one cares about the legitimacy thereof. This is one point of comparison with domestic law, the rules of which are taken to be unquestionably 'legitimate' to regulate the same. From this stage, the further argument is simple: if for this reason the rules of international law cannot regulate uncrewed vessels, it is surely indefensible to state that a vessel under international law would possibly embrace an uncrewed vessel or that an international rule would possibly apply to an uncrewed vessel. If states' consent is presumed, on the opposite, 'the legal challenge is reduced to identifying the key rules that need adjustments and making the amendments.'[100]

---

97 HLA Hart, 'International Law' in HLA Hart, *The Concept of Law* (2nd edn, Clarendon Press, 1997) 208, reprinted in Larry May and Jeff Brown (eds), *Philosophy of Law: Classic and Contemporary Readings* (Wiley-Blackwell, 2010) 175, 180.

98 ibid 181–82.

99 Van Hooydonk (n 3) 406–9.

100 Jordan (n 3) 316.

What might be contrary to the general impression is that state consent to international regulation of uncrewed vessels is not self-evident at the international level. One may argue that the Regulatory Scoping Exercise (RSE) taken by the International Maritime Organization (IMO) in 2018, to which the IMO Members have not voiced objections, may have implied the acquisition by the organization of state consent. In the RSE, the IMO attempted to determine which existing IMO instruments might preclude MASS operations, which instruments do not preclude MASS operations but may need to be amended or clarified, and which instruments are inapplicable to MASS operations.[101] However, it should not be overlooked that the IMO has conducted this exercise in such wise that no findings thereof explicitly acknowledge the innate applicability of the instruments examined. Instead, its focus is whether and how MASS may 'functionally comply' with pertinent legal requirements, '*if* it is determined they should even be made a part of [the] framework.'[102] Under the aegis of the consent theory, where a treaty does not allow room to its applicability to uncrewed vessels, the formal methods for treaty formation or amendment codified in the Vienna Convention on the Law of Treaties should be looked to.[103]

Having crystallized an absence of state consent within the IMO which has taken the lead among the relevant international organizations attempting to regulate uncrewed vessels, we now turn to the will of States to give their consent to international law for such purposes. Like international regulation, domestic regulation has also been a focus of jurisprudence ever since the advent and employment of autonomous technology at sea, encompassing legal issues within the domestic admiralty and maritime law that may impact various aspects of uncrewed naval, administrative, or commercial use of uncrewed vessels.[104] Regulation on those vessels is fragmented across jurisdictions.[105] As countries move forward without international guidance, domestic regulatory regimes are evolving rapidly to accommodate those new technologies.[106]

101 Coito (n 1) at 263; Aldo Chircop, 'Testing International Legal Regimes: The Advent of Automated Commercial Vessels' (2018) 60 German YB Intl L 1, 6.

102 Materna (n 25) 462.

103 Allen (n 3) 513–14.

104 *See*, e.g., Chwedczuk (n 5) 127; Brett (n 3) 27–28; Vice Admiral Darse E. "Del" Crandall Jr., 'Alexander C. Cushing International Law Conference Keynote Address: "International Law Considerations for 21st Century Engagements at Sea"' (2022) 99 Intl L Studies 479, 490.

105 Brett (n 3) 35.

106 ibid.

Competition in domestic legislation between States will be a corollary of the perceived competition therebetween in the development and deployment of autonomous technology.[107] Unsurprisingly, concerns have grown over irreconcilable purposes or values between the international community and individual States. We have been put on some alert that, by the time international regulation is finally complete, existing national regulation may be incompatible with global efforts.[108] As has been advised by one analyst, harmonizing approaches early on at the international level is essential to ensuring effective global governance and avoiding the problem of patchwork regulation that plagues so much of international law, especially in the maritime arena.[109]

We have noted, nonetheless, that there could be exceptions to the consent requirement for the purpose of establishing the legitimacy of international law. According to one authority, two important exceptions are these: the case of a new state (in which a new, independent state is bound by the general obligations of international law including the rules that give binding force to treaties) and the case of a state acquiring territory or undergoing some other changes (in which the state is bought with, for the first time, the incidence of obligations under rules which previously it had no opportunity either to observe or break, and to which it had no occasion to give or withhold consent).[110] These entrenched rules may carry with them some hints to buttress the perceptions that uncrewed vessels must comply with some of the extant international legal doctrines—such as that uncrewed vessels 'must be consistent with the demands of the maritime transportation system for safety of navigation and coastal and port State security interests',[111] and that the use of autonomous weapons at sea in combat missions should comply with rules of humanitarian law.[112]

It is worth clarifying here that prominence given to the legitimacy of international law and the consent theory in the preceding paragraphs does not indicate any disregard for the pivotal role that the existing international legal framework can play in responding to autonomous technology at sea. As one analyst views, we should not underestimate 'the power of general principles to offer sufficient governance during the inevitable hiatus that ensues whilst the impacts of a technological development are sorted through.'[113] Another

107 Crandall Jr. (n 104).
108 Brett (n 3) 35.
109 ibid.
110 Hart (n 97) 182.
111 Allen (n 3) 512.
112 Titiriga (n 60) 76–84.
113 Klein (n 11) 271.

analyst fortifies this view by voicing that, 'the conclusion that the rules governing unmanned systems are derived from broader principles of international law designed for manned ships and aircraft is really the only realistic course.'[114]

What the above analysis aims to crystallize is that legal uncertainty that has pervaded the extant jurisprudence and international institutions regarding international regulation of uncrewed vessels in the past decade can be partially attributed to the absence of due attention which should have been attached to the fundamental legal concerns arising from the legitimacy of international law centering on state consent to such regulation. Hence, in our point of view, a success in effective and efficient regulation of uncrewed vessels at the international level must be premised on a both explicit and vibrant distribution of regulatory power between the international and domestic frameworks. It follows that a detailed scrutiny of the will, values, and approaches held by sovereign States with respect to both domestically regulating uncrewed vessels and transferring their regulatory power to international law is anticipated to engender propositions for a prosperous international uncrewed vessel regime.

5 About This Volume

This policy-oriented jurisprudence was inspired by an international symposium on 'Ocean Governance in the New Era: Current Challenges and the Law of the Sea' held jointly by China Institute for Marine Affairs, Ministry of Natural Resources of the People's Republic of China and the Southern Marine Science and Engineering Guangdong Laboratory (Zhuhai) in November 2022 in Guangzhou, China. The symposium comprises two panels of discussions—one on sea-level rise and international law-making and the other on uncrewed vessels and international law—encompassing a variety of topics under the captioned theme and hosting legal scholars and practitioners from diverse jurisdictions including Belgium, Brazil, Canada, Indonesia, Japan, Korea, Singapore, the United Kingdom, the United States, Hong Kong Special Administrative Region, and Mainland China, as well as legal specialists from such relevant international organizations as the United Nations Food and Agriculture Organization. We should pay our tribute to all the speakers at the symposium, who shared enthusiastically with us their critical and illuminating research findings and opinions relating to the interactions between uncrewed vessels and various

114 ibid.

aspects of international law. Those findings and opinions have proved to be a fascinating source of insights and inspirations for this volume which accommodates the following essays.

In 'Regulations of International Humanitarian Law and Naval Warfare Law on UUV Operations at Sea', Chenhong Liu and Song Pan revisit the legal requirements posited by international humanitarian law and naval warfare law on the use of unmanned underwater vehicles (UUVs). They argue that international norms be reformulated to address, in an expeditious manner, the perceived concerns over the applicability of those requirements to UUVs. In 'Forcing Their Way at Sea: UMS in the Law of Naval Warfare', Zhaoran Lin delves into the interaction between unmanned maritime system (UMS) technology and the law of naval warfare. Three issues discussed therein include the military use of UMS under the law of use of force, the navigational and belligerent rights of UMS, and the rights and obligations of neutral States under maritime neutrality law.

On the premise of the observed tensions and conflicts between the coastal State and the researching State at sea caused by an increasing use of Uncrewed Maritime Vehicles (UMVs) in marine scientific research,Yao Huang and Shuning Zhang, in 'Using Uncrewed Maritime Vehicles for Scientific Research: Legal Challenges and Viable Solutions', focus their discussions on the challenges imposed by such use on the rights and obligations of States concerned under UNCLOS, and explore appropriate responses that can be taken by those States. New pathways for cooperations between the international and domestic frameworks are examined with a view to prompting international regulations in this field. In 'Cybersecurity of Unmanned Ships: A Legal Analysis', Wei Wu and Junming Gong scrutinize cyber risks faced by unmanned ships. Starting from the examination of definition and legal status of unmanned ships, they explore the existing regulations relating to cybersecurity of those ships, and propose legal and policy solutions to the perceived risks.

Mohd Hazmi Mohd Rusli, Dhiana Puspitawati, and Roman Dremliuga critically assess under UNCLOS, in 'Regulating the Passage of Nuclear-Powered Submarines and Autonomous Nuclear Drones: Does International Law Allow Recharacterization of the Straits of Malacca and Singapore?', the legal implications of a predicted increase in the passage of military vessels (including nuclear-powered submarines and potentially autonomous nuclear drones) through the Straits of Malacca and Singapore. They argue for recharacterizing those Straits by virtue of a non-suspendable innocent passage regime which should replace the transit passage regime that currently applies. In 'Is International Law Adequate to Regulate the Underwater Unmanned Vehicles (UUVs)? Legal Challenges beyond the 2016 U.S.-China UUV Incident' by Dan Liu, it is contended that UUVs possess multiple legal statuses by operation of the law of the sea and international humanitarian law, and that different types of legal challenges are issued to international law accordingly.

In 'Challenges Raised by Unmanned Ships and Flag State's Possible Jurisdiction Cooperations with Other Stakeholders', Haibo Chen identifies a possible jurisdictional vacuum on unmanned ships under the law of the sea. She observes that the introduction of new human factors into unmanned ship operations may result in inadequacy of flag State jurisdiction under the current legal framework, and urges jurisdictional cooperation between flag States, on the one side, and other States that are involved in by virtue of those new human factors, on the other. In 'IMO Legal Regulation of Maritime Autonomous Surface Ships: Progress, Trends and China's Response', Xue Yuan and Bo Yu, on the premise of the upcoming MASS Code of the IMO, devise recommendations for China's responses thereto at both domestic and international levels.

Valentin Koshkin critically appraises, in 'From Experimentation to Legislation: Understanding Russia's Approach to Autonomous Vessels', the features and weakness of the most recent legislation on autonomous vessels in Russia. In addition, he deliberates on the legitimacy of the enforcement of domestic regulations of Russia on foreign autonomous vessels passing through the Northern Sea Route, through the lens of the operation of pertinent provisions of UNCLOS. In 'Status Quo, Problems of Shipping Administration and the Counter-Measures on Uncrewed Vessels: From the Perspective of the Guangdong-Hong Kong-Macao Greater Bay Area', Ping Guo looks into the problems and obstacles arising from the laws on shipping management within the captioned area, especially those involving ship registration, crew management, and management of maritime economic activities.

This volume would be the first publication that offers discussions and opinions reflecting a combined international and comparative (especially, eastern) perspective. As has been discerned, 'lack of existing comparative law' has constituted a barrier to international regulation of uncrewed vessels.[115] The preceding analysis on the legitimacy of international law based on state consent also manifests the indispensability of domestic perspective, approach, and will to a leap forward in international regulations of uncrewed vessels. While the extant jurisprudence has brought the world to the legal threshold of an autonomous future, the academic community is now positioned to help both

115 Guerra (n 1) 75.

domestic and international legal frameworks to chart the course on the autonomous ocean amidst the divergent and dubious premises basing the extant literature.

The law of the sea and the international *lex maritima* have enjoyed a reputation for not only stability but also flexibility and openness to embrace new technology. On the one hand, they are regarded as part of the most steadfast areas of the law with many concepts and rules going back hundreds of years.[116] In particular, the *lex maritima* has been persistent for a few centuries 'in the seething currents of technical and political change.'[117] On the other hand, they appear to be relatively well armed for technological innovations and the necessary and undoubtedly extensive adaptations of existing public and private rules.[118] That reputation, in our point of view, indicates a brilliant prospect for international law to finally clinch uncrewed vessels. This volume, we expect, will contribute to raising the prospect of an international regulatory framework that can optimize a balance between the rule-based and goal-based paradigms, with the aim of embracing the advent and use of autonomous technology at sea.

Before closing this Introduction, we should express our deepest gratitude to the Southern Marine Science and Engineering Guangdong Laboratory (Zhuhai) and the colleagues we have closely worked with therein. They have, as always, been a source of our strength and encouragement to move forward. We are incredibly grateful for their endless support, inspiration, and creativity.

Acknowledgements

This project of publication is supported by the Southern Marine Science and Engineering Guangdong Laboratory (Zhuhai) and presents middle-phase research outcomes of its Project No. SML2020SP005.

116 Van Hooydonk (n 3) 403.
117 ibid.
118 ibid 423.

CHAPTER 1

Regulations of International Humanitarian Law and Naval Warfare Law on UUVs Operations at Sea

Chenhong Liu and Song Pan***

1 Introduction

The UUVs is an autonomous propulsion system with operating system or complete automation, or with minimal supervisory control and without cables (except those requiring optical cable data connection),[1] which uses the ocean as an activity space and is an unmanned, intelligent, and functional diverse.[2] It will play an increasingly important role in future national maritime competition. From the perspective of control methods, UUVs can be classified into five types as follows. First, the fully autonomous type with autonomous planning, autonomous navigation, and autonomous environment perception capabilities; second, the program-controlled type that is controlled by pre-built-in programs, sails and performs tasks according to the built-in programs; third, non-autonomous navigation, shore-based remote control type that can be controlled remotely by personnel; fourth, a ship-based remote control type that is released from the working mother ship and controlled by personnel on the working mother ship; fifth, a weapon type used for attack and other combat purposes.[3]

On December 15, 2016, the Chinese Navy seized an UUV being operated by the US Navy ship USNS Bowditch in waters within the nine-dash line in the South China Sea. Although China finally returned the UUV and the incident was resolved peacefully, it involved a series of legal issues, such as the status of UUVs under international law, the legal nature of UUVs carrying out military activities, and jurisdictional immunity of UUVs. This incident has attracted the

* Chenhong Liu, Associate Professor at Dalian Maritime University.

** Song Pan, Master Degree Candidate at Dalian Maritime University.

1 Liu Dan, 'The Rule of International Law Regulating Underwater Unmanned Vehicles: Legal Status, Current Challenges and Solutions' (2021) 3 JOUC 13.

2 Qiu Zhiming, Meng Xiangyao, Ma Yan, Chen Yi, Feng Wei, 'Development and key technologies of Maritime Unmanned Systems' (2023) 3 CJES 75.

3 Song Shuhua, Zhao Jinsong, 'The Legal Status of Unmanned Undersea Vehicles' (2017) 3 JSCSS 21.

 | DOI:10.1163/9789004706279_003

attention and discussion of Chinese scholars.[4] And these legal issues are still under intense discussion and are far from reaching a conclusion. As more and more UUVs are put into use, conflicts between relevant countries will inevitably become more intense. Therefore, the international community should conduct in-depth discussions and research on the legal rules of UUVs and strive to form common rules for the management of UUVs. This article will analyze from the perspective of the military use of UUVs the regulations it may be subject to by international laws such as international humanitarian law and naval warfare law, determine the legal status of UUVs, and focus on the international law regulations related to maritime operations faced by UUVs.

2 Legal Status of Unmanned Underwater Vehicles

As UUVs are widely used in military and non-military tasks such as intelligence reconnaissance, mine clearance, anti-submarine warfare, commercial salvage, scientific expeditions, and environmental monitoring, their maritime activities pose challenges to the application of existing international laws and regulations. Regarding UUVs, there is currently no special international treaty stipulating them. Therefore, we need to rely on existing international legal rules to determine the specific legal status of UUVs when different rules are applied. According to the existing peacetime rules and wartime rules, the legal status of UUV is explored and analysed as follows.

2.1 *Legal Status of UUVs under Peacetime Rules*

For UUVs, peacetime rules mainly include the United Nations Convention on the Law of the Sea (hereinafter referred to as the 'UNCLOS') and relevant conventions issued by the International Maritime Organization. Under the adjustment of these peacetime rules, the first question that needs to be explored and resolved is whether the UUV, is considered a 'ship' in the space of international law.

For 'ship', UNCLOS uses the wording 'ship' directly in a number of articles—such as Articles 91 and 94 which stipulate the nationality of the ship and the obligations of the flag state. However, UNCLOS also uses the wording 'vessel' in

4 Wang Shumin, Tang Xiaocong, 'Research on Legal Status of Unmanned Undersea Vehicles in International Law—Reflections on the Unmanned Undersea Vehicles Event between China and America' (2017) 4 PLS 3, 8; Guo Zhongyuan, Zou Ligang, 'An International Law Analysis on the Incident of Unmanned Underwater Vehicle in the South China Sea' (2017) 4 HSJHU 17, 23.

certain articles—such as Article 211 and Article 292 which deal with pollution from vessels and the prompt release of vessels and crews. However, UNCLOS does not define the two terms, nor does it clarify the legal status of 'ship' and 'vessel' and the differences between them. If it is to be determined whether an UUV can be classified as a ship in the sense of the International Law, it needs to be judged according to the rules of interpretation of the treaty. In accordance with the 'Vienna Convention on the Law of Treaties', a treaty shall be interpreted in good faith in accordance with the ordinary meaning to be given to the terms of the treaty in their context and in the light of its object and purpose. This means that the 'ordinary meaning' of ship or vessel needs to be examined to determine how the above terms are used. From the meaning of the word itself, according to The Oxford English Dictionary, 'vessel' refers to 'a ship or large ship', where 'ship' refers to 'a large boat that transports people or goods by sea.' According to the Wiki definition, 'vessel' refers to any water vehicle, including 'ship'. According to Black's Law Dictionary, 'ship' means a vessel used or capable of being used for navigation on water, whether a brig, sloop or other machine, and 'vessel' means a vessel used or capable of being used for navigation on water or a vessel capable of being used for navigation. Therefore, 'vessel' is used to describe any floating object on the water that can transport people or cargo (even if this definition is not fully accepted), of which the more complex and larger ones are called 'vessel'.[5]

Some important maritime international treaties have some definitions of ship or vessel in their provisions. The 'Convention on the International Regulations for Preventing Collisions at Sea' ('COLREGS') defines 'vessel' as 'every description of water craft, including non-displacement craft and seaplanes, used or capable of being used as a means of transportation on water'; the 'International Convention on Liability and Compensation for Damage in Connection with the Carriage of Hazardous and Noxious Substances by Sea' (HNS Convention) defines 'ship' as 'any seagoing vessel and seaborne craft, of any type whatsoever'; the 'Maritime Labour Convention' defines a 'ship' as 'ship means a ship other than one which navigates exclusively in inland waters or waters within, or closely adjacent to, sheltered waters or areas where port regulations apply'; the 'International Convention for the Prevention of Pollution from Ships' ('MARPOL') defines ship as 'a vessel of any type whatsoever operating in the marine environment and includes hydrofoil boats, air-cushion vehicles, submersibles, floating craft, and fixed or floating platforms'; the 'Hague Rules' specifically emphasizes the shipping function of ship and defines it as

5 Li Rui, 'On the Legal Status of Unmanned Ships' (2019) 4 COLR 170.

'any vessel used for the carriage of goods by sea'; As a modification and supplement to the Hague Rules, the 'Visby Rules' retain this definition, which is also adopted in the 'Rotterdam Rules'. It can be seen that both 'ship' and 'vessel' are used as collective terms for ships in international treaties. Regardless of whether 'vessel' or 'vessel' is used, it only needs to be self-consistent in the treaty, without involving the way the ship is driven or whether there is a crew on board. Therefore, there is no significant difference between the two terms used to refer to ships in UNCLOS and they can be classified as 'ships' under UNCLOS.[6]

Based on the above contents, there are two main standards for judging ships. First, navigation standard, which requires the ability to sail the sea, such as the aforementioned HNS Convention. However, it should be noted that with regard to navigation standards, some international treaties emphasize the provisions of water navigation, such as COLREGS, which emphasizes the 'water raft', which excludes the application of the rules to underwater navigation. In this case, the UUV does not necessarily fall within the scope of the COLREGS, and even if it meets the navigation standard and can be recognized as a ship under other international treaties. Second, functional standard, which requires a certain function to transport people or goods, such as the aforementioned COLREGS.[7] This function of transport is similarly emphasized by legal rules of international transport, such as the Hague Rules. As far as the current application scenarios of UUVs are concerned, engaging in scientific investigations, underwater engineering operations, and operating military tasks are the mainstream application scenarios of UUVs, and carrying out personnel or cargo transportation activities is not its common function. There is controversy in the academic community about the importance of transportation standards.[8] Referring to cases of Anglo-American law, among the above two standards, the navigation standard is the core standard for judging whether it is a ship, and the requirements for functional standards are relatively relaxed.[9] Therefore, it seems that UUVs can be recognized as ships and applicable to relevant laws and regulations.

However, as mentioned above, the specific types of UUVs are diverse, their functions are extensive, and their main functions are always different from

6 Ibid.

7 Liu (n 1) 16.

8 Andrew H. Henderson, 'Murky Waters: The Legal Status of Unmanned Undersea Vehicles' (2006) 53 NLR 70; Oliver Daum, 'The Implications of International Law on Unmanned Naval Craft' (2018) 49 JMLC 80 85.

9 Song, Zhao (n 3) 22.

those of ships, which can but cannot be fully included in the definition of ships under the general concept, nor can they meet the definition of international treaties in any case. So, it is necessary to conduct additional analysis and judgment on UUVs in combination with specific circumstances to determine their legal status. Specifically, fully autonomous, program-controlled, and shore-based remote-controlled UUVs can be recognized to have the legal status of a ship because they can independently perform water or underwater tasks, comply with the most basic navigation standards, and may have certain transportation functions. As for ship-based remote-controlled and weapon-based UUVs, because the former is often deployed on ships or warships to perform specific tasks, there is a tendency in academic circles and precedents to identify them as ship accessories, and they don't have independent legal status.[10] For the latter, because it is a weapon itself or carries torpedoes, missiles and other weapons, its legal status should be directly recognized as a weapon, rather than a ship or ship accessories.

2.2 *Legal Status of UUVs under Wartime Rules*

Under UNCLOS, the definition of 'warship' specifically includes four elements as follows. First, affiliation, a ship that meets the elements of a warship should belong to the armed forces of a country; second, nationality-related signs, a warship should have external signs or symbols that identify their nationality; third, command authority. The command authority of the ship should be vested in the command of an officer formally appointed by the government of a state and listed on the corresponding active service roster or similar roster; fourth if there is a crew to operate or control the ship, the ship should be operated by crew members who obey the discipline of the regular armed forces. Prior to UNCLOS, the 'Manual on the Law of Naval Warfare' adopted by the Oxford Conference in 1913 also held a similar view, stipulating that warships are 'all ships owned by the state, legally flying the national naval flag and pennant, under the command of a military commander, and manned by military crews.'[11] From the perspective of the provisions of international treaties represented by UNCLOS, a 'warship' should at least meet the basic attributes of armed system affiliation, clarity of external signs, clarity of command authority, and manned control.

Since the state to which UUVs belong is clear (the military to which it belongs is generally externally marked), documents such as the German 'Naval

10 Liu (n 1) 17.

11 ICRC Database, 'Manual of the Laws of Naval War' (Oxford, 9 August 1913) <https://ihl-databases.icrc.org/en/ihl-treaties/oxford-manual-1913?activeTab=historical> accessed 19 February 2024.

Commander's Manual' are in support of the 'warship theory'. The aforementioned manual emphasizes that given that military UUVs are controlled and operated by warships in some cases, they should not be excluded from the category of 'warship' but should enjoy the same legal status and immunity.[12] A similar view is taken in the American 'The Commander's Handbook on the Law of Naval Operations', which classifies UUVs under the section on warships and is one of the other naval craft, along with auxiliary vessels, military sealift command vessels, small crafts, and recognizes that they enjoy the same sovereign immunity as warships in general.[13] In fact, the definition of a warship in UNCLOS derives from most of the provisions of Articles 2 to 6 of the 'Convention (VII) relating to the Conversion of Merchant Ships into Warships. The Hague, 18 October 1907'.[14] Proponents of the 'warship theory' argue that this origin reflects the purpose of the definition of warship as to prohibit and prevent privateering.[15] The requirement of 'commanded by an officer' and 'operated or controlled by a crew' in the constituent elements of a warship is in effect conferring belligerent rights on the maritime armed forces under the control of a certain country, denying the legitimacy of private vessels engaged in privateer activities. In the case of UUVs, 'commanded by an officer' can be interpreted as remote command or monitoring by an officer on other warships or command bases, and 'controlled by a crew' can also be interpreted as being operated and controlled by remote operators, and there is no need to carry specific command and control personnel on UUV. The 2022 edition of 'The Commander's Handbook on the Law of Naval Operations' adopts this view, stipulating 'unmanned systems (including UUVs) may be designated as USS if they are under the command of a commissioned officer and manned by a crew under regular armed forces discipline, by remote or other means'.[16] This allows the UUVs to go beyond the limits defined in UNCLOS and be directly recognized as a warship, thereby obtaining the right of belligerent.

The most intuitive problem with the 'warship theory' is that it does not conform to the rules of interpretation of the 'Vienna Convention on the Law of Treaties'. Article 29 of UNCLOS explicitly applies the word 'manned' to emphasize the need for a crew to be present on a warship, while the term 'unmanned' in the UUVs clearly goes beyond the scope of the UNCLOS's definition. Some scholars have put forward similar reason when denying that UUVs are classified

12 2002 Commander's Handbook: Legal Bases for the Operations (GRE) s 2.11.

13 2022 The Commander's Handbook on the Law of Naval Operations (USA).

14 Zhou Yanlin, 'Challenges of Unmanned Underwater Vehicles Concerning Maritime Law Enforcement and China's Responses' (2023) 6 JSCSS 66.

15 Malgorzata Materna, 'Adjusting the Aperture: The International Law Case for Qualifying Unmanned Vessels as Warships' (2023) 100 ILS 475.

16 US Handbook (n 13).

as ships.[17] At the same time, there is also an objection to the 'warship theory' among foreign scholars. Rob McCaughlin took ship-based remote-controlled UUV as an example and proposed the following viewpoints. First, it is difficult for an UUV (released from a mother ship) to be independent of its mother ship and then recognized as a warship; secondly, in practice, due to the greater flexibility of the commander's remote-control command, it is difficult for the word 'command' in the four elements of a warship to include 'command by an officer' to include this type of remote command.[18] Jane Dalton also opposed the characterization of UUVs as warship. Jane Dalton argued that if the navigation rights of the state to which it belongs are considered and UUVs enjoy innocent passage in the territorial sea or the right of passage in the archipelago waters, there is no need to reluctantly classify the UUVs into the category of warships, because UNCLOS has made it clear that its scope of application is 'all' types of ships in the contracting states.[19] The 'warship theory' that regards UUV as warship has neither treaty basis nor state practice support and has few supporters.[20] In fact, the most important reason why the definition of a warship in UNCLOS emphasizes 'officers command' and 'manned crew' is that, as a country's mobile territory, warships have a strong attribute of national sovereignty, and by limiting their command and actual control, warships are guaranteed to exercise their rights of belligerence and self-defense out of the will of the state, so as to avoid serious consequences caused by various unexpected factors. If UUVs are rashly included in the category of warships, the right of passage, the right of immunity of States, and other issues of international law involving national sovereignty will arise, and may affect the behavior of subjects of International Law, resulting in serious consequences that harm the interests of coastal states and even damage national sovereignty. Therefore, accepting the 'warship theory' will give rise to a series of complex controversies, and under the current framework of International Law, it is difficult for UUVs to be directly identified as warships.

One question associated with the 'warship theory' is whether an UUV can be identified as a submarine. As a vessel that was effectively used in the First World War and quickly became an important part of the modern navy, the submarine was highly valued by the naval powers during the interwar period and incorporated into the regulation of international law. After the Washington

17 Michael N. Schmitt, David S. Goddard, 'International law and the military use of unmanned maritime systems' (2016) 98 IRRC 576, 577.

18 Rob McLaughlin, 'Unmanned Naval Vehicles at Sea: USVs, UUVs, and the Adequacy of the Law' (2011) 21 JLIS 108, 114.

19 Jane G. Dalton, 'Future Navies—Present Issues' (2006) 82 ILS 304, 305.

20 Liu (n 1) 14.

Naval Conference in 1922, a series of international treaties dealing with submarine warfare appeared, for example, the 'Treaty for the Limitation and Reduction of Naval Armaments, (Part IV, Art. 22, relating to submarine warfare)' in 1930 and the 'Procès-verbal relating to the Rules of Submarine Warfare set forth in Part IV of the Treaty of London of 22 April 1930' in 1936. After the Second World War, the legal status of submarines was reflected in international treaties, and Article 20 of UNCLOS provides that, 'In the territorial sea, submarines and other underwater vehicles are required to navigate on the surface and to show their flag'. However, like 'ship' and 'vessel', UNCLOS does not provide definitions for 'submarines' and 'other underwater vehicles', but only sets out specific requirements for innocent passage in the section on innocent passage. Therefore, 'submarines' should be understood in the 'ordinary sense'. There is an opinion based on the general working environment of submarines, which is that submarines are vessels that are capable of operating independently on and off the surface of the sea.[21] Considering that submarines have become the main component of the world's navy like warships, and that submarines can be regarded as warships in a broad sense, UNCLOS and earlier international treaties dealing with submarine warfare have not made a clear distinction between the rights and obligations of submarines and warships. Submarines still need to abide by the legal rules applicable to surface ships, have the same belligerent rights, perform the same combat obligations, and bear the same legal liabilities. It is not difficult to see that if an UUV is regarded as a submarine, it will essentially return to the discussion of whether it belongs to a ship and whether it belongs to a warship, and it cannot solve the problem of the ambiguity of the legal status of UUVs. For the sole purpose of Article 20 of UNCLOS, it would be more appropriate to classify UUVs as 'other submersibles' and leave them to be adjusted in the course of the improvement of the rules of international law in the future.

Neither the 'ship theory' based on peacetime rules nor the 'warship theory' based on wartime rules can accurately define the legal status of UUVs, and the two theories themselves have not become the mainstream of academic or national practice. Opponents often strictly adhere to the two standards of ship identification, deny the ship qualification of UUVs, and then deny that UUVs do not have the nature of warships.[22] There is a view that if the UUV is forcibly identified as a ship, it will force the UUV to make unrealistic changes in

21 Kazuhiro Nakatani, 'Submarines', *Max Planck Encyclopedia of Public International Law* (2021) <https://opil.ouplaw.com/view/10.1093/law:epil/9780199231690/law-9780199231690-e1839?rskey=ezH2qr&result=1&prd=MPIL> accessed 24 November 2021.

22 Oliver Daum, 'The Implications of International Law on Unmanned Naval Craft' (2018) 49 JMLC 88.

order to meet the requirements of the corresponding international treaty, and affect the development of UUV technology.[23] In addition, there are perceptions that UUVs are considered to be ship accessories or to link their status to their launch platforms.[24] The common problem of these two perspectives is that they cannot cover the entire UUVs, but can only apply to a part of the UUVs. The former is only suitable for cabled UUVs that do not have much controversy, the latter makes the legal status of the UUVs entirely dependent on the legal status of the corresponding launch platform and increases legal uncertainty by forcing coastal States to struggle to distinguish whether an UUV entering its territorial waters is a warship or has other status.[25] With the development of related technologies, more and more UUVs can perform tasks independently of their launch platforms, and there is no close connection between the two. In the case of shore-based launched UUVs or UUVs launched from other launch platforms that also do not have a clear legal status, the idea of belonging to the launch platform is completely meaningless.

In summary, the legal status of UUVs is ambiguous, and the existing rules of international law do not work effectively against them, nor do they have a widely accepted customary international law. Although the management of UUVs can be realized through interpretation and modification on the basis of the existing rules of international law, this is only a stopgap measure after all. On the basis of the international community's attention to the issue of UUVs and reaching a consensus, the establishment of a new special legal norm for UUVs is the only way to achieve the effective management of UUVs and even the entire unmanned maritime system.

3 Application of Existing Maritime Warfare Rules to Unmanned Underwater Vehicles

3.1 *Interpretation and Application of the Basic Principles of International Humanitarian Law*

The 'Manual on the International Law of Armed Conflict at Sea in San Remo' (hereinafter referred to as the 'San Remo Manual') adopted in 1994 was compiled by the Institute of International Humanitarian Law through a series of roundtable meetings convened by international law and naval experts from various countries. It sets out the rules of International Humanitarian Law to be

23 Lindsay I. McCarl, 'Untethering UMVs from Vessels: Why the United States Should Construct a New Environmental Legal Scheme for Unmanned Maritime Vehicles' (2023) 127 DLR 484.

24 Song, Zhao (n 3) 156.

25 Daum (n 22) 87.

followed in the event of any armed conflicts at sea. According to the provisions of the 'San Remo Manual', the means and methods of maritime warfare are mainly subject to basic principles such as 'being bound by the principles and regulations of International Humanitarian Law from the moment force is used' and 'civilians and combatants are still protected and governed by international law principles derived from established customs, humanitarian principles and public conscience.' Specifically, the San Remo Manual clearly stipulates that in any armed conflict, the right of the parties to the conflict to choose methods or means of war is not unlimited, and requires the followings. First, parties to a conflict must at all times distinguish between civilians or other protected persons and combatants, and between civilian targets or targets protected from attack and military targets; secondly, it is prohibited to use weapons or equipment that cause excessive casualties or unnecessary suffering; thirdly, it is prohibited to issue orders to kill without mercy, threaten opponents with this, or carry out hostilities on this basis.[26]

The San Remo Manual also clearly stipulates various sea and air targets that are protected from attack and exemption conditions, such as the types of enemy ships that are protected from attack, including:

> 1. Hospital ships; 2. Small boats used for coastal rescue operations and other medical transportation; 3. Vessels approved by the warring parties to carry out security operations, including: (i) prisoner of war exchange ships, that is, ships specially used and engaged in transporting prisoners of war; (ii) ships engaged in humanitarian missions, including vessels carrying supplies necessary for the survival of civilians and vessels engaged in relief activities and rescue operations; 4. vessels engaged in transporting cultural relics under special protection; 5. Passenger ships specially used to transport civilian passengers; 6. Vessels carrying religious, non-military scientific or charitable missions and scientific data for military purposes are not protected; 7. Small coastal fishing vessels and boats engaged in local coastal trade, subject to the regulations and inspections of belligerent naval commanders operating in the area; 8. Vessels dedicated or specially modified for the investigation of marine environmental pollution; 9. Surrendered vessels; 10. Life rafts and lifeboats.[27]

Another example is the exemption condition after the transmission of protection from attack,

---

26 ICRC Database, 'San Remo Manual on International Law Applicable to Armed Conflicts at Sea' (12 June 1994) https://ihl-databases.icrc.org/en/ihl-treaties/san-remo-manual-1994?activeTab=default accessed 19 February 2024.

27 Ibid.

> A ship is protected from attack only under the following circumstances: 1. Used harmlessly to perform normal missions; 2. Subject to identification and inspection as required; 3. Unintentional Impede the movement of combatants and comply with orders to stop advance or give way as required.[28]

Since there is no clear legal basis for the wartime legal status of UUVs, specific identification needs to be made based on the actual situation. If an UUV is recognized as a warship or a ship, according to Articles 13 and 45 of the San Remo Manual, the UUVs should be recognized as a warship or an auxiliary vessel of the armed forces of a state and abide by the basic principles and rules of naval warfare law. If an UUV is recognized as a weapon, it can be regulated by international humanitarian law as a means of warfare, and the user can be held accountable if it is used improperly. If an UUV is recognized as a ship attachment, it is subordinate to the ship or warship it is deployed on, and there is no need to consider this issue. Its responsibility belongs to the corresponding ship or warship.

When UUVs carry out attacks, they should abide by the basic operational principles stipulated in International Humanitarian Law and the Law of Armed Conflict represented by the San Remo Manual, mainly including the principles of distinction, proportionality and precautionary measures.[29] The principle of distinction requires that parties to a conflict must distinguish between combatants and civilians, and between military targets and civilian objects, no matter what the circumstances during the conflict.[30] According to the relevant provisions of the 'Protocol Additional to the Geneva Conventions of 12 August 1949, and relating to the Protection of Victims of International Armed Conflicts (Protocol I)' (hereinafter referred to as the Protocol I), the principle of distinction includes the difference between combatants and civilians, military targets and civilian objects; civilians and civilian objects are prohibited from being attacked in principle; if combatants and military targets no longer become military targets , attacks are prohibited, and attacks are allowed if civilians and civilian objects become military targets. Based on past maritime armed rules, the San Remo Manual improves the maritime targets that

---

28 Ibid.

29 Zhai Zhong, 'International Legal Regime of Unmanned Underwater Vehicles in Wartime' (PhD dissertation East China University of Political Science and Law 2022) 113.

30 ICRC Database, 'The Principle of Distinction between Civilians and Combatants' <https://ihl-databases.icrc.org/en/customary-ihl/v1/rule1>; ICRC Database, 'The Principle of Distinction between Civilian Objects and Military Objectives,' <https://ihl-databases.icrc.org/en/customary-ihl/v1/rule7> accessed 19 February 2024.

are prohibited from attacking, including the aforementioned ships and medical aircraft that are protected from attack, aircraft approved to carry out security operations, and civil aviation airliners. In this regard, UUVs must abide by the above regulations when conducting maritime military operations and are not allowed to attack the above-mentioned sea and air targets. As for land targets, unmanned submarines can attack them by carrying missiles. Therefore, for such targets, UUVs should abide by the 'Convention Concerning Bombardment by Naval Forces in Time of War', Protocol I and other relevant rules, and must not target undefended areas, civilian objects, or historical monuments that constitute the cultural or spiritual heritage of the peoples of various countries, works of art or places of worship, objects indispensable to the survival of civilian populations and other land targets. More importantly, UUVs should effectively distinguish combatants from civilians, military targets and civilian objects. This involves issues such as how UUVs identify military targets, how to identify dual-use facilities, how to identify civilians directly involved in combat operations, and how to convert military targets into non-military targets. In actual battlefield environments in the past, these problems often relied on commanders to make comprehensive judgments based on actual battlefield conditions and information, so as to take actions that apply the above rules. However, there is a grey area in the target identification standards of the above rules. It is difficult to use the pre-programmed program of the UUVs decision-making system to have the same judgment ability as the commander and make decisions that are consistent with the actual battlefield conditions.

The principle of proportionality requires that the losses caused by military operations shall not be greater than the expected military benefits. This type of loss includes all civilian lives, property losses and damage to civilian objects caused by military operations.[31] The principle of proportionality is clearly stated in Protocol I. Protocol I stipulates that

> the following types of attacks shall, inter alia, be considered indiscriminate attacks: (a) an attack by bombardment by any methods or means which treats as a single military objective a number of clearly separated and distinct military objectives located in a city, town, village or other area containing a similar concentration of civilians or civilian objects; (b) an attack which may be expected to cause incidental loss of civilian life, injury to civilians, damage to civilian objects, or a combination

31 ICRC Database, 'Customary IHL, Proportionality in Attack' <https://ihl-databases.icrc.org/en/customary-ihl/v1/rule14> accessed 19 February 2024.

> thereof, which would be excessive in relation to the concrete and direct military advantage anticipated.[32]

As far as armed conflicts at sea are concerned, the principle of proportionality has a direct impact on whether UUVs carry out attacks and the specific attack methods, which requires unmanned underwater vehicles to have the ability to effectively identify various types of attacks. Determining its military value and interests, estimating the possible damage results of various attack methods, and weighing the interests in a proportional manner before making corresponding attack decisions should be based on the target. This actually poses a huge challenge to the information evaluation capabilities of the UUV's decision-making system. How to evaluate the military value, collateral damage consequences, and proportional limits of various targets so that attacks comply with the provisions of international humanitarian law and the law of armed conflict is an important issue for the future technological development of UUVs. In addition, environmental factors are also something that needs to be evaluated when UUVs conduct an attack. The San Remo Manual specifically stipulates that the combat methods and means used in maritime operations must take due consideration of the natural environment in accordance with the rules of international law, and prohibits unscrupulous damage and destruction of the natural environment that is not military necessity.

The principle of precautionary measures requires that when conducting military operations, parties to a conflict should take care to avoid harming civilians and civilian objects, and should take all possible preventive measures to reduce or avoid losses to civilian lives, property, and damage to civilian objects.[33] Protocol I clearly stipulates the preventive measures that parties to the conflict should take, including 'precautions in the event of an attack' by the attacking party and 'preventive measures to prevent the impact of an attack' by the defending party. Among them, the attacking party should take the following preventive measures:

> 1. Ascertain as far as possible that the target to be attacked is neither a civilian nor a civilian object, and does not receive special protection, but a military target within the meaning of Article 52, and identify that the attack on the target is not prohibited by the provisions of the Protocol;

32 ICRC Database, 'Protocol Additional to the Geneva Conventions of 12 August 1949, and relating to the Protection of Victims of International Armed Conflicts (Protocol I)' (8 June 1977) <https://ihl-databases.icrc.org/en/ihl-treaties/api-1977/article-51?activeTab=undefined> accessed 19 February 2024.

33 ICRC Database, 'Principle of Precautions in Attack' <https://ihl-databases.icrc.org/en/customary-ihl/v1/rule15> accessed 19 February 2024.

> 2. When selecting the means and methods of attack, take all possible precautions with a view to avoiding and, in any case, reducing incidental loss of civilian life, injury to civilians and civilians. damage to civilian objects;
> 3. Not decide to launch any attack that is likely to cause incidental loss of civilian life, injury to civilians, damage to civilian objects, or a combination of all three and which would be excessive compared with the expected concrete and direct military benefits.[34]

This was fully adopted in the San Remo Manual, which introduced the principle of precautionary measures into the rules of naval warfare. For UUVs, when performing maritime military missions, mostly attack missions, they need to take corresponding preventive measures based on the actual battlefield conditions to achieve the effects of the principles of distinction and proportionality. This requires unmanned underwater vehicles to undertake the obligation to collect and analyse information, select appropriate combat methods, and provide advance warning. However, considering the complex and changeable actual battlefield scenarios, coupled with the large number of applications of dual-use military and civilian facilities, whether it is possible to achieve effective identification of friend or foe, distinction between military and civilians and early warning, thereby effectively reducing civilian casualties and damage to civilian objects, which is also an area that needs to be improved for the future development of UUVs.

In addition, compared with warships, there are some differences in the application of the above principles to UUVs. The above basic principles for conducting maritime operations restrict the various uses of force by both warring parties. Its purpose is to protect civilians and combatants in the event of armed conflicts at sea while still being protected and g authority of the principles of international law derived from established custom, from the principles of humanity and from the dictates of the public conscience.[35] As the most important combat weapon and the most basic large-scale combat platform in naval warfare, warships have the main characteristics of armed system affiliation, clarity of external signs, clarity of command authority, and manned control. This means that if a warship conducts behavior that violates the above basic principles, it may have two consequences. On the one hand, the high power of ship-borne weapons may cause serious harm. On the other hand, during post-event investigations, the four characteristics of warships can

---

34 ICRC Database (n 32).

35 ICRC Database, 'San Remo Manual on International Law Applicable to Armed Conflicts at Sea' (12 June 1994) <https://ihl-databases.icrc.org/en/ihl-treaties/san-remo-manual-1994?activeTab=default> accessed 19 February 2024.

eliminate the possibility of so-called 'accidental firing' or 'accidental attack' to the greatest extent, thereby more accurately determining the responsible party and ascertaining relevant illegal facts, judging the liability under international law. However, the unmanned operation and concealment of UUVs make it obviously impossible to conduct accurate, effective and reliable post-event investigations when violations of international humanitarian law occur. Its concealment and functional diversity make its specific harmful consequences difficult to estimate or even detect, and it is difficult to pursue the liability of relevant subjects.

To sum up, carrying out an attack is a complex behavioral process. Before the final attack, commanders and combatants often need to go through a series of intelligence reconnaissance, target selection, and combat plan evaluation. UUVs also need to go through the above process to carry out an attack. The basic principles for UUVs to conduct maritime operations include the principle of distinction, the principle of proportionality and the principle of preventive measures. These three principles run through the entire process of unmanned underwater vehicles carrying out maritime military missions and carrying out attacks, and mainly include three major links: intelligence reconnaissance, target identification and evaluation, and the formulation and implementation of combat plans. In each link, the principle of preventive measures, the principle of distinction and the principle of proportionality play a leading role. These three principles are often intertwined and closely related in practice, and may be focused on in a particular link, but it is not necessary to apply only one specific principle to a particular link in the process of carrying out an attack. However, it is not easy for UUVs and the entire unmanned maritime system to effectively implement the provisions of these three principles. On the one hand, these three principles are still controversial in theory. The relevant international legal norms are highly generalized and not clear enough. In the actual implementation process, it relies on on-site commanders to judge and take corresponding actions according to specific battlefield conditions, and there is currently a lack of special naval combat rules for UUVs. Faced with the thorny problems of whether to issue effective warnings, whether to accurately identify 'dual-use' items, whether to accurately identify objects that are in the conversion of military targets and non-military targets, and how to assess military interests and collateral casualties or damages, UUVs can only rely on general rules of war to deal when performing military tasks. On the other hand, UUVs may rely on operator instructions to conduct operations, or may take actions based on preset programs within their own systems. The former requires UUVs to be equipped with a complete sensor detection system to provide operators with sufficient information for judgment, while the latter has extremely high requirements for the information collection, analysis, evaluation and judgment capabilities of the preset system. It remains a long distance to develop robust UUVs technology which can determine whether a target meets the exemption conditions in an unmanned and intelligent environment.

3.2 *Interpretation and Application of the Rules of the Naval Warfare Law on the Means and Methods of Warfare*

Means and Methods of Warfare is a legal concept which first appeared in Article 54 of Protocol I. 'Means of Warfare' generally refer to the weapons being used. 'Methods of Warfare' generally refer to the way in which such weapons are used. The difference between the two is that the former stresses whether a specific weapon or equipment can be used, and the latter stresses how a certain weapon can be used or how a certain combat activity should be carried out. If an UUV carries a specific weapon, it involves the Means of Warfare, and if an UUV participates in a certain combat operation, it involves the Methods of Warfare.

According to customary international humanitarian law, there are two main general principles for the use of weapons. First, it is prohibited to use methods and means of warfare that cause excessive harm or unnecessary suffering. Second, the indiscriminate use of weapons is prohibited.[36] UUVs have the characteristics of being unmanned and intelligent. At the same time, it uses underwater submersible as the basic application scenario for performing tasks, making torpedoes, mines and missiles the basic combat methods of UUVs, which then leads to the question of how to comply with the requirements of general international humanitarian law when UUVs are used in military scenarios.

According to the San Remo Manual, maritime warfare means mainly include 'the use of missiles and projectiles, including those with beyond visual range capabilities', and special provisions were also made for torpedoes and mines. The San Remo Manual prohibits the use of torpedoes that do not sink or become harmless after the end of the voyage and it is required that mines be used only for legitimate military purposes, including preventing the enemy from using sea areas; in principle, the use of free-floating mines is prohibited. Regarding the placement and clearance of mines, the San Remo Manual also provides detailed specifications and requirements, and stipulates the

---

36 ICRC Database, 'Weapons of a Nature to Cause Superfluous Injury or Unnecessary Suffering' <https://ihl-databases.icrc.org/en/customary-ihl/v1/rule70; ICRC Database, Customary IHL, Weapons That Are by Nature Indiscriminate, https://ihl-databases.icrc.org/en/customary-ihl/v1/rule71> accessed 19 February 2024.

notification obligations, recording obligations, and clearance obligations of the country using mines, and should provide free access for neutral shipping.

The unmanned, intelligent and underwater combat characteristics of UUVs give them unique advantages in using mines and missiles for combat. Therefore, UUVs must comply with general international legal norms prohibiting the use of specific weapons, and also need to comply with the norms of the law of armed conflict that adjust the above means of combat. As far as mines are concerned, the types of mines carried by UUVs are restricted by relevant international legal norms represented by the San Remo Manual. In principle, free-floating mines are not allowed to be used unless they become inert one hour after losing control. When using UUVs to lay mines, they shall not lay mines in the waters of neutral countries. When deployed in the waters of belligerent countries, they shall provide navigation channels for neutral countries and shall not obstruct the transit of international straits and archipelagic sea lanes. When deployed on the high seas, they shall consider providing convenience to neutral states. After a mine is deployed, if a situation occurs that may endanger ships of other non-belligerent states, the state that deployed the mine should notify the international community of the relevant situation. In addition, UUVs can also be used to fulfil mine clearance obligations. According to the San Remo Manual and relevant international law rules, both belligerents and neutral states can take measures to clear mines or render them harmless, thereby ensuring navigation safety in relevant waters.

As far as torpedoes and missiles are concerned, a torpedo is a traditional naval attack weapon launched from warships, submarines and aircraft to attack various underwater targets. As a basic means of combat in modern warfare, missiles play an important role in three battlefield environments, namely, land, sea and air. In armed conflicts at sea, missiles can be launched from land to assist the navy in maritime operations, or can be used as ship-borne weapons launched from warships or submarines to directly participate in combat. Since there is currently no law of armed conflict at sea that specifically regulates torpedoes and missiles, if UUVs carry torpedoes or small missiles for combat, UUVs should abide by the general principles and rules of the law of armed conflict at sea. That is to say, when unmanned submarines use torpedoes and missiles to attack, they should abide by the principles of distinction, proportionality and precautionary measures, and avoid attacking civilian objects, humanitarian missions and ships and facilities of neutral states.

Blockade, as an ancient and traditional method of naval warfare, began in the early 17th century. Grotius, in his Laws of War and Peace of 1625, recognized the concept of 'naval blockade in time of war', gave it legal status and proposed that the act of breaking the blockade was a crime and its goods could be confiscated as punishment. In more serious cases, the injured party can further pursue the crime. The 1856 Declaration of the Paris Conference on Certain Principles of the Sea regulated maritime blockade for the first time, marking the formation of the rules. The declaration denies the legality of the 'paper blockade' and states that the blockade must be effective. However, the content of the declaration is very small and does not define the effectiveness of the blockade. It cannot meet the needs of regulating maritime blockade behavior.

With the outbreak of World War I, maritime blockade rules were greatly developed and improved. Among the 13 conventions revised and adopted by the Second Hague Peace Conference in 1907, there are seven conventions related to maritime blockades, six conventions of which specifically stipulate the relevant requirements for sea inspections and arrests, and one convention of which clearly regulates mine blockades. The 'London Declaration on the Laws of Naval War' adopted in 1909 reiterated that the blockade must be effective, stating for the first time that 'whether the blockade is effective or not is a question of fact,' and further clarified a series of principles such as declaration of notification, fair application, division of blockade areas, and identification of breach of blockade.[37] Although it did not come into effect in the end, the main principles it established are still recognized by all countries and are of great significance. International treaties such as the 'Treaty on the Use of Submarines and Poisonous Gases in War' adopted in 1922, the 'International Treaty on Limitations and Sanctions of Naval Forces' adopted in 1930, and the 'London Protocol' adopted in 1936 all involve a new area of maritime blockade—the exercise of the power of submarine inspection and capture.

Before the San Remo Manual, the rules on naval blockade were scattered in some chapters and individual articles of various international law conventions, legal documents and international law works. Articles 93 to 104 of the San Remo Manual sorted out and summarized the rules including naval blockade. The rules of naval warfare have made the rules systematic. The San Remo Manual requires that the implementation of the blockade should be announced to all belligerent and neutral countries. The announcement should detail the start time, duration and scope of the blockade, as well as the period within which neutral ships are allowed to leave the blocked coast. The San Remo Manual also requires that 'the blockade must be effective' and stipulates that 'whether the blockade is effective is a question of fact' and 'the troops

37 ICRC Database, 'Treaties, States Parties and Commentaries, Final Protocol to the Naval Conference of London' (26 February 1909) <https://ihl-databases.icrc.org/en/ihl-treaties/london-finprot-1909?activeTab=historical> accessed 19 February 2024.

maintaining the blockade have the right to station at distances determined by military needs.'[38]

Regarding the legality requirements of 'blockade', the San Remo Manual stipulates that

> the implementation and maintenance of a blockade must use a combination of legal combat methods and means, but this combination cannot result in actions that are inconsistent with the rules stipulated in this document;[39]

Regarding merchant ships during the blockade, the 'San Remo Manual' stipulates that

> merchant ships that have reason to prove that they are breaking the blockade have the right to capture, and merchant ships that have obviously resisted capture after being warned in advance have the right to attack.[40]

The San Remo Manual also stipulates the general requirements for blockades, 'the blockade must not prevent access to the ports and coasts of neutral countries', 'the blockade must apply equitably to ships of all countries', 'stop, temporarily lift, re-establish, expand or change the blockade, an announcement and notification must be made in accordance with Articles 93 and 94.'[41]

> It is prohibited to declare or establish a blockade if the following circumstances occur: 1. The sole purpose of the blockade is to starve the civilian population or to cut off the vital resources necessary for survival. 2. The damage caused to the civilian population will or is expected to greatly exceed the specific and direct military benefits expected to be brought about by the blockade;
>
> If the civilian population in the blockaded territory does not receive adequate food and If there are other items indispensable for survival, the blockade must ensure the free passage of such food and other indispensable supplies in accordance with the following provisions: 1. The right to release after making technical arrangements including searches; 2. The

38 ICRC Database (n 35).
39 Ibid.
40 Ibid.
41 Ibid.

> distribution of such supplies must be supervised locally by humanitarian organizations such as the Protecting Power or the International Committee of the Red Cross that can provide impartial guarantees;

'The right to release and blockade parties after making technical arrangements, including searches,' is understood in the following manner:

> The right to release after making technical arrangements, including conducting searches, the blockading party shall allow the passage of medical supplies intended for the civilian population or the wounded and sick of the armed forces.[42]

As for UUVs, existing International Humanitarian Law and the Law of Armed Conflict do not restrict their participation in maritime blockades. If UUVs are used in maritime blockade operations, in addition to complying with the basic principles of maritime conflict such as the principle of distinction, proportionality, and precautionary measures, they must also comply with the maritime blockade requirements stipulated in the San Remo Manual. For example, for unknown ships trying to break through the blockade, UUVs must provide effective advance warning before attacking them. In addition, compared with warships traditionally used for blockades, unmanned underwater vehicles are smaller, carry less powerful weapons, and have higher attack accuracy. When attacking ships trying to undermine a maritime blockade, UUVs can more accurately disable the sailing capabilities of the attacked ship and reduce the occurrence of collateral damage including civilian casualties, damage to civilian objects, and environmental pollution.

In principle, International Humanitarian Law and the Law of Armed Conflict generally do not prohibit any particular method of warfare and permit the use of 'ruses of war', unless the specific method of warfare constitutes 'perfidy' or is a clear violation of the rules of International Humanitarian Law. The prohibition of 'perfidy' and the permissibility of 'ruses of war' are long-standing rules of customary international law, as expressly provided for in Article 37 of Protocol I. Article 37, paragraph 1, defines 'perfidy' as 'acts inviting the confidence of an adversary to lead him to believe that he is entitled to, or is obliged to accord, protection under the rules of international law applicable in armed conflict, with intent to betray that confidence', and lists four specific examples in the article (the feigning of an intent to negotiate under a flag of truce or of a

42 Ibid.

surrender; the feigning of an incapacitation by wounds or sickness; the feigning of civilian, non-combatant status; the feigning of protected status by the use of signs, emblems or uniforms of the United Nations or of neutral or other States not Parties to the conflict). Article 37, paragraph 2, defines 'ruses of war' and explains why they may be used, 'such ruses are acts which are intended to mislead an adversary or to induce him to act recklessly but which infringe no rule of international law applicable in armed conflict and which are not perfidious because they do not invite the confidence of an adversary with respect to protection under that law', and also includes 'the use of camouflage, decoys, mock operations and misinformation' as examples of war tricks. Customary international law and the San Remo Manuals recognize the above provisions and refine the methods and examples of prohibited warfare on this basis. This means that one side takes advantage of the characteristics of UUVs that are small, autonomous and can navigate underwater, and carry out camouflage and imitation, causing the enemy to make mistakes in target identification, thereby misleading the enemy's combat deployment or taking the opportunity to directly attack the enemy. On the premise that it does not constitute an act of perfidy, this falls within the scope of ruses of war and has legitimacy. While this would, in principle, allow belligerents to use UUVs for naval warfare, it still needs to be determined in conjunction with other rules of International Humanitarian Law and the Law of Armed Conflict. For example, the Law of Armed Conflict, such as Protocol I and the San Remo Manual, requires that care be taken to protect the natural environment from extensive, long-term and severe damage and to prohibit wanton destruction of the natural environment that is not justified military necessity. If an UUV camouflages or imitates a marine creature to carry out its mission, in particular an attack, inducing enemy to take an attack that causes irreversible damage to the natural environment, including biomes, such conduct undoubtedly constitutes perfidy. The species of creatures camouflaged by the unmanned underwater vehicle and the sea area in which it is located may also affect the corresponding identification.

In general, with the advancement and development of science and technology, weapon-type unmanned submarines have gradually become a necessary component of the informatization development of the navies of various countries. Although the weapon-type UUV itself does not violate any existing international humanitarian law or the law of armed conflict, as it is gradually installed in the navies of various states, coupled with its own unmanned, autonomous, high concealment and other characteristics, the weapon types of UUVs may still be utilized in ways that violate international humanitarian law or the law of armed conflict. Therefore, when states use weapons or various UUVs, they must abide by the current laws of naval warfare and accept the restrictions of relevant international laws and regulations. For example, when unmanned submarines use torpedoes and missiles to attack, they must abide by the provisions of Chapter 3 of the San Remo Manual on the basic principles and preventive measures of naval warfare, which mainly include the principle of distinction, the principle of proportionality, the principle of preventive measures, and the prohibition of polluting the environment, etc.; Another example is that when unmanned underwater vehicles conduct mine warfare, they must abide by the provisions of Chapter 4, Section 1 of the San Remo Manual on mine types, layout, clearance, etc., and perform relevant warning and clearance obligations; for another example, if a belligerent state uses UUVs to conduct a blockade, in addition to complying with the general rules on blockade stipulated in the San Remo Manual, it should also be noted that UUVs should be equipped with a device that can be used to warn or effectively identify the nature of the target, so as to fulfil notification and warning obligations or correctly identify the nature of the target vessel. In addition, although the San Remo Manual allows the use of ruses of war, belligerents are not allowed to use UUVs in perfidy, such as pretending to be exempt, civilian, neutral, etc., or pretending to express surrender, distress, etc.

4 Conclusion

At present, the rapid development of UUVs technology and the lack of regulation of existing International Law are worthy of attention, and the rules of International Law lack specific rules for UUVs, which are in a state of uncertainty. Academic views either strictly interpret existing legal rules or expand interpretations to apply principles flexibly. As a scholar has pointed out, 'the existing legal regime may or may not apply to maritime drones in its current state'.[43] Although it has been argued that it is easier and more convenient to effectively apply existing laws to entirely new areas of technology than to impose a new framework of legal principles. While the existing legal regime may not have been drafted with the development of ships capable of navigating independently, this condition alone does not preclude the application of these principles to ships adopting these new technologies, and the legal framework itself does not need to be changed.[44] However, the unclear legal status of UUVs and even the entire UMS has not only brought problems at the level of

43 Matt Bartlett, 'Game of Drones: Unmanned Maritime Vehicles and the Law of the Sea' (2018) 24 AULR 80.

44 Materna (n 15) 482.

legal theory, but may also attract the attention of sovereign states and various non-state entities in other fields such as politics, economy, and especially the military. For UUVs, a brand-new thing, the existing rules of International Law such as International Humanitarian Law and the Law of Armed Conflict at sea lack specific provisions, and can only be regulated through general principles and rules, and through the elaboration and analysis of some unclear scope of application and the content of rights and obligations, so that the activities of UUVs can effectively adapt to the existing rules of International Law. Existing technology can embed automatic target recognition devices in UUVs, allowing them to autonomously detect, classify, locate and identify targets. However, the underwater environment is complex, ambiguous and uncertain, and sea conditions will have a significant impact on the platform of UUVs navigating in shallow waters, especially the performance of sensors.[45] This technical level of problems has caused UUVs to pose a series of challenges to the existing law of armed conflict at sea, including the dilemma of algorithmic distinction in target identification and the conversion of ethical protocols into machine language, which makes it difficult to implement the principle of distinction; compliance with the principles of military necessity and proportionality (collateral damage) involves ethical decisions that are difficult to understand and make by machines; dehumanization of fatal decisions results in a lack of accountability (either from the programmer, the commander, or the machine itself).[46]

The renewal of the legal system often lags behind the pace of technological progress. Since there is still room for advancement in the technology of UUVs, and there is still great potential for expansion in future application scenarios. Therefore, in the face of the gaps and ambiguity of the current legal rules related to UUVs, legal regulation of them as early as possible can navigate their future technological development direction, avoid possible humanitarian crises and ethical risks and reduce unnecessary collateral damage in armed conflicts. In future adjustments to the rules of the law of armed conflict at sea, UUVs should be included in the scope of adjustment based on the integration of existing naval warfare rules and the development trend of intelligent integrated warfare, so as to solve the problem of UUVs in maritime operations, status, rights, obligations, operational principles, specific operational rules, and the subject of war responsibility. The establishment of a new legal regime for UUVs and the entire UMS is more effective and fundamental than trying to subjugate or exclude UUVs from the existing definition, and at the same time facilitates the understanding and action of various subjects of international

45 Liu (n 1) 23.

46 Sun Lu, 'Issues of the times in the application of the law of armed conflict and the Chinese solution' (2023) 4JSS 68, 72.

law. A scholar has conceived two options for constructing this new system.[47] However, whether it is the conclusion of a dedicated formal multilateral international treaty or the construction of a relatively less formal framework agreement, in the end, countries around the world need to take active action and work together to promote the renewal and development of the international law system.

References

2002 Commander's Handbook: Legal Bases for the Operations (GRE) s 2.11

2022 The Commander's Handbook on the Law of Naval Operations (USA)

Andrew H. Henderson, 'Murky Waters: The Legal Status of Unmanned Undersea Vehicles' (2006) 53 NLR 55

Annie Brett, 'Regulating the Autonomous Ocean' (2022) 22 BLR 1

Christopher C. Swain, 'Toward Greater Certainty for Unmanned Navigation, a Recommended United States Military Perspective on Application of the 'Rules of the Road' to Unmanned Maritime Systems' (2018) 3GLTR 119

Craig H. Allen, 'Determining the Legal Status of Unmanned Maritime Vehicles: Formalism vs Functionalism' (2018) 49 JMLC 477

Guo Zhongyuan, Zou Ligang, 'An International Law Analysis on the Incident of Unmanned Underwater Vehicle in the South China Sea' (2017) 4 HSJHU 17

ICRC Database 'Customary IHL' <https://ihl-databases.icrc.org/en/customary-ihl> accessed 19 February 2024

ICRC Database, 'San Remo Manual on International Law Applicable to Armed Conflicts at Sea' (12 June 1994) <https://ihl-databases.icrc.org/en/ihl-treaties/san-remo-manual-1994?activeTab=default> accessed 19 February 2024

ICRC Database, Treaties, 'Protocol Additional to the Geneva Conventions of 12 August 1949, and relating to the Protection of Victims of International Armed Conflicts (Protocol I)' (8 June 1977) <https://ihl-databases.icrc.org/en/ihl-treaties/api-1977?activeTab=default> accessed 19 February 2024

Jane G. Dalton, 'Future Navies—Present Issues' (2006) 82 ILS 297

Jeremia Humolong Prasetya Nainggolan, 'Military Application of Unmanned Underwater Vehicles: In Quest of a New Legal Regime?' (2018) 16 IJIL 61

Kazuhiro Nakatani, 'Submarines', *Max Planck Encyclopedia of Public International Law* (2021) <https://opil.ouplaw.com/view/10.1093/law:epil/9780199231690/law-9780199231690-e1839?rskey=ezH2qr&result=1&prd=MPIL> accessed 24 November 2021

47 Bartlett (n43) 88, 90.

Li Rui, 'On the Legal Status of Unmanned Ships' (2019) 4 COLR 165

Lindsay I. McCarl, 'Untethering UMVs from Vessels: Why the United States Should Construct a New Environmental Legal Scheme for Unmanned Maritime Vehicles' (2023) 127 DLR 46

Liu Dan, 'The Rule of International Law Regulating Underwater Unmanned Vehicles: Legal Status, Current Challenges and Solutions' (2021) 3 JOUC 13

Malgorzata Materna, 'Adjusting the Aperture: The International Law Case for Qualifying Unmanned Vessels as Warships' (2023) 100 ILS 452

Matt Bartlett, 'Game of Drones: Unmanned Maritime Vehicles and the Law of the Sea' (2018) 24 AULR 66

Michael N. Schmitt, David S. Goddard, 'International law and the military use of unmanned maritime systems' (2016) 98 IRRC 567

Oliver Daum, 'The Implications of International Law on Unmanned Naval Craft' (2018) 49 JMLC 71

Qiu Zhiming, Meng Xiangyao, Ma Yan, Chen Yi, Feng Wei, 'Development and key technologies of Maritime Unmanned Systems'(2023) 3 CJES 74

Rob McLaughlin, 'Unmanned Naval Vehicles at Sea: USVs, UUVs, and the Adequacy of the Law' (2011) 21 JLIS 100

Song Shuhua, Zhao Jinsong, 'The Legal Status of Unmanned Undersea Vehicles' (2017) 3 JSCSS 21

Sun Lu, 'Issues of the times in the application of the law of armed conflict and the Chinese solution' (2023) 4 JSS 68

Wang Shumin, Tang Xiaocong, 'Research on Legal Status of Unmanned Undersea Vehicles in International Law—Reflections on the Unmanned Undersea Vehicles Event between China and America' (2017) 4 PLS 3

Zhai Zhong, 'International Legal Regime of Unmanned Underwater Vehicles in Wartime' (PhD dissertation East China University of Political Science and Law 2022)

Zhou Yanlin, 'Challenges of Unmanned Underwater Vehicles Concerning Maritime Law Enforcement and China's Responses' (2023) 6 JSCSS 63

CHAPTER 2

Forcing Their Way Out at Sea: UMS in the Law of Naval Warfare

*Zhaoran Lin**

1 Introduction

Although strong artificial intelligence ('AI') that can virtually replace human beings still seems fictitious, it is now getting clearer that the era of 'dehumanization'[1] is arriving. This trend is permeating in all areas, military included. For international lawyers, unmanned aerial vehicles (with a more popular name 'drone') and autonomous weapon systems have long been the superstar that attracted most attentions. In contrast, unmanned maritime systems ('UMS') remained low-key for years due to their once limited capabilities and feasibility to undertake complex military operations at sea. However, it is now a totally different case. The past decade has witnessed a race to make UMS more adaptive in maritime environment, both on surface or undersea.[2] As naval powers are putting more UMS in trials and service, international and domestic legal issues follow.

Military operations at sea can be safely argued as one of the most important catalysts of modern international law. Hugo Grotius, always honored as the father of international law by modern international lawyers, wrote extensively on naval warfare, including the captures of prize and booty, and other war-related sovereign rights.[3] Naval warfare has persisted from an alleged international anarchy to an era we call global ocean governance. While UMS is making a full-scale impact in military fields, the existing literature mostly focuses on their peacetime use. Discussions of the law of naval warfare ('LONW') has

* Postdoctoral Researcher, Institute of Ocean Research/School of Law, Peking University. His research interests include law of the sea, law of war, law of territorial acquisition, history and theory of international law.

1 See Wolff Heintschel von Heinegg, Robert Frau, & Tassilo Singer (eds.), *Dehumanization of Warfare: Legal Implications of New Weapon Technologies* (2018, Springer) 1, 9.

2 See James Kraska & Raul Pedrozo, *Disruptive Technology and the Law of Naval Warfare* (2022, Oxford University Press) 83, 85.

3 Hugo Grotius, *Commentary on the Law of Prize and Booty*, edited and with an introduction by Martine Julia van Ittersum, (2006, Liberty Fund).

 | DOI:10.1163/9789004706279_004

so far remained rather limited with several possible reasons. Rules of LONW have been obscure and scattered. The relevant rules remain mostly customary without accurate written contents, while the latest conventional rules dated back to the beginning of the 20th century.[4] Despite enduring efforts mainly from non-state organizations and professional groups, the codification process never truly caught up with the development of military technology. It is true that many states are still not capable of maintaining independently a modern navy, still less an automated one. Nevertheless, the premature level of this particular system is not a result of long-lasting peace at sea, but rather the desires of naval powers to keep the rules flexible and practice-oriented enough for strategic reasons, with unsettled legal and political debates among them. The lack of immediate interest in this branch of law for the time being is necessarily linked to the postwar UN framework of collectively security, which has brought profound change to the legal picture of use of force and neutrality. But as the armed conflicts of Russia-Ukraine and Israel-Palestine show, both two cores of LONW have not lost their significance.

The revolutionary development of the UMS technology brings both challenges and opportunities to the traditional yet premature systems of law of naval warfare. On the one hand, the application of the law of naval warfare is highly dependent on basic concepts in the law of the sea, but the current vocabulary of the latter seems unprepared for UMS, therefore rendering its status controversial. It may even pose an existential threat to the LONW itself, if the use of UMS in naval warfare, very likely in an asymmetrical way, become common practices in the near future. On the other hand, the advent of UMS can serve to remind states and other international actors the importance of clearer rules, and hopefully push for a progressive and systematic development in this branch of law, as evidenced by the current scholarly discussions on the update and revision of the 1994 *San Remo Manual on International Law Applicable to Armed Conflicts at Sea.*

This chapter consists of five parts. Part 2 deals with the basic questions on the international legal status of UMS. The *jus ad bellum* issue is discussed in Part 3, where the use of UMS is studied under the framework of the use of force or forcible measures. The use of certain UMS may amount to armed attacks or less grave form of force, which triggers the issue of self-defense or other kinds of forcible (counter) measures. The next two parts then consider issues

4 No international treaties on law of naval warfare have been concluded since 1907 Hague Conference on Law of War except Geneva Convention II for the Amelioration of the Condition of the Wounded, Sick and Shipwrecked Members of the Armed Forces at Sea, which focused more on humanitarian issues rather than the traditional concern of belligerent and neutral rights.

concerning *jus in bello*. Part 4 concentrates on what belligerent UMS are entitled to do exactly in naval warfare according to their different legal statuses. In Part 5, special rights and obligations of states that apply to UMS in case of naval warfare are discussed, according to maritime neutrality law. The last part concludes.

2 Categorizing Military UMS

UMS is a concept referring to those which are able to operate and navigate at sea with no human beings on board to remain control. As a considerable volume of literature has already been dedicated to understanding whether military UMS can be categorized into ships and further warships, this chapter will not delve deeper into this question, but simply lists different kinds of possible classifications, thereby laying the foundation of LONW implications under different UMS statuses in the following parts.

2.1 *Legal Status as Ships?*

Normally in domestic law and international law, a ship or vessel is given a legal personality to bear rights and obligations to conduct maritime activities. This leads to a mindset that attaches the rights and obligations to the very status of 'ship' or 'vessel'. Therefore, the lack of a definition of ships or vessels in general international law or United Nations Convention of the Law of the Sea ('UNCLOS') becomes the first obstacle for putting UMS in its right place. It has been commonly argued that negotiators of major maritime treaties failed to foresee the automation technology and all these legal documents presuppose the presence of on-board human staff when they refer to ships or vessels. This argument may tell part of the truth, but still these treaties have not provided us the answer whether UMS can be legally called ships, because they never attempt to offer a general definition beyond the scope of subject matter they deal with. Therefore, there is at least no clear denial of the ship-status of UMS in treaties.[5] Some also argue that even some UMS are not classified as ships and therefore not entitled to certain rights for lack of conventional basis, justifications can be found alternatively in customary law for, e.g., navigational rights.[6] It is also

5 '[T]he definition of a ship is usually disconnected from the question of whether or not the ship is manned.' 'Comité Maritime International Working Group Position Paper on Unmanned Ships and the International Regulatory Framework' 3 <https://comitemaritime.org/wp-content/uploads/2018/05/CMI-Position-Paper-on-Unmanned-Ships.pdf> accessed 1 June 2021.

6 Craig H. Allen, 'Determining the Legal Status of Unmanned Maritime Vehicles: Formalism vs Functionalism' (2018) 49 JMLC 509; Michael N. Schmitt and David S. Goddard, 'International

worth noticing that unmanned underwater vehicles ('UUV') may be entitled to navigational rights by directly referring to Article 20 of UNCLOS as 'other underwater vehicles', even if they are not qualified as submarines, a recognized type of ships.[7] International law leaves the ultimate task of defining ships to states, and states pioneering in this industry are already taking prompt actions to recognize many types of UMS as ships. As specially affected states, their respective efforts may quickly contribute to new customary rules.

It suffices now to say that a final criteria or definition will depend upon state practices and international efforts to create or modify rules. Until then, it is safe to conclude that a great number of them should be classified as ships with certain rights.[8]

2.2 *Legal Status as Warships?*

For the purpose of LONW, it is important whether military UMS can be warships. One can immediately resort to Article 29 of UNCLOS, which reads:

> For the purposes of this Convention, 'warship' means a ship belonging to the armed forces of a State bearing the external marks distinguishing such ships of its nationality, under the command of an officer duly commissioned by the government of the State and whose name appears in the appropriate service list or its equivalent, and manned by a crew which is under regular armed forces discipline.[9]

Obstacles for military UMS thus mainly lie in the requirements of command and manning, which at first glance rule out any considerations of unmanned ships.

Law and the Military Use of Unmanned Maritime Systems', (2016) 98 IRRC567 578. Also see Memorial of the Government of the Republic of Finland (1991), *Case Concerning Passage through the Great Belt* (Finland v Denmark) (1992) ICJ Rep 41 406. Finland argued that 'International Law has never limited rights of passage through territorial sea and straits to an exclusive category of beneficiaries, whether defined as ships, vessels or otherwise. Rather,rights of passage have themselves been conceived in a functional sense, according the right of navigation to all craft which navigate upon the sea'.

7 'In the territorial sea, submarines and other underwater vehicles are required to navigate on the surface and to show their flag.' *United Nations Convention on the Law of the Sea* (UNCLOS), 10 Dec. 1982, 1833 *UNTS* 397, art 20.

8 Natalie Klein et al. 'Maritime Autonomous Vehicles: New Frontiers in The Law of the Sea' (2020) 69 ICLQ 721, 723.

9 The definition under UNCLOS was replicated in the San Remo Manual on International Law Applicable to Armed Conflicts at Sea. See *San Remo Manual on International Law Applicable to Armed Conflicts at Sea* (*San Remo Manual*), (12 June 1994) Rule 13(g).

Although UNCLOS is often crowned as the maritime constitution of the international community, not all maritime rights in international law are included or granted by it. Neither can it be applied in any given situation. The convention is often characterized as international law in peacetime, though with some important exceptions.[10] In general, States are always free to resort to other rules in customary international law, unless those rules are apparently incompatible with UNCLOS.[11] In wartime, even some direct contradictions are allowed on a *lex specialis* basis. For instance, Article 88 unambiguously required the high seas 'be reserved for peaceful purposes'. Yet no one ever questions the general rights of states to conduct belligerent operations on high seas during armed conflicts.

The caveat of 'for the purpose of this convention' implies the functionalist design of Article 29. Arguably, despite the caveat, this provision reflects customary international law definition,[12] because it basically inherits the substantive contents from the *Hague Convention (VII) of 1907 Relating to the Conversion of Merchant Ships into War-Ships* (hereinafter Hague Convention VII), which is often considered parts of customary law. Articles of Hague Convention VII in 1907 showed some differences of wordings:[13]

> A merchant ship converted into a war-ship cannot have the rights and duties accruing to such vessels unless it is placed under the direct authority, immediate control, and responsibility of the Power whose flag it flies.
>
> Merchant ships converted into war-ships must bear the external marks which distinguish the war-ships of their nationality.
>
> The commander must be in the service of the State and duly commissioned by the competent authorities. His name must figure on the list of the officers of the fighting fleet.
>
> The crew must be subject to military discipline.[14]

10 See e.g. art 44 of UNCLOS on duties of states bordering straits which stipulates that '[t]here shall be no suspension of transit passage'. This rule is interpreted to apply to all circumstances, including peacetime and wartime.

11 UNCLOS, art 293.

12 Schmitt & Goddard (n 6) 579.

13 It may be noted that for Schmitt and Goddard, the replicated part is from art 2–6 of Hague Convention VII. art 5 requires '[e]very merchant ship converted into a war-ship must observe in its operations the laws and customs of war'. *Ibid.*

14 Convention (VII) of 1907 Relating to the Conversion of Merchant Ships into War-Ships (18 October 1907) 205 *CTS* 319, art 4.

It is very likely that neither UNCLOS nor the Hague Convention VII foresaw the development of complicated UMS,[15] but the difference between the requirements of warships is telling that manning is not necessarily an essential element.[16] Moreover, the mere fact that a new technology is unforeseen in the law does not automatically render the law inapplicable or unable to adapt to new scenarios, as the case of submarines have enlightened.[17] For negotiators in the 1907 Hague Conference, the main concern is to ensure state control and the responsibility to command the warring ships, thereby eliminating privateering for good.[18] There is no evidence showing that UNCLOS changed the definition substantially due to different underlying purposes. Article 29, therefore, is more likely an adjusted and laconic restatement of the Hague Convention VII that coincidentally creates a misconception of extra requirements.

It is worth noticing that as commercial UMS can be converted into military ones, the process should be in compliance with Hague Convention VII if the relevant UMS are ships.

There may also be legal problems other than definitions. In some cases, although UMS can be categorized as warships, it can still be prohibited from participating in hostilities because of their inability to carry out certain obligations. This type of obstacles mainly come from international humanitarian law ('IHL'). While UMS warships are in principle not under protection in IHL because there is no one on board, they are normally expected to fulfil the legal obligations to protect people or other objects. It should be noted that these obligations fall directly on states or other armed groups, so they are not necessarily related to the status of a UMS.

For example, some UMS may also be considered as autonomous weapon systems as in the case of drones. The principle of distinction as the core element in IHL has already been extensively discussed in the context of autonomous weapons. In the present phase, UMS is far from autonomous navigation

15 It should be noted that remote-controlled unmanned vehicles have been used for naval purpose even before World War II. See S. Campbell, W. Naeem & G. W. Irwin, 'A Review on Improving the Autonomy of Unmanned Surface Vehicles through Intelligent Collision Avoidance Manoeuvres' (2012) 36 ARC2 267, 268.

16 For example, '[i]n the United States, all Navy ships designated "USS" and Coast Guard vessels designated "USCGC" are considered "warships" whether manned or unmanned under international law.' James Kraska et al, 'The Newport Manual on the Law of Naval Warfare' (2023) 101 ILS 38.

17 The introduction of submarines into the law of naval warfare and the category of warships has met with the same doubts. See Malgorzata Materna, 'Adjusting the Aperture: The International Law Case for Qualifying Unmanned Vessels as Warships', (2023) 100 ILS 452, 453.

18 Klein et al. (n 8) 723, 724.

and operation. The use of UMS is likely to be less controversial than drones in IHL, as drones are mostly directed against persons whose statuses remain difficult to determine even for human soldiers, but the main targets of UMS are different ships and aircraft that are usually more identifiable,[19] and tend to cause fewer direct casualties. Certain ships are exempt from attacks and other belligerent measures, but there are relatively clear rules on how these ships should be marked and identified.[20] Doubts have also been raised whether unmanned systems can recognize surrenders and stop attacks accordingly.[21] For UMS the problems may also be of minor concerns, because acts of surrender in armed conflicts at sea are always displayed with clearer signals than in land battlefields. It remains unanswered that whether UMS with the status of ship are subject to weapon reviews, to ensure that 'in the study, development, acquisition or adoption of a new weapon, means or method of warfare, a High Contracting Party is under an obligation to determine whether its employment would, in some or all circumstances, be prohibited by this Protocol or by any other rule of international law applicable to the High Contracting Party'.[22] Whatever conclusion for the question is reached,[23] it is clear that any systems, vehicles or devices that are not able to comply with the principle of distinction cannot be applied for the purpose of attacks in armed conflicts. The definition of attacks in the era of UMS, however, will be another question that will be addressed below.

---

19 The main targets of attack, warships and military aircraft, are legally expected to have significant external marks. *San Remo Manual*, Rule 13(g) (j). Also see Jeffrey S. Thurnher, 'The Law that Applies to Autonomous Weapon Systems', 17 *American Society of International Law Insights* (Jan. 18, 2013), <www.asil.org/insights/volume/17/issue/4/law-applies-autonomous-weapon-systems> accessed on Sep 20, 2021.

20 See Protocol additional to the Geneva Conventions of 12 August 1949, and relating to the protection of victims of international armed conflicts (Protocol I), (8 Jun. 1977) 1125 UNTS 3 Annex I.

21 Cf. Robert Sparrow, 'Twenty Seconds to Comply: Autonomous Weapon Systems and the Recognition of Surrender', (2015) 91 ILS 699.

22 Protocol I, art 36. Also see Klein et al, (n 8) 725,726. A distinction between means and methods of warfare may be needed, while the latter category is not necessary included in the article. See Kenneth Anderson, Daniel Reisner & Matthew Waxman, 'Adapting the Law of Armed Conflict to Autonomous Weapon Systems' (2014) 90ILS 386, 398.

23 The answer is likely affirmative for autonomous or AI weapons. See James Farrant & Christopher M. Ford 'Autonomous Weapons and Weapon Reviews: The UK Second International Weapon Review Forum', (2017) 93 ILS 389 However, the problems remain for UMS that are not fully autonomous or AI-driven, and whether UMS as a whole system can be regarded as new weapons or weapon systems.

Search and rescue (SAR) by UMS has also attracted attention.[24] A UMS can hardly comply with the obligations of search and rescue for *hors de combat*, persons who are incapable of performing their combat duties during war, people in distress or other sick and wounded people due to its limited capacity, as required for ordinary warships. The status or rights of UMS *per se* are not affected because the obligation is not placed on certain types of ships, and there are no treaties that incorporated SAR duty into any definitions of vessels or ships, including those regarding humanitarian aids. However, it would likely lead to brutal irresponsibility if UMS were completely free from SAR duty. In a typical asymmetrical battle, naval powers can conduct maritime operations solely by UMS and avoid their duties to a large extent. Therefore, new rules are expected in order to urge for full use of UMS in SAR, based on their respective functions, such as sending out SOS signals, providing temporary shelter, or even taking people on board.

Nevertheless, there seems to be no absolute difficulties for military UMS to be recognized as warships, if a certain level of military control and command is guaranteed. When a UMS satisfies the standards of a ship, it is up to states to decide whether to designate a warship status.

Other questions arise when UMS are released from warships. In this case, it may be argued the released UMS as attachments to the warships and are not entitled to warship status. However, it would be more reasonable to make distinctions under different circumstances. If UMS released are tethered to or can only operate in the immediate vicinity of the mother warships under strict control, they certainly should be treated the same as any other devices that can be temporarily separated from the mother ships. But when UMS can travel far away from their mother ships, there seems to be no practical difference from those harbor-based UMS. The situation should be similar in the case of UMS released from other UMS. The most practical criterion is the capability of the UMS to conduct independent operations, rather than its original platform.

2.3 *Legal Status as Auxiliary Vessels or Other 'Military Devices'?*

What if UMS, albeit recognized as ships, failed to satisfy international or domestic legal standards to become warships? Considerations of domestic legal or strategic factors may encourage states to avoid granting warship status to some military UMS. According to *San Remo Manual*, 'a vessel, other than a warship, that is owned by or under the exclusive control of the armed forces of

24 See Robert Sparrow, Rob McLaughlin & Mark Howard, 'Naval Robots and Rescue', (2017) 99 IRRC 1139.

a State and used for the time being on government non-commercial service',[25] can be defined as an auxiliary vessel. This is hardly a useful definition which tells us no more than its non-warship status. It does provide a status of military ship without the requirement of manning, but as demonstrated above, manning is not really an obstacle for states. States like the US, the UK and Japan have lists of naval auxiliaries,[26] but none of them provide a more sophisticated definition. The distinction between warships and naval auxiliaries is highly functional,[27] and the latter aims to support rather than directly engage in attacks, including refueling, replenishment and disembarking materials or troops. Accordingly, auxiliaries are not entitled to any belligerent rights other than self-defense. A UMS can perfectly perform nearly all tasks of a traditional auxiliary (except transporting troops or other people). But again, there are no rules in international law on when to designate a ship as auxiliary, so it's up to individual states to decide the case. Naval powers want more than supportive functions from UMS and would not limit these systems as auxiliaries unless they find it more beneficial.

The 'identity crisis' remains for those military UMS which are not qualified as ships. The concept of 'military device' undefined in Article 19(2)(f) of UNCLOS come to us, which probably refers to those with military characters operating at sea yet not qualified as ships. In the 1991 Convention on the Marking of Plastic Explosives for the Purpose of Detection we can find a definition of 'duly authorized military devices', though no link has ever been established between the two instruments. In the 1991 Convention, military devices include but are not restricted to 'shells, bombs, projectiles, mines, missiles, rockets, shaped charges, grenades, and perforators exclusively for military or police purposes according to the laws and regulations of the State Party concerned'.[28] In Section 845 of Title 18 of the United States Code in 2006, which concerns military-related crimes and criminal procedures, similar definition was adopted, with 'similar devices manufactures' added into the category.[29] The aforementioned definition is for the main purpose of dealing with explosives rather than providing a comprehensive understanding of military

25 *San Remo Manual*, Rule 13(h).

26 See Kraska et al. (n 16) 45.

27 'UK Royal Navy unmanned vessels (of which there are 23 at the time of writing) are currently listed as auxiliaries in the experimentation section of the UK Defence Shipping Register, but with the aspiration that they be classified as warships where appropriate once the capabilities under experimentation are proven.' Ibid 40, 41.

28 Convention on the Marking of Plastic Explosives for the Purpose of Identification, (3 Jan. 1991) 2122 UNTS 359, art 1(5).

29 18 *U.S.C.* §845(c)(3) (2006).

devices, and military devices at sea may be well beyond its concern, but it does shed some lights on a rough image of what these devices really are. Some UMS can be qualified as these devices as long as they possess capability of spontaneous explosion and causing physical damages. Conventions governing the use of mines and torpedoes are already applicable, if UMS are themselves designed for prepared detonations,[30] because neither mines nor torpedoes have been clearly defined[31] to exclude autonomous or AI systems. For those UMS without warheads within and cannot participate in attacks directly, they may also be classified as military devices, at least for the purpose of UNCLOS. The term in Article 19(2)(f) must consist of devices other than those weapons, otherwise it would render Article 19(2)(b) meaningless.[32]

Under this framework, UMS are almost treated as mere weapons, effectively transforming them into sole objects of weapon laws, without any rights or obligations in their own. This is exactly the same logic that has been applied to unmanned aerial vehicles. Though it sounds unproblematic in a theoretical sense, this framework in practice can be too restrictive for UMS to function properly. Drones do not lose many of their strategic values when classified as ordinary weapons,[33] but for UMS, their military values mainly come from their capacity of multiple functions,[34] including navigation. When categorized as weapons, the navigational capacity of UMS may face serious legal challenges. For some states, UMS will lose most strategic and tactical values if they cannot be warships,[35] not to mention the case where they are mere weapons. UMS of very small size and designed for one-off use could be reasonably considered as weapons, but for other UMS, such categorization would not be satisfying enough.

To summarize, military UMS can be classified as warships or auxiliary vessels if they enjoy the legal status of ships. In a practical sense, individual states have the final say on these two categories. Otherwise, they can be classified as military devices, though it is not entirely clear what this means legally. For those UMS released from warships or other UMS, the most reasonable criterion is to tell by their capacity to operate independently. It should be noted that

---

30 Convention (VIII) Relative to the Laying of Automatic Submarine Contact Mines, (18 Oct. 1907) 36 Stat. 2332, T.S. No. 541.

31 See Hitoshi Nasu & David Letts, 'The Legal Characterization of Lethal Autonomous Maritime Systems: Warship, Torpedo, or Naval Mine?', (2020) 96 ILS 79.

32 A comparison with art 19(2)(b) of UNCLOS also supports this interpretation.

33 Belligerent rights of naval warfare are limited to military aircraft, but for now UAV is much more often deployed in targeted killings than launching attacks in maritime battles.

34 See Kraska et al (n 16) 41.

35 Nasu & Letts (n 31) 86.

non-ship UMS may also be entitled to some rights that ships enjoy, if they are provided in sources of international law other than UNCLOS. UMS may fall into categories of weapons if certain standards are met. UMS may therefore have more than one status, and be regulated under different legal regimes.

3 UMS and the Law Relating to Use of Force

Modern law of war in a broad sense can be divided into two parts, namely *jus ad bellum* and *jus in bello*. Traditional law of naval warfare does not deal with legal issues on use of force. This specific branch was for long considered to apply only after an intense armed conflict begins, which means it consists of *jus in bello* at sea and law of maritime neutrality. Nevertheless, the line has been blurred in modern maritime military operations. The International Tribunal for the Law of the Sea ('ITLOS') has specifically noted that: '[T]he traditional distinction between naval vessels and law enforcement vessels in terms of their roles has become considerably blurred … it is not uncommon today for States to employ the two types of vessels collaboratively for diverse maritime tasks.'[36] War is now seldom declared, so the start of an armed conflict now depends on the assessment of actual behaviors of states. Naval operations can be seemingly the same during peacetime and wartime, but they have different legal basis and hence are subject to different limitations. When violent incidents occur at sea, it is challenging for states and international lawyers to distinguish between law enforcement by military vessels and wartime naval operations. States have been making use of this ambiguity to conduct the so-called 'maritime hybrid warfare'[37] or 'hybrid naval warfare'[38] in order to maximize their strategic interests. With the application of UMS, this strategy is likely to become more militarily effective but legally perplexing. Therefore, before looking into narrow-sense LONW issues, it is necessary to understand the potential role of UMS in triggering naval warfare. In this regard, several hypothetical scenes will be examined below.

---

36 The *Case concerning the detention of three Ukrainian naval vessels* (Ukraine v. Russian Federation), ITLOS Order of (25 May 2019) para. 64.

37 Martin Murphy, Frank G Hoffman & Gary Schaub, Jr, *Hybrid Maritime Warfare and the Baltic Sea Region*, University of Copenhagen (2016) <https://cms.polsci.ku.dk/publikationer/Hybrid_Maritime_Warfare_and_the_Baltic_Sea_Region.pdf> accessed 1 September 2022.

38 Alexander Lott, Hybrid Threats and the Law of the Sea: Use of Force and Discriminatory Navigational Restrictions in Straits, (2022,Brill/Nijhoff) 28.

3.1 *Naval Navigation*

As military UMS are becoming more capable of conducting direct attacks, they are expected to play a much bigger role in potential violent conflicts at sea. UMS are now able to use force in the way traditional warships do,[39] which should be examined through the lens of use of force. Firing heavy gunshots or launching missiles are clear examples use of force. However, given its unclear status, a UMS may be considered to conduct attacks even when no force in traditional sense is used.

Consider several military UMS with warheads navigating through the territorial sea of another state. If these UMS enjoy the status of warships or auxiliary vessels, the rights to conduct an expedient and continuous passage may apply, although there may be some domestic restrictions. If they are only 'military devices', it is highly unlikely they can enjoy the rights of innocent passage in foreign territorial sea. The same applies to UMS that are only considered as weapons.

Theoretically speaking, violations of rules regarding innocent passage by military vessels, or military non-innocent passage in short, are essentially different from use of force or armed attacks. In the former case, the coastal State may take the necessary steps in its territorial sea to prevent passage which is not innocent,[40] without referring to any kind of self-defense. However in practice, it is better to view them as a conceptual continuum varying in degrees.

Firstly, when warships in the course of innocent passage release UMS, they are clearly in violation of the rules of Article 19(2)(f) of UNCLOS. If the released UMS are regarded as weapons, not only Article 19(2)(b) may be breached, but the action may be deemed by the coastal state as use of force in certain situations.

Secondly, in the case where UMS as weapons enter the territorial sea of another state, it is not a violation of rules on innocent passage but likely an act of force, because there is no ship at all. As shown in the *Nicaragua* case of the International Court of Justice ('ICJ'), sending a considerable number of mines into the territorial sea of another state can amount to an armed attack.[41]

Lastly, it is also possible that a UMS-using state list a small-size UMS as a warship, while the coastal state see it as a weapon. In this case, it may never

39 Cf. Julian Turner, 'Sea Hunter: Inside the US Navy's Autonomous Submarine Tracking Vessel' (*Naval Technology*, 3 May 2018, Last Updated 30 January, 2020), <https://www.naval-technology.com/features/sea-hunter-inside-us-navys-autonomous-submarine-tracking-vessel/> accessed 20 September 2021.

40 UNCLOS, art 25(1).

41 *Military and Paramilitary Activities in and against Nicaragua* (Nicaragua. v. U.S.), Judgment, (1986) ICJ Rep 14, 227, 251.

undertake such a passage, because the navigation is itself an 'exercise or practice with weapons of any kind'. As mentioned above, its passage may also conflict with Article 19(2)(a).

Therefore, UMS with warheads, especially for those that are small in size and capable of spontaneous explosion, may find it hard to conduct innocent passages, whatever status they are granted. Moreover, their entering the territorial seas *per se* can be regarded as use of force by coastal states. In a similar vein, it could be regarded as use of force when UMS of this type approach constructions on the continental shelf or in the exclusive economic zone ('EEZ') of another state.

Even if certain acts of UMS do not amount to use of force, some may nevertheless qualify as threat of force. According to Ian Brownlie, '[a] threat of force consists in an express or implied promise by a government of a resort to force conditional on non-acceptance of certain demands of that government'.[42] As generally accepted, threats of force include:

> [U]nder certain circumstances, rearmament, military manoeuvres, establishment of military bases on the territory of a foreign state, bellicose declarations, concentration of troops along the borders, general mobilization, and propaganda in favour of a war of aggression.[43]

Though, for example, the entering of territorial seas of another state by some military UMS does not exactly fit in the categories listed above, it can demonstrate an implied promise and somehow resemble the concentration of troops. Accompanied by political requests and pressures, this act seems to fulfil the requirements of threats.

It should be noted that use of force does not necessarily amount to an armed attack in the sense of self-defense. ICJ has made a distinction between armed attacks and use of force short of armed attacks, or use of force of less grave form,[44] and created some rather vague and controversial terms like 'frontier incidents'.[45] The use of military UMS lack of intense attacks, therefore, are

---

42 Ian Brownlie, International Law and the Use of Force by States, (1963, Clarendon Press) 364.

43 FranÇois Dubuisson & Anne Lagerwall, 'The Threat of the Use of Force and Ultimata', in Marc Weller (ed.), *The Oxford Handbook of the Use of Force in International Law* (2015, Oxford University Press) 913.

44 *Nicaragua* case (n 41) 114; *Oil Platforms* (Islamic Republic of Iran v. United States of America), Judgment, I. C. J. Reports (2003) 187.

45 *Nicaragua* case (n 41) 113. The logic was followed later in Eritrea-Ethiopia case. 'Eritrea Ethiopia Claims Commission, Partial Award, *Jus ad Bellum* (Ethiopia's Claims 1–8), 2005' (2006) 45 ILM 430.

most likely to be characterized as use of force short of armed attacks. As a result, victim states are not entitled to resort to self-defense of Article 51 of the UN Charter in these cases. That said, there is generally no clear prohibitions in international law on victim states' resort to self-help, including pacific and forcible (counter) measures.[46]

3.2 *Naval Law Enforcement and Use of Force*

Naval law enforcement, especially navigational restriction is now a common operation usually carried out by naval vessels, both in peacetime and wartime. Military UMS prove more than competent to perform these tasks. In a navigational restriction operation, force is a frequent resort in order to deter vessels that fail to comply with restrictions. In international law, however, using force against ships can lead to serious results, as force against even commercial vessels may constitute an 'aggression' against a State.[47] Using UMS in this scenario seems to be a rather good choice, as their attacks are more likely of lower intensity that fail to reach the level of armed attack in international law. However, if UMS become commonly used in naval operations, law enforcement against UMS—rather than by UMS—can be a thorny question. It has been argued by some scholars that use of force against one single unmanned warship can amount to an armed attack which can lead to an armed conflict.[48]

Using force on UMS in case they are threatening or harming the peace, good order or security, seems to be a reasonable option, for the purpose of self-defense or less intensive self-help. Victim states might capture, disable or destroy a UMS that is using force, as long as the response can fulfill a test similar to the standard of lawful self-defense.[49] Normally, using force against one warship or government ship of another State is already an armed attack. However, as McLaughlin has argued, using force on UMS with the status of naval ships may be considered an armed attack, but may not reach the same level as the use of force on traditional warships or auxiliary vessels, for there are supposed to be less significant losses of financial, strategic values or human lives.[50]

---

46 *Nicaragua* case (n 41) 110; *Oil Platforms* (Islamic Republic of Iran v. United States of America), Judgment, Separate Opinion of Judge Simma, I. C. J. Reports (2003) 331, 332.

47 *Definition of Aggression*, General Assembly Resolution 3314 (XXIX) (14 December 1974) art 3(d).

48 See Kraska et al, (n 16) 21, 22.

49 See Patrick O. Jackson, 'Drone Interdiction: Use of Force as a Countermeasure against Unmanned Vehicles at Sea', (2018) 226 MLR 223.

50 Rob McLaughlin, 'Unmanned Naval Vehicles at Sea: USVs, UUVs, and the Adequacy of the Law', (2011) 21 JLIS 100.

Attacking military UMS as warships under certain circumstances would not be in violation of international law, including law of immunity that protect warships. Warships are certainly not entitled to immunity in the context of self-defense or armed conflicts. In the context of forcible measures in law enforcement, some scholars are of the opinion that forcible measures can be taken against warships if they are in breach of the rules of innocent passage and refuse to correct their wrongs, for example, submarines that keep submerged and refuse to surface.[51] It seems safe to say that when foreign warships are releasing UMS in the territorial sea of the coastal State that constitute use of force, force may be used against the warships themselves and the UMS. Logically, using force on UMS with auxiliary vessels or other status should not become a problem either.

Self-defense can take place theoretically anywhere, including the territory of a third state, though immediate urgency and danger should be proved.[52] Military units thus can fight back wherever they are under armed attack by military UMS. This does not apply to forcible measures. These measures, though forcible, are not normally attributed to acts of war but law enforcement activities. They are thus strictly confined by national jurisdictions in different maritime areas. In areas where freedom of navigation applies, forcible measures can be taken, in due regard of rights of other states,[53] but it seems difficult to be justified under the framework of law enforcement. When in territorial sea or archipelagic waters of a third State, or an international strait, the legal basis to use forcible countermeasures becomes even more shaky, if there is any. This arguably weakens the ability of States to respond to UMS operations in an alleged hybrid warfare. The most viable basis thus lies on unit self-defense independent of the self-defense of States.[54]

4 Navigational and Belligerent Rights of UMS in Armed Conflicts at Sea

For the purpose of LONW, the different types and characters of ships are always recognized as deciding factors of their respective rights and obligations during

51 Cf. Ingrid Delupis, 'Foreign Warships and Immunity for Espionage', (1984) 78 AJIL53 72,73; Francesco Francioni, 'Peacetime Use of Force, Military Activities, and the New Law of the Sea, (1985) 18 CILJ203 209, 210.

52 San Remo Manual, Rule 30.

53 UNCLOS, arts. 58, 79, and 87.

54 Cf. Standing Rules of Engagement for U.S. Forces, CJCSI 3121.01B, ¶6(b) (13 June 2005).

armed conflicts. Warships, auxiliary vessels, other governmental ships and merchant ships are strictly distinguished from each other in theory. The use of UMS in naval warfare also has to comply with these rules. But the new technology has posed great challenges to LONW, and even question the basic foundation of the law.

4.1 *Navigational Rights*

Navigation used to be of critical significance for naval warfare before long-range technology of attacks were available to states. It is still important for power projection in modern military strategies, especially for naval hegemony. In a traditional sense, only a ship is entitled to wartime navigational rights, while other types of devices or equipment in the sea are mostly excluded. In particular, weapons are sole objects under international law that is not associated with navigation, even for torpedoes and autonomous mines that do navigate physically. The development of UMS technology may serve as an important turning point, as it blurs the line between different types of ships and between ships and other devices. For the time being, to what extent UMS will challenge this framework remains highly unforeseeable.

In an international armed conflict ('IAC') at sea, states have self-evident 'rights' or more exactly, 'privilege',[55] to navigate in all sea areas under sovereignty of belligerent states, including belligerent internal waters, territorial seas and archipelagic waters. Belligerent UMS of whatever status can navigate in these areas, as there is no need for 'navigational rights' proper in this case. There seems to be no difficulties in applying this conclusion to the high seas, belligerent EEZs and continental shelves, although with slight modifications due to the requirements of due regard for the rights of other states, unless prohibited by specific conventional or customary rules.[56] Article 88, with Article

55 In a Hohfeldian legal analysis, rights are to be exercised with obligatory assistance by corresponding duty-bearers, when privileges are only freedoms to do something where no one is legally obliged to ensure its fulfillment. Navigation in belligerent seas is obviously a 'privilege' that can only be exercised by the belligerent State on its own, and the opposing State is never obliged to ensure the fulfillment. See Wesley N. Hohfeld, 'Some Fundamental Legal Conceptions as Applied in Judicial Reasoning', (1913–1914) 23YLJ16 30, 44.

56 *San Remo Manual*, Rule 10. There are disputes on whether belligerents are obliged to have due regards toward neutral states in case of naval warfare, although *San Remo Manual* explicitly mentions the obligation in Rule 34 and 35. See Kraska et al, (n 16) 77, 78. The reluctance may be mainly due to some 'expansionist' interpretations of due regards as including procedural obligations to inform and consult. Cf. Yurika Ishii, 'The "Due Regard" Obligation and the Peaceful and Economic Uses of the EEZ Other than Fisheries' (2019) 34I CML 73, 74; Jinyuan Su, 'Is the Establishment of Air Defence Identification Zones Outside National Airspace in Accordance with International Law?' (2021) 32 EJIL 1309, 1326.

58(2) of UNCLOS, cannot apply in this case to prevent the use of UMS with whatever status in battles, as these areas are all areas of war in customary LONW, which in wartime serve as *lex specialis*.[57]

Neutral EEZs and continental shelves are also areas of war. But different rules may apply in respect of military UMS apart from the requirement of due regard. Since the law of peacetime apply between belligerent and neutral states in principle,[58] neutral coastal states having interests in securing normal activities under their jurisdiction sometimes resort to law enforcement to keep out hostile acts. Unfortunately, there has not been a comprehensive and exhausted list of rights for coastal States' jurisdictions in these zones, just as there is none for maritime belligerent rights. Therefore, while belligerent military UMS as ships can navigate almost freely in these zones, those that are not qualified as such may be subject to coastal law enforcement for security considerations. In practice, coastal states may more likely choose to stay tolerant in order to maintain neutrality. However, whether this kind of tolerance can be understood as *opinio juris* of accepting a new type of belligerent rights, is hard to determine. Coastal states can argue that they are acting restraint out of strategic reasons instead of legal convictions. This is particularly convincing in the case where states believe the law of neutrality has become obsolete. It is

---

57 UNCLOS, art 88: 'The high seas shall be reserved for peaceful purposes', art 58(2): 'Articles 88 to 115 and other pertinent rules of international law apply to the exclusive economic zone in so far as they are not incompatible with this Part.' Comparisons can be made with the 'peaceful-purpose' clause in the Antarctic Treaty and the Outer Space Treaty, both of which provide specific military examples and are recognized as general prohibitions on use of force. 'Antarctica shall be used for peaceful purposes only. There shall be prohibited, *inter alia*, any measures of a military nature, such as the establishment of military bases and fortifications, the carrying out of military maneuvers, as well as the testing of any type of weapons.' The Antarctic Treaty, (1 Dec. 1959) 402 UNTS 5778, art 1(1); 'The moon and other celestial bodies shall be used by all States Parties to the Treaty exclusively for peaceful purposes. The establishment of military bases, installations and fortifications, the testing of any type of weapons and the conduct of military maneuvers on celestial bodies shall be forbidden. The use of military personnel for scientific research or for any other peaceful purposes shall not be prohibited. The use of any equipment or facility necessary for peaceful exploration of the moon and other celestial bodies shall also not be prohibited.' 'Treaty on Principles Governing the Activities of States in the Exploration and Use of Outer Space, including the Moon and Other Celestial Bodies', UNGA Res 2222 (XXI), 19 December 1966, Annex, art 4.

58 Committee on Maritime Neutrality, International Law Association, *Helsinki Principles on the Law of Maritime Neutrality*, in *International Law Association Report of the 68th Conference*, Taipei (1998) 496, Principle 1.3, <https://archive.org/stream/pdfy-zwUMQoiwLk5e3kj_/Helsinki%20Principles%20On%20The%20Law%20Of%20Maritime%20Neutrality_djvu.txt> accessed 20 September 2021.

now still too early to predict how the relevant practices (and hopefully, rules) will develop.

The 1907 Hague Convention (XIII) concerning the Rights and Duties of Neutral Powers in Naval War ('Hague Convention XIII'), grants belligerent warships a right of mere passage in neutral territorial seas instead of innocent passage,[59] which can be one of the 'other rules of international law' in Article 19(1) of UNCLOS. The *San Remo Manual*, allegedly codifying customary law, extended the scope to cover auxiliary vessels.[60] Therefore, only belligerent UMS with the status of warships or auxiliaries may enjoy the right of mere passage. The customary status of this rule is certainly questionable, as even peacetime innocent passage of warships are still under considerable debates. Meanwhile, a weapon-like UMS should be excluded from the regime of mere passage, because its entry effectively turns the neutral territorial seas into areas of military operations. In this case, a neutral coastal State should not be too concerned about the unclear status of UMS. It would have a wide discretion to restrict or prohibit such belligerent passages in their territorial seas, as long as the restrictions or prohibitions are enforced on all belligerents in an impartial manner,[61] which is distinct from the rights recognized by Article 25 of UNCLOS. The belligerent naval vessels in the course of mere passage, in addition to complying with the requirement of innocent passage, cannot in effects base their naval operations or seek sanctuary in neutral territorial seas. It could be technically and economically burdensome to tell whether a UMS is actually basing its naval operations during a passage, so neutral coastal states may prefer to prohibit all passages of belligerent UMS to avoid violating the rules of neutrality.

Rights of transit passage and archipelagic sea lanes passage and innocent passage in international straits are not suspendable according to UNCLOS,[62] which also applies in times of war as evidenced by state practices. Warship and auxiliary UMS therefore may not be legally barred from these waters.[63] However, as mentioned before, the navigational rights in these areas of UMS without the status of ships, if any, can only be based in customary law. Even if such customary rights are justified, they are not rights of 'transit passage' or 'archipelagic sea lanes passage' proper. They are thus more likely to be suspended in

59 Convention (XIII) Concerning the Rights and Duties of Neutral Powers in Naval War (18 Oct. 1907) 36 Stat. 2415, art 10.

60 San Remo Manual, Rule 19.

61 Hague Convention XIII, art 9.

62 UNCLOS, arts 44, 45(2), 54; *San Remo Manual*, Rule 29.

63 See UNCLOS, arts 34, 39, 45.

times of war at the discretion of neutral coastal states, in the lack of permanent guarantee of UNCLOS.

In the context of a non-international armed conflicts ('NIAC'), the belligerent parties in principle are not entitled to any special wartime navigational rights in areas under jurisdiction of other states. History also shows that such rights are not usually militarily necessary for the warring Parties.[64] In this case, the navigational rights of UMS is virtually the same as in peacetime. Also, it has been commonly agreed by most (western) international lawyers, that Parties in NIAC are only allowed to conduct hostile military operations within their own territorial sea, but this argument is becoming more disputed in our time when more NIACs take place and spread seawards.

4.2 *Belligerent Rights*

In a *lex lata* sense, for states to justify their employment of UMS in navigational operations, the most important legal task is to interpret their UMS as ships. Paradoxically, when it comes to actual use of force in wartime, the status of ship can somehow become a legal setback. Under traditional understandings of LONW, the rights to use belligerent measures, or shortly 'belligerent rights' in a broad sense, has been granted to warships only.[65] Other vessels, including naval auxiliaries, are prevented from using belligerent measures and are not allowed to do direct harm to belligerent or neutral vessels.[66] It is true that devices other than ships do not have any belligerent rights either, but in fact they don't need any rights of this kind because they can become weapons themselves. No one would ever ask if a sea-to-air missile has belligerent rights. Therefore, when a military UMS ship fails to be recognized as warships, it can only display very limited functions in case of engagement, while a UMS as other devices is 'permitted' to use force. This will soon become more than a theoretical dilemma, for maritime powers have already been experimenting on medium-size UMS that aims to perform navigational operations as well as striking targets at sea.

---

64 During the American Civil War, the Spanish Civil War (1936–1939), the 1983–2009 armed conflict in Sri Lanka, the Gaza conflict and Yemeni conflict that can be regarded as NIACs, Parties resort to belligerent measures outside their sovereign waters, but seldom claim wartime navigational rights to pass through neutral waters.

65 *Declaration Respecting Maritime Law* (Apr. 16, 1856) 115 *CTS* 1, reprinted in (1907) 1AJILM 89; Hague Convention VII, Preamble.

66 See Terry D. Gill & Dieter Fleck, 'The Law of Military Operations at Sea', in Terry D. Gill, Dieter Fleck (eds.), *The Handbook of the International Law of Military Operations* (2nd edn.) (2015, Oxford University Press) 385, 392.

It should be noted that belligerent rights is exclusively a concept applied to IACs at sea, and there are far fewer restrictions on similar rights in NIACs, where non-warship UMS, especially auxiliary UMS are generally not barred from using direct force and performing other wartime operations, if applicable,[67] as long as the target is one of another Party in the conflict.[68]

In practice, the traditional distinction between warships and auxiliaries sometimes creates more problems than it answers. Without a clear definition of belligerent rights and belligerent measures, there remains a vast gray zone of what tasks auxiliary vessels are entitled to carry out in wartime. It is most common for auxiliaries to conduct resupply at sea operations, carry troops and war materiel and undertake defensive mine countermeasures,[69] and the most explicit prohibition is that these vessels cannot engage in direct attacks against other vessels in IACs, except for their own self-defense.[70] However, it is interesting to note that for the UK:

> Warships and *auxiliary vessels*, however, are *prohibited from launching an attack whilst flying a false flag*, and at all times from actively simulating the status of those vessels exempt from attack listed in paragraph 13.33.[71]

From this plain wording, auxiliary vessels for the UK should be permitted to launch an attack in normal circumstances, otherwise this provision would not have included this specific requirement for this type of ships. That means even the most essential difference between warships and auxiliaries are somehow ambivalent.

---

67 The law of naval warfare in NIACs is a least developed branch of international law, where there are seldom practices or specific rules. See generally Wolff Heintschel von Heinegg, 'Methods and Means of Naval Warfare in Non-International Armed Conflicts', (2012) 88 ILS 211.

68 In NIACs at sea, the legality of 'belligerent' measures that have effects on ships of other states is more controversial. While the state governments in NIACs may be entitled to exercise the right of visit and search, the opposition group is hardly considered to have any rights against ships of other states, unless it is recognized by the flag states as a belligerent. Ibid.

69 Klein et al. (n 8) 725.

70 Institute of International Law, 'The Law of Naval Warfare Governing the Relations between Belligerents (1913)', reprinted in Dietrich Schindler & Jiri Toman (eds.), *The Laws of Armed Conflicts: A Collection of Conventions, Resolutions and Other Documents* (2004, Brill/Nijhoff) 1125, art 12.

71 United Kingdom Ministry of Defence, *The Manual of the Law of Armed Conflict* (2005, Oxford University Press) 365 The Paragraph 13.33 mentioned here is a list including twelve classes of vessels exempt from attack, 356–57.

Belligerent rights that are related to warships usually include the rights to commit attacks, undertake prize measures or similar operations, and establish blockades or other military zones.

4.2.1 Attacks

Direct attacks usually can be agreed to mean firing guns and cannons, launching missiles and torpedoes, or the use of weapons that aims to neutralize or destroy targets in a relative short period. Other 'less direct' actions, including conducting electronic warfare, launching cyber attacks or laying mines, can also be attacks under LONW, but disagreement exists.[72] Small-size UMS may be suitable or even specifically designed for these operations.[73] For example, a small UMS may carry EMP weapons and paralyze the control system of a belligerent warship after approaching it unnoticed. It would be pointless to deprive this right from UMS of whatever status, otherwise the user state may just claim that the UMS is only a military device launched elsewhere. States may also deploy UMS to conduct mine laying and mine countermeasures, which is traditionally regarded as a belligerent right.[74] The mines that are laid may well be another type of UMS. In the above scenes, the use of UMS appears a more economic and humanitarian choice. In modern warfare, where the meaning of attack grows more ambiguous every day, it seems inevitable that UMS will play a more active role in military attacks, even they are not warships and therefore not allowed to attack directly in a traditional sense. Also, countering UMS (by using UMS) will likely become an important part in naval operations. In that case, denial of rights to attack is even more meaningless.

4.2.2 Prize Measures

Prize taking is an important method of traditional naval warfare, but its significance has been on decline continuously in modern times. Prize measure has also been considered a part of belligerent rights confined to warships only. These measures may typically include visit and search, interception and capture of neutral merchant vessels.

---

72 For example, some scholars argue that '[l]aying a minefield, either at sea or on land, never in itself constitutes an attack … it is the activation of the mine that constitutes an attack.' Kraska et al, (n 16) 132.

73 See Kara Chadwick, 'Unmanned Maritime Systems Will Shape the Future of Naval Operations: Is International Law Ready?', in Malcolm D. Evans and Sofia Galani (eds.), *Maritime Security and the Law of the Sea: Help or Hindrance?* (2020, Edward Elgar) 146.

74 During the Iran-Iraq War (1980–1988), Iran has employed auxiliary vessels to lay naval mines during naval warfare. See e.g. Bradley Peniston, 'Capturing the Iran Ajr', <http://www.navybook.com/nohigherhonor/pic-iranajr.shtml> accessed 1 September 2022.

It is doubtful whether UMS as warships have the capacity to undertake prize measures. UMS can provide military assistance but seems incapable of finishing the tasks on their own, because they cannot conduct physical visit, search or capture. One may argue that a visual visit and search into the data of the target ships is already available. In fact, boarding and inspection *in situ* by human beings has become less effective since World War II. The purpose of prize measures has largely changed, from making economic benefits and controlling contraband to maintaining control over strategically important areas. It serves no purpose stopping ships and checking on thousands of containers, when the inspecting warship becomes a static target for enemies. The same strategic goals can be fulfilled by diversion, which means requiring vessels to change their courses or even sending them to certain locations.[75] A UMS on mission is able to intercept and force the target vessel to designated ports or harbors. This new method is preferable to captures or visit-and-search operations for economic and strategic reasons.[76] Meanwhile, the regime of contraband can be largely replaced by the system of navigational certificates, or navicerts,[77] which grants neutral vessels clearances for undisturbed voyage in advance. In these new methods, UMS is a perfect choice.

If one insists that we should apply the traditional rules that have not been seriously challenged for almost a century, then only UMS as warships are entitled to undertake prize measures in IACs.[78] However, one should also bear in mind that auxiliaries usually also serve in peacetime law enforcement, and therefore carry out similar measures. Visit, search and capture has completely different legal basis under law in peacetime and wartime, but between a belligerent and neutral state, both these two legal regimes can be in effect at the same time. This ultimately leads to the phenomenon of 'maritime hybrid warfare'. In any case, auxiliary UMS can always be designed to accompany warships and help enforce prize measures. Moreover, diversion is not generally recognized as a traditional belligerent measure *per se* but emerged as accepted practices in modern times, meaning that UMS other than warships could be able to undertake such measure during armed conflicts at sea. As the relatively new measures is gaining more importance, UMS may in fact end up taking a larger part in these military operations, replacing the roles traditional warships play.

75 Paragraph 119 of the *San Remo Manual* requires the consent of the neutral vessel before diversion, but is not necessarily considered as reflective of state practices. Kraska et al (n 16) 173.

76 See James Farrant, 'Modern Maritime Neutrality Law' (2014) 90ILS 198.

77 Ibid 243, 245.

78 Gill & Fleck (n 66) 387.

4.2.3 Blockades and Establishment of War Zones

Different types of area control are repeatedly established in naval warfare, such as blockades,[79] and war zones including exclusion zones, control zones, defensive bubbles, etc.

Blockades are carried out mainly by warships and military aircraft in the past. The requirement of effectiveness used to suggest strict controls on site by warships in order to actually lock down the blockaded coastlines and harbors. With the development of military technology, this legal requirement has nearly gone obsolete.[80] 'Paper blockade' can be now enforced effectively with missiles, military GPS and other systems. It is inevitable that UMS will be applied to enforce blockades in future warfare, no matter in what legal status. Mines have always been common in blockades,[81] which means that even weapon-like UMS can participate in blockades in some way without the presence of traditional warships. Therefore, there is no reason to prevent auxiliary UMS from taking a part, but they may be barred from capturing or conducting direct attacks on the vessels in case of attempts of blockade running. The same can be applied to the establishment of exclusion zones.[82] The real concern is whether UMS with a certain level of autonomy can independently and correctly characterize a breach of zonal controls, and conduct responsive measures that are necessary and proportionate. But this technical question does not seem a fatal legal obstacle.

In certain types of war zones, like the immediate vicinity of naval operations, ships are excluded for protecting their safety because of the battles in the area. The standard measures to be taken are warning and diversion, which are not likely to 'harm' other ships. UMS can thus serve effectively in maintaining these war zones as long as they can display proper signals for warning and guidance.[83]

---

79 Blockades are normally not considered as 'war zones' as they usually serve to establish one or multiple fictitious lines and take measures to prevent the crossing of the line(s), namely blockade running, while leaving activities unaffected on both sides the line. This is different from war zones which create zonal effects within the established line.

80 See Farrant (n 76) 257, 258.

81 See D. R. Humphrey, 'Belligerent Interdiction of Neutral Shipping in International Armed Conflict' (1997) 2 JCSL 23.

82 For the introduction of modern law of exclusion zones, see generally Sandesh Sivakumaran, 'Exclusion Zones in the Law of Armed Conflict at Sea: Evolution in Law and Practice' (2016) 92 ILS 153.

83 Schmitt and Goddard limit this right to warships but no reasoning is provided, only with a footnote referring to Rule 108 of San Remo Manual which says nothing about warships. See Schmitt & Goddard (n 6) 581.

Defensive bubbles, mobile zones, or a new type of 'cordon sanitare',[84] are set up to protect moving units in naval warfare.[85] Any vessel or aircraft that comes closer than a given distance without proper permissions or identifications, may be subjected to necessary military measures, including attacks.[86] Though the zones are often assigned to a military unit, for example, a fleet on operation, it is theoretically possible to set up such a zone for unmanned fleets. Whether UMS in the bubbles can undertake attacks is uncertain, but UMS short of warship status are not necessarily deprived of the right to resort to force, for their acts may be considered (unit) self-defense in *jus ad bellum*, instead of belligerent rights of attacks in *jus in bello*.

4.2.4 Rethinking the Regime of Belligerent Rights?

As demonstrated above, in an era where unmanned crafts of different sizes and forms are capable of fighting at sea, the regime of belligerent rights, though never a clear and systematic one, is now under great pressure. John Westlake a century ago correctly described the regime of belligerent-neutral rights as more than anarchic but much less than theoretically coherent and timeless:

> The aggregate possibilities of enjoyment which any such system can furnish are inadequate to meet the demands made on them in the name of rights, and yet no right which has been recognised as primary can consistently be asked to give way to others. The very notion of a precedence among rights supposes some standard by which to judge them, lying deeper than the so-called rights and excluding them from a really primary position. And the result of a system placed on such a basis can only be a working compromise between demands, reached with reference at once to their justice and to the forces behind them, but veiled under a philosophically sounding nomenclature of rights.[87]

Neither the rules nor the whole system changed much since Westlake wrote. The distinction between warships and other vessels are mainly for the purpose of prohibiting privateering,[88] which in modern time is hardly an important

84 See James Kraska & Raul A. Pedrozo, *International Maritime Security Law*, (2013, Martinus Nijhoff Publishers) 880, 882.

85 Farrant (n 76) 270. See also S. F. Gilchrist, 'The Cordon Sanitaire: Is It Useful? Is It Practical?', (1982) 35 NWCR 60; William J. Fenrick, 'The Exclusion Zone in the Law of Naval Warfare', (1986) 24 CYIL 91, 92.

86 Ibid 270–72.

87 John Westlake, *International Law, Part II: War*, (1907, Cambridge University Press) 166.

88 Klein et al. (n 8) 723, 724.

problem. Meanwhile, the dichotomy of warships and auxiliary vessels are mostly functional under domestic discretion, only implying that ships should be designed for specific aims and assigned with given tasks.[89] When the sizes and structures of maritime vehicles varied, and these vehicles are equipped with multiple functions and complex capabilities, the logic underlying traditional distinctions is seriously undermined. According to Stephen Neff, 'the single greatest lesson of our historical survey is that the evolution of the law of neutrality has been determined far more by events on the ground than by the theories of scholars'.[90] To insist that all belligerent rights are limited to narrowly defined warships are therefore neither reasonable nor practical to reach 'a working compromise between demands'.

Two approaches seem available if we are to preserve the theoretical integrity of the legal system while adapting to new changes. The first one is to maintain the sacred distinction of warship and other vessels, which means a wider understanding of warships will be necessary; the second is to reallocate the rights in naval warfare to meet the changing demands in a more practice-oriented way. Belligerent rights for example can be designed for certain circumstances instead of different types of ships, while the fundamental distinction of military and civilian vessels is still in place (which means every military vehicle is required to have a special external mark for identification). The former approach may find it hard to deal with various kinds of unmanned systems in practice. The latter approach, though at first glance complicated, could be understood as a return to the earlier legal design reminiscent of 19th century. Concrete solutions and agreements may not appear soon, but the system is resilient enough to allow the weighing of pros and cons.

5 Special Rights and Obligations of UMS-Using States in Armed Conflicts at Sea

Part 4 has addressed rights to navigate and undertake military operations in the perspective of belligerents. This part turns to problems of maritime neutral law and focuses on rights and obligations of neutral states. The recent

89 No conventional rules have been settled down to draw the line between the two mutually exclusive categories and they are almost left to States to decide what their real differences are and what they are entitled to do. For example, the United States has re-designated some naval auxiliaries (USNS) to warships (USS). See Kraska et al (n 16) 46.

90 Stephen C. Neff, *The Rights and Duties of Neutrals: A General History* (2022, Manchester University Press) 218.

Russian-Ukraine conflict has particularly reaffirmed the continuing relevance of neutrality in international law.[91] This specific branch of law may not directly involve warfare as commonly understood, yet also has important implications on the use of UMS.

5.1 *Neutral Navigational Rights and Limitations*

As a default rule, vessels of neutral States continue to enjoy navigational rights during wartime.[92] UMS of neutral States thus enjoy navigational rights through maritime areas under jurisdiction of belligerent states under different regimes of navigation as in peacetime, as long as they enjoy certain legal status. As noted above, belligerent States can suspend innocent passage in parts of their territorial seas,[93] or resort to the non-innocent character of the navigation of armed UMS, in order to keep out neutral military UMS as they see fit.[94] Although transit passage in international straits are not suspendable, belligerent coastal states may require advanced notice before the exercise of transit passage by neutral states. In practice, restrictions or even prohibitions on transit passage in international straits during wartime have been occasionally taken without receiving protests.[95] In any case, belligerent states have a full legal toolkit to keep suspicious vessels out of their sovereign waters if they want, including establishing zones of operations. UMS of neutral states are theoretically under tight control in belligerent waters.

5.2 *Neutral Rights and Obligations Regarding Ports and Harbors*

Neutral States are permitted to offer certain supplies and services for belligerents in an impartial manner without breaking rules of neutrality, which usually include refueling, repairs and revictualing for warships.[96] That means neutral ports and harbors are not necessarily closed to belligerents. UMS of bigger sizes and designed for long-term use are certainly in need of frequent refueling

91 Cf. Martin Fink, 'Naval Blockade and the Russia-Ukraine Conflict', (2022) 69 Netherlands International Law Review 411. Martin Fink, 'How Qualified Neutrality Impacts the Law of Contraband' (Lieber Institute West Point) <https://lieber.westpoint.edu/how-qualified-neutrality-impacts-law-contraband/> accessed on Jul 11, 2023; John C. Tramazzo Santicola Ian, 'Russia's Interdiction of Neutral Merchant Vessels and the Law of the Sea' (Lieber Institute West Point) <https://lieber.westpoint.edu/russias-interdiction-neutral-merchant-vessels-law-sea/> accessed on Sep 11, 2023.

92 See Helsinki Principles on the Law of Maritime Neutrality, 496, Principle 1.3; San Remo Manual, Rule 26.

93 UNCLOS, art 25.

94 UNCLOS, art 19(2).

95 See von Heinegg (n 67) 264, 267.

96 Hague Convention XIII, arts 17, 19.

(or recharging) and repairs. The delicate balance should be struck between the rights of neutral states to offer normal support to foreign warships, and the neutral obligation not to provide base or sanctuary for belligerent operations. A narrow interpretation of the rules is unfavorable for including belligerent UMS, even when they are warships. It could be argued that the neutral rights of refueling, repairs and revictualing are exceptional rules in wartime, and that the reason for these exceptional rules is almost solely humanitarian, though not explicitly.[97] Refueling serves to enable foreign warships to make their way home, instead of undertaking military missions, though neutral states are generally not obliged to ensure the motives;[98] repairs are also permitted in order to maintain the seaworthiness of foreign warships.[99] With no human beings on board, UMS warships may not enjoy such humanitarian treatments. A neutral state that offers refueling or repairs to UMS may be effectively making contributions to operations undertaken by the UMS, and therefore in breach of the law of neutrality. In a similar case, UMS warship can not take refuge in a neutral harbor after being seriously damaged, as no one is truly in distress at sea.[100] This conclusion reasonably extends to UMS other than warships, unless they are tasked with humanitarian or similar missions. It should be noted, however, not all LONW rules concerning neutral harbors are based on humanitarian considerations. Some of the rules are applicable to UMS, especially for those regulating the leaving of neutral harbors by warships, and the prohibition of engagement of belligerent warships upon leaving neutral harbors.[101]

5.3 *Neutral Rights and Obligations in Neutral Waters*

Neutral States are obliged to exhaust all their reasonable efforts, including use of force, to avoid making contributions to any belligerent Party if they wish to

97 In a widespread understanding, the underlying logic for this whole regime is 'enough to get you home' based on a peacetime standard. See Farrant, (n 76) 221, 226. This is primarily a British understanding that is not shared with all continental European states.

98 France instead argued for a 'full-tanker' approach. The different methods of restrictions ultimately lied in the discretion of neutral states. See James Brown Scott (ed.), *The Proceedings of the Hague Peace Conference, The Conference of 1907*, Vol. 3, (1921, Oxford University Press) 634, 639.

99 Art 17 of *Hague Convention XIII* provides: 'In neutral ports and roadsteads war-ships may only carry out such repairs as are absolutely necessary to render them seaworthy, and may not add in any manner whatsoever to their fighting force. The local authorities of the neutral Power shall decide what repairs are necessary, and these must be carried out with the least possible delay.'

100 Geneva Convention II for the Amelioration of the Condition of the Wounded, Sick and Shipwrecked Members of the Armed Forces at Sea (12 Aug. 1949) 75 UNTS 85, arts 12, 18.

101 Hague Convention XIII, art 12; *San Remo Manual*, Rules 15, 16.

remain in neutral status.[102] For instance, they can open fires to expel belligerent ships which are trying to base the neutral territorial seas for operations, if necessary. If a neutral State fail to carry out neutral obligations, while it does not immediately lose its neutral status, belligerent states may undertake necessary measures, including use of force, to enforce neutrality.[103] In that case, belligerent parties may engage in battles in neutral waters where the violation of neutrality takes place.[104] It would become more complex when UMS are involved. As noted above, it can be difficult for some neutral States to tell whether UMS are basing their territorial seas, and to effectively expel all of the belligerent UMS. If a coastal neutral State concerned is unable or unwilling to enforce necessary neutrality measures, other belligerent Parties may enter the territorial seas and use force on their own, maybe by sending more UMS. In that case, the territorial sea involved will become a war zone in effect. The neutral State involved will be in great disadvantage. This can be the gravest concerns for states that are not technically capable of developing and countering military UMS. The lawmaking efforts of maritime neutrality ought to prepare for the use of armed military UMS on a large scale and the following asymmetric situations in wars. Considering the introduction of *jus ad bellum* restriction on belligerent self-help may be helpful. Belligerents should not be allowed to enforce neutrality themselves except for extreme situations, otherwise the measures should be regarded as illegal use of force against the neutral coastal States.

6 Conclusion

This chapter serves as a preliminary study into the particular legal issue on using UMS in naval warfare. The use of UMS in a large scale in naval warfare,

102 Hague Convention XIII, art 8; See also Geoffrey S. Corn et al., *The Law of Armed Conflict: An Operational Approach* (2012, Wolters Kluwer Law & Business) 432.

103 Hague Convention XIII, art 25. The *Altmark* Incident in World War II could serve as a typical case for the neutral obligation to take active actions. For a detailed analysis of the incident, see James Farrant, 'The Altmark Incident', in David Letts & Rob Mclaughlin, *Maritime Operations Law in Practice: Key Cases and Incidents*, (2022, Routledge) 179, 190.

104 However, we should note that according to Rule 22 '[t]he *San Remo Manual* provides that a belligerent must first notify the neutral State and give the neutral a reasonable time to terminate the violation of its neutrality by another belligerent before it can exercise the right of self-help … The limitations reflected in the San Remo Manual are not reflected in State practice or *opinio juris* and represent a progressive statement of the law.' Kraska et al (n 16) 230, 231.

or even fully unmanned naval warfare, is highly possible in the future. The discussions on the law of naval warfare have regained attentions, though still developing at a relatively slow pace with limited political impacts. The current understanding on how UMS and the law of naval warfare may impact each other is still underdeveloped, mainly focusing on the core principles of international humanitarian law. This chapter therefore aims to enrich the discussions on the issues such as means and methods of naval warfare, and maritime neutrality. The debates on the legal status of UMS are far from settled, for which we can keep an open mind, think of different potentials and possibilities, and respectively ponder their respective legal implications. Thus, there is actually no final conclusion given, rather than an invitation to keep a close watch on the practices to come.

As far as this chapter is concerned, the law of naval warfare as a traditional branch of international law should deserve more academic and political attentions, and the development of UMS technology can catalyze a comprehensive reflexion or even reconstruction of this legal regime, especially the part of belligerent rights. Special regimes of rights can be designed for military UMS; or, the distinction of warships and auxiliary vessels can be abolished, at least for UMS. A thoughtful consideration of the functions, normative settings and contextual factors of LONW is needed, before a more desirable path is chosen.

States have long lived with vague legal terms of belligerent rights and obscure conceptual divides between different regimes, and the most powerful and bellicose ones may have benefited from these legal gray zones in maritime battlefields. But the development of UMS may sharpen the contradictions theoretically and practically, so that the international community can find it increasingly hard to neglect the coming challenges. As so many terms are only defined in customary international law, and subject to subsequent practices to be clarified and developed, there is always enough room to reflect and reconceptualize the law of naval warfare and discuss the way we should move forward. To do this, however, a turn to look at history in a critical way maybe more constructive than we normally imagine. The past has not long gone, and what seems new in the present is often a result of what we have missed in the past.

Acknowledgements

This research is supported by Southern Marine Science and Engineering Guangdong Laboratory (Zhuhai) (No. SML2020SP005).

References

Allen, Craig H, 'Determining the Legal Status of Unmanned Maritime Vehicles: Formalism vs Functionalism' (2018) 49 *Journal of Maritime Law and Commerce* 477.

Anderson, Kenneth, et al, 'Adapting the Law of Armed Conflict to Autonomous Weapon Systems', (2014) 90 *International Law Studies* 386.

Brownlie, Ian, *International Law and the Use of Force by States* (Clarendon Press 1963).

Campbell, Sable, et al, 'A Review on Improving the Autonomy of Unmanned Surface Vehicles through Intelligent Collision Avoidance Manoeuvres' (2012) 36(2) *Annual Reviews in Control* 267.

Case Concerning Passage through the Great Belt (Finland v Denmark) (1992) ICJ Rep 41.

Chadwick, Kara, 'Unmanned Maritime Systems Will Shape the Future of Naval Operations: Is International Law Ready?', in Evans, Malcolm D and Galani, Sofia (eds), *Maritime Security and the Law of the Sea: Help or Hindrance?* (Edward Elgar 2020).

Chang, Yen-Chiang, et al, 'The International Legal Status of the Unmanned Maritime Vehicles', (2020) 113 *Marine Policy* 103830.

Coito, Joel, 'Maritime Autonomous Surface Ships: New Possibilities-and Challenges-in Ocean Law and Policy, (2021) 97 *International Law Studies* 259.

Committee on Maritime Neutrality, *Helsinki Principles on the Law of Maritime Neutrality*, in 68 *International Law Association Report of the 68th Conference*, Taipei, 1998.

Convention (VII) of 1907 Relating to the Conversion of Merchant Ships into War-Ships, 18 Oct 1907, 205 *CTS* 319.

Convention (VIII) Relative to the Laying of Automatic Submarine Contact Mines, 18 Oct 1907, 36 Stat. 2332, T.S. No. 541.

Convention (XIII) Concerning the Rights and Duties of Neutral Powers in Naval War, 18 Oct 1907, 36 Stat. 2415.

Convention on the Marking of Plastic Explosives for the Purpose of Identification, 3 Jan 1991, 2122 *UNTS* 359.

Coogan, John W, *The End of Neutrality: The United States, Britain, and Maritime Rights, 1899–1915* (Cornell University Press 1981).

Corn, Geoffrey S,et al., *The Law of Armed Conflict: An Operational Approach* (Wolters Kluwer Law & Business 2012).

Daum, Oliver, 'The Implications of International Law on Unmanned Naval Craft', (2018) 49 *Journal of Maritime Law and Commerce* 71.

Declaration Respecting Maritime Law, Apr 16, 1856, 115 *CTS* 1.

Definition of Aggression, UNGA Res 3314 (XXIX), 14 Dec 1974.

Delupis, Ingrid, 'Foreign Warships and Immunity for Espionage', (1984) 78 *American Journal of International Law* 53.

Dinstein, Yoram, and Dahl, Arne W, *Oslo Manual on Select Topics of the Law of Armed Conflict: Rules and Commentary* (Springer International Publishing 2020).

Doswald-Beck, Louise (ed), *San Remo Manual on International Law Applicable to Armed Conflicts at Sea* (Cambridge University Press 1995).

Drew, Phillip, *The Law of Maritime Blockade: Past, Present, and Future* (Oxford University Press, 2017).

Dubuisson, FranÇois and Lagerwall, Anne 'The Threat of the Use of Force and Ultimata', in Weller, Marc (ed), *The Oxford Handbook of the Use of Force in International Law* (Oxford University Press 2015).

'Eritrea Ethiopia Claims Commission, Partial Award, *Jus ad Bellum* (Ethiopia's Claims 1–8), 2005', (2006) 45 *International Law Materials* 430.

Farrant, James, 'Modern Maritime Neutrality Law', (2014) 90 *International Law Studies* 198.

Farrant, James, 'The Altmark Incident', in Letts, David and Mclaughlin, Rob, *Maritime Operations Law in Practice: Key Cases and Incidents* (Routledge 2022).

Farrant, James and Ford, Christopher M, 'Autonomous Weapons and Weapon Reviews: The UK Second International Weapon Review Forum', (2017) 93 *International Legal Studies* 389.

Fenrick, William J, 'The Exclusion Zone in the Law of Naval Warfare', (1986) 24 *Canadian Yearbook on International Law* 91.

Fink, Martin, 'Naval Blockade and the Russia-Ukraine Conflict', (2022) 69 Netherlands International Law Review 411.

Francioni, Francesco, 'Peacetime Use of Force, Military Activities, and the New Law of the Sea, (1985) 18 *Cornell International Law Journal* 203.

Frei A. Gabriela, *Great Britain, International Law & the Evolution of Maritime Strategic Thought, 1856–1914* (Oxford University Press, 2020).

Geneva Convention II for the Amelioration of the Condition of the Wounded, Sick and Shipwrecked Members of the Armed Forces at Sea, 12 Aug 1949, 75 UNTS 85.

Gilchrist, SF, 'The Cordon Sanitaire: Is It Useful? Is It Practical?', (1982) 35 *Naval War College Review* 60.

Gill, Terry D and Fleck, Dieter, 'The Law of Military Operations at Sea', in Gill, Terry D and Fleck, Dieter (eds), *The Handbook of the International Law of Military Operations* (Oxford University Press 2015).

Gill, Terry D, and Tibori-Szabó, Kinga, *The Use of Force and the International Legal System* (Cambridge University Press 2023).

Grotius, Hugo (edited and with an introduction by Martine Julia van Ittersum), *Commentary on the Law of Prize and Booty* (Liberty Fund, 2006).

Hagemeyer-Witzleb, Teoman M, *The International Law of Economic Warfare* (Springer International Publishing 2021).

Hohfeld, Wesley N, 'Some Fundamental Legal Conceptions as Applied in Judicial Reasoning', (1913–1914) 23 *Yale Law Journal* 16.

Humphrey, DR, 'Belligerent Interdiction of Neutral Shipping in International Armed Conflict', (1997) 2 *Journal of Conflict and Security Law* 23.

Institute of International Law, 'The Law of Naval Warfare Governing the Relations between Belligerents (1913)', reprinted in Schindler, Dietrich and Toman, Jiri (eds), *The Laws of Armed Conflicts: A Collection of Conventions, Resolutions and Other Documents* (Brill/Nijhoff 2004).

Ishii, Yurika, 'The "Due Regard" Obligation and the Peaceful and Economic Uses of the EEZ Other than Fisheries', (2019) 34 The International Journal of Marine and Coastal Law 73.

Ishii, Yurika, 'Attacks on Commercial Maritime Autonomous Surface Ships at Sea', (2023) 8 *Asia-Pacific Journal of Ocean Law and Policy* 266.

Jackson, Patrick O, 'Drone Interdiction: Use of Force as a Countermeasure against Unmanned Vehicles at Sea', (2018) 226 *Military Law Review* 223.

Kalmanovitz, Pablo, *The Laws of War in International Thought* (Oxford University Press 2020).

Kalshoven, Frits, *Belligerent Reprisals* (Brill, 2005).

Keefer, Scott A, *The Law of Nations and Britain's Quest for Naval Security: International Law and Arms Control, 1898–1914* (Palgrave Macmillan, 2016).

Klein, Natalie, 'Maritime Autonomous Vehicles within the International Law Framework to Enhance Maritime Security', (2019) 95 *International Law Studies* 244.

Klein, Natalie, et al, 'Maritime Autonomous Vehicles: New Frontiers in the Law of the Sea', (2020) 69 *International and Comparative Law Quarterly* 719.

Kraska, James and Pedrozo, Raul, *Disruptive Technology and the Law of Naval Warfare* (Oxford University Press 2022).

Kraska, James and Pedrozo, Raul, *International Maritime Security Law* (Martinus Nijhoff Publishers 2013).

Kraska, James, et al, 'The Newport Manual on the Law of Naval Warfare', (2023) 101 *International Law Studies* 1.

Kraska, James, *Maritime Power and the Law of the Sea: Expeditionary Operations in World Politics* (Oxford University Press 2011).

Liu Dan and Li Rui, *Wuren haiyang xitong yu guoji fa* [Unmanned Maritime System and International Law] (Beijing: Haiyang chubanshe, 2021).

Lott, Alexander, *Hybrid Threats and the Law of the Sea: Use of Force and Discriminatory Navigational Restrictions in Straits* (Brill/Nijhoff 2022).

Materna, Malgorzata, 'Adjusting the Aperture: The International Law Case for Qualifying Unmanned Vessels as Warships', (2023) 100 *International Law Studies* 452.

McKenzie, Simon, 'Sovereign Immunity of Uncrewed Surveillance Vehicles and the Limits of Enforcement Jurisdiction', (2023) 92 *Nordic Journal of International Law* 573.

McLaughlin, Rob, 'Unmanned Naval Vehicles at Sea: USVs, UUVs, and the Adequacy of the Law', (2011) 21 *Journal of Law, Information and Science* 100.

Military and Paramilitary Activities in and against Nicaragua (Nicaragua. v. U.S), (1986) ICJ Rep 14.

Nasu, Hitoshi and Letts, David, 'The Legal Characterization of Lethal Autonomous Maritime Systems: Warship, Torpedo, or Naval Mine?', (2020) 96 *International Law Study* 79.

Neff, Stephen C, *The Rights and Duties of Neutrals: A General History* (Manchester University Press 2022).

O'Connell, Daniel P, *The Influence of Law on Sea Power* (Manchester University Press, 1975).

Oil Platforms (Islamic Republic of Iran v. United States of America), Judgment, ICJ Reports 2003.

Politakis, George, *Modern Aspects of the Laws of Naval Warfare and Maritime Neutrality* (Kegan Paul International 1998).

Protocol additional to the Geneva Conventions of 12 August 1949, and relating to the protection of victims of international armed conflicts (Protocol I), 8 Jun. 1977, 1125 UNTS 3.

Saito, Yusuke, 'Reviewing Law of Armed Conflict at Sea and Warfare in New Domains and New Measures: Submarine Cables, Merchant Missile Ships, and Unmanned Marine Systems' (2019) 44 *Tulane Maritime Law Journal* 107.

Schmitt, Michael N and Goddard, David S, 'International Law and the Military Use of Unmanned Maritime Systems', (2016) 98 *International Review of the Red Cross* 567.

Scott, James B (ed), *The Proceedings of the Hague Peace Conference, The Conference of 1907*, Vol. 3 (Oxford University Press 1921).

Sivakumaran, Sandesh, 'Exclusion Zones in the Law of Armed Conflict at Sea: Evolution in Law and Practice', (2016) 92 *International Legal Studies* 153.

Sparrow, Robert, 'Twenty Seconds to Comply: Autonomous Weapon Systems and the Recognition of Surrender', (2015) 91 *International Law Studies* 699.

Sparrow, Robert, et al, 'Naval Robots and Rescue', (2017) 99 *International Review of the Red Cross* 1139.

Standing Rules of Engagement for U.S. Forces, CJCSI 3121.01B.

Sturchler, Nikolas, *The Threat of Force in International Law* (Cambridge University Press 2007).

Su, Jinyuan, 'Is the Establishment of Air Defence Identification Zones Outside National Airspace in Accordance with International Law?', (2021) 32 *European Journal of International Law* 1309.

The Antarctic Treaty, 1 Dec 1959, 402 UNTS 5778.

The *Case concerning the detention of three Ukrainian naval vessels* (Ukraine v. Russian Federation), ITLOS Order of 25 May 2019.

Tracy, Nicolas, *Sea Power and the Control of Trade: Belligerent Rights from the Russian War to the Beira Patrol, 1854–1970* (Routledge 2005).

'Treaty on Principles Governing the Activities of States in the Exploration and Use of Outer Space, including the Moon and Other Celestial Bodies', UNGA Res 2222 (XXI), 19 Dec 1966.

Übersetzung aus dem Deutschen, Commander's Handbook: Legal Bases for the Operations of Naval Forces, Bundessprachenamt-Referat SM 3, Auftragsnummer 2002U-01441 (2002).

United Kingdom Ministry of Defence, *The Manual of the Law of Armed Conflict* (Oxford University Press 2005).

United Nations Convention on the Law of the Sea, 10 Dec 1982, 1833 *UNTS* 397.

U.S. Navy, U.S. Marine Corps & U.S. Coast Guard, *The Commander's Handbook on the Law of Naval Operations*, NWP 1-14M/MCTP 11-10B/COMDTPUB P5800.7A (2022).

Veal, Robert, et al, 'The Legal Status and Operation of Unmanned Maritime Vehicles', (2019) 50 *Ocean Development & International Law* 23.

von Heinegg, Wolff H, 'Methods and Means of Naval Warfare in Non-International Armed Conflicts', (2012) 88 International Law Studies 211.

von Heinegg, Wolff H, et al (eds), *Dehumanization of Warfare: Legal Implications of New Weapon Technologies* (Springer 2018).

Westlake, John, *International Law, Part II: War* (Cambridge University Press 1907).

Xing Guangmei, *Guoji haishang wuzhuang chongtu fa de lishi yanjin* [*The History on the International Law of Armed Conflict at Sea*] (Beijing: Falv chubanshe, 2010).

CHAPTER 3

Using Uncrewed Maritime Vehicles for Scientific Research: Legal Challenges and Viable Solutions

Yao Huang * *and Shuning Zhang* **

1 Introduction

The explosion in Uncrewed maritime vehicles (UMVs) used for marine scientific research (MSR) is a paradigm shift for oceanographic research, which in the past has been primarily conducted on research cruises that are extremely limited in geographic scope and temporal coverage.[1] UMVs can cover more terrain than research vessels at a fraction of the cost.[2] Data collected by UMVs is already contributing to important scientific insights, from a better understanding of baseline ocean conditions to more accurate global models of climate change.[3] And these new, important insights are not only useful to scientists but also significant to relevant industries and even the world.

However, UMVs, unlike unmanned aerial vehicles or unmanned underground vehicles, have not prompted significant social and legal discussion despite their increased usage. The legal literature on UMVs' use for MSR remains limited. The current academic literature has not yet analyzed and solved the related issues sufficiently which is primarily focused on narrow regulatory questions centered around compliance with existing safety laws or whether UMVs should be considered vessels.[4]

* Yao Huang, Professor at Sun Yat-sen University School of Law; Lead Expert, Innovation Team of Marine Strategy and Law, Southern Marine Science and Engineering Guangdong Laboratory (Zhuhai).

** Shuning Zhang, Ph.D. candidate of international law at Sun Yat-sen University School of Law.

1 Annie Brett, 'Regulating the Autonomous Ocean' (2022) 88 BLR 1, 2.

2 See Paul G. Fernandes et al. 'AUVs as Research Vessels: The Pros and Cons' (2002) <https://www.ices.dk/sites/pub/CM%20Doccuments/2002/J/J0202.PDF> accessed 15 July 2023.

3 See Lijing Cheng et al. 'How Fast are the Oceans Warming?' (2019) 363 Science.

4 See Annie Brett (n 1) 8; Henrik Ringbom. 'Regulating Autonomous Ships-Concepts, Challenges and Precedents'(2019) 50 ODIL; Craig H. Allen. 'The Seabots Are Coming Here: Should They Be Treated as 'Vessels'?'(2012) 65 JN; Rob McLaughlin. 'Unmanned Naval Vehicles at Sea: USVs, UUVs, and the Adequacy of the Law' (2011) 21 JLIS.

 | DOI:10.1163/9789004706279_005

In the past, ocean scientific data was primarily collected by fully staffed research vessels. The advent of UMVs that can be operated free from remote control is allowing scientists to break new ground, expanding the range of what it is possible to observe and discover in the oceans. In 2020, ProMare and IBM launched the Mayflower, an autonomous ship designed to gather data about the ocean with no human captain or onboard crew.[5] The majority of UMVs currently used in the oceans today collect baseline information on ocean conditions. Generally speaking, based on their characteristics, they may be classified easily by the environment in which they operate: on the surface of the water (uncrewed surface vehicles, USVs) or underneath it (uncrewed underwater vehicles, UUVs).[6] However, UMVs used for MSR should be roughly divided into three categories: the simple drifting floats that do not have navigable power and float with ocean currents, USVs, and UUVs.[7]

The simple drifting floats, including many scientific floats which are small sensor platforms that drift with global currents, sending information to shore at regular intervals via satellite,[8] are already deployed throughout the world's oceans. For example, the Argo (Array for Real-time Geostrophic Oceanography) program has nearly four thousand profiling floats deployed around the globe and there are still some areas of the ocean that are over-populated while others have gaps that need to be filled with additional floats. The reliability of float has improved almost every year.[9] Argo floats and other similar systems have dramatically improved scientific understanding of global marine ecosystems in the more than twenty years they have been active.[10]

Unlike the simple drifting floats, other more sophisticated UMVs can move independently of ocean currents, which rely on propulsion driven by wave, wind, or solar energy to stay at sea for years. These UMVs can travel and collect data across entire ocean basins.[11] For example, Wave Gliders and Saildrones

5 'Mayflower Autonomous Ship Launches' (IBM, 15 September 2020) <https://newsroom.ibm.com/2020-09-15-Mayflower-Autonomous-Ship-Launches> accessed 15 July 2023.

6 Shuning Zhang. 'The Legal Status of Unmanned Maritime System' (in Chinese) (2021) 6 SHJL.

7 See Katharina Bork et al. 'The Legal Regulation of Floats and Gliders—In Quest of a New Regime?'(2008) 39ODIL 299.

8 Ibid.

9 'Argo's status' (Argo) <https://argo.ucsd.edu/about/status/> accessed 15 July 2023.

10 *See* Dean Roemmich et al. 'The Argo Program: Observing the Global Ocean with Profiling Floats' (2009) 22 Oceanography.

11 Gloria Dickie, 'Ocean Cleanup Struggles to Fulfill Promise to Scoop Up Plastic at Sea' (REUTERS, 16 September 2021) <https://www.reuters.com/business/environment/ocean-cleanup-struggles-fulfill-promisescoop-up-plastic-sea-2021-09-16/> accessed 15 July 2023.

are two of the most advanced propulsive UMVs used for MSR that are already being used to collect oceanographic data globally. Wave Gliders, built by Liquid Robotics, is a USV that operates individually or in fleets delivering real-time data with no fuel but powered by wave and solar energy.[12] Likewise, Saildrone USVs combine wind-powered propulsion technology and solar-powered meteorological and oceanographic sensors to perform autonomous long-range data collection missions in the harshest ocean environments. They have sailed in every ocean on the planet, carrying payloads of sophisticated science-grade instruments, sensors, and cameras.[13] There is a large-scale deployment of UMVs used for MSR, with both scientific organizations and States using these UMVs to gather scientific data. In addition to these USVs, scientists are also increasingly leveraging UUVs. In practice, tethered submersible UUVs have been used for decades to complement research vessel capabilities.[14]

To stimulate the development of UMVs, many organizations incentivize the creation of new, more sophisticated types of UMVs. For instance, to incentivize the development of UMVs capable of high-resolution seafloor mapping, XPrize launched a competition sponsored by Shell with a bonus prize from the US National Oceanic and Atmospheric Administration (NOAA). It also announced a continuing partnership with the SeaBed 2030 Project, which is aiming to produce a publicly available map of the entire seafloor by 2030 and already has the backing of a range of organizations including the United Nations.[15]

To close the gap, this paper aims to illuminate the legal questions raised by using UMVs for MSR are significant, from whether UMVs can be considered vessels[16] and may be regulated by the United Nations Convention on the Law of the Sea (UNCLOS) as scientific research installations and equipment, to whether the activities conducted by UMVs are regarded as MSR, to whether uncontrolled drifting of UMVs can apply the relevant rules of UNCLOS.

The structure of this article is as follows: moving from the introduction, Section 2 analyses whether the use of UMVs for MSR can be regulated by UNCLOS, particularly around the recognition of the legal status of UMVs and the

12 'Homepage' (LIQUID ROBOTICS) <https://www.liquid-robotics.com/wave-glider/overview/> accessed 15 July 2023.

13 'Homepage' (SAILDRONE) <https://www.saildrone.com/> accessed 15 July 2023.

14 See 'History of Alvin' (Woods Hole Oceanographic Inst) <https://www.whoi.edu/what-we-do/explore/underwater-vehicles/hov-alvin/history-of-alvin/> accessed 15 July 2023.

15 Scott K.Johnson, 'XPRIZE selects winners of autonomous seafloor-mapping competition' (ARS TECHNICA, 1 June 2019) <https://arstechnica.com/science/2019/06/xprize-selects-winners-of-autonomous-seafloor-mapping-competition/> accessed 15 July 2023.

16 Craig H. Allen, 'Determining the Legal Status of Unmanned Maritime Vehicles: Formalism vs Functionalism' (2018) 49 JMLC.

definition or scope of MSR. Section 3 analyses the legal challenges arising from UMVs' unique operation of uncontrolled drifting. It may challenge the rights and obligations of States concerned under UNCLOS and therefore may raise legal issues. The conflict between researching State and coastal State is considered for the case of entering waters subject to the jurisdiction of foreign states. Section 4 concludes with a few suggestions on both domestic and international paths to regulate using UMVs for MSR.

2 Difficulties in the Identification of Legal Status and Activities of Using UMVs for Scientific Research under UNCLOS

UMVs are the new things of scientific and technological development. There are some difficulties when regulating UMVs under UNCLOS, mainly including how to define UMVs, identify their legal status, and activities of using UMVs for MSR.

2.1 *Defining Uncrewed Maritime Vehicles (UMVs)*

There are numerous types, technologies, and functions of UMVs. Generally, UMVs are water-borne systems that are capable of operating without onboard personnel.[17] UMVs are also commonly referred to as unmanned maritime systems (UMSs). As a result of most UMVs having different levels of autonomy to operate without onboard personnel, some scholars use the term autonomous maritime vehicles (AMVs).[18] Two subcategories of UMVs include UUVs and USVs. As the name indicates, UUVs operate primarily submerged and USVs operate solely on water surfaces.[19] As stated above, smaller UMVs include 'float' and 'gliders' that often conduct MSR.[20] For this chapter, the focus is on the use of UMVs for MSR and they could be roughly divided into three categories: Float, USVs, and UUVs (see Figure 3.1).[21]

17 See Robert Veal, Michael Tsimplis, and Andrew Serdy, 'The Legal Status and Operation of Unmanned Maritime Vehicles' (2019) 50 ODIL; Craig H. Allen (n 16).

18 For additional terms and acronyms for the same or similar systems, see Natalie Klein, 'Maritime Autonomous Vehicles Within the International Law Framework to Enhance Maritime Security' (2019) 95 ILS 248.

19 David S. Goddard, 'International Law and the Military Use of Unmanned Maritime Systems' (2016) 98 IRRC.

20 Natalie Klein et al. 'Maritime Autonomous Vehicles: New Frontiers in The Law of the Sea' (2020) 69ICLQ; see also Katharina Bork et al. (n 4).

21 See Katharina Bork et al. (n 4) 299.

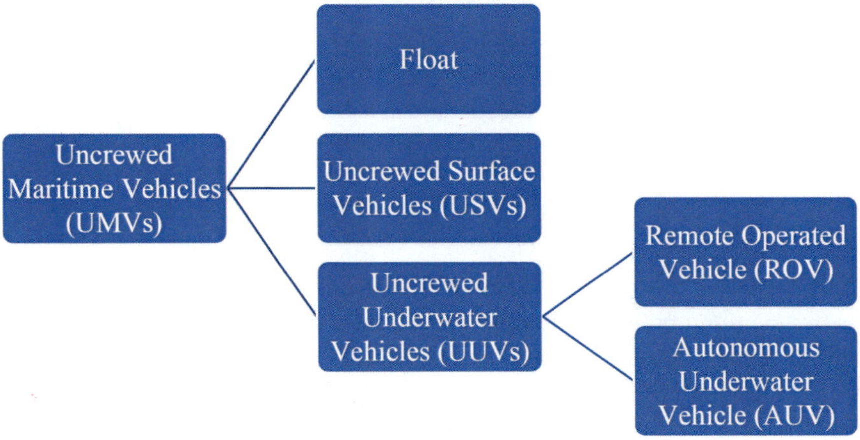

FIGURE 3.1 Types of Uncrewed Maritime Vehicles (UMVs)

2.2 *The Legal Status of Uncrewed Maritime Vehicles*

So far there is no internationally recognized definition of 'vessel' or 'ship', and therefore it is often challenging to determine whether the relevant provisions of UNCLOS can apply to various kinds of UMVs. Given the breadth of types, functions, and technology used by UMVs, it is quite taxing to fit UMVs within a 'vessel' or 'ship' legal scheme that provides a bright-line rule. Nonetheless, legal scholars have attempted to compartmentalize the legal status of UMVs for decades within the international legal framework of 'vessel' or 'ship'.[22]

According to the relevant provisions of international treaties and domestic laws of various States, it is not shown that a 'vessel' or 'ship' must be manned. In summary, the important factors that constitute a 'vessel' or 'ship' should include navigational capability and functional capability.[23] For instance, Article 2 of the United Nations Convention on Conditions for Registration of Ships

22 Lindsay I. McCarl, 'Untethering UMVs from Vessels: Why the United States Should Construct a New Environmental Legal Scheme for Unmanned Maritime Vehicles' (2023) 127 DLR 2.

23 See Ramböll, Core Advokatfirma, 'Analysis of Regulatory Barriers to the Use of Autonomous Ships-Final Report' <https://dma.dk/Media/637745499808186153/Analysis%20of%20Regulatory%20Barriers%20to%20the%20Use%20of%20Autonomous%20Ships.pdf> accessed 15 July 2023; Daum Oliver. 'The Implications of International Law on Unmanned Naval Craft', (2018) 49 JMLC; Yuqing Sun. 'The Legal Status of Commercial Unmanned Ships' (in Chinese). (2019) 6I LRWU 127, 128.

(UNCCRS)[24] makes no mention of personnel requirements. In 2017, the UK Ship Register signed its first-ever uncrewed vessel to the flag,[25] certifying that inadequate staffing does not prevent UMVs from being registered as a 'vessel' or 'ship'. As a result, this section will analyze whether UMVs can be regarded as 'vessel' or 'ship' with the two standards—navigational capability and functional capability.

2.2.1 The Legal Status of Float

According to the Intergovernmental Oceanographic Commission (IOC), 'Float' means an autonomous vehicle used for the collection of data and floating passively at a preprogrammed pressure level until at predetermined time intervals rising to the ocean surface to broadcast its position and, as the case may be, collected data to a satellite.[26] Currently, floats are designed to float or dive underwater. Compared with other UMVs, the biggest feature of float is that it does not have the power to achieve horizontal movement independently, and can only float with the ocean current. The Argo Global Ocean Observatory is the most famous project using floats for MSR, collecting data on temperature and salinity from thousands of floats.[27]

It is debatable whether or not being 'self-powered' should be a necessary element for a 'vessel' or 'ship'. Some domestic laws and international conventions provide that being self-propelled is not essential for a ship. PART I (2) of the Merchant Shipping Act of Singapore particularly emphasizes that a ship shall be 'used in navigation by water' no matter how 'propelled or moved'. This implies that a 'vessel' or 'ship' that is not self-propelled, and where only the winds and the waves and no human power direct it, may also be considered to be a ship under Singapore law. However, UNCLOS establishes a legal regime of international navigation, which requires the flag State to ensure the safety of its ships at sea (UNCLOS, Article 94.3) and assigns navigational rights for a flag

---

24 Article 2 of the *United Nations Convention on Conditions for Registration of Ships:* 'ship' means any self-propelled sea-going vessel used in international seaborne trade for the transport of goods, passengers, or both with the exception of vessels of less than 500 gross registered tons.

25 See 'First Unmanned Vessel Joins UK Ship Register' (Offshore Energy, 14 November 2017) <https://www.offshore-energy.biz/first-unmanned-vessel-joins-uk-ship-register/> accessed 15 July 2023.

26 Intergovernmental Oceanographic Commission Advisory Body of Experts on the Law of the Sea (IOC/ABE-LOS). 'Seventh Meeting of The Advisory Body of Experts on The Law of The Sea'. IOC/ABE-LOS-VII/7 (2007) 2.

27 Argo, 'Technological Innovations'. <https://argo.ucsd.edu/how-do-floats-work/technological-innovations/> accessed 15 July 2023.

State to sail ships flying its flag on the high seas (UNCLOS, Article 90), and it is the person who controls and steers the ships that have such rights. As a result, one may conclude that a marine device that moves solely by winds and waves without any human intervention is not eligible to enjoy navigational rights under the UNCLOS.[28] In addition, several given definitions of 'ship' require that it be self-powered (e.g., Article 2 of the UNCCRS), and the Merchant Shipping Ordinance of HK explicitly excludes the devices 'propelled by oars' from ships. Therefore, being 'self-powered' is necessary for a ship to navigate.

Without being 'self-powered' and having the navigational capability, floats cannot be regarded as 'vessel' or 'ship'.

2.2.2 The Legal Status of Uncrewed Surface Vehicles (USVs)

As for USVs, they have a wide range of application prospects in both civil and military fields, such as maritime surveying and mapping, maritime surveillance and reconnaissance, and their navigation capability can be confirmed by their transport function or operation function easily. Although some scholars suspect that some USVs being too small and not capable of transport are impossible to constitute a 'vessel' or 'ship',[29] the size does not prevent USVs from being recognized as a 'vessel' or 'ship'.

Firstly, as far as the typical existing USVs are concerned, their size is consistent with their research and development purpose. For example, the Greeno Advanced Rescue Craft (GARC),[30] which is designed to complete rescue missions, has a payload of only 0.4 tons but is enough to provide survivors with medical care, water, and shelter for up to three days.

Secondly, in the long run, the development trend of USVs is diversified, and their intelligence degree will be further enhanced. Their size can theoretically be divided into small (less than 1 ton), medium (less than 100 tons), large (less than 1,000 tons), and super large (greater than 1,000 tons).[31] In the fiscal year 2020 defense budget, the U.S. Navy allocated $400 million for research and development of the Ghost Fleet large USV, with an initial test load of 2,000 tons and a length of 60.96–91.44 meters, which would be a major advance in the development of large USV. We can reasonably predict that, according to

28 Wangwang Xing, Ling Zhu, 'A functional approach to reassessing the legal status and navigational rights of ships and ship-shaped structures' (2021) 106 TP 122.

29 See Robert Veal, Michael Tsimplis, and Andrew Serdy (n 17); Wangwang Xing, Ling Zhu, (n 28).

30 See 'Naval Sea Systems' <https://www.navsea.navy.mil/Home/Team-Ships/Media-Gallery/PhotoGallery/igphoto/2002217172/> accessed 15 July 2023.

31 Qing Wu, Le Wang, Jialun Liu, 'Research status and prospect of autonomous surface cargo ship' (in Chinese) (2019) 14 CTIS1 59.

their theoretical classification, with the continuous development of USVs technology, there will be ultra-large USVs greater than 1,000 tons.

Hence, in the long run, it is not in line with the development trend of the field that USVs cannot be recognized as 'vessel' or 'ship' just because of their small size.

2.2.3 The Legal Status of Uncrewed Underwater Vehicles (UUVs)

Being different from the discussion on the status of USVs, the debate on the status of UUVs is more intense. UUVs are defined as self-propelled submersibles whose operation is either fully autonomous (pre-programmed or real-time adaptive mission control) or under minimal supervisory control and is untethered except, possibly, for data links such as a fiber optic cable.[32] According to the different control methods, UUVs can be divided into Remote Operated Vehicle (ROV) and Autonomous Underwater Vehicle (AUV). Their commonality is that they usually need to be equipped with a specialized mother ship to provide surface support, but the closeness between the two and the mother ship is different. According to the analysis of navigational capability and functional capability, the navigational capability of UUV should not be questioned. As for its functional capability, UUVs are not designed to transport personnel or goods at the beginning of their development, and the main application purpose is MSR and marine resource exploitation. As early as the 1960s, about 20 countries in the world developed nearly 200 types of UUVs, serving military, ocean engineering applications, and other fields. With the continuous development of science and technology, UUVs will develop in the direction of miniaturization, intelligence, etc., to further meet the needs of MSR.[33] As a result, despite their small size, UUVs can also have functional capability.

However, unlike AUV, which can achieve its energy and operation independence, and can be deployed directly from the dock without the need for the mother ship to complete the task, the ROV requires the mother ship to provide energy and maneuvering. From the feature that it needs the assistance of the mother ship, ROV cannot become an independent 'vessel' or 'ship', it is like a part of the mother ship, rather than being an independent ship, ROV should be regarded as parts or attachments of the mother ship, which can only reflect the legal status of its mother ship. So ROV does not constitute a 'vessel' or 'ship'.

---

32 See U.S. Dep't of Navy, 'The Navy Unmanned Underwater Vehicle (UUV) Master Plan' (9 November 2004) 4 <https://www.hsdl.org/?view&did=708654> accessed 15 July 2023.

33 Feng Xu, *Underwater Acoustic Sensing Technology for Unmanned Underwater Vehicle (in Chinese)* (2020, Science Press) 2.

In addition, some scholars point out that although USVs and AUVs can meet the requirement of navigational capacity and functional capacity and constitute 'ship', they cannot automatically apply the relevant provisions of international conventions.[34] Therefore, to clarify whether UMVs can be regulated by UNCLOS, an 'evolutionary approach' to treaty interpretation should be used.[35] The evolutionary interpretation of UNCLOS is consistent with not only the Vienna Convention on the Law of Treaties in 1969 (VCLT) but also the intention of the parties to UNCLOS. After providing an evolutionary interpretation of the term 'vessel' or 'ship' in UNCLOS, it can be concluded that the meaning of 'vessel' or 'ship' has changed over time, and regarding UMVs as 'vessel' or 'ship' is consistent with the object and purpose of UNCLOS. Thus, UMVs (except float and ROV) may be regarded as 'vessel' or 'ship' under UNCLOS.

It should also be pointed out here that although float and ROV cannot be regulated by UNCLOS as 'vessel' or 'ship', they can easily be regarded as 'scientific research installations or equipment' which is stipulated in Article 258 of UNCLOS.[36] UNCLOS does not define the term 'scientific research installations or equipment'. According to the Oxford English Dictionary, 'equipment' refers to anything used in equipping.[37] Consequently, 'scientific research equipment' can be defined as encompassing all items necessary for the conduct of a scientific research project. In contrast, installations would denote a facility or a grouping of facilities, located in the same vicinity, for a particular function or purpose. The difference between installation and equipment would appear to consist of a time and size element as follows: while installation is intended to remain in place for an extended period or even permanent, the equipment has the connotation of being quickly deployed and removed in the course of a single experiment; an installation may consist of several various parts with a variety of functions, while equipment is only intended for one specific objective.[38] Due to the relatively small size and deployment of float and ROV in practice,

34 Yuqing Sun (n 23).

35 See Robert Veal, Michael Tsimplis, and Andrew Serdy (n 17); Yen-Chiang Chang, Chao Zhang, Nannan Wang, 'The international legal status of the unmanned maritime vehicles' (2020) 113 MP 2; David S. Goddard (n 19).

36 UNCLOS, art 258 ('The deployment and use of any type of scientific research installations or equipment in any area of the marine environment shall be subject to the same conditions as are prescribed in this Convention for the conduct of marine scientific research in any such area.')

37 Oxford English Dictionary https://www.oed.com/dictionary/equipment_n?tab=meaning_and_use#5378431.

38 Florian H.Th. Wegelein, *Marine Scientific Research: The Operation and Status of Research Vessels and Other Platforms in International Law* (2005, Maritinus Nijhoff Publishers) 138.

they are more likely to be identified as 'scientific research equipment'. And with the development of technology, they may develop further in the future to be recognized as 'scientific research installation' and even 'ship' or 'vessel'. But anyway, like other UMVs, float and ROV can also apply the relevant provisions of UNCLOS.

2.3 *Controversy over the Nature of Uncrewed Maritime Vehicles' Scientific Research*

MSR involves the sovereignty, security, and economic interests of coastal States, as well as the marine exploration and exploitation rights of other States. Part XIII of UNCLOS lays out a comprehensive legal framework for the conduct of MSR and aims to achieve a balance between rights and interests of coastal States and that of other States. Yet the term 'MSR' is not defined in the UNCLOS to enable the negotiating parties of the Third United Nations Conference on the Law of the Sea to reach a compromise as soon as possible.[39] Since the lack of a clear definition for MSR in the UNCLOS, States, and scholars diverge in classifying some activities as MSR. Although international law scholars from various countries have tried to define MSR, in the end, the differences are large because of the different positions of the countries they are in.

The most controversial point is whether 'MSR' includes hydrographic surveys and military survey which is key to figuring out whether coastal State has jurisdiction over these activities. UNCLOS does not define 'survey', 'survey activities', or 'hydrographic surveys', nor does it clearly answer questions such as whether 'MSR' and 'survey' are inclusive or parallel, whether 'military survey' is a kind of 'survey', and whether 'military survey' falls into the category of 'MSR'. Scholars have different views on these issues. Captain J. Ashley Roach[40] indicates that activities that do not appear in or are excluded from Part XIII of UNCLOS are excluded from the scope of 'MSR' based on the relevant provisions of UNCLOS, and the relevant provisions of Part XIII of UNCLOS do not apply to these activities. But Dr. Haiwen Zhang and Dr. Sam Bateman do not agree with the point of view and indicate that it is impossible to draw a sharp distinction between MSR and other activities of marine data collection. As Bateman has noted, "Many of the technologies now used for hydrographic surveying and MSR are both similar and relatively recent innovations. Furthermore, technological developments with MSR equipments in recent decades have made this similarity even more the case than it may have been at the time of the Third

39 See Mron H. Nordquist. *UNCLOS* 1982 Commentary (vol.4) Translated by Wenzheng Lv and Bin Mao (2018,China Ocean Press) 420, 427.

40 See J. Ashley, Roach. Excessive Maritime Claims (4th Edn) (2021, Brill Nijhoff) 486, 540.

UN Conference on the Law of the Sea."[41] They state that marine data collecting activities should be categorized as MSR.[42]

In terms of the provisions of UNCLOS, UNCLOS does not make clear provisions on hydrographic survey and military survey, nor does it directly make clear provisions on the relationship between them and MSR. The term 'hydrographic survey' is mentioned in Articles 21 and 40 of UNCLOS is in juxtaposition to MSR, which implies that UNCLOS considers these activities as being different and mutually exclusive,[43] but they have the same means and methods, and even the same purpose to a large extent. As with hydrographic survey, the relationship between military survey and MSR is difficult to determine. Some scholars suggest that because the data collected by military survey may be used for scientific research, the activity could also be classified as 'MSR'.[44] The view that military marine data collection is one component of the general concept of MSR, is backed up by some commentators.[45] In support, they point to several factors, including the similarity of the technology used to carry out military survey and scientific research, and the difficulty of knowing what sort of activities a device is undertaking.[46] However, some scholars put forward different opinions on this and state that just because the data collected may be used for scientific research, it is biased to include military survey in the

41 Sam Bateman. 'Hydrographic Surveying in Exclusive Economic Zones-Is It Marine Scientific Research?' in Nordquist, Koh and Moore (eds.), *Freedom of Seas, Passage Rights and the 1982 Law of the Sea Convention.* (2009, Martinus Nijhoff Publishers) 122.

42 Haiwen Zhang, 'Is It Safeguarding the Freedom of Navigation or Maritime Hegemony of the United States?—Comments on Raul (Pete) Pedrozo's Article on Military Activities in the EEZ' (2010) 9 CJIL; Sam Bateman, 'A Response to Pedrozo: The Wider Utility of Hydrographic Surveys' (2011) 10 CJIL.

43 Tobias Hofmann, Alexander Proelss, 'The operation of Gliders Under the International Law of the Sea' (2015) 46 ODIL3 169.

44 Yongming Jin, ' Military Activities in Exclusive Economic Zone and State Practice'(in Chinese) (2008) 3 LS.

45 Haiwen Zhang, (n 42); WU Jilu, *The Concept of Marine Scientific Research' in Peter A. DUTTON, ed., Military Activities in the EEZ: A U.S.-China Dialog on Security and International Law in the Maritime Commons* (2010, Newport, RI: Naval War College Press) 65, 71.

46 YU Zhirong, 'Jurisprudential Analysis of the U.S. Navy's Military Surveys in the Exclusive Economic Zones of Coastal Countries' in Peter A. DUTTON, ed., *Military Activities in the EEZ: A U.S.-China Dialog on Security and International Law in the Maritime Commons* (2010, Newport, RI: Naval War College Press) 37,47; XUE Guifang. 'Surveys and Research Activities in the EEZ: Issues and Prospects' in Peter A. DUTTON, ed., *Military Activities in the EEZ: A U.S.-China Dialog on Security and International Law in the Maritime Commons* (2010, Newport, RI: Naval War College Press) 89, 103.

category of MSR.[47] Some scholars point out that the purpose for which the information is collected is the main criterion distinguishing between MSR and other forms of maritime information collection.[48] Military survey is conducted for military purposes and is different from MSR.[49]

It is true that, according to the *literal interpretation* of the UNCLOS's provisions, there is a certain logical difficulty in bringing hydrographic and military survey directly into the scope of MSR.[50] But 'MSR' should be a practical concept, which needs to be understood and applied based on the development of the international community's practices. As for the scope of MSR, given the highly dynamic nature of the marine environment, survey or hydrographic survey is an important method of MSR and an important path to achieve the objectives of MSR. Using the contents of Part XIII of UNCLOS to establish the meaning of MSR, Professor Stephens, and Professor Rothwell define it as 'any form of scientific investigation, fundamental or applied, concerned with the marine environment, i.e. that marine environment as its object'.[51] Therefore, the scope of MSR could include hydrographic survey and military survey in highly dynamic marine environments.[52]

As stated above, whether the using UMVs for MSR can be regulated by UNCLOS includes two legal issues: whether UMVs are 'vessel' or 'ship' or 'scientific research installations or equipment'; whether the UMVs' activities can be regarded as MSR. While USVs and AUVs can be regarded as 'vessel' or 'ship', float and ROVs cannot be regulated by UNCLOS as 'vessel' or 'ship' but as 'scientific research installations or equipment' (see Table 3.1). Due to the unclear definition of MSR, whether the UMVs' activities can be regarded as MSR is still in debate which needs more state practice, and interpretation of existing or new international rules to be solved. However, for regulating the increasing use of UMVs for MSR, it is better to take 'MSR' stipulated in Part XIII as a general and basic concept to cover as far as possible all research activities with the marine

47 Boleslaw Adam Boczek, 'Peacetime Military Activities in the Exclusive Economic Zone of Third Countries', (1988) 19 ODIL 447, 448.

48 Simon Mckenzie, 'Autonomous Technology and Dynamic Obligations: Uncrewed Maritime Vehicles and the Regulation of Maritime Military Surveillance in the Exclusive Economic Zone' (2021) 11 AJIL 161.

49 Qu Ya-nan, Xu Xuan, 'International Law Analysis of U.S. Military Survey Activities in China's EEZ' (2022) 19 UCLR10 459.

50 Zan He, 'The Limited Freedom of Military Activities in the Exclusive Economic Zone' (in Chinese) (2015) 4 TPSL 163.

51 Tim Stephens and Donald Rothwell. 'Marine Scientific Research' in Donald Rothwell, Alex Oude Elferink, Karen Scott, and Tim Stephens, eds., *The Oxford Handbook of the Law of the Sea* (2015, Oxford: Oxford University Press) 562.

52 Haibo Chen, 'Competent International organizations and the development of the system of international rules for Marine scientific research' (in Chinese) (2023) 1 SJTULR.

TABLE 3.1 The legal status of Uncrewed Maritime Vehicles (UMVs)

<table>
<tr><th colspan="2">Uncrewed Maritime Vehicles (UMVs)</th><th>Legal Status</th></tr>
<tr><td colspan="2">Float</td><td>scientific research installations or equipment</td></tr>
<tr><td colspan="2">Uncrewed Surface Vehicles (USVs)</td><td>ship/vessel</td></tr>
<tr><td rowspan="2">Uncrewed Underwater Vehicles (UUVs)</td><td>Remote Operated Vehicle (ROV)</td><td>scientific research installations or equipment</td></tr>
<tr><td>Autonomous Underwater Vehicle (AUV)</td><td>ship/vessel</td></tr>
</table>

environment as the research object. In this sense, the use of UMVs for MSR should apply the relevant rules of UNCLOS.

3 The Challenges to the Rights and Obligations of States Concerned under UNCLOS during UMVs' Conducting Scientific Research

As noted above, the UMVs used for MSR include float, USVs, and UUVs, and Part XIII of UNCLOS can apply to UMVs. While the deployment of UMVs by a research vessel is controllable by researching State or international organizations, the control over the profiling UMVs is reduced once they have been deployed, given that profiling UMVs follow the flow of currents which makes it nearly impossible to precisely predict their route or to influence them. After deploying on the ocean, the float is only driven by currents and can only float randomly. While gliders have a programmed course and follow it as far as possible, strong currents may nevertheless influence the course of gliders resulting in their uncontrolled drifting.[53] As a result, either float drifting with global currents and without being self-powered, or other UMVs, like Wave Glider, moving independent of ocean currents and relying on propulsion driven by wave or other energy, may get caught up in issues caused by uncontrolled drifting.

53 Katharina Bork et al. (n 4) 311.

3.1 *The Issues of Using UMVs for Scientific Research in Territorial Sea and EEZ*

Since the deployment and use of UMVs for MSR is subject to the conditions of UNCLOS, it is necessary to seek the consent of foreign coastal States for the deployment and use of UMVs if they are to operate within the maritime zones under the sovereignty or jurisdiction of the coastal State.

According to Article 245 of UNCLOS, MSR shall be conducted in the territorial sea only with the express consent of and under the conditions set forth by the coastal State. UNCLOS leaves the right to formulate relevant regulations in the territorial sea to the coastal State without interference. In the territorial sea, coastal States have the exclusive right to grant consent for MSR and the discretion to impose requirements. However, many coastal States have not established detailed regulations for MSR activities within their territorial sea. For example, Article 11 of the Law of the People's Republic of China on the Territorial Sea and the Contiguous Zone in 1992 only stipulates that all international organizations, foreign organizations, or individuals shall obtain approval from the Government of the People's Republic of China for carrying out scientific research, marine operations or other activities. All illegal entries into the territorial sea of the People's Republic of China for carrying out these activities shall be dealt with by the relevant organs of the People's Republic of China. The Philippines makes no reference to its rights in the territorial sea in its law establishing the so-called baselines and limits of the territorial sea.[54] Without clear domestic rules, it is hard for researching States to figure out how to obtain the consent of coastal States to use UMVs for MSR in the territorial sea of coastal States. Moreover, with the characteristic of uncontrolled drifting, UMVs that conduct MSR in other maritime zones may drift into the territorial sea which may be regarded as 'illegal entries' and be dealt with by the relevant organs of the coastal State. This situation may discourage the researching State from using UMVs for MSR and cause conflicts between the researching State and the coastal State.

Article 248 of UNCLOS makes detailed provisions on MSR in the EEZ or on the continental shelf, States and competent international organizations that intend to undertake MSR in the exclusive economic zone or on the continental shelf of a coastal State shall, not less than six months in advance of the expected starting date of the MSR project, provide that State with a full description of the precise geographical areas, the expected date of first appearance and final departure of the research vessels, etc. In this regard, many coastal States have not made further detailed provisions. For example, the 1984

54 Haiwen Zhang and Hongyun Li, *Translation Series on the International Law of the Sea: Asia'* (in Chinese) (2017, Qingdao Publishing) 169, 171.

Exclusive Economic Zone Act of Malaysia stipulates the regime of MSR in Part V, but the five provisions of this part are basically the same as the relevant provisions of Part XIII of UNCLOS.[55]

However, with the characteristic of uncontrolled drifting, it is nearly impossible to know ahead of time where an observing UMV will be taking the observations for some observing UMVs.[56] So it is hard for researching States to provide the necessary and relevant information on using UMVs for MSR with coastal States. It is uncertain whether the project's geographical location and the date of first appearance and departure, which must be informed in the pre-cruise phase, include just the site of data collection or also areas of transiting.[57] The solution would be to obtain, the researching State to predict a range of possible geographical areas and time and provide this information to all coastal States of which the slightest possibility exists that UMVs might enter their EEZ or continental shelf. Such a requirement would, however, place a disproportionately heavy burden on the researching State. This would disproportionately inhibit the freedom of MSR, which is an important part of the UNCLOS legal regime.[58]

3.2 *The Issues of Using UMVs for Scientific Research in the Waters beyond EEZ*

According to Article 257 of UNCLOS, all States and competent international organizations have the right to conduct MSR in the water column beyond the limits of the EEZ in conformity with UNCLOS.

With the characteristic of uncontrolled drifting of UMVs, although States and international organizations conduct MSR with UMVs in the water column beyond national jurisdiction, it is unpredictable when and where a profiling UMV might enter the EEZ or other maritime zones under national jurisdiction, which may raise conflict with the coastal States because of lacking the prior consent of the coastal State and other prior processes. And in practical terms, the prior consent of the coastal State cannot be obtained in advance. Tobias Hofmann and Alexander Proelss recommend that prior consent be obtained where UMVs' activities are planned to take place near the EEZ of a foreign

55 1984 Exclusive Economic Zone Act, Act No.3 11. <https://www.un.org/Depts/los/LEGISLATIONANDTREATIES/PDFFILES/MYS_1984_Act.pdf> accessed 30 July 2023.

56 IOC Circular Letter No 2938 (15 March 2023) 6.

57 Luciana Fernandes Coelho, Roland Rogers, 'The Use of Marine Autonomous Systems in Ocean Observation Under the LOSC: Maintaining Access to and Sharing Benefits for Coastal States' in Tafsir Matin Johansson, Dimitrios Dalaklis, etc., *Smart Ports and Robotic Systems, Navigating the Waves of Techno-Regulation and Governance* (2023, Palgrave Macmillan).

58 Katharina Bork et al. (n 4) 311.

coastal State.[59] Obviously, this places a disproportionately heavy burden on the researching State too. Moreover, there is no legal basis to require the researching State to obtain prior consent when conducting MSR in the water column beyond national jurisdiction. But for the coastal State, although in such a situation entry into EEZ is unintentional, Article 246(2) of UNCLOS is not limited to activities that are undertaken deliberately. Unintentional entry without prior consent constitutes an infringement of the coastal State's jurisdiction.

4 The Responses to the Legal Challenges of Using Uncrewed Maritime Vehicles for Scientific Research

Based on the above analysis of the relevant legal questions, this section suggests that we should strengthen the regulations on UMVs used for MSR from both domestic and international paths.

4.1 *To Regulate Using UMVs for MSR in Domestic Laws*

Before reaching a consensus on relevant international rules, States can start with domestic laws, which is also a good opportunity to take a stand on controversial issues, like the legal status of UMVs.

Specifically speaking, firstly, the legal status of various kinds of UMVs could be clarified in domestic law, which is the most basic regulation of UMVs, and will enable relevant domestic regulations to clearly apply to the using UMVs for MSR. Before clarifying the legal status of UMVs, it is not clear whether using UMVs for MSR should apply the relevant domestic rules, whether the different kinds of UMVs may apply the same domestic rules, etc. This uncertainty will hamper not only the right of the researching State to apply for MSR but also the jurisdiction of the coastal State which is detrimental to the interests of States and the international marine order. As analyzed above, except for float and ROV which do not constitute 'ships' but can be regarded as 'scientific research installations or equipment', other UMVs constitute 'ship'.

Secondly, clarifying the concept of MSR in domestic laws. Indeed, because of the interests of different States, it is hard to reach a consensus on whether hydrographic survey and military survey can be regarded as MSR. But for the sake of the coastal State's interests, China and other coastal States with the same position should make it clear that hydrographic and military survey are part of MSR which shall obtain the consent of coastal States in domestic laws.

59 Tobias Hofmann et al. (n 43) 179.

Moreover, the domestic rules should emphasize MSR projects 'for peaceful purposes'.

Thirdly, States may amend the existing relevant rules or make new detailed rules to regulate the using UMVs for MSR according to the characteristics of UMVs, like 'uncontrolled drifting'. In the territorial sea, the coastal States, in the exercise of their sovereignty, have the exclusive right to regulate, authorize, and conduct MSR. Although coastal States tend to retain the right to conduct MSR in the territorial sea for themselves and they are not active in refining the relevant rules, they should improve the relevant rules in response to the new characteristics of UMVs, like 'uncontrolled drifting'.

According to Article 255 of UNCLOS, States shall endeavor to adopt reasonable rules, regulations, and procedures to promote and facilitate MSR conducted under UNCLOS beyond their territorial sea. States should clarify the requirements of foreign States for conducting MSR in maritime zones under their jurisdiction and make new appropriate rules to adapt to the new development of using UMVs for MSR. For example, in 2016, Vietnam issued the Decree on Elaborating the Authorization of Foreign Organizations and Individuals to Conduct Science Research in the Marine Waters of Vietnam which specifies the authorities in charge of MSR activities conducted by foreign individuals and research institutions in the marine waters of Vietnam and clarified many details. The annex of the Decree also provides a sample of the researching State's project submission, the permit of MSR issued by the Vietnamese government, and the preliminary report to be submitted after the completion of the research project.[60]

Regarding the approval of MSR projects, there are problems with the existing rules for MSR in some States. For example, some scholars indicate that the Philippines has problems in the approval and management of MSR projects: in terms of the approval process, the evaluation and approval process of MSR projects is too slow; in some cases, the Philippine Department of Foreign Affairs refused to allow foreign research ships to proceed days before departure.[61] Obtaining the consent of coastal States is the most important constraint on MSR. If States' mechanisms for approving MSR are not improved, and

60 2016 Decree on Elaborating the Authorization of Foreign Organizations and Individuals to Conduct Science Research in the Marine Waters of Vietnam. No. 41/2016/ND-CP <https://vanbanphapluat.co/decree-41-2016-nd-cp-authorization-foreign-organizations-individuals-science-research-marine-waters-vietnam>accessed 30 July 2023.

61 Factsasia. 'FNI, UP MSI, MERF and US Embassy Manila Convened a Webinar on Improving Filipino MSR Framework' <https://www.factsasia.org/blog/fni-up-msi-merf-and-us-embassy-manila-convened-a-webinar-on-improving-filipino-msr-framework> accessed 15 July 2023.

regulations on UMVs for MSR are not included, it will be difficult to move forward with the development of using UMVs for MSR.

4.2 *To Regulate Using UMVs for MSR at the International Level*

Except for strengthening the regulations on UMVs used for MSR from the domestic path, it also suggests to regulate using UMVs for MSR at the international level. In the short term, the interpretation and application of relevant provisions of UNCLOS may be clarified to regulate the use of UMVs for MSR. In the long term, States may push forward the development of relevant international rules or guidelines and promote international cooperation on using UMVs for MSR.

4.2.1 Clarifying the Interpretation and Application of Relevant International Rules

In the short term, the formation of new international rules cannot be achieved overnight, and the international community needs to work together to gradually reach a consensus on how to regulate the using UMVs for MSR. Therefore, as the core of the international law of the sea, UNCLOS has always been an important basis for States to regulate the using UMVs for MSR.

Several provisions of UNCLOS are vague, and on major issues of safeguarding national interests, States have actively interpreted the relevant provisions of UNCLOS and claimed their rights. As mentioned above, on whether UMVs constitute 'ship' or whether the relevant provisions of Part XIII of UNCLOS apply to UMVs, UNCLOS will inevitably be interpreted and applied. The coastal State and the researching State hold different views from the standpoint of safeguarding national interests. In this regard, at present, it is necessary to clarify that the relevant provisions of Part XIII of UNCLOS shall apply to UMVs through the interpretation of 'ships', 'MSR', and other terms or rules in UNCLOS. On one hand, 'MSR' stipulated in Part XIII should be taken as a general and basic concept to cover as far as possible all research activities with the marine environment as the research object. On the other hand, most of the provisions of Part XIII on rights, obligations, responsibilities, and liability related to 'MSR' should be applied to all MSR activities as general and fundamental provisions.[62] At the same time, based on the overall understanding and application

62 The general and fundamental provisions of Part XIII of UNCLOS run through each section, mainly including the provisions of Section 1 'General Provisions', the provisions of Section 2 'International Cooperation', Section 3 'Conduct and promotion of Marine scientific research', other than the basis for the determination of 'consent' of the coastal State, the provisions of Section 4 'Scientific research installations or equipment in the Marine

and cross-guidance of the relevant provisions of Part XIII of UNCLOS and other parts of UNCLOS, the general and basic provisions of Part XIII of UNCLOS still apply to research activities that focus on the marine environment but are not characterized as 'MSR'.

Before the formation of new international rules, the interpretation and application of international conventions such as UNCLOS will be an important way for States to strengthen the regulation. Based on the relevant rules of VCLT, States should not be limited to literal interpretation but apply different treaties' interpretation ways to interpret and flexibly apply the relevant provisions of UNCLOS to govern the using UMVs for MSR.

4.2.2 Pushing Forward the Development of Relevant International Rules or Guidelines on Using UMVs for MSR

Some scholars have proposed that there are two possible ways to regulate UMVs: to conclude a treaty, and to establish criteria to set out the principles of how States should deploy UMVs.[63] In addition, a formal amendment of UNCLOS is also a possible avenue. However, the legal issues related to the use of UMVs for MSR are highly controversial, and it is hard for UNCLOS to be amended to include relevant provisions.

In terms of the formulation of new treaty rules or customary law, the technology of UMVs still develops continuously, which means that UMVs will be in an 'unpredictable' and 'unstable' state for a long time in the future, and relevant state practices and specific ways of deploying UMVs are difficult to predict. This brings great challenges to the formation of treaty rules or customary law. However, in the long run, based on the active promotion of the regulation in domestic laws and the increasing state practice, the formulation of new international rules on the use of UMVs for MSR is undoubtedly the best solution to the relevant legal challenges.

Moreover, according to Article 251 of UNCLOS, States shall promote the establishment of generally accepted guidelines and criteria to assist States in ascertaining the nature and implications of MSR. In practice, relevant international organizations have formulated or contributed to the formulation of many 'criteria and guidelines'. For example, in 2010, the Division for Ocean Affairs and the Law of the Sea (DOALOS) adopted Marine Scientific Research: A Revised Guide to the Implementation of the Relevant Provisions of the United

environment', the provisions of Section 5 'responsibility and liability', and the relevant provisions of Section 6 'settlement of disputes and interim measures'.

63 See Matt Bartlett, 'Game of Drones: Unmanned Maritime Vehicles and the Law of the Sea' (2018) 24 AULR 66.

Nations Convention on the Law of the Sea and other 'criteria and guidelines'. This guide provides draft standard forms for States to use when they request an MSR project clearance and draft standard forms for the States in providing clearance. Due to the new technology development, maybe it is time to update the Guide prepared by the DOALOS in 2010. The idea is that updated guidance could reflect the issues raised by the use of UMVs for MSR, providing a new 'best practice' for granting MSR clearance for sustained observing that would address the issues of MSR process and advanced notification when using UMVs for MSR. However, it was also suggested that a 'lighter' approach could be in the form of issuing additional guidance to the existing Guide.[64]

Although these criteria and guidelines are soft law in nature and cannot have the legal effect of amending the rules relating to MSR of UNCLOS, they can serve as important arguments and practices for the interpretation and application of the rules of international law on MSR and make the content of MSR's international rules more specific and the application of rules more targeted. Shortly that it is difficult to formulate new international rules or modify the existing legal framework for UMVs conducting MSR, the efforts of States to promote the establishment of generally accepted 'guidelines and criteria' with the nature of soft law can not only strengthen the regulation of using UMVs for MSR in the short term but also in the long run, it can gradually reach an international consensus to form new international rules to regulate UMVs' carrying out MSR.

4.2.3 Promoting International Cooperation in the Using UMVs for MSR

UMVs' uncontrolled drifting challenges the relevant provisions of UNCLOS and affects the interest of both the coastal State and researching State. To achieve a balance of interests between the coastal State and the researching State, UNCLOS requires that the consent of the coastal State and the relevant requirements shall be obtained when MSR is conducted in the territorial sea, EEZ, or continental shelf of the coastal State. Obtaining the consent of coastal States is the most important constraint on MSR. But as stated above, with the characteristic of uncontrolled drifting of UMVs, the applicant, including the researching State and competent international organizations, may not meet the requirements under UNCLOS to obtain the consent of the coastal State. Therefore, in addition to developing new international rules for using UMVs for MSR or amending the relevant rules of UNCLOS, promoting international cooperation in using UMVs for MSR is another viable way to address these legal challenges.

64 IOC (n 56) 7.

Article 242(1) of UNCLOS mandates States and competent international organizations to promote international cooperation in MSR for peaceful purposes under the principle of respect for sovereignty and jurisdiction and based on mutual benefit. International cooperation is an effective way to solve the problem of imbalance in MSR capacity among States.[65] There are two ways for States to promote international cooperation in using UMVs for MSR.

Firstly, States can cooperate directly with each other. However, due to the difficulty of balancing the interests between the coastal State and the researching State and between developing and developed countries, it has been so hard to achieve effective cooperation between States for a long time.

Secondly, according to Article 247 of UNCLOS, two relations may exist between the coastal State and the international organization conducting or hosting MSR: the coastal State is a member of the international organization; or, the coastal State has bilateral agreements with the international organization. Those kinds of States can promote international cooperation in using UMVs for MSR through competent international organizations. For example, IOC has a successful history of developing a cooperative framework for the real-time sharing of ocean data. In particular, the IOC was successful in creating a Member State-agreed framework and mechanism, in compliance with UNCLOS, for the provision of data from floats in the global Argo Programme that drift into EEZs. The Argo programme was formally accepted and defined by IOC Resolution XX-6 (1999), which was jointly developed by the IOC, World Meteorological Organization (WMO), and other organizations and has been convened by more than 30 States to monitor and recognize the state of the global ocean in real-time and continuously.[66] In 2006, the IOC acknowledged that international cooperation is capital to deploy floats in EEZs and remote areas in the sixth meeting of the IOC Advisory body of experts on the law of the sea.[67]

Competent international organizations have been key in creating favorable conditions for MSR and enhancing capacities. They conduct or host MSR can fully demonstrate the coordinating role of international organizations,

---

65 See P. Bernal & A. Simcock. 'Chapter 30 Marine Scientific Research'. In L. Inniss and A. Simcock. The First Global Integrated Marine Assessment: World Ocean Assessment I, United Nations (2016) 7.

66 See IOC, Resolution XX 6: the Argo Project, the 20th Executive Council (June 1999, IOC). EC XLI.4: Guidelines for the Implementation of Resolution XX 6 of the IOC Assembly Regarding the Deployment of Profiling Floats in the High Seas within the Framework of the Argo Programme (2008, IOC).

67 IOC. Sixth Meeting of the IOC Advisory Body of Experts on the Law of the Sea (April 2006).

achieve benefit sharing and data exchange, and have advantages that sovereign States do not have when conducting MSR in the territorial sea or other maritime zones under their jurisdiction, which is conducive to the reconciliation of interests and the sharing of results.[68] MSR involves important public interests, and its results are also important international public goods, reflecting the mutual promotion between the collective interests of mankind and the national interests of States. However, the hardware and software capabilities of States to conduct MSR with UMVs and manage marine data and information are uneven.[69] The participation of developing countries in international collaborations still is asymmetrical.[70] Joint international action becomes an important means of overcoming these deficiencies. As an important professional organization within the framework of the United Nations, the IOC can promote the coordination of interests through the United Nations mechanism, work with other intergovernmental organizations and non-governmental organizations to promote functional coordination, ensure the integrity and coordination of research projects, and practice, facilitating the exchange or sharing of key data and information, helping to promote capacity building, etc. The Argo project is a good example. It is necessary to adhere to the United Nations cooperation mechanism led by the IOC, adhere to the United Nations institutional mechanism as the basic path for the diversified development of MSR, and create a friendly and efficient atmosphere for South-South cooperation and regional cooperation, and build a practical cooperation mechanism for MSR and development. Similar to the successful example of the Argo project, in South-South cooperation and regional cooperation, we can actively promote the sharing and exchange of experience on best practices and play an exemplary role. There was agreement on the importance of regional governance and that working to develop a regional multi-State agreement to help facilitate observations in waters under national jurisdiction could be useful in some circumstances.[71]

Part XIII of UNCLOS does not specify whether 'competent international organizations' include regional international organizations, but regional States have more consistent common interests, concerns, and needs in using UMVs

68 Haibo Chen (n 52) 39.

69 UNFCCC, 'Global Ocean Science Report 2020' (2020) <https://unfccc.int/documents/568127?gclid=CjwKCAjw5MOlBhBTEiwAAJ8e1ruOFpIIRALrzwduG2lAFLnyP-rxk_ok_p4jjtosEjId_6cWAdLy8RoCSz0QAvD_BwE> accessed 15 July 2023.

70 Luciana Fernandes Coelho, Roland Rogers (n 56).

71 IOC (n 56) 7.

for MSR. Coordination through regional international organizations can provide a good basis for cooperation. Therefore, the 'competent international organizations' for MSR should not be limited to global international organizations, but should also include regional and even subregional organizations.[72] Accordingly, States in the region can also promote cooperation in the use of UMVs for MSR through regional international organizations in addition to global international organizations.

5 Conclusion

The rising use of UMVs for MSR has cast a spotlight on the inadequacy of current legal frameworks under UNCLOS. It's observed that both UNCLOS and the draft guidelines formulated by relevant international organizations or domestic laws of States concerned fall short of addressing the challenges posed by UMVs in MSR. This paper mainly focuses on the legal issues of whether UMVs can be regarded as 'ship' or 'vessel', whether the activities conducted by UMVs can be regarded as MSR and the challenge of UMVs' uncontrolled drifting to the rights and obligations of States concerned under UNCLOS.

This paper examines the complex legal recognition of UMVs and their activities in MSR. Beyond textual analysis, it employs various treaty interpretations to scrutinize the relevant UNCLOS provisions, suggesting that UMVs be governed as either 'ship' or 'scientific research installations and equipment'. Despite debates over classifying UMV-conducted hydrographic and military surveys as MSR, this study advocates for their inclusion under MSR, subject to relevant regulations of UNCLOS.

On the challenges of UMVs to the rights and obligations of States concerned under UNCLOS, due to the characteristic of UMVs' uncontrolled drifting, using UMVs for MSR may not apply some relevant provisions of UNCLOS, such as Articles 247 and 258 of UNCLOS which may cause maritime jurisdictional conflict between researching State and coastal State. These challenges result primarily from the application of relevant provisions of UNCLOS that were not designed to and are not adequate to, regulate the deployment of UMVs. On one hand, the researching State using UMVs for MSR within the maritime zones under the sovereignty or jurisdiction of coastal States may not meet the requirements of UNCLOS and domestic laws of coastal States. On the other

72 Haibo Chen (n 52).

hand, without establishing detailed regulations for using UMVs for MSR, it is hard for coastal States to solve the maritime jurisdictional conflict with the researching State arising from the characteristic of UMVs' uncontrolled drifting. Hence, MSR projects that use UMVs are hampered by Part XIII of UNCLOS for the reason that the requirements stipulated in relevant provisions of UNCLOS are hard to meet.

To conclude, it is recommended for States concerned to make efforts on both domestic and international fronts to regulate the use of UMVs for MSR. From the domestic perspective, States should define UMVs' legal classifications and refine MSR definition within their legal frameworks, utilizing comparative legal research to adapt or create precise regulations tailored to UMVs features, such as their propensity for 'uncontrolled drifting'. From the international perspective, immediate efforts may focus on clarifying the provisions of UNCLOS, while long-term objectives should aim at developing new international standards to govern the operation of UMVs effectively. Additionally, enhancing international cooperation via international organizations will be critical in establishing and enforcing these regulations.

Acknowledgment

This research is supported by the National Social Foundation of China (Project No. 20VHQ005).

References

Annie Brett. 'Regulating the Autonomous Ocean' (2022) 88 BLR 1.

Boleslaw Adam Boczek, 'Peacetime Military Activities in the Exclusive Economic Zone of Third Countries', (1988) 19 ODIL 447.

Craig H. Allen, 'Determining the Legal Status of Unmanned Maritime Vehicles: Formalism vs Functionalism' (2018) 49 JMLC.

Craig H. Allen. 'The Seabots Are Coming Here: Should They Be Treated as 'Vessels'?' (2012) 65 JN.

Daum Oliver. 'The Implications of International Law on Unmanned Naval Craft', (2018) 49 JMLC.

David S. Goddard, 'International Law and the Military Use of Unmanned Maritime Systems' (2016) 98 IRRC.

Dean Roemmich et al. 'The Argo Program: Observing the Global Ocean with Profiling Floats' (2009) 22 Oceanography.

Feng Xu, Underwater Acoustic Sensing Technology for Unmanned Underwater Vehicle (in Chinese) (2020, Science Press).

Haibo Chen, 'Competent International organizations and the development of the system of international rules for Marine scientific research' (in Chinese) (2023) 1 SJTULR.

Haiwen Zhang and Hongyun Li, Translation Series on the International Law of the Sea: Asia' (in Chinese) (2017, Qingdao Publishing) 169.

Haiwen Zhang, 'Is It Safeguarding the Freedom of Navigation or Maritime Hegemony of the United States? — Comments on Raul (Pete) Pedrozo's Article on Military Activities in the EEZ' (2010) 9 CJIL.

Henrik Ringbom. 'Regulating Autonomous Ships-Concepts, Challenges and Precedents' (2019) 50 ODIL.

J. Ashley, Roach. Excessive Maritime Claims (Fourth Edition) (2021, Brill Nijhoff) 486.

Katharina Bork et al. 'The Legal Regulation of Floats and Gliders—In Quest of a New Regime?' (2008) 39 ODIL.

Lijing Cheng et al. 'How Fast are the Oceans Warming?' (2019) 363 Science.

Lindsay I. McCarl, 'Untethering UMVs from Vessels: Why the United States Should Construct a New Environmental Legal Scheme for Unmanned Maritime Vehicles' (2023) 127 DLR2.

lorian H.Th. Wegelein, Marine Scientific Research: The Operation and Status of Research Vessels and Other Platforms in International Law (2005, Maritinus Nijhoff Publishers).

Luciana Fernandes Coelho, Roland Rogers, 'The Use of Marine Autonomous Systems in Ocean Observation Under the LOSC: Maintaining Access to and Sharing Benefits for Coastal States' in Tafsir Matin Johansson, Dimitrios Dalaklis, etc., Smart Ports and Robotic Systems, Navigating the Waves of Techno-Regulation and Governance (2023, Palgrave Macmillan).

Matt Bartlett, 'Game of Drones: Unmanned Maritime Vehicles and the Law of the Sea' (2018) 24 AULR 66.

Mron H. Nordquist. UNCLOS 1982 Commentary (vol. 4) Translated by Wenzheng Lv and Bin Mao (2018,China Ocean Press) 420.

Natalie Klein, 'Maritime Autonomous Vehicles Within the International Law Framework to Enhance Maritime Security' (2019) 95 ILS 248.

Natalie Klein et al. 'Maritime Autonomous Vehicles: New Frontiers in The Law of the Sea' (2020) 69 ICLQ.

P. Bernal & A. Simcock, 'Chapter 30 Marine Scientific Research' in L. Inniss and A. Simcock (eds) The First Global Integrated Marine Assessment: World Ocean Assessment I, United Nations (2016).

Qing Wu, Le Wang, Jialun Liu, 'Research status and prospect of autonomous surface cargo ship' (in Chinese) (2019) 14 CTISI 59.

Qu Ya-nan, Xu Xuan, 'International Law Analysis of U.S. Military Survey Activities in China's EEZ' (2022) 19 UCLR10 459.

Rob McLaughlin. 'Unmanned Naval Vehicles at Sea: USVs, UUVs, and the Adequacy of the Law' (2011) 21 JLIS.

Robert Veal, Michael Tsimplis, and Andrew Serdy, 'The Legal Status and Operation of Unmanned Maritime Vehicles' (2019) 50 ODIL.

Sam Bateman, 'A Response to Pedrozo: The Wider Utility of Hydrographic Surveys' (2011) 10 CJIL.

Shuhua Song, Jinsong Zhao, 'The Legal Status of Unmanned Undersea Vehicles' (in Chinese) (2017) 3JSCSS3.

Shuning Zhang, 'The Legal Status of Unmanned Maritime System' (in Chinese) (2021) 6 SHJL.

Simon Mckenzie, 'Autonomous Technology and Dynamic Obligations: Uncrewed Maritime Vehicles and the Regulation of Maritime Military Surveillance in the Exclusive Economic Zone' (2021) 11 AJIL 161.

Tim Stephens and Donald Rothwell. 'Marine Scientific Research' in Donald Rothwell, Alex Oude Elferink, Karen Scott, and Tim Stephens, eds., The Oxford Handbook of the Law of the Sea (2015, Oxford: Oxford University Press) 562.

Tobias Hofmann, Alexander Proelss, 'The operation of Gliders Under the International Law of the Sea' (2015) 46ODIL3 169.

Wangwang Xing, Ling Zhu, 'A functional approach to reassessing the legal status and navigational rights of ships and ship-shaped structures' (2021) 106 TP 122.

WU Jilu, The Concept of Marine Scientific Research' in Peter A. Dutton, ed., Military Activities in the EEZ: A U.S.-China Dialog on Security and International Law in the Maritime Commons (2010, Newport, RI: Naval War College Press).

XUE Guifang. 'Surveys and Research Activities in the EEZ: Issues and Prospects' in Peter A. DUTTON, ed., Military Activities in the EEZ: A U.S.-China Dialog on Security and International Law in the Maritime Commons (2010, Newport, RI: Naval War College Press) 89.

Yen-Chiang Chang, Chao Zhang, Nannan Wang, 'The international legal status of the unmanned maritime vehicles' (2020) 113 MP 2.

Yongming Jin, 'Military Activities in Exclusive Economic Zone and State Practice'(in Chinese) (2008) 3 LS.

Yuqing Sun. 'The Legal Status of Commercial Unmanned Ships' (in Chinese) (2019) 6ILRWU 127.

YU Zhirong, 'Jurisprudential Analysis of the U.S. Navy's Military Surveys in the Exclusive Economic Zones of Coastal Countries' in Peter A. Dutton, ed., Military Activities in the EEZ: A U.S.-China Dialog on Security and International Law in the Maritime Commons (2010, Newport, RI: Naval War College Press) 37.

Zan He, 'The Limited Freedom of Military Activities in the Exclusive Economic Zone'(in Chinese) (2015) 4TPSL 163.

CHAPTER 4

Cybersecurity of Unmanned Ships: a Legal Analysis

Wei Wu and Junming Gong***

1 Introduction

The shipping industry is responsible for transporting over 95% of all goods traded around the world today, making the shipping community constantly look for ways to increase profits while still considering human and environmental safety.[1] In recent years, shipping companies are continuously transforming to digital management. Currently, the main technologies is for the development of intelligent ships in the shipbuilding and marine sectors have focused on data platforms, telecommunications and cyber security.[2]

Digitalization of ship management can also reduce the risk of reducing collision, grounding and stranding accidents at sea.[3] With the maturity and cost reduction of satellite broadband technology, more and more core parameters of ships have been able to achieve remote monitoring and real-time transmission from land, which greatly facilitates ship management. The rise of the Internet of Things (IoT) also provides the means to gain an integrated view of ships and improve transportation efficiency.[4] The aforementioned development allows shipping companies to make more effective decisions with the help of big data and advanced algorithms, thereby gaining a competitive

* Wei Wu, Associate Professor, Wuhan University China Institute of Boundary and Ocean Studies, Wuhan, China.

** Junming Gong, Master's Student, Wuhan University China Institute of Boundary and Ocean Studies, Wuhan, China.

1 Kimberly Tam and Kevin Jones, 'Cyber-Risk Assessment for Autonomous Ships' in Cyber Security 2018 Programme Committee, *2018 International Conference on Cyber Security and Protection of Digital Services (Cyber Security)* (IEEE 2018) 1, 1.

2 Jin-Hong Lim, Jae-Hwan Kim and Jun-Ho Huh 'Recent trends and proposed response strategies of international standards related to shipbuilding equipment big data integration platform' (2023) 57 Quality & Quantity 863, 864.

3 Anete Vagale, Rachid Oucheikh, Robin T. Bye, Ottar L. Osen and Thor I. Fossen, 'Path planning and collision avoidance for autonomous surface vehicles I: a review' (2021) 26 Journal of Marine Science and Technology 1292.

4 KVH Industries 'How Maritime loT Connectivity Transforms Performance & Profits' (2021) 1–5, <https://www.kvh.com/> accessed 27 February 2024.

 | DOI:10.1163/9789004706279_006

advantage.[5] With the development comes with hidden dangers that cannot be ignored, especially in the field of unmanned ships, which could become the major transportation vessel in the future based on its cost efficiencies. The dependence of unmanned ships' operation on internet remote control also leads to the high possibility of suffering from cyberattacks at the same time.[6] The prospect of unmanned ships addresses a very fundamental feature in shipping. After listing out the definition of unmanned ships, the focus of this paper is on risks concerned about the network in unmanned ships and the international rules related to the risks.

2 Definition of Unmanned Ships

Exploring the definition and legal nature of a subject is the basis to conduct further researches. Regarding the concept of unmanned ships, this part illustrates its definition and legal nature.

2.1 *Historical Development of Unmanned Ships*

In illustrating the concept of unmanned ships, it is imperative to explore the contributions of academia and organizations on other pertinent concepts. Synthesizing and clarifying other existing terms could supply revealment for the definition of unmanned ships. In the 1980s, the concept of autonomous ships was introduced. It was expected that in the future, the captain will perform his duties from an office building ashore, while the ship will be navigated through the use of computers.[7] Based on this concept, academia, organizations and states have developed other pertinent concepts in practice.

In 2017, Lloyd's Register published the Design Code for Unmanned Marine Systems (hereinafter referred to as the 'DCUMS'). The DCUMS used the term 'Cyber Enabled Ships' to describe unmanned ships, and the automation level of the ship is classified into six levels from ALO to AL6.[8] In this hierarchy, the

5 Martin Jes Iversen, 'Maritime Digital Business Models: The Case of D/S Norden, 2015–2020' in Byoung-Wook Ko Dong-Wook Song, *New Maritime Business* (Springer 2021) 113, 121.

6 Georgios Kavallieratos, Sokratis Katsikas and Vasileios Gkioulosm, 'Cyber-Attacks Against the Autonomous Ship' in Sokratis K. Katsikas and Others (eds), *Computer Security* (Springer 2019) 20, 21–25; Chia-Hsun Chang, Christos Kontovas, Qing Yu and Zaili Yang, 'Risk assessment of the operations of maritime autonomous surface ships' (2021) 207 Reliability Engineering & System Safety 1, 1–11.

7 Jurgen Lusch, *Ships and Shipping of Tomorrow*, (Cornell Maritime Pr/Tidewater Pub 1983).

8 Lloyd's Register, 'Design Code for Unmanned Marine Systems' (2017) 1–2, <https://www.lr.org/en/unmanned-code/> accessed 19 February 2024.

intelligence increases and the human involvement decreases, as the ship moves from no automation with full human operation, to semi-automation with human-machine collaboration, to a full automation level completely free from human will. With increased automation, relevant personnel's burden involved in ship management could be reduced, and the shipping companies can handle the complex communications and operation of ships with more efficiency.[9]

The Maritime Safety Committee of the International Maritime Organization (hereinafter referred to as the 'IMO'), at its 98th session in 2017, proposed the concept of 'Maritime Autonomous Surface Ships' (hereinafter referred to as the 'MASS') and considered the concept to include ships

> with different levels of automation, from partially automated systems that assisted the human crew to fully autonomous systems which were able to undertake all aspects of a ship's operation without the need for human intervention.[10]

In 2018, the IMO defined the MASS as 'a ship which, to a varying degree, can operate independent of human interaction.'[11] The degree of automation of the MASS is illustrated as follows,

> Degree one: Ship with automated processes and decision support: Seafarers are on board to operate and control shipboard systems and functions. Some operations may be automated and at times be unsupervised but with seafarers on board ready to take control. Degree two: Remotely controlled ship with seafarers on board: The ship is controlled and operated from another location. Seafarers are available on board to take control and to operate the shipboard systems and functions. Degree three: Remotely controlled ship without seafarers on board: The ship is controlled and

---

9 Hanan Hindy, David Brosset, Ethan Bayne, Amar Seeam and Xavier Bellekens, 'Improving SIEM for Critical SCADA Water Infrastructures Using Machine Learning' in Sokratis K. Katsikas and Others (eds), *Computer Security* (Springer 2018) 3, 4.

10 IMO 'Outcome of the Regulatory Scoping Exercise for the use of Maritime Autonomous Surface Ships (MASS)' (2021) 1–2, <https://wwwcdn.imo.org/localresources/en/MediaCentre/HotTopics/Documents/MSC.1-Circ.1638%20-%20Outcome%20Of%20The%20Regulatory%20Scoping%20ExerciseFor%20The%20Use%20Of%20Maritime%20Autonomous%20Surface%20Ships...%20(Secretariat).pdf> accessed 19 February 2024.

11 IMO, 'Framework for the Regulatory Scoping Exercise for the Use of Maritime Autonomous Surface Ships (MASS)' (2020) 1 <https://maiif.org/wp-content/uploads/2019/06/MSC-100_20-Annex-20-1.pdf> accessed 19 February 2024.

> operated from another location. There are no seafarers on board. Degree four: Fully autonomous ship: The operating system of the ship is able to make decisions and determine actions by itself.[12]

These four degrees provide guidance for the development and application of fully autonomous ships within the limits of technology.[13]

In 2023, China Classification Society (hereinafter referred to as the 'CCS') released its latest Rules for Intelligent Ships (hereinafter referred to as the 'RIS'), stating that

> intelligence refers to the application of modern communication and information technology, computer network technology, intelligent control technology, etc. for an object, which These applications usually include, but are not limited to, assessment, diagnosis, prediction and decision making.[14]
>
> Intelligence generally has the following characteristics: (1) the ability to perceive, i.e., the ability to perceive the ship itself and equipment, the external world, and obtain external information; (2) the ability to remember and think, i.e., the ability to store perceived external information and knowledge generated by thinking, and the ability to use existing knowledge to analyze, calculate, compare, judge, associate, and make decisions about information; (3) the ability to learn (3) Learning ability and self-adaptive ability, i.e., through the interaction with the environment, continuously learning and accumulating knowledge, so that they can adapt to environmental changes; (4) Behavioral decision-making ability, i.e., responding to external stimuli, forming decisions and conveying corresponding information.[15]

---

12 IMO 'Outcome of the Regulatory Scoping Exercise for the use of Maritime Autonomous Surface Ships (MASS)' (2021) 3–4 <https://wwwcdn.imo.org/localresources/en/MediaCentre/HotTopics/Documents/MSC.1-Circ.1638%20-%20Outcome%20Of%20The%20Regulatory%20Scoping%20ExerciseFor%20The%20Use%20Of%20Maritime%20Autonomous%20Surface%20Ships...%20(Secretariat).pdf> accessed 19 February 2024.

13 Young-Soo Han, Kyung Ho Lee, Yang Ouk Kim, Young Su Kim and Hyun Bin Yeo 'A Study on Augmented Reality Remote Maintenance Support System for Ships and Offshore Structures' (2022) 1 <https://avestia.com/ICCSTE2022_Proceedings/files/paper/ICCSTE_161.pdf> accessed 19 February 2024.

14 CCS, 'Rules for Intelligent Ships' (2023) 1 <https://www.ccs.org.cn/ccswz/articleDetail?id=202303061016018608> accessed 19 February 2024.

15 Ibid.

As the carrier of intelligence, intelligent ship refers to,

> ships that use technical means such as sensors, communication, Internet of Things, Internet, etc., automatically sense and obtain information and data of the ship itself, marine environment, logistics, port, etc., and realizes intelligent operation in terms of ship navigation, management, maintenance, cargo transportation, etc. based on computer technology, automatic control technology and big data processing and analysis technology in ship navigation, management, maintenance, cargo transportation, etc. with the purpose of making ships safer, more environmentally friendly, more economical and more efficient.[16]

For intelligent navigation, the RIS stipulates that

> intelligent navigation refers to the use of advanced sensing technology and sensor information fusion technology to obtain and sense the state information required for ship navigation, and through computer technology, control technology to analyze and process, to provide speed and route optimization decisions for the ship's navigation Suggestions. When it is feasible, the ship can achieve autonomous navigation in different navigation scenarios and complex environmental conditions such as open water, narrow waterway, entering and leaving ports, and docking and departing from terminals. The basic function of intelligent navigation is route and speed design and optimization. Intelligent navigation can also have the following advanced functions: (1) Autonomous navigation in open water; (2) Autonomous navigation at full range.[17]

In addition to ship service organizations, national and regional organizations and their scholars have different definitions regarding unmanned ships. RAND Corporation defines Unmanned Surface Vehicle (hereinafter referred to as the 'USV') as 'maritime vehicles uninhabited by personnel that maintain continuous, substantial contact with the surface.'[18] European Commission defines Unmanned Autonomous Vessel (hereinafter referred to as the 'UAV') as vessels

16 Ibid.

17 Ibid.

18 RAND 'U.S. Navy Employment Options for Unmanned Surface Vehicles (USVs)' (2013) 16 <https://www.rand.org/content/dam/rand/pubs/research_reports/RR300/RR384/RAND_RR384.pdf> accessed 19 February 2024.

> equipped with modular control systems and communication technology to enable wireless monitoring and control, including advanced decision support systems and the capabilities for remote and autonomous operation.[19]

Robert Veal defines the USV as 'vehicles that are capable of controlled, self-propelled movement in water without any personnel onboard.'[20] In Chinese academia, the terms 'unmanned ship' and 'intelligent ship' are the most common-used terms among all regarding ships with autonomous nature.

2.2 *Synthesized Definition of Unmanned Ships*

Based on the aforementioned regulations and opinions, it could be summarized that IMO classifies MASS based on degrees of automation, thereby allowing subtle and specific regulations on different MASS. Different from IMO, CCS' definition of intelligent ships focuses on the use of cyber technologies. RAND Corporation attaches importance to the basic functions that USV must possesses, which is the contact with surface, while the scholars and the European Commission mainly elaborate the unmanned nature of autonomous ships. The different definitions concentrate on various aspects.

To ensure the wide application and inclusiveness of the definition, by integrating and synthesizing the views of the organizations and academia, this paper defines unmanned ships as ships with different levels of automation, from partially automated systems that assist human crews to fully autonomous systems that can take on all aspects of ship operation without human intervention and maintain continuous and substantial contact with the water, using technological means such as sensors, communications, the Internet of Things, and the Internet. Based on this detailed definition, this paper could further illustrate the risks faced by unmanned ships and propose related legal responses in the following analysis without being cumbersome or unspecific.

19 European Commission 'Maritime Unmanned Navigation through Intelligence in Networks' (2016) 1 <http://www.unmanned-ship.org/munin/wp-content/uploads/2016/02/MUNIN-final-brochure.pdf> accessed 19 February 2024.

20 Robert Veal, Michael Tsimplis and Andrew Serdy, 'The Legal Status and Operation of Unmanned Maritime Vehicles' (2019) 50 Ocean Development & International Law 23, 24.

3 The Cyber Risks of Unmanned Ships and the Existing Legal Regulation

The unmanned ships have a great potential to save energy consumption and reduce ship crew, and have become a hot spot in the shipping industry in recent years, but their security issues should not be ignored. Unmanned ships highly rely on computer, automatic control, internet communication and artificial intelligence (hereinafter referred to as 'AI') technologies. Therefore, hackers may attack the ship's communication system, operating system and information technology system, and may also remotely control the satellite communication and navigation system to change the ship's route.[21] All of these attacks can cause irreparable damage to shipping. Legal regulations, no matter whether they are international or domestic, are of great importance in preventing and punishing these attacks.

3.1 *The Cyber Risks of Unmanned Ships*

The maritime industry is rapidly evolving and technological advances bring new challenges, such as increased cyber risks. Remote control or monitor operations of unmanned ships require additional communication channels, which introduces new system vulnerabilities and increases the severity and likelihood of cyber intrusions.[22] When these systems are not well protected, they cannot withstand cyberattacks.[23] In 2019, a deep-draft vessel suffered a cyber malware intrusion that severely impacted the ship's network. It was an incident that exposed potential security vulnerabilities on merchant ships, for which the United States Coast Guard (hereinafter referred to as 'USCG') issued a Maritime Security Alert.[24] From the results of this investigation, the USCG believes that this accident is not a simple Internet Technology (hereinafter referred to as 'IT') problem. They noted that ensuring cybersecurity

21 NATO Cooperative Cyber Defence Center of Excellence 'Cybersecurity Considerations in Autonomous Ships' (2022) 4–22 <https://ccdcoe.org/library/publications/cybersecurity-considerations-in-autonomous-ships/> accessed 19 February 2024.

22 Comité Maritime International 'Cyber-risks in unmanned vessel industry and adapting current U.S. and International legal framework to New Challenges' (2019) 3 <https://comitemaritime.org/wp-content/uploads/2019/09/yCMI-Essay-AB0015.pdf> accessed 19 February 2024.

23 Georgios Kavallieratos, Vasiliki Diamantopoulou and Sokratis K. Katsikas, 'Shipping 4.0: Security requirements for the Cyber-Enabled Ship' (2020) 16 IEEE Transactions on Industrial Informatics 6617.

24 United States Coast Guard 'Cyber Incident Exposes Potential Vulnerabilities Onboard Commercial Vessels' (2019) 1 <https://www.dco.uscg.mil/Portals/9/DCO%20Documents/5p/CG-5PC/INV/Alerts/0619.pdf> accessed 19 February 2024.

is a fundamental operation in the 21st-century maritime environment. The USCG strongly recommends that all ships, ship owners and their operators conduct a cybersecurity assessment to better understand their potential cyber deficiencies.[25]

With the wide application of maritime network technology in the shipping industry, ship network plays an increasingly important role in many critical systems involving ship safety and pollution prevention, regardless of whether it is a ship with a captain or an unmanned ship. However, along with the use of network comes cyber risks, especially in unmanned ships. Cyber risks come from a variety of sources, such as operational errors in the program, software defects,[26] unauthorized access to systems,[27] and management failure to adopt effective risk control procedures. Through the survey, it was found that there are many systems that are vulnerable to cyberattacks. These systems include bridge systems, cargo operation and management systems, propulsion and mechanical equipment management and power control systems, access control systems, passenger service and management systems, passenger public network management and crew protection systems, and communication systems.

Generally, maritime networks can be divided into two categories. The first category is networks for information gathering and information management services. These services include reporting, scheduling, inventory management, operations and maintenance management, e-mail, telephone, printing services and ship-to-shore communication. This type of network is often called as the information network. Its major components include the computers used by the crew, gateways, routers, file servers, database servers, application servers, and other devices. The second category is the network responsible for collecting, monitoring and controlling the operation status of the whole ship equipment and serving the ship control system. This type of network is often called as the control network. It mainly involves the main propulsion monitoring system, auxiliary engine monitoring system, power station monitoring system, fire alarm system, navigation system and the integrated bridge system.

Among the various systems, the unmanned ships have the greatest risks in terms of power unit stability, remote control reliability, crew management, information transmission security and software security. The human factor

25 Ibid.

26 Eray Yağdereli, Cemal Gemci and A Ziya Aktaş, 'A study on cyber-security of autonomous and unmanned vehicles' (2015) 12 The Journal of Defense Modeling and Simulation 369.

27 Victor Bolbot, Gerasimos Theotokatos, Evangelos Boulougouris and Dracos Vassalos, 'A novel cyber-risk assessment method for ship systems' (2020) 131 Safety Science 1.

remains critical in the remote control of vessels. Controllers who are performing watchkeeping duties may improperly operate the ships during the navigation. Systems' shutdown can also lead to the consequences of loss of control or even loss of connection of a ship. These risks may lead to ships' collision and grounding, and the damages to equipment. These hazards could impair the natural and navigable environment in which the ship is navigating.

Development is bound to bring new issues. Maritime cyber risk refers to

> a measure of the extent to which a technology asset is threatened by a potential circumstance or event, which may result in shipping-related operational, safety or security failures as a consequence of information or systems being corrupted, lost or compromised.[28]

Specifically, the gradual development of the unmanned ships may encounter problems such as data collection issues, data storage issues, and data usage issues. The first one is data collection issue, meaning the intelligent system record may be wrong. Errors in the system lead to discrepancies in fuel records or speed and wind records, which can seriously hinder the investigation and evidence collection after the occurrence of accidents. In particular, when two unmanned ships collide, the misinformation recorded on the network could give rise to disputes about which party should be held responsible for information errors.

Second, data storage issues such as the infringement of AI information records may cause damages. When there is a cyberattack on the shipping network that causes system operation failure, a large amount of information such as voyage records may be lost. In this case, not only one specific ship will be damaged, but all ships under the coverage of the same network could be affected. Like the jammed Suez Canal could do to the shipping industry, a downed cloud storage system or loss of information would most likely bring the entire shipping industry's operations to a halt. It is difficult to timely identify the infringing the person or institution that launched the cyberattack. Even if the infringer is eventually identified, shipping enterprises are often unable to afford such a huge data loss and economic losses. Currently, there is no relevant international law on how to manage these incidents and attribute responsibility for the losses incurred.

28 IMO 'Guidelines on maritime cyber risk management' (2017) 1, <https://www.gard.no/Content/23896593/MSC-FAL.1-Circ.3.pdf> accessed 19 February 2024.

Finally, data usage issues could impinge navigational security. The vulnerability of satellite navigation systems, particularly the Global Positioning System (hereinafter referred to as the 'GPS'), is of particular concern as an important branch of cyber threats affecting many maritime systems.[29] Unmanned ship are supposed to rely on communication devices to input control signals, and it is easily to be a target of hackers. Hackers could cooperate with pirates to locate unmanned ships for robbery. For unmanned ships with high autonomy level, they could stop the ships or even guide the ships to other port so they could occupy the cargo or sample and record of scientific researches. Even if unmanned ships are equipped with the necessary defensive measures, it is difficult for them to escape from the pirates' aggression.

3.2 *Existing Legal Regulation Regarding Cyber Risks of Unmanned Ships*

The existing international conventions clearly stipulate the crew on board and manual control as the basic measures to ensure the safety of ships, and the existing conventions use a lot of 'alarms' and 'manual operation', which is inconsistent with the development goal of intelligent ships to achieve unmanned control eventually. International Convention for the Safety of Life at Sea (hereinafter referred to as 'SOLAS') emphasize that providing adequate number of competent crew is the obligation of state parties.[30] International Convention on Standards of Training, Certification and Watchkeeping for Seafarers (hereinafter referred to as 'STCW') regulates that, 'it is of special importance that at all times the officer of the watch ensures that an efficient look-out is maintained.'[31] The International Regulations for Preventing Collisions at Sea (hereinafter referred to as 'COLREGS') provides rules for the safety of navigation, such as 'good seamanship', which should be used to avoid ship collisions.[32]

Over the decades, ship crewing has been gradually reduced to the point where unmanned ships are in operation. The operator of an intelligent ship may be in a remote control center on land, and the duty officer may be away

29 Andrej Androjna, Tanja Brcko, Ivica Pavic and Harm Greidanus, 'Assessing Cyber Challenges of Maritime Navigation' (2020) 8(10) Journal of Marine Science and Engineering 776.

30 International Convention for the Safety of Life at Sea (adopted 1 November 1974, entered into force 25 May 1980) 1184 UNTC 278 Chapter V Safety of Navigation.

31 International Convention on Standards of Training, Certification and Watchkeeping for Seafarers (adopted 7 July 1978, entered into force 28 April 1984) 1361 UNTC 76 Annex. Recommendation on Operational Guidance for Officers in Charge of 1 Navigational Watch.

32 Convention on the International Regulations for Preventing Collisions at Sea (adopted 20 October 1972, entered into force 15 July 1977) 1050 UNTC 16 Part B Rule 8.

from the bridge or a location directly connected to it. The mixing of conventional ships and unmanned ships in the same sea area also poses a challenge to the existing collision avoidance rules.[33] The development of unmanned ships has brought new challenges to maritime traffic safety in terms of maritime cyber risks, and has also impacted on international rules and standards related to ship management and crew management.

In terms of legal regulations regarding the risks of unmanned ships, the relevant international laws can be summarized into three main categories. Firstly, there are jurisdictional rules. General international treaties represented by the UNCLOS stipulate the rights and obligations of states to take measures regarding ships. Secondly, there are technical rules concerning safety, environment, training and watchkeeping standards, which are mainly developed by international organizations represented by the IMO. Thirdly, in the field of domestic law, states could legislate and develop regulations to regulate and coordinate the development of unmanned ships.

3.2.1 Rules of International Law

In recent years, with the development of digitalization, intelligence and networking of ships, more and more control systems, communication and navigation systems, information management systems and equipment are constantly connected to the ship network to realize external information interaction. Ships are increasingly 'online', making them more vulnerable to cyber threats than traditional communications.[34] In such a context, cybersecurity of ships is particularly important.

Uniform rules of international law are still lacking.[35] There is currently no clear global regulation on how to regulate the risks posed by AI, including the cyber risks of unmanned ships. However, the IMO and International Association of Classification Societies (hereinafter referred to as 'IACS'), which are influential international organizations in the maritime field, have developed a series of rules concerning unmanned ships. Awareness of ships' cyber risk is growing in the international maritime community as IACS released

---

33 Tae-eun Kim, Lokukaluge Prasad Perera, Magne-Petter Sollid, Bjørn-Morten Batalden, Are Kristoffer Sydnes, 'Safety challenges related to autonomous ships in mixed navigational environments' (2022) 21 Journal of Maritime Affairs 141, 144.

34 Andrea Antolini 'Cyber security in maritime transport and question of cyber security measures for autonomous ships' (2020) 1, <https://www.jttri.or.jp/document/2019/andrea42.pdf> accessed 19 February 2024.

35 Young-Soo Park, Jung-Sik Jeong and Yusuf Volkan Aydogdu, 'Advances in Maritime Safety' (2022) 10 Journal of Marine Science and Engineering 1721.

12 recommendations for ship cybersecurity in 2018.[36] These recommendations include recommended procedures for software maintenance of shipboard equipment and systems, recommendation concerning manual / local control capabilities for software dependent machinery systems, contingency plan for onboard computer based systems, network architecture, data assurance, physical security of onboard computer based systems, network security of onboard computer based systems, vessel system design, inventory list of computer based systems, integration, remote update / access, and communication and Interfaces.[37] In 2019, the Baltic and International Maritime Council (hereinafter referred to as 'BIMCO') also released contractual provisions for cybersecurity to clarify the responsibilities of each party and avoid losses due to cybersecurity risks.[38] In 2019, with the support of the American Bureau of Shipping Group (hereinafter referred to as 'ABS Group'), the IMO and BIMCO jointly produced a free white paper on maritime cybersecurity.[39] The white paper combines the analysis of five years of survey results and matches them to online behavior and investment trends in the maritime industry. It also provides a comprehensive overview of the key cyber security issues facing the maritime industry and practical advice from industry experts on assessing cyber risks, preventing cyberattacks, and developing business recovery methods. In 2021, the BIMCO released the fourth edition of Guidelines on Cyber Security Onboard Ships (hereinafter referred to as 'GCSOS'). This is an important milestone in maritime safety and security and is the result of a collaborative effort between shipping industry leaders and IMO member countries. The GCSOS further refines the IMO guidelines and provides the industry with a new set of specific operational guidance regarding ship protection.[40]

Regarding the cyber security of seaports, the GCSOS points out that in the shipping industry, ships and port facilities are part of the whole, and both have

36 International Association of Classification Society '12 IACS Recommendations on Cyber Safety Mark Step Change in Delivery of Cyber Resiliant Ships' (2018), <https://iacs.org.uk/news/12-iacs-recommendations-on-cyber-safety-mark-step-change-in-delivery-of-cyber-resilient-ships/> accessed 19 February 2024.

37 Ibid.

38 The Baltic and International Maritime Council 'Cyber Security Clause 2019' (2019), <https://www.bimco.org/contracts-and-clauses/bimco-clauses/current/cyber-security-clause-2019> accessed 19 February 2024.

39 IHS Markit and BIMCO 'Safety at Sea and BIMCO cyber security white paper' (2019), <https://cdn.ihsmarkit.com/www/pdf/1019/Safety-at-Sea-and-bimco-cyber-security-white-paper.pdf> accessed 19 February 2024.

40 BIMCO 'Guidelines on Cyber Security Onboard Ships' (2021), <https://www.ics-shipping.org/wp-content/uploads/2021/02/2021-Cyber-Security-Guidelines.pdf> accessed 19 February 2024.

equal importance.[41] However, there is no similar set of principles. With the GCSOS being entered into implementation phase, member states and shipping industry leaders could once again fully cooperate with each other to develop unified cybersecurity standards for port facilities.

3.2.2 Chinese Domestic Law

Intelligent ships have been listed as the key development object of many national strategies such as Made in China 2025,[42] and the Outline of the Construction of a Strong Transportation Country (hereinafter referred to as the 'OCSTC').[43] The Fourteenth Five-Year Plan for water transportation in 2022 also includes the level of water transportation intelligence as one of the basic principles.[44] On policy level, China has released the Action Plan for the Development of Intelligent Ships (2019–2021) (hereinafter referred to as the 'APDIS'), which stipulates that the major tasks of governments at all levels include comprehensive strengthening of top-level design, breakthroughs in key intelligent technologies, promote intelligent upgrading of marine equipment, enhance network and information security protection capabilities, strengthen testing and verification capacity building, build a standardized standards system, promote pilot demonstrations of engineering applications, create a collaborative development ecosystem, and promote deep civil-military integration.[45]

On 16 May 2019, the Ministry of Transport and seven other departments jointly issued the Guidance on the Development of Intelligent Ships, which put forward clear requirements for preventing the safety risks of intelligent shipping. For example, the Guidance specifies ten major tasks for the development of intelligent shipping, namely, strengthening top-level design and system planning, enhancing the information and intelligence level of port

41 Ibid.

42 Center for Security and Emerging Technology 'Made in China 2025' (2015), <https://cset.georgetown.edu/wp-content/uploads/t0432_made_in_china_2025_EN.pdf> accessed 19 February 2024.

43 The State Council of the People's Republic of China 'Outline of the Construction of a Strong Transportation Country' (2019), <http://www.gov.cn/zhengce/2019-09/19/content_5431432.htm> accessed 19 February 2024.

44 Ministry of Transport of the People's Republic of China 'Fourteenth Five-Year Plan for water transportation' (2022), <https://xxgk.mot.gov.cn/2020/jigou/zhghs/202204/P020220407576099539088.pdf> accessed 19 February 2024.

45 The State Council of the People's Republic of China 'Action Plan for the Development of Intelligent Ships' (2019), <https://www.baidu.com/link?url=niRSVa2ptOQgX_zGM4WAy01w_I723FvbmIoKZPmzDEZlWjeFLT3TTRIcrYNp731CqkvoCqcKeIYlMuEt1lje1t607jk-RT25rCwsyNxUDVJuYPFiE2lIGcdU6tndXVoGLk27MzjejmAt_DnvEqUmlq&wd=&eqid=9c1898b3003f49210000000005641cd7c5> accessed 19 February 2024.

terminals and shipping infrastructure, promoting the application of intelligent ship technology, strengthening the technological innovation of intelligent shipping, accelerating the construction of intelligent navigation guarantee system for ships, enhancing the design and construction of ports and their major equipment and intelligent shipping instruments, equipment and systems, cultivating new business models of intelligent shipping services, preventing intelligent shipping safety risks, strengthening the construction of intelligent shipping regulations and standards and regulatory mechanisms, and strengthening the training of intelligent shipping talents. Equipment, system design and construction (manufacturing) capacity, cultivate new business and new modes of intelligent shipping service, prevent intelligent shipping safety risk, strengthen intelligent shipping regulations and standards and regulatory mechanism construction, and strengthen intelligent shipping personnel training.[46] After the release of the theoretical Guidance, the Ministry of Transport further organized a pilot application of intelligent shipping in 2021.[47] On the implementation level, in recent years, China has delivered intelligent ships of several vessel types, including bulk carriers, ore carriers, container ships and crude oil carriers. In addition, to promote the development of unmanned ship-related technologies, the Ministry of Transport has also entered into cooperation with several Chinese universities, such as Dalian Maritime University and Wuhan University of Technology.[48]

Regarding specific legal regulations, China promulgated the Cybersecurity Law on 7 November 2016, and it came into effect on 1 June 2017.[49] This is China's first fundamental law that comprehensively regulates issues related to

---

46 Ministry of Transport of the People's Republic of China 'Guidance on the Development of Intelligent Ships' (2019) <https://xxgk.mot.gov.cn/2020/jigou/haishi/202006/t20200630_3319468.html> accessed 19 February 2024.

47 Ministry of Transport of the People's Republic of China 'Notice on the organization of pilot application of autonomous driving and intelligent shipping' (2021) <https://xxgk.mot.gov.cn/2020/jigou/kjs/202111/t20211110_3625462.html> accessed 19 February 2024.

48 Ministry of Transport of the People's Republic of China 'Opinions on Wuhan University of Technology to carry out intelligent technology and equipment engineering of waterway traffic safety and other pilot work of the construction of a strong transportation' (2020) <https://xxgk.mot.gov.cn/2020/jigou/zhghs/202110/t20211026_3623064.html>; Ministry of Transport of the People's Republic of China 'Opinions on Dalian Maritime University's pilot work on unmanned cargo transport vessel technology research and other construction of a strong transportation country' (2020), <https://xxgk.mot.gov.cn/2020/jigou/zhghs/202011/t20201120_3492627.html> accessed 19 February 2024.

49 The National People's Congress of the People's Republic of China 'Cybersecurity Law of the People's Republic of China' (2019) <http://www.gov.cn/zhengce/2019-09/19/content_5431432.htm> accessed 19 February 2024.

cyberspace security management, and is an important milestone in the construction of the rule of law in China's cyberspace, as well as a legal weight for governing the network and resolving network risks in accordance with the law. In addition, the implementation of the Basic Requirements for Network Security Level Protection,[50] which began on 1 December 2019, marks the entry of network security level protection into the new era, adapting to the needs of new technologies and new application areas such as cloud computing, mobile Internet, Internet of Things, industrial control and big data network security protection. A series of laws and national standards have been introduced one after another, which also provide practical legal protection and fundamental followings for ship network security management.

Optional soft law is also developed to cope with the cybersecurity of unmanned ships. In 2020, the CCS released the latest Guidelines for Requirement and Security Assessment of Ship Cyber System, which provides guidance on software, hardware and risk to further assess the security of network conditions and network products to assist the shipping industry in preventing cyber risks.[51] Without the stability and predictability provided by the rule of law in cyberspace, it is virtually impossible for nations to pursue their common interests through international cooperation.[52] In this regard, the Guidance is significant. The Guidance aims to standardize the design, construction, operation, maintenance and inspection of ship network, make relevant managers and technicians understand the importance of ship network security, form a new concept of comprehensively improving the construction level of ship network system and threat defense capability, guarantee the stability of ship network environment, and provide basic conditions and guarantee for the intelligence, digitalization and networking of ships. This Guidance is divided into five chapters. The preface introduces the background and significance of ship network security construction and assessment. The first part specifies the scope of application of the guide, the general requirements, the definition of the guide and the normative references to documents. Part 2 management requirements

50 Standardization Administration of the People's Republic of China 'Basic Requirements for Network Security Level Protection' (2019) <https://openstd.samr.gov.cn/bzgk/gb/newGbInfo?hcno=BAFB47E8874764186BDB7865E8344DAF> accessed 19 February 2024.

51 CCS 'Guidelines for Requirement and Security Assessment of Ship Cyber' (2020) <https://www.baidu.com/link?url=iKyV9PP9WkFAZpZGa1xAhrYoFN9UnkADrktFQKzIZg0MBO_Bcrl3h6Rbff8uno hbsEk7pWky7IOlwholqlY2ukMNqUTcP8uua4vi1daF8NS&wd=&eqid=8141a453001987bd00000005641ca9f7> accessed 19 February 2024.

52 Zhixiong Huang and Yaohui Ying, 'Chinese approaches to cyberspace governance and international law in cyberspace' in NicholasTsagourias and Others (eds), *Research Handbook on International Law and Cyberspace* (Edward Elgar Publishing Limited 2021) 547.

stipulate the ship network construction requirements. Part 3 introduces the technical requirements that should be met by ship network security. Part 4 specifies the requirements related to the product security assessment process for ship network systems. Part 5 specifies the requirements related to the ship network security assessment process and the granting of additional marks. Regarding appendixes: Appendix 1 is in the ship network risk assessment guidance content; Appendix 2 is the ship network security pre-assessment form; Appendix 3 bit the ship network security equipment assessment form; Appendix 4 is the ship network system (product) assessment form; Appendix 5 is the ship network assessment form; Appendix 6 is the ship industrial control system firewall additional recommendations.

In December 2023, the Guangdong Maritime Safety Administration of the People's Republic of China submitted the Code of Practice for the Management of Sea Testing of Unmanned Surface Craft and Intelligent Vessels (Draft for Review) to the provincial government of Guangdong.[53] The Code puts forward the standardization and management requirements for small unmanned surface craft and intelligent ships to conduct autonomous navigation and remote control navigation tests at sea, guides the relevant research, development, production and testing institutions in their test management, ensures the safety of water traffic during the tests, and promotes the rapid and healthy development of the unmanned surface craft and intelligent ships industry in Guangdong. If the Code is approved, it would become the first official document that regulates the operation of unmanned ships.

From the analysis of the above-mentioned Chinese domestic law, it seems China's domestic AI legislation is in the principium stage, with no formal legislative plans or related drafts. The existing legislation like the Cybersecurity Law does not offer specific regulation on the cyber risks of unmanned ships. However, China still attaches great importance to the development of unmanned ships from the perspective of national strategy. For the stable development of the industry of unmanned ships and the detailing of current Cybersecurity Law, China could start drafting specific navigational regulations that enumerate the preventative measures regarding unmanned ships' cyber risks, the punishment on the conducts that inflicts cyber risks of unmanned ships, and the technical standards in constructing unmanned ships. Considering that CCS is a public institution directly under the Ministry of Communications of China, its

53 Guangdong Maritime Safety Administration of the People's Republic of China 'Announcement on Soliciting Opinions on Local Standard Code of Practice for the Management of Sea Testing of Unmanned Surface Craft and Intelligent Vessels (Draft for Review) of Guangdong Province' (2023) <https://www.gd.msa.gov.cn/253eedc62a0607177087e3a951b1d8ad/e6a8e3dc4c384d3d8d10172f9eaaf275.jhtml> accessed 19 February 2024.

Guide can be directly transformed into national legislation when appropriate, thus allowing China to further adapt to the development of unmanned ships.

In conclusion, regarding the current cyber risks of unmanned ships, namely data collection issues, data storage issues, and data usage issues, the international society did not provide adequate corresponding measures. The international law lacks uniform rules to govern the risks at a global level. As for China's domestic law, relevant rules and regulations are mainly in soft law nature while a modicum of hard law is rather general than specific regarding the cyber risks of unmanned ships.

4 Measures for the Development of Unmanned Ships based on Cooperation and Risk Prevention

The dependence of unmanned ships on cyber operation and the intelligence of ships will bring a range of legal and practical issues related to AI. At the same time, the development of unmanned ships and the intelligence of ships pose a risk of occupational innovation. Meanwhile, the new services that unmanned ships bring to the shipping market have great potential to create new jobs. In order to maximize economic gains and minimize potential negative impacts on crews and shipping workers, policymakers should act in the interest of society as a whole. Policymakers in of all states need to accelerate the pace and prepare for technological change or risk falling further behind. Specifically, personnel and facility upgrades and international cooperation constitutes two major methods that all stakeholders should adopt to address the aforementioned cyber risks and inadequate regulation regarding the unmanned ships.

4.1 *Personnel and Equipment Upgrades*

Personnel and equipment are the two essential factors for the operation and development of shipping industry. The sustainable development of unmanned ships is also dependent upon its solution regarding the challenges presented by personnel and equipment changes. Stakeholders could take the following measures to ensure the two essential factors are improved in accordance with the unmanned ships' development thereby solving the issues regarding data collection, data storage, and data usage.

4.1.1 Personnel Upgrades

The growing influence of unmanned systems in working life, like most technological revolutions affecting works, is a double-edged sword that will affect the livelihood of crews and shipping workers, posing a risk of unemployment for skilled and semi-skilled trades. Workers who are quicker to adapt to technological change will be able to be benefitted by taking on more work that complements the networked controls and intelligence of unmanned ships and abandoning traditional ways of operating.

To make a better utilization of unmanned ships, studying and developing the training programs for the human resources are needed. Companies could establish a mechanism for transitioning traditional crew members to unmanned ships' operators and other related shore-based staff to stabilize the existing crew. For this purpose, developing corresponding talent training objectives and reforming the existing talent training programs are imperative. Also, shore-based control personnel should sail with the ship on a regular or fixed route, so that the shore-based control personnel of unmanned ships could have rich experience in marine navigation to cultivate the awareness of marine scenarios, emergency handling ability, and the expertise in data processing. Maintaining a crew that can manually maneuver the ship at sea is also important to provide maritime safety. In addition, unmanned ships' maritime supervisory personnel, especially ship inspection and safety inspection personnel, should master the basic knowledge and relevant skills of unmanned ships.

In terms of ship's manning, the ship's crew reduction guidelines should be formulated for different autonomous ship classes. The minimum safety manning certificate of gradual reduction should be issued in due course, and the operation manning of unmanned ships should be regulated under the premise of ensuring navigation safety. In the meantime, stakeholders in the autonomous ship industry could endeavor to identify and hire talent, focusing resources on attracting, recruiting, training and retaining employees who can truly innovate in digitally relevant jobs. It is also necessary to identify and train non-technical personnel to lead and oversee the innovation culture and promote the responsible use and application of data, analysis and artificial intelligence capabilities.

4.1.2 Equipment Upgrades

The integration of ship hardware and software systems should be further promoted, which is, after all, a fundamental requirement for the design and implementation of networked ship systems with AI.[54] Besides, cybersecurity assessments should be conducted for all ships, ship owners and their operators

54 Kjeld Dittmann, 'Autonomy for Ships: System Thinking and Engineering' in IEEE, *Proceedings of International Conference on Software, Telecommunications and Computer Networks 2022* (IEEE 2022) 1.

to better understand their potential cyber deficiencies. At the same time, a more uniform arrangement of facilities could allow the ship to better respond to emergencies, such as rescue in the event of natural disasters.[55] Installing an intrusion detection system on unmanned ships is also essential to detect, react and stop any incoming network threats.[56] Ship owners, operators and other interested parties can take the following basic measures to improve their cybersecurity.

Firstly, it is recommended that the network can be divided into 'subnets' so that adversaries do not have easy access to critical systems and devices. Secondly, limit access to the level required for each employee's job, and only use administrator accounts discreetly when necessary. Also, any external media must be scanned for malware on a separate system before accessing either shipboard network. Never run an executable file without a trusted certificate. Lastly, it is essential to install basic antivirus software and update it regularly, and remember to patch vulnerabilities in a timely manner. These measures could reduce the cyber risks of data loss and network system infringement.

The usage of data is also of importance since analyzing previous information could facilitate the prevention of risks in the future. Shipowners and policy makers could focus on advancing data analysis technology and continuously improving data quality to provide more comprehensive information for personnel and systems related to unmanned ships, so that they can better respond and make proactive decisions. At the same time, stakeholders can advocate that various departments under their jurisdiction increase investment in resources such as personnel and funds in areas involving unmanned ship data analysis. For example, the ocean and river environments that unmanned ships may encounter are simulated in the experimental site to verify and improve the data analysis capabilities of the unmanned ship system. These rigorously tested data and analysis methods can gain more support and be adopted on a large scale to promote the evolution of decision-making systems for unmanned ships.

---

55 Jorge F. Victoria, H. Murat Afsar, and Christian Prins, 'Metaheuristic Framework for a Disaster Logistics Problem with Time-Dependent Demands' in Tolga Bektas and Others (eds), *Computational Logistics 8th International Conference, ICCL 2017 Southampton, UK, October 18–20, 2017 Proceedings* (Springer 2017) 143.

56 Center for Maritime Research and Experimentation NATO, 'Maritime Cyber Situational Awareness Elaboration for Unmanned Vehicles' (2019) 3–4 <https://www.cmre.nato.int/msaw-2019-home/msaw2019-papers/1363-msaw2019-jacq-maritimecybersituationalawarenesselaborationforunmannedvehicles/file> accessed 19 February 2024.

4.2 *International Cooperation*

Current international regulation is inadequate regarding setting uniform standards on unmanned ships and relevant cyber risks. On the one hand, amending existing treaties could establish general consent and mechanisms without undermining current systems. Promoting regional cooperation, on the other hand, could facilitate setting specific requirements in the new field of unmanned ships and control pertinent cyber risks based on the differentiated interests of States.

4.2.1 Amending Existing Treaties

The STCW can be amended to increase its fitness for different classes of intelligent ship operators. Also, the STCW's implicit restriction on the use of unmanned ships could be conditionally amended to leave room for the unmanned ships' development. In this way, all classes of intelligent ships could be subject to the STCW, which will also ensure the Convention's adaptation to the time. Also, special rules concerning unmanned ships and remote control centers could be developed and added to the SOLAS as separate chapters so as to exclude SOLAS's restrictions and regulatory barriers on unmanned and intelligent ships.

At the same time, standards related to the certification of intelligent ship equipment, systems and algorithms should be developed to promote interaction and information exchange between ships to ensure that ship equipment and systems are safe and reliable.[57] Also, the intelligent ship cyber security solution and related standards could be further improved, and a proposal could be made to incorporate the relevant requirements into the International Safety Management Code (hereinafter referred to as 'ISMC').

4.2.2 Promoting Regional Cooperation

Regional international organizations are demonstrating regulations on AI. On 21 April 2021, the European Commission published the Proposal for a Regulation laying down harmonized rules on AI (Artificial Intelligence Act) and Amending Certain Union Legislative Acts.[58] This proposal aims to strengthen thegovernance of AI systems and apply the current flag s (hereinafter referred

57 Melih Akdağ, Petter Solnør and Tor Arne Johansen, 'Collaborative collision avoidance for Maritime Autonomous Surface Ships: A review' (2022) 1.

58 European Commission 'Proposal for a Regulation laying down harmonized rules on artificial intelligence (Artificial Intelligence Act) and Amending Certain Union Legislative Acts' (2021) <https://digital-strategy.ec.europa.eu/en/library/proposal-regulation-laying-down-harmonised-rules-artificial-intelligence> accessed 19 February 2024.

to as the 'EU') laws regarding fundamental rights and security requirements to AI systems. Meanwhile, the proposal requires member states to establish at least one AI-related regulatory agency responsible for ensuring that the necessary AI-related procedures are followed. Deducing from the proposal, regarding the regulation of unmanned ships, responsible agencies and risk assessment frameworks should be established, but not affected by international organizations or domestic governments.

The international community has also held numerous discussions on the security of cyberspace, interpreting and justifying the application of existing rules of international law in cyberspace. Scholars have developed the Tallinn Manual Version 2.0, which proposes to impose precautionary obligations on states to prevent cyber acts against other states in the field.[59] Indeed, due to the difference in the development of science and technology among states, the ability to ensure the harmlessness of unmanned ships is very different. In the present time, when IT is highly developed and commonly used, strengthening international cooperation is still an optional strategy to avoid risks. Countries could cooperate to disclose suspicious ships and share the information in a timely manner to make up for the lack of technologies in some countries for the reference and vigilance of relevant countries to strengthen the law enforcement monitoring of the ship.

States could jointly explore the strategies regarding the cybersecurity of unmanned ships. Building risk monitoring and early warning systems, as well as developing corresponding international cooperation mechanisms are also of importance could be two of the effective measures. For example, countries could jointly explore the relevant factors affecting the risk of maritime network and exert their comparative advantages to jointly solve the tasks.[60] EU member states and EU institutions have been actively promoting the consolidation of maritime security at the international level,[61] which sets an example of how states could cooperate to make higher achievement. China can take advantage of its communication technology to study the application of quantum communication, a technology that completely eliminates spy eavesdropping and cracking, to ship and shore-based communication.

---

59 Michael N. Schmitt, *Tallinn Manual 2.0 on the International Law Applicable to Cyber Operations* (Cambridge University Press 2017).

60 'Situational Awareness Examining Factors that Affect Cyber-Risks in the Maritime Sector' (2019) 4 International Janitorial Cleaning Services Association 1.

61 European Commission 'Report on the implementation of the revised EU Maritime Security Strategy Action Plan' (2020) <https://oceans-and-fisheries.ec.europa.eu/system/files/2021-03/swd-2020-252_en.pdf> accessed 19 February 2024.

It is worth noting that in the field of unmanned ship research and development, no one party can succeed alone. The international community needs to promote the establishment of strong national and international systems to improve intergovernmental, academic, industrial and international cooperation in data analysis and artificial intelligence technologies. It is also critical to continue exporting key technologies and sharing data to ensure partners maintain agility and the ability to rapidly adopt advanced analytics and AI innovation. Within a country, the government can provide more scientific research funds to academia to develop cutting-edge technologies related to artificial intelligence and data analysis, and provide relevant tax and subsidy incentives to industry to promote the practice of new technologies. Also, ensuring that enterprises, especially small and medium-sized enterprises, can independently develop artificial intelligence solutions and avoid undue pressure from certain industry giants who are powerful enough to control the price and supply chain. The industry can work closely with academia to speed up the transformation of cutting-edge scientific and technological achievements into practical civilian technologies. Within the region, governments can establish cooperation mechanisms to promote the sharing of relevant technologies and data, jointly determine trial routes for unmanned ships, and establish mutual funds to promote the development of unmanned ships. Covid-19 has ended, and barriers to academic exchange across borders have been significantly reduced. Universities and scientific research institutions in various countries can also increase academic exchanges and send visiting scholars to each other to facilitate the communication and understanding of crucial technologies' development. In addition, companies from different countries can set up transnational cooperative companies to share the technology patents they own, so as to develop highly autonomous unmanned ships that can sail safely as soon as possible, thereby acquiring market advantages in the region. These cooperative measures can improve countries' understanding of unmanned ship-related technologies and thus promote their research and practice in the field of cybersecurity for unmanned ships.

Take East Asia as an example. In China, in July 2023, two unmanned vessels were put on trial at the Gaogang Tower of Taizhou Maritime Bureau to jointly carry out effectiveness and application tests in the field of maritime daily law enforcement.[62] The trial unmanned ships are the latest generation of intelligent unmanned ship in China. Specifically, the L30 unmanned ship

62 Jiangsu Maritime Bureau of the People's Republic of China 'Latest Generation of Intelligent Unmanned Vessels to Conduct Efficacy and Application Tests in Taizhou' (2023), <https://js.msa.gov.cn/art/2023/7/14/art_51_1415961.html> accessed 19 February 2024.

has the following characteristics: two modes of unmanned and manned driving; two driving seats; a length of 7.5 meters; a hull made of all aluminum alloy materials; and a full load weight of 5 tons; adaptable to class 5 sea state; gasoline-powered propulsion; maximum speed up to 40 knots; range over 300 nautical miles; and fully watertight hull arrangement. The characteristics of the "M75B" unmanned ship are slightly different: pure unmanned mode; length of 5.3 meters; hull made of carbon fiber composite material; full loaded weight of 1.3 tons; adaptable to class 4 sea state; diesel-powered propulsion; maximum speed of up to 30 knots; a range of more than 150 nautical miles; and self-righting capability. The latest generation of intelligent unmanned vessels are equipped with navigation radar, laser radar, photoelectric camera, police flashing lights, acoustic system, VHF, AIS and other devices. Relying on intelligent equipment and software system integration, the new unmanned ships can effectively perceive the environment around the ship and the navigational situation in real time, establish communication with other ships in a timely manner, autonomously carry out tasks such as cruising in the water area or fixed-point guarding, intelligently capture the ship's target, automatically realize obstacle avoidance actions such as circling, decelerating or stopping, and transmit the screen back to the base station in real time, so that the operator can discover abnormal targets or behaviors in time and complete remote warning, VHF reminder, fixing evidence and other actions. The unmanned ship can realize automatic return under abnormal conditions such as signal interruption. In December 2023, the dual-use ship for intelligent research and practical training, which was developed by Dalian Maritime University in cooperation with relevant departments of Liaoning Province with an investment of about 180 million yuan, was completed.[63] The ship has the following features: length 69.83; beam 10.9m; depth 5m; service speed 17.5km; crew 15; researchers 5. The ship will obtain the i-Ship intelligent class notation to realize the full coverage of intelligentization, and meet the highest requirements of intelligent specification of CCS. The ship is expected to be delivered in June 2024 for use. In Japan, in 2022, the Mikage, a 194 TEU domestic container ship, completed an autonomous voyage of 270 kilometers.[64] In addition to an automatic identification system and radar, the ship was equipped with a visible light camera and

63 Dalian Maritime University 'Dalian Maritime University's Intelligent Research and Practical Training Dual Purpose Vessel Officially Launched' (2023), <https://www.dlmu.edu.cn/info /1096/64798.htm> accessed 19 February 2024.

64 The Nippon Foundation '3rd and 4th Demonstration Tests of Fully Autonomous Ship Navigation Successfully Completed' (2022) <https://www.nippon-foundation.or.jp/en/news /articles/2022/20220207-67748.html> accessed 19 February 2024.

infrared camera for night recording, as well as an artificial intelligence learning system capable of detecting other ships. In November 2023, HOKUREN MARU No.2 completed a 1,600-kilometer round-trip voyage between the ports of Hitachi and Kushiro via autonomous navigation.[65] The vessel has been tested since October 2023 for a total of three voyages on existing service routes. In the experiments, the autonomous navigation system was independent of normal crew navigation, and in cases where avoidance was required, the autonomous navigation system proposed an avoidance course and controlled steering to safely avoid other vessels. The results showed that the autonomous navigation system achieved an average system operation rate of about 96% within the set operational design domain (ODD) sea area. In December 2023, as one of the most important ports in East Asia, Singapore released its updated National Artificial Intelligence Strategy 2.0.[66] It calls for fostering collaboration among industry, government, and research organizations to promote AI development in four areas: talent, capabilities, community, infrastructure, and environment. From the above information, it could be found that China attaches importance on the law enforcement use of unmanned vessels, while Japan focuses on the commercial value of unmanned vessels. China and Japan may carry out international cooperation to complement each other's differences in research fields and technical deficiencies. In addition, the maritime trade routes between China and Japan are moderately distant, which can be used as a site for cross-border maritime experiments of new unmanned vessels regarding the ships' cybersecurity development. Considering Singapore's emphasis on artificial intelligence, China and Japan could further collaborate with Singapore to develop unmanned vessels capable of ocean voyages. The aforementioned cooperation could offer states the opportunities to gain more experiences and data regarding the cybersecurity of unmanned ships' operations.

Safeguarding cybersecurity and promoting orderly development are of great importance. Security and development are interrelated twins. Security is the guarantee of development; development is the purpose of security. Cybersecurity is a global challenge, and no country can stay out of it or do it alone, and it is the common responsibility for the international community to maintain

---

65 KAWASAKI KISEN KAISHA, LTD. 'The Nippon Foundation MEGURI2040 Fully Autonomous Ship Project -Demonstration test of autonomous navigation system on large RORO cargo-' (2023) <https://www.kline.co.jp/en/news/csr/csr-20231127.html> accessed 19 February 2024.

66 Smart Nation Singapore 'National Artificial Intelligence Strategy 2 to uplift Singapore's social and economic potential' (2023) <https://www.smartnation.gov.sg/media-hub/press-releases/04122023/> accessed 19 February 2024.

cybersecurity. Countries should work together to curb the misuse of information technology, oppose network eavesdropping and cyberattacks.

4.3 *Drafting Domestic Laws and Regulations*

It is important to ensure data security and national security information protection in the process of unmanned ships being used. Regulations must combine algorithm regulation and data regulation. In the exploration of algorithm regulation mechanisms, the types of subjects and algorithm decision-making should be fully considered to develop scenario-based and refined algorithm governance mechanisms. It is recommended that states should strengthen relevant legislation at the national level to regulate the balance between data protection and data processing. Drafting domestic laws and regulations could be beneficial in addressing the issues deriving from being general rather than specific in the prevention of unmanned ships' cyber risks and the punishment of relevant conducts.

Countries can develop practical trial regulatory laws regarding unmanned ships to govern matters, including the management of test waters and maritime safety and environmental protection requirements. The jurisdiction of the coastal state cannot provide a strong guarantee by technical assurance alone. The technical standards need to be raised to a legal level to be binding and enforceable. Also, it is necessary to re-examine the rules of ship manning, from the examination of personnel on board to the requirements of shore-based personnel, and to clarify the responsibilities of all parties by legal provisions. Meanwhile, AI algorithm technology could be used to ensure the control of the coastal state. The developers and manufacturers of unmanned ships should be required to design intelligent systems to meet certain standards during the construction of the ship. It is understandable that due to the inevitable algorithmic vulnerabilities and environmental complexities of AI technology, developers usually do not take responsibility for relevant accidents. Otherwise, the demanding requirements would be detrimental to the improvement and progress of the technology. Also, artificial intelligence systems used in unmanned ship-related industries and the general artificial intelligence models they are based on must meet transparency requirements, and specific standards can vary from country to country. These requirements include drafting technical documentation, complying with intellectual property laws and publishing detailed summaries of content for training purposes. For general artificial intelligence models with systemic risks and high impact, more stringent requirements can be set. Once these models meet certain standards, they must be evaluated by an independent third party and registered with a government agency. Specifically, system risks should be assessed and mitigated, adversarial testing should be conducted, critical events should be reported to relevant regulatory agencies, the network should be secured and its energy efficiency should be reported. Regarding transitional adaption, until unified and harmonized standards are published, companies using general artificial intelligence that poses systemic risks can act in accordance with their industry codes.

Taking China as an example, China has been adhering to the principle of strict regulation for data security, and has established a strict regulatory system including a series of laws, regulations, departmental rules, and regulatory documents based on the Cybersecurity Law. Thus, the application of unmanned ships' network must consider strict regulations for all aspects of data collection, use and disposal. First, the accuracy of the data samples obtained by the use of the relevant technology should be regulated from the source. The database should be checked and updated in a timely manner, and the specific data content that may have network risks should be removed. The legal and regulatory system of the algorithm and the regulatory mechanism should also be improved. Secondly, to establish the accountability system of the algorithm of unmanned ships' network intelligence technology, it is necessary to improve the corresponding attribution system, and clarify the responsible subjects that lead to network risks and the legal responsibilities that each subject should bear. Also, it is necessary to strengthen the security of information and data, especially the protection of national information security, at the level of unmanned ships' network technology and system. Establishing a sound data classification and grading protection system could be one of the choices. For example, the training data set can be categorized and managed according to the data subject, the degree of data processing, and the attributes of data rights. The data can also be graded according to the value of the data to the data right subject and the degree of harm to the data subject after the data is maliciously manipulated. Regarding the cross-border flow of data, reasonable cross-border data security enforcement rules should be formulated based on consideration of internationally prevailing standards and practices. The synchronization with rules of other countries and regions should be strengthened to promote cross-border data security enforcement cooperation. Finally, on the technical level, the application of privacy computing technologies in the field of unmanned ships' network should be accelerated.

In conclusion, China should effectively implement domestic laws and regulations to effectively promote digital transformation, strictly implement security-related legal and regulatory requirements, and improve information security under digitalization and digital economy. In the planning and implementation process of digital transformation, it should ensure that information technology construction and network security construction are planned, built and operated simultaneously, and security is carried through the whole stage of planning, construction and use. From the policy level, monitoring and supervision, emergency response, adequate network security awareness and security capabilities, system management, and cybersecurity review are the aspects of focus.

5 Conclusion

The application of unmanned ships in the maritime industry is evolving, although there are still many immature technologies and regulations. This paper examines the definition and legal nature of unmanned ships, proposing that unmanned ships are ships with different levels of automation, from partially automated systems that assist human crews to fully autonomous systems that can take on all aspects of ship operation without human intervention and maintain continuous and substantial contact with the water, using technological means such as sensors, communications, the Internet of Things, and the Internet. Secondly, this paper illustrates the cyber risks of unmanned ships and the existing legal regulations and the measures for the development of unmanned ships based on cooperation and risk prevention from international and domestic levels, with a view to providing reference for countries in their future international and domestic legislation. While promoting the development of unmanned ship-related science and technology, countries could also work together and actively participate in international rule-making. Specifically, China could take the initiative to cooperate with regional countries so the participating states may explore the efficient ways to enhance the cybersecurity of unmanned ships together.

Unmanned ships bring more opportunities for the development of digital innovation and have become one of the key directions of future global competition and innovation. While promoting the development of unmanned ship-related science and technology, countries should also work together and actively participate in international rule-making. We must also face up to the potential legal risks behind the rapid development of unmanned ships and timely update and scientifically improve the relevant laws and regulations in this field. It is of paramount importance that we should establish and improve the relevant code of conduct and ethical guidelines, promote the standardized, systematic, and make sustainable development of unmanned ships' cybersecurity.

References

Andrea Antolini 'Cyber security in maritime transport and question of cyber security measures for autonomous ships' (2020) <https://www.jttri.or.jp/document/2019/andrea42.pdf> accessed 19 February 2024.

Andrej Androjna, Tanja Brcko, Ivica Pavic and Harm Greidanus, 'Assessing Cyber Challenges of Maritime Navigation' (2020) 8(10) Journal of Marine Science and Engineering 776.

Anete Vagale, Rachid Oucheikh, Robin T. Bye, Ottar L. Osen and Thor I. Fossen, 'Path planning and collision avoidance for autonomous surface vehicles I: a review' (2021) 26 Journal of Marine Science and Technology 1292.

BIMCO 'Guidelines on Cyber Security Onboard Ships' (2021), <https://www.ics-shipping.org/wp-content/uploads/2021/02/2021-Cyber-Security-Guidelines.pdf> accessed 19 February 2024.

BIMCO 'Guidelines on Cyber Security Onboard Ships' (2021), available at <https://www.ics-shipping.org/wp-content/uploads/2021/02/2021-Cyber-Security-Guidelines.pdf> accessed 19 February 2024.

CCS 'Guidelines for Requirement and Security Assessment of Ship Cyber' (2020) <https://www.baidu.com/link?url=iKyV9PP9WkFAZpZGa1xAhrYoFN9UnkADrktFQKzIZg0MBO_Bcrl3h6Rbff8un0hbsEk7pWky7IOlwh0lqlY2ukMNqUTcP8uua4vi1daF8NS&wd=&eqid=8141a453001987bd000000005641ca9f7> accessed 19 February 2024.

CCS, 'Rules for Intelligent Ships' (2023) <https://www.ccs.org.cn/ccswz/articleDetail?id=202303061016018608> accessed 19 February 2024.

CCS, 'Rules for Intelligent Ships' (2023) <https://www.ccs.org.cn/ccswz/articleDetail?id=202303061016018608> accessed 19 February 2024.

CCS, 'Rules for Intelligent Ships' (2023) <https://www.ccs.org.cn/ccswz/articleDetail?id=202303061016018608> accessed 19 February 2024.

CCS, 'Rules for Intelligent Ships' (2023) <https://www.ccs.org.cn/ccswz/file/download?fileid=202303061061897887> accessed 19 February 2024.

Center for Maritime Research and Experimentation NATO, 'Maritime Cyber Situational Awareness Elaboration for Unmanned Vehicles' (2019) <https://www.cmre.nato.int/msaw-2019-home/msaw2019-papers/1363-msaw2019-jacq-maritime cybersituationalawarenesselaborationforunmannedvehicles/file> accessed 19 February 2024.

Center for Security and Emerging Technology 'Made in China 2025' (2015), available at <https://cset.georgetown.edu/wp-content/uploads/t0432_made_in_china_2025_EN.pdf> accessed 19 February 2024.

Chia-Hsun Chang, Christos Kontovas, Qing Yu and Zaili Yang, 'Risk assessment of the operations of maritime autonomous surface ships' (2021) 207 Reliability Engineering & System Safety 1.

Comité Maritime International, 'Cyber-risks in unmanned vessel industry and adapting current U.S. and International legal framework to New Challenges' (2019) <https://comitemaritime.org/wp-content/uploads/2019/09/yCMI-Essay-AB0015.pdf> accessed 19 February 2024.

Convention on the International Regulations for Preventing Collisions at Sea (adopted 20 October 1972, entered into force 15 July 1977) 1050 UNTC 16 Part B Rule 8.

Dalian Maritime University 'Dalian Maritime University's Intelligent Research and Practical Training Dual Purpose Vessel Officially Launched' (2023) <https://www.dlmu.edu.cn/info/1096/64798.htm> accessed 19 February 2024.

Eray Yağdereli, Cemal Gemci and A Ziya Aktaş, 'A study on cyber-security of autonomous and unmanned vehicles' (2015) 12 The Journal of Defense Modeling and Simulation 369.

European Commission 'Proposal for a Regulation laying down harmonized rules on artificial intelligence (Artificial Intelligence Act) and Amending Certain Union Legislative Acts' (2021) <https://digital-strategy.ec.europa.eu/en/library/proposal-regulation-laying-down-harmonised-rules-artificial-intelligence> accessed 19 February 2024.

European Commission 'Report on the implementation of the revised EU Maritime Security Strategy Action Plan' (2020) <https://oceans-and-fisheries.ec.europa.eu/system/files/2021-03/swd-2020-252_en.pdf> accessed 19 February 2024.

European Commission, 'Maritime Unmanned Navigation through Intelligence in Networks' (2016) <http://www.unmanned-ship.org/munin/wp-content/uploads/2016/02/MUNIN-final-brochure.pdf> accessed 19 February 2024.

Georgios Kavallieratos, Sokratis Katsikas and Vasileios Gkioulosm, 'Cyber-Attacks Against the Autonomous Ship' in Sokratis K. Katsikas and Others (eds), *Computer Security* (Springer 2019) 20.

Georgios Kavallieratos, Vasiliki Diamantopoulou and Sokratis K. Katsikas, 'Shipping 4.0·Security requirements for the Cyber-Enabled Ship' (2020) 16 IEEE Transactions on Industrial Informatics 6617.

Guangdong Maritime Safety Administration of the People's Republic of China 'Announcement on Soliciting Opinions on Local Standard Code of Practice for the Management of Sea Testing of Unmanned Surface Craft and Intelligent Vessels (Draft for Review) of Guangdong Province' (2023) <https://www.gd.msa.gov.cn/253eedc62a0607177087e3a951b1d8ad/e6a8e3dc4c384d3d8d10172f9eaaf275.jhtml> accessed 19 February 2024.

Hanan Hindy, David Brosset, Ethan Bayne, Amar Seeam and Xavier Bellekens, 'Improving SIEM for Critical SCADA Water Infrastructures Using Machine Learning' in Sokratis K. Katsikas and Others (eds), *Computer Security* (Springer 2018) 3.

IHS Markit and BIMCO 'Safety at Sea and BIMCO cyber security white paper' (2019), <https://cdn.ihsmarkit.com/www/pdf/1019/Safety-at-Sea-and-bimco-cyber-security-white-paper.pdf> accessed 19 February 2024.

IMO, 'Framework for the Regulatory Scoping Exercise for the Use of Maritime Autonomous Surface Ships (MASS)' (2020) <https://maiif.org/wp-content/uploads/2019/06/MSC-100_20-Annex-20-1.pdf> accessed 19 February 2024.

IMO, 'Guidelines on maritime cyber risk management' (2017) <https://www.gard.no/Content/23896593/MSC-FAL.1-Circ.3.pdf> accessed 19 February 2024.

IMO, 'Outcome of the Regulatory Scoping Exercise for the use of Maritime Autonomous Surface Ships (MASS)' (2021) <https://wwwcdn.imo.org/localresources/en/MediaCentre/HotTopics/Documents/MSC.1-Circ.1638%20-%20Outcome%20Of%20The%20Regulatory%20Scoping%20ExerciseFor%20The%20Use%20Of%20Maritime%20Autonomous%20Surface%20Ships...%20(Secretariat).pdf> accessed 19 February 2024.

International Association of Classification Society '12 IACS Recommendations on Cyber Safety Mark Step Change in Delivery of Cyber Resiliant Ships' (2018) <https://iacs.org.uk/news/12-iacs-recommendations-on-cyber-safety-mark-step-change-in-delivery-of-cyber-resilient-ships/> accessed 19 February 2024.

International Convention for the Safety of Life at Sea (adopted 01November 1974, entered into force 25 May 1980) 1184 UNTC 278 Chapter V Safety of Navigation.

International Convention on Standards of Training, Certification and Watchkeeping for Seafarers (adopted 07 July 1978, entered into force 28 April 1984) 1361 UNTC 76 Annex. Recommendation on Operational Guidance for Officers in Charge of A Navigational Watch.

Jiangsu Maritime Bureau of the People's Republic of China 'Latest Generation of Intelligent Unmanned Vessels to Conduct Efficacy and Application Tests in Taizhou' (2023) <https://js.msa.gov.cn/art/2023/7/14/art_51_1415961.html> accessed 19 February 2024.

Jin-Hong Lim, Jae-Hwan Kim and Jun-Ho Huh 'Recent trends and proposed response strategies of international standards related to shipbuilding equipment big data integration platform' (2023) 57 Quality & Quantity 863.

Jorge F. Victoria, H. Murat Afsar, and Christian Prins, 'Metaheuristic Framework for a Disaster Logistics Problem with Time-Dependent Demands' in Tolga Bektas and Others (eds), *Computational Logistics 8th International Conference, ICCL 2017 Southampton, UK, October 18–20, 2017 Proceedings* (Springer 2017) 143.

Jurgen Lusch, *Ships and Shipping of Tomorrow*, (Cornell Maritime Pr/Tidewater Pub 1983).

KAWASAKI KISEN KAISHA, LTD. 'The Nippon Foundation MEGURI2040 Fully Autonomous Ship Project -Demonstration test of autonomous navigation system on large RORO cargo-' (2023) <https://www.kline.co.jp/en/news/csr/csr-20231127.html> accessed 19 February 2024.

Kimberly Tam and Kevin Jones, 'Cyber-Risk Assessment for Autonomous Ships' in Cyber Security 2018 Programme Committee, *2018 International Conference on Cyber Security and Protection of Digital Services (Cyber Security)* (IEEE 2018) 1.

Kjeld Dittmann, 'Autonomy for Ships: System Thinking and Engineering' in IEEE, *Proceedings of International Conference on Software, Telecommunications and Computer Networks 2022* (IEEE 2022) 1.

KVH Industries 'How Maritime loT Connectivity Transforms Performance & Profits' (2021) <https://www.kvh.com/> accessed 19 February 2024.

Lloyd's Register, 'Design Code for Unmanned Marine Systems' (2017) <https://www.lr.org/en/unmanned-code/> accessed 19 February 2024.

Martin Jes Iversen, 'Maritime Digital Business Models: The Case of D/S Norden, 2015–2020' in Byoung-Wook Ko Dong-Wook Song, *New Maritime Business* (Springer 2021) 113.

Melih Akdağ, Petter Solnør and Tor Arne Johansen, 'Collaborative collision avoidance for Maritime Autonomous Surface Ships: A review' (2022) 1.

Michael N. Schmitt, *Tallinn Manual 2.0 on the International Law Applicable to Cyber Operations* (Cambridge University Press 2017).

Ministry of Transport of the People's Republic of China 'Fourteenth Five-Year Plan for water transportation' (2022), available at <https://xxgk.mot.gov.cn/2020/jigou/zhghs/202204/P020220407576099539088.pdf> accessed 19 February 2024.

Ministry of Transport of the People's Republic of China 'Guidance on the Development of Intelligent Ships' (2019) <https://xxgk.mot.gov.cn/2020/jigou/haishi/202006/t20200630_3319468.html> accessed 19 February 2024.

Ministry of Transport of the People's Republic of China 'Notice on the organization of pilot application of autonomous driving and intelligent shipping' (2021) <https://xxgk.mot.gov.cn/2020/jigou/kjs/202111/t20211110_3625462.html> accessed 19 February 2024.

Ministry of Transport of the People's Republic of China 'Opinions on Dalian Maritime University's pilot work on unmanned cargo transport vessel technology research and other construction of a strong transportation country' (2020) <https://xxgk.mot.gov.cn/2020/jigou/zhghs/202011/t20201120_3492627.html> accessed 19 February 2024.

Ministry of Transport of the People's Republic of China 'Opinions on Wuhan University of Technology to carry out intelligent technology and equipment engineering of waterway traffic safety and other pilot work of the construction of a strong transportation' (2020) https://xxgk.mot.gov.cn/2020/jigou/zhghs/202110/t20211026_3623064.html.

NATO Cooperative Cyber Defence Center of Excellence, 'Cybersecurity Considerations in Autonomous Ships' (2022) <https://ccdcoe.org/library/publications/cybersecurity-considerations-in-autonomous-ships/> accessed 19 February 2024.

RAND, 'U.S. Navy Employment Options for Unmanned Surface Vehicles (USVs)' (2013) <https://www.rand.org/content/dam/rand/pubs/research_reports/RR300/RR384/RAND_RR384.pdf> accessed 19 February 2024.

Robert Veal, Michael Tsimplis and Andrew Serdy, 'The Legal Status and Operation of Unmanned Maritime Vehicles' (2019) 50 Ocean Development & International Law 23.

'Situational Awareness Examining Factors that Affect Cyber-Risks in the Maritime Sector' (2019) 4 International Janitorial Cleaning Services Association 1.

Smart Nation Singapore 'National Artificial Intelligence Strategy 2 to uplift Singapore's social and economic potential' (2023) <https://www.smartnation.gov.sg/media-hub/press-releases/04122023/> accessed 19 February 2024.

Standardization Administration of the People's Republic of China 'Basic Requirements for Network Security Level Protection' (2019) <https://openstd.samr.gov.cn/bzgk/gb/newGbInfo?hcno=BAFB47E8874764186BDB7865E8344DAF> accessed 19 February 2024.

Tae-eun Kim, Lokukaluge Prasad Perera, Magne-Petter Sollid, Bjørn-Morten Batalden, Are Kristoffer Sydnes, 'Safety challenges related to autonomous ships in mixed navigational environments' (2022) 21 Journal of Maritime Affairs 141.

The Baltic and International Maritime Council 'Cyber Security Clause 2019' (2019), <https://www.bimco.org/contracts-and-clauses/bimco-clauses/current/cyber-security-clause-2019> accessed 19 February 2024.

The National People's Congress of the People's Republic of China 'Cybersecurity Law of the People's Republic of China' (2019) <http://www.gov.cn/zhengce/2019-09/19/content_5431432.htm> accessed 19 February 2024.

The Nippon Foundation '3rd and 4th Demonstration Tests of Fully Autonomous Ship Navigation Successfully Completed' (2022) <https://www.nippon-foundation.or.jp/en/news/articles/2022/20220207-67748.html> accessed 19 February 2024.

The State Council of the People's Republic of China 'Action Plan for the Development of Intelligent Ships' (2019), <https://www.baidu.com/link?url=niRSVa2ptOQgX_zGM4WAy01w_I723FvbmIOKZPmzDEZlWjeFLT3TTRICrYNp731Cqkv0CqcKeIYlMuEt1lje1t607jk-RT25rCwsyNxUDVJUYPFiE2lIGcdU6tndXV0GLk27MzjejmAt_DnvEqUmlq&wd=&eqid=9c1898b3003f492100000005641cd7c5> accessed 19 February 2024.

The State Council of the People's Republic of China 'Outline of the Construction of a Strong Transportation Country' (2019), available at <http://www.gov.cn/zhengce/2019-09/19/content_5431432.htm> accessed 19 February 2024.

United States Coast Guard 'Cyber Incident Exposes Potential Vulnerabilities Onboard Commercial Vessels' (2019) <https://www.dco.uscg.mil/Portals/9/DCO%20Documents/5p/CG-5PC/INV/Alerts/0619.pdf> accessed 19 February 2024.

Victor Bolbot, Gerasimos Theotokatos, Evangelos Boulougouris and Dracos Vassalos, 'A novel cyber-risk assessment method for ship systems' (2020) 131 Safety Science 1.

Young-Soo Han, Kyung Ho Lee, Yang Ouk Kim, Young Su Kim and Hyun Bin Yeo 'A Study on Augmented Reality Remote Maintenance Support System for Ships and

Offshore Structures' (2022) <https://avestia.com/ICCSTE2022_Proceedings/files/paper/ICCSTE_161.pdf> accessed 19 February 2024.

Young-Soo Park, Jung-Sik Jeong and Yusuf Volkan Aydogdu, 'Advances in Maritime Safety' (2022) 10 Journal of Marine Science and Engineering 1721.

Zhixiong Huang and Yaohui Ying, 'Chinese approaches to cyberspace governance and international law in cyberspace' in Nicholas Tsagourias and Others (eds), *Research Handbook on International Law and Cyberspace* (Edward Elgar Publishing Limited 2021) 547.

CHAPTER 5

Regulating the Passage of Nuclear-Powered Submarines and Autonomous Nuclear Drones: Does International Law Allow Recharacterization of the Straits of Malacca and Singapore?

Mohd Hazmi Mohd Rusli, Dhiana Puspitawati**, and Roman Dremliuga****

1 Introduction

Southeast Asia is home to the significant maritime highways of the Straits of Malacca and Singapore and Indonesia's archipelagic straits.[1] On daily basis, there are more than 200 vessels passing the Straits of Malacca and Singapore carrying an estimated 15–16 million barrels of oil.[2] While Indonesia's archipelagic straits are often regarded as alternative routes,[3] the Straits of Malacca and Singapore remains the primary maritime highway linking the Indian Ocean and the Pacific Ocean.[4]

The closure of these important shipping ways would not only violate international law but would also affect the wellbeing of the global economy.[5] As

* Mohd Hazmi Mohd Rusli, Universiti Sains Islam Malaysia Faculty of Syariah and Law; Universiti Utara Malaysia Asian Institute of International Affairs and Diplomacy.

** Dhiana Puspitawati, Universitas Brawijaya Faculty of Law, Indonesia.

*** Roman Dremliuga, Far Eastern Federal University School of Law, Vladivostok, Russia.

1 Mohd Hazmi bin Mohd Rusli, 'Maritime highways of Southeast Asia: Alternative Straits?' (10 February 2012) RSIS Commentaries <https://www.rsis.edu.sg/rsis-publication/rsis/1686-maritime-highways-of-southeast/#.YeeDEXpBzIU> accessed 26 February 2024.

2 Jagan Jeevan, Nurul Haqimin Mohd Salleh and Mohamad Rosni Othman, 'Thai Canal and Malacca Straits: Complementing or Competing Strategem for Trade Development in South East Asia' (2018) 3JSDTL2 34–48.

3 Stephen Kuper, 'The Indo-Pacific's Maritime Choke Points: Sunda and Lombok', *Defence Connect* (2019) <https://www.defenceconnect.com.au/maritime-antisub/4240-the-indo-pacific-s-maritime-choke-points-sunda-and-lombok> accessed 26 February 2024.

4 Hanizah Idris and Muhammad Faiz Ramli, 'Southeast Asian Region Maritime Connectivity and the Potential Development of the Northern Sea Route for Commercial Shipping' (2018) 23JSAS2 25–28.

5 N. S. F. Abdul Rahman, A. H. Saharudiin and R. Rasdi, 'Effect of the Northern Sea route opening to the shipping activities at Malacca Straits' (2014) 11JNM 85 <https://www.sciencedirect.com/science/article/pii/S2405535214000096> accessed 26 February 2024.

 | DOI:10.1163/9789004706279_007

crucial maritime superhighways, thousands of vessels traverse these waterways each year, including vessels carrying hazardous nuclear substances such as Japanese vessels carrying nuclear waste bound for reprocessing facilities in Europe[6] and nuclear-powered submarines belonging to superpower nations of the world.[7]

When a ship merely navigates through the territorial sea of a state without entering any of its ports, that state is considered a coastal state.[8] The coastal state has jurisdiction over its territorial sea, which is subject to the right of innocent passage,[9] a passage regime where the coastal state has the power to regulate but not to control.[10] The powers of a coastal state to take action against recalcitrant vessels are subject to the jurisdictional balance, which, based on the practice of international law, leans heavily in favor of navigational interests.[11]

Unlike the innocent passage regime, which can be temporarily suspended,[12] states bordering straits possess more limited powers because they have no legal right under international law to impede navigation via the transit passage

6 Yann-huei Song, 'Security in the Strait of Malacca and the Regional Maritime Security Initiative: Responses to the US proposal' in Michael D. Carsten (ed), Global Legal Challenges: Command of the Commons, Strategic Communications, and Natural Disasters (Naval War College, Newport, Rhode Island, 2007) 97 <https://apps.dtic.mil/sti/pdfs/ADA605285.pdf> accessed 26 February 2024.

7 Mark J. Valencia, 'International conflict over marine resources in South-East Asia: Trends in politicization and militarization' in Lim Teck Ghee and Mark J. Valencia (eds), *Conflict over Natural Resources in South-East Asia and the Pacific* (United Nations University Press, 1990) <https://archive.unu.edu/unupress/unupbooks/80a04e/80A04E00.htm#Contents> accessed 26 February 2024; Zia Mian, MV Ramana and AH Nayyar, 'Nuclear Submarines in South Asia: New Risks and Dangers' (2019) 2 JPND1 185–187.

8 Ana G. Lopez Martin, International Straits: Concept, Classification and Rules of Passage (2010).

9 The right of innocent passage is considered customary international law as reflected in the *Corfu Channel Case* (*United Kingdom v. Albania*), Judgment, ICJ Reports 1949. In this case, the ICJ held that navigation of warships in times of peace through straits used for international navigation connecting two parts of the high seas without previous authorization of the coastal state, provided the passage is innocent, is permissible. This ruling is now embedded in Article 17 of the United Nations Convention on the Law of the Sea 1982 which reads '… ships of all States, whether coastal or land-locked, enjoy the right of innocent passage through the territorial sea'.

10 Alan E. Boyle, 'Marine pollution under the Law of the Sea Convention' (1985) 79 AJIL 2 357.

11 Ibid.

12 Article 25(3) of UNCLOS stipulates that a coastal state may temporarily suspend passage of vessels through its territorial sea if such suspension is essential for the protection of its security.

regime.[13] Submarines are not required to surface while exercising transit passage prescribed by UNCLOS.[14]

Malaysia and Indonesia have expressed uneasiness about the tripartite security pact between Australia, the United Kingdom, and the United States (AUKUS), which was announced in September 2021.[15] The pact envisages that Australia will eventually construct at least eight nuclear-powered submarines through this trilateral security partnership.[16]

Australia has reiterated that the development of its nuclear-powered submarines program is not in contravention of international law.[17] Developing nuclear-powered submarines is not in any way similar to developing nuclear weapons.[18] Australia is projected to possess its first nuclear-powered submarine by the year 2040.[19] This means that apart from the existing nuclear-powered submarines navigating Southeast Asia's sea lines of communication, it is projected that Australia's nuclear-powered submarines will all navigate these sea lanes by 2040.

In addition, Russia has developed 'The *Poseidon*', an autonomous, nuclear-powered drone capable of delivering both conventional and nuclear warheads. The first batch of the *Poseidon* was reported to have been manufactured and

13 Article 44 of UNCLOS mentions clearly that there shall be no suspension of transit passage.

14 See Articles 39(1) (c) and 54 of UNCLOS. United Nations Convention on the Law of the Sea, adopted 10 December 1982, entered into force 16 November 1994, 1833 UNTS.

15 Mohd Hazmi Mohd Rusli, 'Is it too little too late to protect the Strait of Malacca?' (31 August 2022) *The Straits Times* <https://www.straitstimes.com/asia/se-asia/is-it-too-little-too-late-to-protect-the-strait-of-malacca-jakarta-post-contributor> accessed 26 February 2024.

16 James Chin, 'Why is Southeast Asia so concerned about AUKUS and Australia's plans for nuclear submarines?' (20 September 2021) *The Conversation* <https://theconversation.com/why-is-southeast-asia-so-concerned-about-aukus-and-australias-plans-for-nuclear-submarines-168260> accessed 26 February 2024.

17 Ryan A. Musto, 'Does AUKUS violate the pledge of a nuclear-free south Pacific? China thinks it might' (22 October 2021) *The Diplomat* <https://thediplomat.com/2021/10/does-aukus-violate-the-pledge-of-a-nuclear-free-south-pacific-china-thinks-it-might/> accessed 26 February 2024.

18 Julian Kerr, 'Australia to build at least eight nuclear-powered submarines in place of discontinued attack-class programme' (16 September 2021) *Janes* <https://www.janes.com/defence-news/news-detail/australia-to-build-at-least-eight-nuclear-powered-submarines-in-place-of-discontinued-attack-class-programme>accessed 26 February 2024.

19 Matt Coughlan, 'Australia in deal for nuclear submarines' (16 September 2021) *The Canberra Times* <https://www.canberratimes.com.au/story/7432533/australia-in-deal-for-nuclear-submarines/> accessed 26 February 2024.

is set to be commissioned into Russian fleet in 2023.[20] The trials of the *Poseidon* are conducted from Belgorod, a nuclear-powered submarine with the main focus on assessing the performance of its nuclear engine.[21] With Russia's success in developing state-of-the-art *Poseidon*, it is not surprising that other superpowers would follow suit given the geopolitical and military tensions in the South China Sea, which forms part of the Straits of Malacca and Singapore maritime route.[22]

Given that the unimpeded transit passage regime applies to the Straits of Malacca and Singapore, Malaysia and Indonesia have reasons to feel apprehensive on potential maritime threats caused by these new developments.[23] Malaysia reiterated its concerns over AUKUS during Australian Foreign Minister Penny Wong's visit to Kuala Lumpur in July 2022.[24]

International law has placed the obligation on Malaysia and Indonesia to allow its territorial sea within the Straits of Malacca and Singapore to be open for international navigation, and this obligation includes passage for vessels carrying hazardous nuclear substances and for nuclear-powered submarines.[25]

It is important to consider whether such navigation could be detrimental to the security of Malaysia and Indonesia and whether it could adversely affect the sensitive marine environment of the Straits of Malacca and Singapore.[26]

---

20 'Russia's unmanned Poseidon underwater drone to start first sea trials' (23 June 2023) *Xinhuanet* <https://english.news.cn/20230623/fa4c5a9ab3bc47778e4e776633898110/c.html> accessed 26 February 2024.

21 ibid.

22 'China, US in war of words over South China Sea navigation' (24 March 2023) *South China Morning Post* <https://www.aljazeera.com/news/2023/3/24/china-us-militaries-in-war-of-words-over-south-china-sea-access> accessed 26 February 2024.

23 Mohd Hazmi Mohd Rusli and Izyan Munirah Mohd Zaideen, 'AUKUS and Malaysia: Cats on hot bricks?' (8 October 2021) *New Straits Times* <https://www.nst.com.my/opinion/columnists/2021/10/734789/aukus-and-malaysia-cats-hot-bricks> accessed 26 February 2024.

24 Katharine Murphy, 'Malaysian foreign minister says concerns remain about Aukus pact after meeting with Penny Wong' 28 June 2022) *The Guardian* <https://www.theguardian.com/world/2022/jun/28/malaysian-foreign-minister-says-concerns-remain-about-aukus-pact-after-meeting-with-penny-wong> accessed 26 February 2024.

25 Article 44 of UNCLOS stipulates that 'States bordering straits shall not hamper transit passage … There shall be no suspension of transit passage.

26 Masha Menhat et al, 'The Impact of Covid-19 Pandemic: A Review on Maritime Sectors in Malaysia' (2021) Aug 1(209) *Ocean and Coastal Management* <https://www.sciencedirect.com/science/article/pii/S0964569121001228?via%3Dihub> accessed 26 February 2024; Danson Cheong, 'Keeping Straits of Malacca and Singapore Open to Shipping Key to Success of Maritime Silk Road, Says DPM Teo', *Straits Times* (2017) <https://www.straitstimes.com/singapore/keeping-straits-of-malacca-open-to-shipping-key-to-success-of-maritime-silk-road-says-dpm> accessed 26 February 2024.

It is also important to examine whether there is any preventive remedy applicable to coastal states that can protect their territorial waters from unprecedented collision involving nuclear-powered submarine and autonomous nuclear-powered drones.

International law provides foreign vessels unimpeded right of transit passage through the Straits of Malacca and Singapore.[27] Nevertheless, coastal states should be provided with adequate measures to ensure their respective maritime domains will not be adversely affected in the unexpected event of leakage of radioactive substances as a result of scuttling or maritime accidents involving nuclear-powered military vessels. This article therefore discusses the pertinent issue of whether or not in such a scenario, the stricter regime of non-suspendable innocent passage would replace the application of the more liberal transit passage regime.

2 The Status of the Straits of Malacca and Singapore under UNCLOS

The Straits of Malacca and Singapore route is the shortest maritime passageway connecting oil exporter nations in West Asia to their East Asian consumers. In 2017, the Singapore-based Nippon Maritime Center reported that one vessel leaves or enters the Straits of Malacca and Singapore every six minutes.[28]

The Straits of Malacca and Singapore are now the second busiest shipping way after the Dover Strait.[29] An estimated 15 million barrels of oil pass through the Straits of Malacca and Singapore daily.[30]

Statistical data have demonstrated that most of the world's busiest ports are located in East Asian countries, including China and South Korea.As indicated in Table 5.1, Singapore and Port Klang in Malaysia are ranked as the busiest ports which are located along the Straits of Malacca and Singapore.

27 Mohd Hazmi Mohd Rusli, 'Are nuclear-powered submarines a problem in Southeast Asia?' (27 May 2022) *Policy Forum* <https://www.policyforum.net/are-nuclear-powered-submarines-a-problem-in-southeast-asia/>.

28 Marcus Hand, 'Exclusive: Malacca Straits VLCC traffic doubles in a decade as shipping traffic hits all time high in 2017' (19 February 2018) *Seatrade Maritime News* <https://www.seatrade-maritime.com/asia/exclusive-malacca-straits-vlcc-traffic-doubles-decade-shipping-traffic-hits-all-time-high-2017> accessed 26 February 2024.

29 Izyan Munirah Mohd Zaideen, 'Should the Straits of Malacca and Singapore be designated as special area?' (2019) 49EPL4–5 236.

30 'Strait of Malacca key chokepoint for oil trade' (27 August 2018) *The Maritime Executive* <https://www.maritime-executive.com/article/strait-of-malacca-key-chokepoint-for-oil-trade> accessed 26 February 2024.

TABLE 5.1 World's top 12 busiest ports 2021

Container Traffic 2021			
Rank	**Port**	**Country**	TEUs **(Million)**
1	Shanghai	China	47.03
2	**Singapore**	**Singapore**	**37.49**
3	Ningbo-Zhoushan	China	31.07
4	Shenzhen	China	28.77
5	Guangzhou	China	24.18
6	Busan	South Korea	22.71
7	Qingdao	China	23.71
8	Hong Kong	China	17.8
9	Tianjin	China	20.27
10	Rotterdam	Netherlands	15.3
11	Jebel Ali	United Arab Emirates	13.74
12	**Port Klang**	**Malaysia**	**13.72**

SOURCE: WORLD SHIPPING COUNCIL
Note: Ports in bold are located along the Straits of Malacca and Singapore. TEU=twenty-foot equivalent units.

If for any reason the Straits of Malacca and Singapore are not available for international navigation, shipping companies will have no other choice but to traverse through the Indonesian archipelagic Straits of Lombok and Makassar, which will lead to higher shipping costs that could affect the wellbeing of the global economy.[31]

As straits used for international navigation that is subjected to Part III of UNCLOS, the caretaker states of the Straits of Malacca and Singapore, namely Malaysia, Singapore and Indonesia have no rights to impede, suspend or impair navigation of vessels exercising transit via the straits. International law dictates that the Straits of Malacca and Singapore must always be open to international navigation.

On average, the Straits of Malacca and Singapore are navigated by about 70, 000 vessels per year. Nevertheless, according to INFOMARE, total transits

31 Mohd Hazmi Mohd Rusli and Rahmat Mohamad, 'A priceless maritime heritage' (28 June 2014) *New Straits Times* <https://www.nst.com.my/news/2015/09/priceless-maritime-heritage> accessed 26 February 2024.

in the first nine months of 2023 were 66, 083, indicating a rise of 8.6 percent of transits if compared to the year 2022. This may include passage of nuclear-powered submarines flying Chinese,[32] Indian,[33] and United States flags, as well as flags of other nations.[34]States bordering the Straits of Malacca and Singapore have do not possess rights to impede navigation of vessels exercising transit passage. As maritime technology develops, the Straits would also accommodate the passage of nuclear-powered and autonomous submarines in the future, bringing together risks of environmental repercussions.

3 Nuclear-Powered Submarines and Autonomous Drones—Aspirations of Maritime Nations

A nuclear submarine is a submarine powered by a nuclear reactor, but not necessarily nuclear-armed,[35] possessing considerable performance advantages over conventional diesel-electric submarines.[36] There are three major types of submarines which are ballistic missile submarines, attack submarines and cruise missile submarines.[37] Nuclear-powered submarines could operate at high speed for long unlimited period without the constant need of refuelling, limiting their detection by adversaries.[38]

The first nuclear-powered submarine, *USS Nautilus* plied the oceans back in 1955. During the Cold War, the Americans and the Soviets built more than 400 nuclear-powered submarines.[39] As reported by Janes, the following nations

---

32 Rob Taylor, 'China's submarines add nuclear-strike capability, altering strategic balance' (27 October 2014) *WSJ* <https://www.wsj.com/articles/chinas-submarine-fleet-adds-nuclear-strike-capability-altering-strategic-balance-undersea-1414164738> accessed 26 February 2024.

33 Defense World, 'Nuclear submarine INS Chakra spotted in Straits of Malacca escorted by Russian naval ships' (2020) *Defense World* <https://www.defenseworld.net/news/29732/Nuclear_Submarine_INS_Chakra_Spotted_in_Straits_of_Malacca_Escorted_by_Russian_Naval_Ships#.YeoQanpBzIU> accessed 26 February 2024.

34 Zia Mian, M. V. Ramana and A. H. Nayyar, 'Nuclear submarines in South Asia: New risks and dangers' (2019) 2 JPND1 184.

35 Frank von Hippel, 'Mitigating the Threat of Nuclear-Weapon Proliferation via Nuclear-Submarine Programs' (2019) 2JPND1 133–150.

36 Lukas Trakimavičius, 'The Future Role of Nuclear Propulsion in the Military' (2021) EH 2–5.

37 Ibid.

38 James Campbell, 'Seoul's Misguided Desire for a Nuclear Submarine' (2021) 74 NWCR 4 1–3.

39 Alec Luhn, 'Russia's 'slow-motion Chernobyl' at sea' (2 September 2020) *BBC* <https://www.bbc.com/future/article/20200901-the-radioactive-risk-of-sunken-nuclear-soviet-submarines> accessed 26 February 2024.

possess nuclear-powered submarines: the United Kingdom, France, China, Russia, India,[40] and the United States.[41] In fact, nuclear-powered shipbuilding programmes account for more than half of the shipbuilding account in the US Navy fiscal year 2023 budget request.[42] As of 2021, China has 12 nuclear submarines, Russia 29, the United Kingdom 11, France 8, and India with one.[43] The United States military still has the most, with a fleet of more than 68 nuclear-powered submarines.

Several other countries, such as Argentina, Brazil, and Australia, have ongoing projects in different phases to construct nuclear-powered submarines.[44]

Russia's success in developing autonomous nuclear-powered vehicles would potentially prompt other superpower nations to do the same, following their mutual aspirations as global power. This would, one way or the other, cause possible threats to coastal states if such vehicles are to exercise the right of transit passage when navigating via the Straits of Malacca and Singapore.

4 Implications of Radioactive Pollution

According to the website of the World Nuclear Association, the safety record of the United States nuclear navy is impeccable, which is attributed to a high level of standardization in naval power plants and their maintenance.[45] Despite this, a number of American nuclear-powered submarines have foundered in 1960s including USS *Trasher*, USS *Scorpion* and USS *Guitarro*. Early Soviet endeavors

---

40 Rahul Bedi, 'India to Approve Plans for Six-Boat Nuclear Submarine Fleet', *Janes* (2021) <https://www.janes.com/defence-news/news-detail/india-to-approve-plans-for-six-boat-nuclear-submarine-fleet> accessed 26 February 2024.

41 Julian Kerr, 'Australian Nuclear Sub Decision Driven by Technology and Chinese Assertiveness', *Janes* (2021) <https://www.janes.com/defence-news/news-detail/australian-nuclear-sub-decision-driven-by-technology-and-chinese-assertiveness> accessed 26 February 2024.

42 Michael Fabey, 'Pentagon Budget 2023: US Navy Nuclear-Powered Fleet Drives Ship Procurement Costs', *Janes* (2022) <https://www.janes.com/defence-news/news-detail/pentagon-budget-2023-us-navy-nuclear-powered-fleet-drives-ship-procurement-costs> accessed 26 February 2024.

43 Data extracted from The Military Balance 2021, International Institute for Strategic Studies as reported in Mohammed Haddad, 'Infographic: Are nuclear submarines better' (21 September 2021) *Al-Jazeera* <https://www.aljazeera.com/news/2021/9/21/infographic-how-many-submarines-does-each-country-have-interactive> accessed 26 February 2024.

44 Ibid.

45 World Nuclear Association, 'Nuclear-powered ships' (November 2021) *World Nuclear Association* <https://world-nuclear.org/information-library/non-power-nuclear-applications/transport/nuclear-powered-ships.aspx> accessed 26 February 2024.

in developing nuclear-powered submarines also resulted in serious mishaps, resulting in radiation leaks.

Research work commissioned by Greenpeace International toward the end of the Cold War indicated that there are many nuclear weapons and fully fueled nuclear reactors lying in the depths of the ocean.[46] However, studies also show that there was no evidence of radioactive contamination measurable on the sea floor. In addition, there have been no radioactive materials above the legal limits measured in organisms captured on and around this point source of high-level radioactive material.

Scientists have been monitoring radioactive levels of the 1963-sunken United States nuclear-powered attack submarine *Thresher* and the 1968-sunken nuclear-armed and nuclear-powered attack submarine *Scorpion* in 1968. The results of this work, most of which was conducted in the early to mid-1980s, indicated that there has been no release or dispersion of contamination to dangerous or illegal levels. However, these were studies conducted four decades ago and recent studies have found otherwise.[47] For example, a joint Russian–Norwegian study on the *K-278*, a Soviet nuclear-powered submarine that sank to the bottom of the Norwegian Sea in 1989 after it caught fire, was conducted in 2019. This expedition discovered that K-278 was leaking radiation up to 800,000 times above normal levels.

Realizing the potential environmental threat, international collaborations have been sought to salvage nuclear powered submarines.[48] In 2012. Russia has announced plans to collaborate with companies from France, Netherlands, South Korea and the United States to salvage sunken nuclear submarines in the northern Barents and Kara Seas.[49] Recently, the European Union (EU) has also announced that it is willing to co-fund such efforts with Russia in salvaging two old Soviet submarines *K-159* and *K-27*, both rusting on the Arctic seabed with highly radioactive spent nuclear fuel elements in their reactors.[50]

---

46 Raphael Vartanov and Charles D. Hollister, 'Nuclear legacy of the Cold War: Russian policy and ocean disposal' (1997) 21 MP 1, 1.

47 AFP, 'Russia to measure radioactivity at sunk nuclear sub' (19 May 2021) *The Moscow Times* <https://www.themoscowtimes.com/2021/05/19/russia-to-measure-radioactivity-at-sunk-nuclear-sub-a73949> accessed 26 February 2024.

48 SV Antipov and Koroleva N.S., 'International Collaboration on Salvaging Nuclear-Powered Submarines' in *At Energy* (Springer Nature, 2004) 796–801.

49 'Russia to Salvage Sunken Nuclear Subs—Media', *Azernews* (2012) <https://www.azernews.az/region/44787.html> accessed 26 February 2024.

50 Thomas Nilsen, 'EU Willing to Co-Fund Lifting of Sunken Nuclear Subs from Arctic Seabed', *The Barents Observer* (2021) <https://thebarentsobserver.com/en/nuclear-safety/2021/11/europe-offers-pay-russia-raise-sunken-nuclear-subs> accessed 26 February 2024.

These sunken submarines will contaminate the marine environment if left as they are because they contain a large amount of spent nuclear fuel or radioactive waste that will eventually leak into the surrounding area and affect the marine environment.[51] It must be remembered that radioactive waste is more hazardous than other waste because it emits dangerous radiation. These materials can remain radioactive and dangerous to human health for thousands of years.[52]

In 2021, Japan announced its plan to release radioactive water from the Fukushima Nuclear Plant into the Pacific Ocean.[53] Once radioactive water is dumped into waters off the coast of Fukushima, the strong currents will disseminate radioactive materials to most parts of the Pacific Ocean within 57 days of discharge and will reach all oceans of the world within a decade. This can be expected to have adverse implications in various areas, including global fish migration, pelagic fisheries, human health, and ecological security.

So far, there have been nine incidents of sunken nuclear submarines worldwide, either by accident or scuttling.[54] However, none of these incidents have occurred within Southeast Asian waters. These sunken nuclear submarines may pose threats to the marine environment by leaking radiation into the sea.[55] In addition, the recent incident involving a United States nuclear-powered submarine that collided with an undersea mountain in the South China Sea has raised concerns about potential maritime accidents or worse, a nuclear meltdown.[56]

---

51 Ibid.

52 World Nuclear Association, 'Radioactive waste—Myths and realities' (January 2022) *World Nuclear Association* <https://world-nuclear.org/information-library/nuclear-fuel-cycle/nuclear-wastes/radioactive-wastes-myths-and-realities.aspx> accessed 26 February 2024.

53 Justin McCurry, 'UN to review Japan's plan to release Fukushima water into Pacific' (18 February 2022) *The Guardian* <https://www.theguardian.com/environment/2022/feb/18/un-to-review-japans-plan-to-release-fukushima-water-into-pacific> accessed 26 February 2024.

54 The Soviet and Russian Navies have lost five and two nuclear-powered submarines respectively. The United States Navy have lost two. All sank in the Atlantic and Arctic Oceans. See Dorian Archus, 'How many nuclear submarines have been sunk' *Naval Post* (26 April 2020) <https://navalpost.com/how-many-nuclear-submarines-have-been-sunk/> accessed 26 February 2024.

55 James Rogers, 'Sunken nuclear submarine leaking radiation into sea up to 800,000 times normal level' (26 July 2019) *NY Post* <https://nypost.com/2019/07/11/sunken-nuclear-submarine-leaking-radiation-into-sea-up-to-800000-times-normal-level/> accessed 26 February 2024.

56 Brad Lendon, 'How did a $3 billion US navy submarine hit an undersea mountain?' (5 November 2021) *CNN* <https://edition.cnn.com/2021/11/04/asia/submarine-uss

An article published in the *South China Morning Post* reported that the alleged 'undersea mountain" was actually an abandoned oil rig.[57] Needless to say, this recent development and fears about future events that could lead to nuclear waste leaking into seas must be taken under serious consideration.

5 Protection of the Marine Environment

As caretaker states of these important sea lines of communication, Malaysia, Indonesia, and Singapore are obliged to give effect to applicable international regulations to balance navigational rights and the protection of the marine environment. International law clearly states that the navigational rights of all vessels through straits that are used for international navigation must not be subjected to obstruction and must be impaired by the coastal states.

Part XII of UNCLOS is dedicated to protecting and preserving the marine environment. Article 233 of UNCLOS is specifically included in the Convention as a mechanism for protecting straits used for international navigation. In practice, this article is collectively read with Articles 42(1) (a) and (b)[58] and Article 42(2)[59] of UNCLOS.[60] However, Article 236 of UNCLOS clearly states that the provision of Article 233 does not apply to military vessels that enjoy sovereign immunity.

This means that the states bordering the Straits of Malacca and Singapore not only have no rights to impede navigation of vessels passing through the straits but are also left with limited options for enforcing preventive measures against potential marine pollution caused by passage of ships such as nuclear-powered submarines.

Nevertheless, Article 236 of UNCLOS states that such vessels or aircraft must act in a manner consistent, so far as is reasonable and practicable, with the

---

-connecticut-accident-undersea-mountain-hnk-intl-ml-dst/index.html> accessed 26 February 2024.

57 Kristin Huang, 'US nuclear sub 'may have hit an oil rig' in South China Sea' (13 November 2021) *South China Morning Post* <https://www.scmp.com/news/china/military/article/3155777/us-nuclear-sub-may-have-hit-oil-rig-south-china-sea> accessed 26 February 2024.

58 Articles 42(1)(a) and (b) of UNCLOS allow states bordering straits to give effect to applicable international regulations relating to safety of navigation and prevention of vessel-source pollution.

59 Article 42(2) of UNCLOS states clearly that such regulations shall not hamper or deny the application of transit passage.

60 John Warren Kindt, *Marine Pollution and the Law of the Sea* (William S. Hein & Co., Inc, 1986) 1193.

Convention. The question then is what is meant by the wording "so far as is reasonable and practicable with this Convention.' Does the phrase "so far as is reasonable and practicable' connote that states bordering straits could hamper or intercept the passage of nuclear-powered submarines if such passage is deemed detrimental to the security of the coastal state?

Before answering this question, it is vital to examine the provisions of the Vienna Convention on the Law of Treaties 1969 (Vienna Convention). The UNCLOS is a multilateral treaty and should therefore be interpreted in accordance with Article 26 of the Vienna Convention, which provides the following:

> Every treaty in force is binding upon the parties to it and must be performed by them in good faith.[61]

The term "good faith' has been commented on in several cases by the International Court of Justice (ICJ). In the *Nuclear Tests Case* (*Australia* v. *France*), the court reiterated that one of the basic principles governing the creation and performance of legal obligations, whatever their source, is the principle of good faith. Trust and confidence are inherent in international cooperation, particularly in an era when cooperation in many areas is becoming increasingly necessary.[62] In *Gabčíkovo-Nagymaros Project* (*Hungary v. Slovakia*), the ICJ commented that the principle of good faith obliges the parties to apply a treaty in a reasonable way and in such a manner that its purpose can be realized.[63]

The term "good faith' indeed carries legal significance, as seen in Article 300 of UNCLOS where it provides that "state parties shall fulfil in good faith the obligations assumed under this Convention and shall exercise the right, jurisdiction and freedoms recognized in this Convention in a manner which would not constitute an abuse of right.'[64] However, in justifying states bordering

---

61 Article 26 of Vienna Convention on the Law of Treaties (23 May 1969) entered into force 27 January 1980, 1155 UNTS.

62 Nuclear Tests Case (Australia v. France), Judgment, ICJ Reports 1974, 268.

63 Gabčíkovo-Nagymaros Project (Hungary v. Slovakia), Judgment, ICJ Reports 1997, 78.

64 The ongoing Cooperative Mechanism in the Straits of Malacca and Singapore is a good example to illustrate this. Because of the lack of support given by the users, particularly private stakeholders of the Straits, there were proposals in 2007 that the littoral states consider lodging a report to the International Tribunal of the Law of the Sea citing the users for violating Article 300 of UNCLOS on good faith and abuse of rights. See Mohd Hazmi bin Mohd Rusli, 'Protecting vital Sea Lines of Communication: A study of the proposed designation of the Straits of Malacca and Singapore as a Particularly Sensitive Sea Area' (2012) 57OCM 79.

straits intercepting the transit of recalcitrant ships, Article 300 of UNCLOS may not carry as much weight as Article 42(1) (a) and (b), Article 42(2) and Article 233, which explicitly limit the enforcement powers of states bordering straits to intercept the transit of such ships.

Thus, international law has placed restrictions on states bordering straits to impede navigation of vessels, particularly in straits where vessels are permitted to exercise transit passage. Thus, it is important to consider whether there are any options under international law for states bordering straits to replace the application of transit passage with a more liberal navigation regime.

6 The Application of Non-suspendable Innocent Passage in the Strait of Malacca

The Straits of Malacca and Singapore are located between two main oceans: the Indian Ocean to the west via the Andaman Sea and the Pacific Ocean to the east via the South China Sea.[65] The straits form a waterway linking these two regions of the world together.[66] In relation to maritime navigation, these straits have always been considered a single strait,[67] despite the waterway being formed by two different straits: the Strait of Malacca and the Strait of Singapore (see Map 5.1).[68]

65 Mohd Hazmi Mohd Rusli, 'Straits of Malacca and Singapore: Pride of the Malay Archipelago, priceless maritime heritage of the world' (2012) Special Ed *Jurnal Hadhari* 109.

66 Catherine Zara Raymond, 'Piracy and armed robbery in the Malacca Strait' (2009) 62 NWCR3 31.

67 Similar characterization also applies to Canada's Northwest Passage. See Don M McRae, 'The Negotiation of Article 234' in F Griffiths (ed), *Politics of the Nortwest Passage* (McGill-Queen's University Press, 1987) 110.

68 Tommy Koh stated that 'The Straits of Malacca and Singapore, which are interconnected … should be treated as one watercourse.' See Tommy Koh, 'Opening remarks by Prof Tommy Koh, Chair of the IMO-IPS Conference on the Straits of Malacca and Singapore; Ambassador-At-Large, Ministry of Foreign Affairs, Singapore' (1999) 3SJICL 295. This view is also shared by Beckman, who contends the following: 'The Malacca Strait and the Singapore Strait are connected. They are treated by the three littoral States of Indonesia, Malaysia and Singapore and by the IMO, as a single strait, which is referred to as the Straits of Malacca and Singapore.' See Robert Beckman, 'Singapore strives to enhance safety, security and environmental protection in its port and in the Straits of Malacca and Singapore' (2009) 14(2) OCJL167.

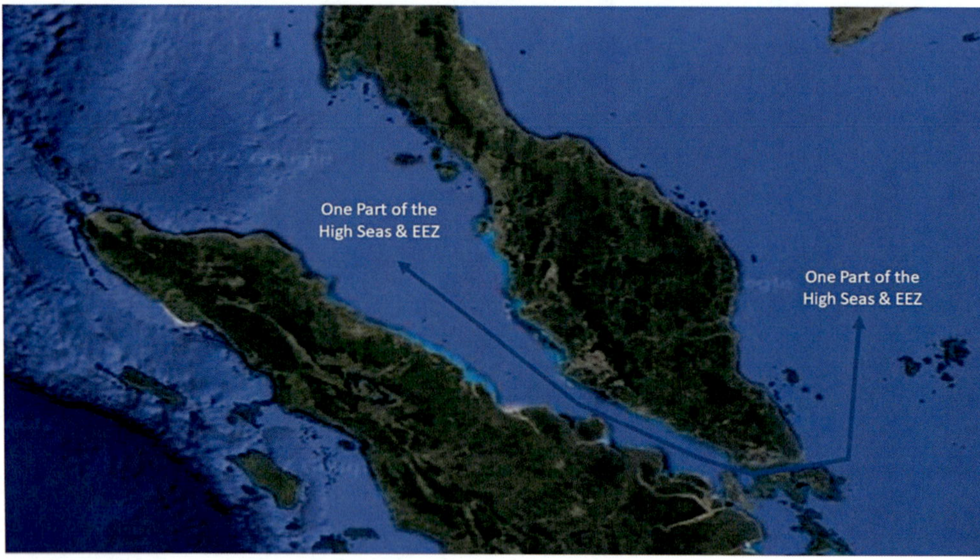

MAP 5.1 The straits of Malacca and Singapore
SOURCE: MODIFIED FROM GOOGLE MAPS

The Straits of Malacca and Singapore fit the definition of a strait used for international navigation in Article 37[69] and Article 38(1)[70] of UNCLOS because these straits connect one part of the high seas to another part of the high seas. Thus, the transit passage regime is applicable in these straits and inevitably opens them to international shipping traffic, which creates the burden for the littoral states of accommodating unlimited shipping traffic.[71] This burden exists when the Straits of Malacca and Singapore are considered one entity. However, the International Hydrographic Organization considers the Straits of Malacca and Singapore as two distinct straits and specifies the limits of these straits distinctly.[72] The limits of these two straits are illustrated in Maps 5.2 and 5.3.

69 Article 37 of UNCLOS states that transit passage applies to 'straits which are used for international navigation between one part of the high seas or an exclusive economic zone and another part of the high seas or an exclusive economic zone.'

70 Article 38 (1) of UNCLOS states the following: 'In straits referred to in article 37, all ships and aircraft enjoy the right of transit passage, which shall not be impeded.'

71 Mohd Hazmi bin Mohd Rusli, Maizatun Binti Mustafa and Wan Izatul Asma Binti Wan Talaat, 'Replacing the Transit Passage Regime with Freedom of Navigation in the Strait of Malacca: A case study with special reference to the Korea Strait' (2013) 78 OCM 25.

72 International Hydrographic Organization, 'Limits of Oceans and Seas' (150-XII-1971, International Hydrographic Organization, 1953) 23.

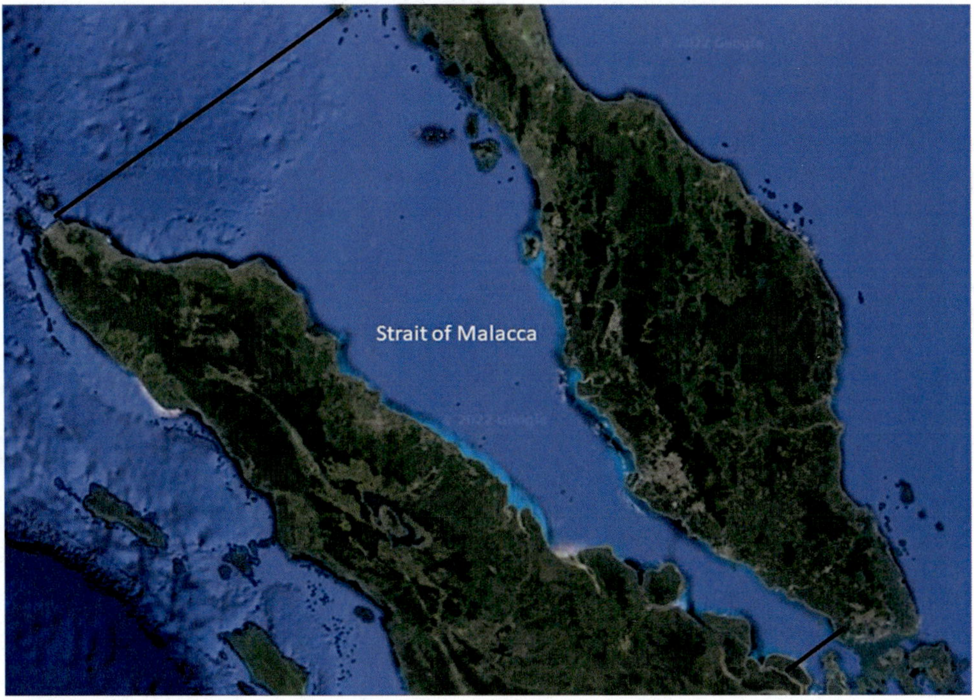

MAP 5.2 Limits of the strait of Malacca
SOURCE: MODIFIED FROM GOOGLE MAPS

MAP 5.3 Limits of the strait of Singapore
SOURCE: MODIFIED FROM GOOGLE MAPS

MAP 5.4 Strait of Malacca—a strait that connects one part of the high seas/EEZ to the territorial sea of Singapore
SOURCE: MODIFIED FROM GOOGLE MAPS

As can be seen in Map 5.4, if the Straits of Malacca and Singapore were not treated as one single strait, the transit passage regime would no longer apply to foreign vessels plying the Strait of Malacca because it would be a strait that connects one part of the high seas to the territorial sea of another state. Therefore, if considered separately from the Strait of Singapore, the Malaysian side of the Strait of Malacca would fulfil the requirements needed for non-suspendable innocent passage to apply as provided in Article 45(2) of UNCLOS.[73]

Similarly, if the Indonesian side of the Strait of Malacca were considered separately from the Strait of Singapore, it would be a strait that connects one part of the high seas or the exclusive economic zone (EEZ) to the territorial sea of Singapore. However, it could also be argued that if the Indonesian side of the Strait of Malacca were not considered to form one single strait with its Singaporean counterpart, it would be a strait that connects one part of the high

73 Article 45(1) (b) of UNCLOS states the following: 'The regime of innocent passage, in accordance with Part II, section 3, shall apply in straits used for international navigation between a part of the high seas or an exclusive economic zone and the territorial sea of a foreign State.' The difference between this navigational regime and that of innocent passage in Part II of UNCLOS is that this regime is non-suspendable. This is reiterated in Article 45(2) of UNCLOS.

seas or EEZ to the territorial seas of both Singapore and Indonesia as well as to the archipelagic waters of Indonesia.

It is not too simplistic to state that if the Strait of Malacca and the Strait of Singapore are considered separate straits, the Strait of Malacca may be seen as a strait that connects one part of the high seas or EEZ to the territorial sea of a foreign state, and therefore, non-suspendable innocent passage would apply in the Strait of Malacca rather than the principles of transit passage.[74]

7 Political and Legal Implications

If Malaysia and Indonesia, as states bordering the Strait of Malacca, supported such an interpretation of the strait's status, the navigational regime in the Strait of Malacca would be viewed differently by these states, who would contend that foreign vessels would cease to have the right to exercise transit passage in the strait. The application of non-suspendable innocent passage would allow both Malaysia and Indonesia to impose more stringent shipping control mechanisms on ships and aircraft transiting the strait. Under the non-suspendable innocent passage regime, submarines are required to travel on the surface while exercising innocent passage.[75] These military vessels like nuclear-powered submarines and autonomous nuclear drones traversing the Straits of Malacca and Singapore would no longer be able to exercise their normal mode of navigation because the vessels would need to surface. The application of a non-suspendable innocent passage regime would ultimately strengthen the regulatory powers of the littoral states, which are more limited under the transit passage regime.

Article 45(1) of UNCLOS stipulates that the application of non-suspendable innocent passage shall be subjected to the rules of innocent passage underlined in Part II of UNCLOS. Under this navigational regime, Malaysia and Indonesia could then apply Article 30 of UNCLOS, which provides regulatory powers to states bordering straits to require any recalcitrant warships to leave the territorial sea immediately.[76]

---

74 Rusli, Mustafa and Wan Talaat (n 71).

75 Bernard H. Oxman, 'The New Law of the Sea' (1983) 69 ABAJ 156.

76 Article 30 of UNCLOS states the following: 'If any warship does not comply with the laws and regulations of the coastal State concerning passage through the territorial sea and disregards any request for compliance therewith which is made to it, the coastal State may require it to leave the territorial sea immediately.'

This reinterpretation or recharacterization would also nullify the application of Article 42(1) (a) and (b), Article 42(2), and Article 44 of UNCLOS, which disallow states bordering straits to implement regulations that could impede navigation. However, this does not in any way mean that the littoral states could suspend the passage of vessels plying the Strait of Malacca without any valid or compelling reason to do so. The fact remains that unlike the innocent passage regime, vessels exercising non-suspendable innocent passage are not subjected to suspension, as the name of this regime implies.[77]

This reinterpretation of the navigational regime applicable in the Strait of Malacca would be highly contentious among maritime States like the United States, the United Kingdom and China. The fact that the non-suspendable innocent passage regime is less liberal than that of transit passage may incite mixed reactions, particularly among the states that are heavily dependent on the Strait of Malacca.[78]

During the ministerial meeting that concluded the 1971 Joint Statement of the Governments of Indonesia, Malaysia and Singapore on the Malacca Strait, the three littoral states agreed, for the purposes of safety of navigation and the protection of the environment of the straits, to treat the Straits of Malacca and Singapore as one single strait.[79]

However, in response to potential objections against this proposed recharacterization, Malaysia and Indonesia could argue that the 1971 Joint Statement was simply a joint statement and was never intended to be treated as an international treaty. The 1971 Joint Statement was agreed on 50 years ago, at a time when the volume of shipping traffic transiting the Strait of Malacca was not as great as it is now. In addition, there was far less focus on environmental issues at this time. From 1970 until 1986, the average number of shipping transits did not exceed 50,000 per year.[80] However, at the turn of the twenty-first century, the traffic reached 60,000 shipping transits per year.[81] Currently, there are

77 Article 45(2) of UNCLOS states the following: 'There shall be non-suspension of innocent passage through such straits.'

78 Rusli, Mustafa and Wan Talaat (n 71).

79 Robert C. Beckman and Zhen Sun, 'The Cooperative Mechanism for the Straits of Malacca and Singapore' in Robert C. Beckman, Tore Henriksen, Kristine Dalaker Kraabel et al. (eds), *Governance of Arctic Shipping* (Brill, 2017) 379.

80 Muhammad Razif bin Ahmad, 'The financial cost of risk management in the Straits of Malacca' in Hamzah Ahmad (ed), *The Straits of Malacca: International Co-Operation in Trade, Funding & Navigational Safety* (Pelanduk Publications, 1997) 187.

81 Hand (n 28).

approximately 85,000 transits per year, an increase of approximately 70 percent from the number of transits the straits accommodated five decades ago.[82]

Moreover, with the growing military and economic influence of China, the establishment of AUKUS and the rapid development of autonomous nuclear-powered submarines, it is anticipated that the Straits of Malacca and Singapore will accommodate an increasing number of both merchant and military vessels,[83] which may include nuclear-powered submarines and autonomous nuclear drones. Indeed, the agreement expressed in the 1971 Joint Statement was never intended to be a treaty. Therefore, given the increasing volume of shipping traffic, the littoral states, unilaterally or collectively, have the option to consider reviewing the 1971 Joint Statement taking into account the well-being of the security of their territorial sea.[84]

The assertion that the replacement of the transit passage regime with non-suspendable innocent passage would hamper international maritime traffic passing through the straits is flawed. Vessels and ships would continue to enjoy non-suspendable innocent passage through the Strait of Malacca. As stated earlier, the application of this navigational regime would neither impede nor hamper free passage of shipping because there is no right of suspension.[85]

While ships comply with accepted international rules and do not commit any acts in violation of the marine pollution laws of the littoral states, then these states would not interrupt their passage. With user states enjoying non-suspendable passage through the Strait of Malacca, the development of the cooperation mechanism existing between the littoral states and the users of the straits would be unlikely to be inhibited.

---

82 Mohd Hazmi Mohd Rusli, 'Will Nusantara affect Straits of Malacca?' (30 May 2022) *New Straits Times* <https://www.nst.com.my/opinion/letters/2022/05/800884/will-nusantara-affect-straits-malacca#:~:text=Until and unless East Asian,Straits of Malacca and Singapore.> accessed 26 February 2024.

83 Mohd Hazmi Mohd Rusli, 'Asia's busy straits must not become the playground of superpower navies' (25 May 2022) *South China Morning Post* <https://www.scmp.com/comment/letters/article/3178546/asias-busy-straits-must-not-become-playground-superpower-navies>accessed 26 February 2024.

84 Mohd Hazmi bin Mohd Rusli, 'The application of compulsory pilotage in straits used for international navigation: A study of the Straits of Malacca and Singapore' (2011) 3ASPP4; 'The 1971 Joint Statement of the Government of Indonesia, Malaysia and Singapore on the Malacca Strait as quoted in Michael Leifer, 'Malacca, Singapore and Indonesia' in Gerard J. Mangone (ed), International Straits of the World (Sijthoff & Noordhoff, 1978), 204.

85 See Article 45(2) of UNCLOS.

Unlike Iran which had previously closed the Strait of Hormuz to international shipping, Malaysia and Indonesia have never engaged in such acts.[86] In fact, Malaysia, Indonesia, and Singapore have always worked together with user states via Cooperative Mechanism to ensure that the maritime community can enjoy safe and uninterrupted passage via the straits.[87]

Although recharacterizing the Strait of Malacca might be a viable option for Malaysia and Indonesia, particularly in enhancing the regulatory powers of these littoral states, this proposed measure may be extremely controversial, particularly among the other maritime users of the Strait of Malacca.

Malaysia's 2017 proposal to designate an area between Kukup and Tanjung Piai, located at the southern portion of the Strait of Malacca, failed to proceed because Indonesia did not support the proposal.[88] From this perspective, little is known about whether both Malaysia and Indonesia would jointly agree to reinterpret the navigational regimes applicable to foreign vessels traversing the Straits of Malacca and Singapore. However, Malaysia could still unilaterally proceed with recharacterizing the Strait of Malacca, even if Indonesia were reluctant to do so.

8 Recharacterizing the Straits

Although UNCLOS has clearly specified the character and definition of straits used for international navigation, states have differed in their interpretation of the provision of Part III of the Convention.

The Northwest Arctic Channel, otherwise known as the 'Northwest Passage', is a clear example of this. The Northwest Passage is the sea route between the Atlantic and Pacific Oceans through the Arctic Ocean, along the northern coast of North America via waterways through the Canadian Arctic Archipelago, often considered a strait between the Atlantic and the Pacific Oceans.[89] The navigational distance required for transit via the Northwest Passage is

86 Yelena Dzhanova, 'The Suez Canal has a contentious history and has been blocked and closed several times since opening' (28 March 2022) <https://www.businessinsider.com/the-suez-canal-blocked-and-closed-several-times-since-opening-2021-3> accessed 26 February 2024.

87 Robert C. Beckman and Zhen Sun (n 79).

88 'Designation of Malaysia's Particularly Sensitive Sea Areas (PSSAs) Kukup to Tanjung Piai' in *Regional Workshop on PSSAs in Southeast Asia: Trends and Prospects* (International Maritime Organization, 2017).

89 Andrea Charron, 'The Northwest Passage: Is Canada's sovereignty floating away?' (2005) 60IJCJGPA3 831–848.

considerably less than that of the conventional route via the Panama Canal. That is, transit between East Asia and Western Europe would require approximately 13,600 km using the Northwest Passage, compared with 24,000 km using the Panama Canal.[90]

The United States government has persistently argued that the Northwest Passage is a strait used for international navigation stipulated under Article 37 of UNCLOS.[91] In contrast, Canada has consistently asserted that the Northwest Passage is part of its internal waters and therefore is not subject to the application of the transit passage or innocent passage regimes.[92]

As a result, both governments concluded the 1988 Canada–United States Agreement on Arctic Cooperation.[93] Although Washington and Ottawa have agreed to disagree, both are determined to work together and cooperate in resolving issues of mutual interest and concern involving the Northwest Passage.[94]

Although Canada considers the Northwest Passage as its internal waters, shipping traffic in the channel has been increasing. There were only two occasions where United States vessels traversed the Northwest Passage without Canada's prior consent.[95] These occasions occurred in 1969 and 1985 under the pretext of the exercise of transit passage.

---

90 Rebecca Sheehan, Dimitrios Dalaklis and Anastasia Christodoulou et al., 'The Northwest Passage in the Arctic: A brief assessment of the relevant marine transportation system and current availability of search and rescue services' (2021) 5*Logistics*2 23.

91 Adam Lajeunesse, 'The Northwest Passage in Canadian Policy' (2008) 63(4) *Nuclear Strategy in the Age of Weapons of Mass Destruction* 1037–52; Suzanne Lalonde and Frédéric Lasserre, 'The Position of the United States on the Northwest Passage: Is the Fear of Creating a Precedent Warranted?' (2013) 44ODIL1 28–32; 'The potential-use test and the Northwest Passage' 10 June 2020, <https://harvardlawreview.org/2020/06/the-potential-use-test-and-the-northwest-passage/> accessed 26 February 2024.

92 Donat Pharand, 'The Arctic Waters and the Northwest Passage: A Final Revisit' (2007) 38ODIL1–2 3–10; Bing Bing Jia, 'The Northwest Passage: An Artificial Waterway Subject to a Bilateral Treaty Regime?' (2013) 44ODIL2 123–144; Rebecca Rowe, 'Legal article: The Northwest Passage—What is its status under the International Law of the Sea?' 27 February 2019, <https://www.ukpandi.com/news-and-resources/articles/2019/legal-article-the-northwest-passage-what-is-its-status-under-the-international-law-of-the-sea/> accessed 26 February 2024.

93 Agreement Between the Government of Canada and the Government of the United States of America on Arctic Cooperation, adopted 11 January 1988, E101701—CTS No. 1988/29.

94 Donald R. Rothwell, 'The Canadian–US Northwest Passage dispute: A reassessment' (1993) 26 CILJ 2, 345.

95 Adam Lajeunesse, 'The Northwest Passage in Canadian policy: An approach for the 21st Century' (2008) 63 IJ 4, 1037.

According to the Protection of the Arctic Marine Environment (PAME), shipping in the Arctic increased by 25 per cent in six years, from 1,298 ships in 2013 to 1,628 ships in 2019.[96] While these numbers are far lower than the shipping traffic passing through the Straits of Malacca and Singapore, this increase demonstrates the growing importance of the Northwest Passage to international shipping activities. Despite Canada's position that the Northwest Passage is part of its internal waters, the melting of ice and the projected increase of shipping traffic may result in a recharacterization of these waters as straits used for international navigation governed by UNCLOS in the coming years, which would be in line with the interpretation of the United States.[97] It should also be remembered that via the 1988 Agreement, Canada has always guaranteed that permission for the purpose of transit would always be granted.[98] This is an indication that Canada acknowledges the increasing importance of the Northwest Passage as a significant international shipping way.

The Torres Strait, which separates Australia and Papua New Guinea, has always been considered a strait used for international navigation.[99] However, in the past decade, the Torres Strait was subjected to recharacterization, and the exercise of transit passage has been reinterpreted via the application of compulsory pilotage for certain types of ships.[100] This was undertaken to protect the sensitive marine environment of these waters from shipping activities. The application of compulsory pilotage was implemented via the designation of the Torres Strait as a Particularly Sensitive Sea Area (PSSA) in 2005.[101]

These developments allow consideration of whether the recharacterization of the Straits of Malacca and Singapore is possible. As strategic waterways adjacent to the much-contested South China Sea, it is not surprising that the Straits of Malacca and Singapore would accommodate not only the increasing

---

96 PAME, 'Arctic Shipping' 2022 <https://www.pame.is/arctic-shipping> accessed 26 February 2024.

97 M. D., 'Who owns the Northwest Passage?' (22 May 2019) *The Economist* <https://www.economist.com/the-economist-explains/2019/05/22/who-owns-the-northwest-passage> accessed 26 February 2024.

98 Will Greaves, 'As Russia upends the global order, Canada must secure the Arctic' (23 March 2022) *National Observer* <https://www.nationalobserver.com/2022/03/23/opinion/russia-upends-global-order-canada-must-secure-arctic> accessed 26 February 2024.

99 Donald R Rothwell, 'Compulsory Pilotage and the Law of the Sea: Lessons Learned from the Torres Strait,' Securing the Safety of Navigation in East Asia, eds. Shicun Wu and Keyuan Zou (Oxford: Chandos, 2013) 51.

100 Ibid.

101 Mohd Hazmi bin Mohd Rusli, 'Protecting vital Sea Lines of Communication: A study of the proposed designation of the Straits of Malacca and Singapore as a Particularly Sensitive Sea Area' (2012) 57 OCM 79.

number of merchant vessels but also transit of nuclear-powered submarines and autonomous nuclear drones. Although the reinterpretation or recharacterization of the Straits of Malacca and Singapore could be highly controversial, the proposed application of non-suspendable innocent passage replacing the transit passage regime may not directly impede, hamper, or impair passage of vessels plying the straits.

Article 45 (2) of UNCLOS has ensured that navigation via straits is not subjected to suspension. The exercise of non-suspendable innocent passage would result in a more equitable balance because it enables user states to exercise unobstructed navigational rights but at the same time empowers the regulatory capacity of states bordering straits against recalcitrant ships—a privilege that is not available under the transit passage regime.

9 Conclusion

Table 2 demonstrates that traffic passing through the Straits of Malacca and Singapore has been consistently increasing over the years. With the rise of China's military capability against the might of the forces of the United States and its allies, passage of military vessels via these crucial straits is anticipated to increase, including passage of nuclear-powered submarines. As the main maritime conduit connecting the Pacific Ocean via the South China Sea to the Indian Ocean, the significance of this maritime link is indisputable.

Nuclear-powered submarines flying United States, Chinese, and Indian flags have been reported to have traversed the straits in recent years. With the creation of AUKUS, Australia will be the next country in the region to possess nuclear-powered submarines by the 2040. In addition, Russia has also developed '*The Poseidon*', a state-of-the-art autonomous nuclear-powered drone. As such, it is not too simplistic to state that the Straits of Malacca and Singapore will potentially accommodate increasing number of nuclear-powered submarines in coming years.

The application of the transit passage regime has restricted the regulatory capacity of states bordering straits because it prevents passage of foreign vessels being hampered, impaired, or impeded. However, incidents such as the United States nuclear-powered submarine colliding with an unknown underwater object in the South China Sea in 2021 have led to fears of potential nuclear disaster in the region and of the risk that similar incidents could occur in the busy waters of the Straits of Malacca and Singapore.

To remedy this situation, this analysis proposes that Malaysia and Indonesia could jointly declare that as far as navigation is concerned, the Straits of

Malacca and Singapore are not part of the same strait, thus recharacterizing their position as straits where transit passage applies.

Geographically speaking, without the Strait of Singapore, the Strait of Malacca could be viewed as a strait that connects one part of the high seas or an EEZ to a territorial sea of a third state. This would fit the definition under Article 45 (1) (b) of UNCLOS of a strait in which non-suspendable innocent passage applies. If Malaysia, unilaterally or collectively with Indonesia, were to declare that the status of the strait had changed, both these states could contend that the stricter navigational regime of non-suspendable innocent passage would apply in the Strait of Malacca. This would mean that transit passage would cease to apply, which would in turn mean that nuclear-powered submarines and autonomous nuclear drones would no longer be allowed to navigate in normal mode because these vessels are required to surface under the regime of non-suspendable innocent passage.

Malaysia and Indonesia could also apply the provision of Article 30 of UNCLOS that empowers coastal states to suspend navigation of recalcitrant naval vessels; applying this provision would put these states in a better position to protect their maritime sovereignty—a right that is not available under the regime of transit passage.

Nevertheless, this article concludes that any proposed measures that could impede or hamper free passage through the Straits of Malacca and Singapore would spark various reactions from numerous states, particularly the maritime powers. It is submitted that such a declaration would be rejected by most maritime states, and that these states would argue that the regime of transit passage in the Strait of Malacca had achieved the status of customary international law.

Closing important maritime highways to vessels carrying hazardous nuclear substances would, one way or another, violate the spirit of UNCLOS. However, it could also be argued that UNCLOS places an obligation on each member state to protect and preserve its marine environment.

An analogy of this situation is that owners of houses located next to a busy road in the city center have no right to impede movement of road-users. However, if the road is consistently used by large trucks, lorries, or tractors that eventually damage the road to the extent of affecting the surrounding neighborhood, special measures should be implemented to ensure that the safety and comfort of residents are not compromised.

This analogy applies *mutatis mutandis* to the passage of nuclear-powered submarines and autonomous nuclear drones via the busy Straits of Malacca and Singapore. Treaties such as UNCLOS are not static and are subject to legal evolution and reinterpretation. The UNCLOS was drafted in the 1970s when there were not as many nuclear-powered submarines transiting the seas as there are today. Thus, it seems that based on state practices, recharacterizing the Straits of Malacca and Singapore is not unrealistic. Strong political will from the states bordering these straits would be key in making this recharacterization a reality.

The preamble of UNCLOS clearly promotes 'peaceful uses of the seas and oceans' and 'preservation of the marine environment'. Thus, the navigational regime of vessels carrying hazardous substances, such as nuclear-powered submarines and autonomous nuclear drones should be reinterpreted to further protect the interests of the coastal states concerned. Nevertheless, any attempts to reinterpret the existing navigational regime must not have the practical effect of denying or impairing passage of vessels genuinely exercising passage through the Straits of Malacca and Singapore.

References

Journal Articles and Books

Adam Lajeunesse, 'The Northwest Passage in Canadian Policy' (2008) 63 NSAWMD 4.

Antipov, SV and Koroleva N.S., 'International Collaboration on Salvaging Nuclear-Powered Submarines' in *At Energy* (Springer Nature, 2004).

Beckman, Robert C. and Zhen Sun, 'The Cooperative Mechanism for the Straits of Malacca and Singapore' in Robert C. Beckman, Tore Henriksen, Kristine Dalaker Kraabel et al. (eds), *Governance of Arctic Shipping* (Brill, 2017) 379.

Beckman, Robert, 'Singapore strives to enhance safety, security and environmental protection in its port and in the Straits of Malacca and Singapore' (2009) 14 OCLJ2 167.

Boyle, Alan E., 'Marine pollution under the Law of the Sea Convention' (1985) 79 AJIL2 357.

Campbell, James, 'Seoul's Misguided Desire for a Nuclear Submarine' (2021) 74NWCR4.

Charron, Andrea, 'The Northwest Passage: Is Canada's sovereignty floating away?' (2005) 60IJCJGPA3 838.

'Designation of Malaysia's Particularly Sensitive Sea Areas (PSSAs) Kukup to Tanjung Piai' in *Regional Workshop on PSSAs in Southeast Asia: Trends and Prospects* (International Maritime Organization, 2017).

Hippel, Frank von, 'Mitigating the Threat of Nuclear-Weapon Proliferation via Nuclear-Submarine Programs' (2019) 2JPND1.

Idris, Hanizah and Muhammad Faiz Ramli, 'Southeast Asian Region Maritime Connectivity and the Potential Development of the Northern Sea Route for Commercial Shipping' (2018) 23JSAS2.

International Hydrographic Organization, 'Limits of Oceans and Seas' (150-XII-1971, International Hydrographic Organization, 1953).

Jeevan, Jagan, Nurul Haqimin Mohd Salleh and Mohamad Rosni Othman, 'Thai Canal and Malacca Straits: Complementing or Competing Strategem for Trade Development in South East Asia' (2018) 3 JSDTL 2.

Jia, Bing Bing, 'The Northwest Passage: An Artificial Waterway Subject to a Bilateral Treaty Regime?' (2013) 44 ODIL 2.

Kindt, John Warren, *Marine Pollution and the Law of the Sea* (William S. Hein & Co., 1986).

Koh, Tommy, 'Opening remarks by Prof Tommy Koh, Chair of the IMO-IPS Conference on the Straits of Malacca and Singapore; Ambassador-At-Large, Ministry of Foreign Affairs, Singapore' (1999) 3 SJICL 295.

Lajeunesse, Adam, 'The Northwest Passage in Canadian policy: An approach for the 21st Century' (2008) 63(4) *International Journal* 1037.

Lalonde, Suzanne and Frédéric Lasserre, 'The Position of the United States on the Northwest Passage: Is the Fear of Creating a Precedent Warranted?' (2013) 44 ODIL 1.

Martin, Ana G Lopez, *International Straits: Concept, Classification and Rules of Passage* (Springer, 2010).

McRae, Don M, 'The Negotiation of Article 234' in F Griffiths (ed), *Politics of the Nortwest Passage* (McGill-Queen's University Press, 1987) 110.

Menhat, Masha et al, 'The Impact of Covid-19 Pandemic: A Review on Maritime Sectors in Malaysia' (2021) Aug 1(209) *Ocean and Coastal Management* <https://www.sciencedirect.com/science/article/pii/S0964569121001228?via%3Dihub>accessed 26 February 2024.

Mian, Zia, M. V. Ramana and A. H. Nayyar, 'Nuclear submarines in South Asia: New risks and dangers' (2019) 2 JPND 1.

Muhammad Razif bin Ahmad, 'The financial cost of risk management in the Straits of Malacca' in Hamzah Ahmad (ed), *The Straits of Malacca: International Co-operation in Trade, Funding & Navigational Safety* (Pelanduk Publications, 1997).

Oxman, Bernard H, 'The new Law of the Sea' (1983) 69 ABAJ 156.

Pharand, Donat, 'The Arctic Waters and the Northwest Passage: A Final Revisit' (2007) 38 ODIL 1.

Rahman, N. S. F. Abdul, A. H. Saharudiin and R. Rasdi, 'Effect of the Northern Sea Route opening to the shipping activities at Malacca Straits' (2014) 1 IJNME 85.

Raymond, Catherine Zara, 'Piracy and armed robbery in the Malacca Strait' (2009) 62 NWCR 3.

Rothwell, Donald R, 'The Canadian–US Northwest passage dispute: A reassessment' (1993) 26 CILJ 345.

Rothwell, Donald R, 'Compulsory Pilotage and the Law of the Sea: Lessons Learned from the Torres Strait,' Securing the Safety of Navigation in East Asia, eds. Shicun Wu and Keyuan Zou (Oxford: Chandos, 2013).

Rusli, Mohd Hazmi bin Mohd, 'The application of compulsory pilotage in straits used for international navigation: A study of the Straits of Malacca and Singapore' (2011) 3 APP 4 501.

Rusli, Mohd Hazmi bin Mohd, 'Protecting vital Sea Lines of Communication: A study of the proposed designation of the Straits of Malacca and Singapore as a Particularly Sensitive Sea Area' (2012) 57 OCM 79.

Rusli, Mohd Hazmi Mohd, 'Straits of Malacca and Singapore: Pride of the Malay Archipelago, priceless maritime heritage of the world' (2012) Special Ed *Jurnal Hadhari* 109.

Rusli, Mohd Hazmi bin Mohd, Maizatun Binti Mustafa and Wan Izatul Asma Binti Wan Talaat, 'Replacing the transit passage regime with freedom of navigation in the Strait of Malacca: A case study with special reference to the Korea Strait' (2013) 78 OCM 25.

Sheehan, Rebecca, Dimitrios Dalaklis and Anastasia Christodoulou et al., 'The Northwest Passage in the Arctic: A brief assessment of the relevant marine transportation system and current availability of search and rescue services' (2021) 5(2) *Logistics* 23.

Song, Yann-huei, 'Security in the Strait of Malacca and the Regional Maritime Security Initiative: Responses to the US proposal' in Michael D. Carsten (ed), *Global Legal Challenges: Command of the Commons, Strategic Communications, and Natural Disasters* (Naval War College, Newport, Rhode Island, 2007) 97 <https://apps.dtic.mil/sti/pdfs/ADA605285.pdf> accessed 26 February 2024.

Trakimavičius, Lukas, 'The Future Role of Nuclear Propulsion in the Military' (2021) *Energy Highlights.*

Valencia, Mark J., 'International conflict over marine resources in South-East Asia: Trends in politicization and militarization' in Lim Teck Ghee and Mark J. Valencia (eds), *Conflict over Natural Resources in South-East Asia and the Pacific* (United Nations University Press, 1990) <https://archive.unu.edu/unupress/unupbooks/80a04e/80A04E00.htm#Contents> accessed 26 February 2024.

Vartanov, Raphael and Charles D. Hollister, 'Nuclear legacy of the Cold War: Russian policy and ocean disposal' (1997) 21 MP 1.

Zaideen, Izyan Munirah Mohd, 'Should the Straits of Malacca and Singapore be designated as special area?' (2019) 49 EPL 4–5 236.

News Articles

AFP, 'Russia to measure radioactivity at sunk nuclear sub' (19 May 2021) *The Moscow Times* <https://www.themoscowtimes.com/2021/05/19/russia-to-measure-radioactivity-at-sunk-nuclear-sub-a73949> accessed 26 February 2024.

Archus, Dorian, 'How many nuclear submarines have been sunk' (26 April 2020) *Naval Post* <https://navalpost.com/how-many-nuclear-submarines-have-been-sunk/> accessed 26 February 2024.

Bedi, Rahul, 'India to Approve Plans for Six-Boat Nuclear Submarine Fleet' *Janes* (29 November 2021) <https://www.janes.com/defence-news/news-detail/india-to-app rove -plans-for-six-boat-nuclear-submarine-fleet> accessed 26 February 2024.

Cheong, Danson, 'Keeping Straits of Malacca and Singapore Open to Shipping Key to Success of Maritime Silk Road, Says DPM Teo' (13 July 2017) *Straits Times* <https://www.straitstimes.com/singapore/keeping-straits-of-malacca-open-to-shipping-key-to-success-of-maritime-silk-road-says-dpm> accessed 26 February 2024.

Chin, James, 'Why is Southeast Asia so concerned about AUKUS and Australia's plans for nuclear submarines?' (20 September 2021) *The Conversation* <https://theconversation.com/why-is-southeast-asia-so-concerned-about-aukus-and-australias-plans-for-nuclear-submarines-168260> accessed 26 February 2024.

'China, US in war of words over South China Sea navigation' (24 March 2023) *South China Morning Post* <https://www.aljazeera.com/news/2023/3/24/china-us-militaries-in-war-of-words-over-south-china-sea-access> accessed 26 February 2024.

Coughlan, Matt, 'Australia in deal for nuclear submarines' (16 September 2021) *The Canberra Times* <https://www.canberratimes.com.au/story/7432533/australia-in-deal-for-nuclear-submarines/> accessed 26 February 2024.

Defense World, 'Nuclear submarine INS Chakra spotted in Straits of Malacca escorted by Russian naval ships' (2020) *Defense World* <https://www.defenseworld.net/news/29732/Nuclear_Submarine_INS_Chakra_Spotted_in_Straits_of_Malacca_Escorted_by_Russian_Naval_Ships#.YeoQanpBzIU> accessed 26 February 2024.

Dzhanova, Yelena, 'The Suez Canal has a contentious history and has been blocked and closed several times since opening' 28 March 2022, *Business Insider* https://www.businessinsider.com/the-suez-canal-blocked-and-closed-several-times-since-opening-2021-3.

Fabey, Michael, 'Pentagon Budget 2023: US Navy Nuclear-Powered Fleet Drives Ship Procurement Costs' (29 March 2022) *Janes* <https://www.janes.com/defence-news/news-detail/pentagon-budget-2023-us-navy-nuclear-powered-fleet-drives-ship-procurement-costs> accessed 26 February 2024.

Greaves, Will, 'As Russia upends the global order, Canada must secure the Arctic' (23 March 2022) *National Observer* <https://www.nationalobserver.com/2022/03/23/opinion/russia-upends-global-order-canada-must-secure-arctic> accessed 26 February 2024.

Haddad, Mohammed, 'Infographic: Are nuclear submarines better' (21 September 2021) *Al-Jazeera* <https://www.aljazeera.com/news/2021/9/21/infographic-how-many-submarines-does-each-country-have-interactive> accessed 26 February 2024.

Hand, Marcus, 'Exclusive: Malacca Straits VLCC traffic doubles in a decade as shipping traffic hits all time high in 2017' 19 February 2018, *Seatrade Maritime News* https://www.seatrade-maritime.com/asia/exclusive-malacca-straits-vlcc-traffic-doubles-decade-shipping-traffic-hits-all-time-high-2017.

Huang, Kristin, 'US nuclear sub 'may have hit an oil rig' in South China Sea' (13 November 2021) *South China Morning Post* <https://www.scmp.com/news/china/military/article/3155777/us-nuclear-sub-may-have-hit-oil-rig-south-china-sea> accessed 26 February 2024.

Kerr, Julian, 'Australia to build at least eight nuclear-powered submarines in place of discontinued attack-class programme' (16 September 2021) *Janes* <https://www.janes.com/defence-news/news-detail/australia-to-build-at-least-eight-nuclear-powered-submarines-in-place-of-discontinued-attack-class-programme> accessed 26 February 2024.

Kuper, Stephen, 'The Indo-Pacific's Maritime Choke Points: Sunda and Lombok' (14 June 2019) *Defence Connect* https://www.defenceconnect.com.au/maritime-antisub/4240-the-indo-pacific-s-maritime-choke-points-sunda-and-lombok.

Lendon, Brad, 'How did a $3 billion US navy submarine hit an undersea mountain?' (5 November 2021) *CNN* <https://edition.cnn.com/2021/11/04/asia/submarine-uss-connecticut-accident-undersea-mountain-hnk-intl-ml-dst/index.html> accessed 26 February 2024.

Luhn, Alec, 'Russia's 'slow-motion Chernobyl' at sea' (2 September 2020) *BBC* <https://www.bbc.com/future/article/20200901-the-radioactive-risk-of-sunken-nuclear-soviet-submarines> accessed 26 February 2024.

M. D., 'Who owns the Northwest Passage?' (22 May 2019) *The Economist* <https://www.economist.com/the-economist-explains/2019/05/22/who-owns-the-northwest-passage> accessed 26 February 2024.

McCurry, Justin, 'UN to review Japan's plan to release Fukushima water into Pacific' (18 February 2022) *The Guardian* <https://www.theguardian.com/environment/2022/feb/18/un-to-review-japans-plan-to-release-fukushima-water-into-pacific> accessed 26 February 2024.

Murphy, Katharine, 'Malaysian foreign minister says concerns remain about Aukus pact after meeting with Penny Wong' (28 June 2022) *The Guardian* <https://www.theguardian.com/world/2022/jun/28/malaysian-foreign-minister-says-concerns-remain-about-aukus-pact-after-meeting-with-penny-wong> accessed 26 February 2024.

Musto, Ryan A., 'Does AUKUS violate the pledge of a nuclear-free South Pacific? China thinks it might' (22 October 2021) *The Diplomat* <https://thediplomat.com/2021/10/does-aukus-violate-the-pledge-of-a-nuclear-free-south-pacific-china-thinks-it-might/> accessed 26 February 2024.

Nilsen, Thomas, 'EU Willing to Co-Fund Lifting of Sunken Nuclear Subs from Arctic Seabed' (22 November 2021) *The Barents Observer* <https://thebarentsobserver.com/en/nuclear-safety/2021/11/europe-offers-pay-russia-raise-sunken-nuclear-subs> accessed 26 February 2024.

Page, Jeremy, 'China's submarines add nuclear-strike capability, altering strategic balance' 27 October 2014, *WSJ* https://www.wsj.com/articles/chinas-submarine-fleet-adds-nuclear-strike-capability-altering-strategic-balance-undersea-1414164738.

PAME, 'Arctic Shipping' 2022 https://www.pame.is/arctic-shipping.

Rogers, James, 'Sunken nuclear submarine leaking radiation into sea up to 800,000 times normal level' (26 July 2019) *NY Post* <https://nypost.com/2019/07/11/sunken-nuclear-submarine-leaking-radiation-into-sea-up-to-800000-times-normal-level/> accessed 26 February 2024.

Rowe, Rebecca, 'Legal article: The Northwest Passage—What is its status under the International Law of the Sea?' (27 February 2019) *Thomas Miller Group* <https://www.ukpandi.com/news-and-resources/articles/2019/legal-article-the-northwest-passage-what-is-its-status-under-the-international-law-of-the-sea/>accessed 26 February 2024.

Rusli, Mohd Hazmi bin Mohd, 'Maritime highways of Southeast Asia: Alternative Straits?' (10 February 2012) *RSIS Commentaries* <https://www.rsis.edu.sg/rsis-publication/rsis/1686-maritime-highways-of-southeast/#.YeeDEXpBzIU> accessed 26 February 2024.

Rusli, Mohd Hazmi Mohd, 'Asia's busy straits must not become the playground of superpower navies' (25 May 2022) *South China Morning Post* <https://www.scmp.com/comment/letters/article/3178546/asias-busy-straits-must-not-become-playground-superpower-navies> accessed 26 February 2024.

Rusli, Mohd Hazmi Mohd 'Are nuclear-powered submarines a problem in Southeast Asia?' (27 May 2022) *Policy Forum* <https://www.policyforum.net/are-nuclear-powered-submarines-a-problem-in-southeast-asia/> accessed 26 February 2024.

Rusli, Mohd Hazmi Mohd, 'Will Nusantara affect Straits of Malacca?' (30 May 2022) *New Straits Times* <https://www.nst.com.my/opinion/letters/2022/05/800884/will-nusantara-affect-straits-malacca#:~:text=Until and unless East Asian,Straits of Malacca and Singapore.> accessed 26 February 2024.

Rusli, Mohd Hazmi Mohd, 'Is it too little too late to protect the Strait of Malacca?' (31 August 2022) *The Straits Times* <https://www.straitstimes.com/asia/se-asia/is-it-too-little-too-late-to-protect-the-strait-of-malacca-jakarta-post-contributor> accessed 26 February 2024.

Rusli, Mohd Hazmi Mohd and Izyan Munirah Mohd Zaideen, 'AUKUS and Malaysia: Cats on hot bricks?' (8 October 2021) *New Straits Times* <https://www.nst.com.my/opinion/columnists/2021/10/734789/aukus-and-malaysia-cats-hot-bricks> accessed 26 February 2024.

Rusli, Mohd Hazmi Mohd and Rahmat Mohamad, 'A priceless maritime heritage' (28 June 2014) *New Straits Times* <https://www.nst.com.my/news/2015/09/priceless-maritime-heritage> accessed 26 February 2024.

'Russia to Salvage Sunken Nuclear Subs—Media' (11 October 2012) *Azernews* <https://www.azernews.az/region/44787.html> accessed 26 February 2024.

'Russia's unmanned Poseidon underwater drone to start first sea trials' (23 June 2023) *Xinhuanet* <https://english.news.cn/20230623/fa4c5a9ab3bc47778e4e776633898110/c.html> accessed 26 February 2024.

'Strait of Malacca key chokepoint for oil trade' (27 August 2018) *The Maritime Executive* <https://www.maritime-executive.com/article/strait-of-malacca-key-chokepoint-for-oil-trade> accessed 26 February 2024.

'The potential-use test and the Northwest Passage' (10 June 2020) *Harvard Law Review* <https://harvardlawreview.org/2020/06/the-potential-use-test-and-the-northwest-passage/> accessed 26 February 2024.

World Nuclear Association, 'Nuclear-powered ships' (November 2021) *World Nuclear Association* <https://world-nuclear.org/information-library/non-power-nuclear-applications/transport/nuclear-powered-ships.aspx> accessed 26 February 2024.

World Nuclear Association, 'Radioactive waste—Myths and realities' (January 2022) *World Nuclear Association* <https://world-nuclear.org/information-library/nuclear-fuel-cycle/nuclear-wastes/radioactive-wastes-myths-and-realities.aspx> accessed 26 February 2024.

Cases

Corfu Channel Case (*United Kingdom v. Albania*) (*Judgment*) [1949] ICJ Reports.

Gabčíkovo-Nagymaros Project (*Hungary v. Slovakia*) (*Judgment*) [1997] ICJ Reports.

Nuclear Tests Case (*Australia v. France*) (*Judgment*) [1974] ICJ Reports.

Treaties/Agreement

Agreement Between the Government of Canada and the Government of the United States of America on Arctic Cooperation, (11 January 1988) E101701—CTS No. 1988/29.

United Nations Convention on the Law of the Sea, (10 December 1982) entered into force 16 November 1994, 1833 UNTS.

Vienna Convention on the Law of Treaties, (23 May 1969) entered into force 27 January 1980, 1155 UNTS.

CHAPTER 6

Is International Law Adequate to Regulate Underwater Unmanned Vehicles (UUVs)? Legal Challenges beyond the 2016 U.S.–China UUV Incident

*Dan Liu**

1 Introduction

An 'unmanned undersea vehicle,' or a UUV, is a self-propelled submersible whose operation is either fully autonomous or under minimal supervisory control and is untethered except, possibly, for data links such as a fiber optic cable.[1] In terms of modes of operation, UUVs can be classified into 5 categories: (1) fully autonomous UUVs that are capable of autonomous planning, navigation and environment detection; (2) pre-programed UUVs that navigate and perform tasks in accordance with pre-set control programs; (3) shore-based remote-controlled UUVs that are incapable of autonomous navigation but require remote control by a shore-based operator; (4) platform-based remote-controlled UUVs that are deployed and controlled by a mother ship; and (5) weaponized UUVs that are used for attacks and other military purposes.[2] Weaponized UUVs are known as 'force multipliers' for the modern navy. For example, Russia's nuclear-powered UUV 'Poseidon' can travel within a range of 6000 km and to a depth maximum of 3000 feet. The UUV is also capable of launching nuclear warheads.[3] With the battle over 'command of the sea' expanding from the surface to the underwater space, the deployment of UUVs in the South China Sea (SCS), the East China Sea (ECS) and other sea areas has become a 'new normality' for the U.S., Japan and other regions. Since 2015, the U.S. Navy has been using long-endurance and wide-range Wave Gliders to

* Associate Research Professor, KoGuan School of Law, Shanghai Jiao Tong University. Email: liudan2015@sjtu.edu.cn.

1 U.S. Dep't of Navy, 'The Navy Unmanned Undersea Vehicle (UUV) Master Plan' (Novenber 9, 2004)4 <https://www.navy.mil/navydata/technology/uuvmp.pdf> accessed 2 Feburary 2024.

2 Song Shuhua and Zhao Jinsong, 'The legal status of UUV' (2017) NX 21.

3 Fang Xiaozhi and Lin Weimin, 'Russian Poseidon unmanned underwater vehicle'(2018) 15SB

 | DOI:10.1163/9789004706279_008

perform oceanographic surveys and to gather data on marine environments for potential underwater military operations.[4]

In December 2016, the Chinese Navy seized such a UUV (the 'China–U.S. UUV incident').[5] Military equipment tends to confuse military use and civilian use. Military or diplomatic disputes triggered by UUVs are pressing issues faced by China.

The legal issues brought about by the 'China–U.S. UUV incident' include the following: First, should a UUV be characterized as a vessel, a warship, or a weapon? Will the legal status of a UUV impact the rights and obligations of its owner State? Second, how will the coastal State's jurisdiction under the United Nations Convention on the Law of the Sea (UNCLOS) be challenged by the deployment of a foreign UUV in its territorial sea, archipelagic waters, exclusive economic zone (EEZ), or other maritime zones? Third, is a UUV entitled to immunity under international law? Fourth, shall the owner State assume state responsibility for the use of force by a weaponized UUV? Parts Two to Four of this paper will focus on the above four questions.

2 The Diversified Legal Status of UUVs

For UUVs, whether fully or semiautonomously or whether they are deployed from shore or from a vessel (warship or submarine), UUVs may enter waters under the jurisdiction of other states to conduct their activities, but the vehicles or operators of the owner state are often not required to do so. When discussing the legal issues of UUVs, their legal status is both the starting point and the difficult point. The legal status of UUVs is crucial for the rights and obligations of their owner State in time of peace and war.[6]

The doctrinal discussion on the legal status of UUVs can be categorized into three types of doctrines, namely, 'warships and submarines theory', 'ship's apparels doctrine and vessel theory', and 'autonomous weapons systems theory', taking into account the manner in which they operate.

4 Xu Yihang, 'How Underwater Spy Unmanned Underwater Vehicles Threaten Our National Security' (*China Youth News*, February 16, 2017) 11.

5 Liu Dan 'The Chinese Navy captured a U.S. Unmanned Underwater Vehicle, who has the upper hand in international law in this matter?' (*Pengpai Xinwen*, December 22, 2016) <https://www.thepaper.cn/newsDetail_forward_1585150> accessed 2 Feburary 2024.

6 See Michael N. Schmitt and David S. Goddard, 'International law and the military use of unmanned maritime systems', (2016) 98 IRRC 567–592.

2.1 *The 'Warship Theory' and the 'Submarine Theory' in the Context of UNCLOS*

The definition of 'warship', which is representative of that contained in UNCLOS, includes four elements: (1) Affiliation. A warship belongs to the armed forces of a State. (2) Nationality-related symbols. A warship bears the external marks distinguishing such ships of its nationality. (3) Command. A warship is under the command of an officer duly commissioned by the government of the State and whose name appears in the appropriate service list or its equivalent. (4) Crew operated or controlled. A warship is manned by a crew member who is under regular armed force discipline.[7] The four elements reference and incorporate most of the regulations of Articles 2–6 of the 1907 Hague Convention VII Relating to the Conversion of Merchant Ships Into Warships (the 1907 Hague Convention).[8] According to the regulations of the international conventions represented by UNCLOS, 'warships' include at least the basic attributes of affiliation with an armed system, clarity of external markings, clarity of command and manned control.

Since military UUVs are clearly identified as owner States and marked on the hull with military affiliation, the 'warship theory' is represented by the German Navy 'Commander's Handbook'. It emphasizes that the military UUV should not be excluded from the category of 'warships' because, in some cases, UUVs are controlled and operated by warships and should have the same legal status and immunities.[9] Rob McLaughlin, one of the opponents of the 'warship theory,' cited ship-based remotely operated UUVs as an example to raise two challenges: (1) difficulty identifying UUVs (released from a mother ship) independent of its mother ship as a warship and (2) difficulty in practice due to the greater flexibility of the commander's remote control command at a distance, the word 'command' of 'under the command of an officer' in the four elements of warships; additionally, it is difficult to include such remote control commands.[10] Jane Dalton also objected to the characterization of UUVs as warships. He argued that there was no need for UUVs to be reluctantly categorized as warships. UUVs enjoy the right to the innocent passage or the right to the archipelagic sea lane passage if considering the navigation rights of the owner state. Because UNCLOS has made it clear that its scope of application is to 'all'

7 1982 The United Nations Convention on the Law of the Sea, Article 29.

8 See the 1907 Hague Convention VII Relating to the Conversion of Merchant Ships Into Warships (October, 1907) <http://avalon.law.yale.edu/20th_century/hague07.asp> access 21 December 2023.

9 German Navy, *Commander's Handbook: Legal Bases for the Operations* (2002) s 2.11.

10 Rob McLaughlin, 'Unmanned Naval Vehicles at Sea: USVs, UUVs, and the Adequacy of the Law' (2011) 21 JLIS100 108, 109.

types of ships of States Parties.[11] The 'warship theory', which considers UUVs warships, is not supported by the treaty basis and has few supporters.

If characterizing UUVs as 'warships' is not accurate, can they be considered 'submarines' or 'other underwater vehicles' under UNCLOS? In analyzing the feasibility of characterizing UUVs as submarines, some scholars have pointed to the Code for Unplanned Encounters at Sea (CUES), adopted by the 14th Western Pacific Naval Forum in 2014, Part II, 'Safety Protocols', Article 2.7.[12] The biggest problem with the 'submarine theory' based on CUES is that CUES itself has no treaty effect, and there is no definition of 'submarine' in the entirety of the rule, so it is impossible to infer whether UUVs fall within the scope of 'submarines'.[13] The terms 'submarines' or 'other underwater vehicles' are referred to in parallel in Article 20 of Part II (Territorial Sea) of UNCLOS. Article 20 states that 'submarines and other underwater vehicles' passing through the territorial sea of the coastal State are required to navigate on the surface and to show their flag'. Article 14 of the Convention on Territorial Sea and Contiguous Zone,[14] concluded at the first Conference on the Law of the Sea in 1958, contains a similar provision. Interestingly, Article 14 refers only to 'submarines' and not to 'other underwater vehicles'. The differences in terminology between the two Conventions need to be analyzed in the context of the 'ordinary meaning' of the terms of the treaties and the negotiating documents of the Third Conference on the Law of the Sea, as described below:

First, what is the understanding of 'other underwater vehicles' in Article 20 of UNCLOS, and are 'submarines' and 'other underwater vehicles' the same thing? In 1956, the International Law Commission's 'Articles concerning the Law of the Sea with commentaries' proposed applying the requirement to 'navigate on the surface of the sea and display its flag' to submarine vessels 'both military and commercial'.[15] This requirement applies equally to other submersibles of any design (except for submarines) at the third Conference

11 See Jane Dalton, 'Future Navies-Present Issues', (2006) 59UNWR17 304.

12 *Code for Unplanned Encounters at Sea* (version 1.0) (China, 22 April, 2014) at the 2014 Western Pacific Navy Symposium, art 7.

13 Wang Shumin and Tang Xiaocong, 'Research on Legal Status of Unmanned Undersea Vehicles in International Law—Reflections on the Unmanned Undersea Vehicles Event between China and America' (2017) 4PLS.

14 Geneva Convention on Territorial Sea and Contiguous Zone Article 14(6).

15 'The International Law Commission (ILC), Articles concerning the Law of the Sea with commentaries' In ILC, Yearbook of the International Law Commission, (1956) vol. II., 273 <http://legal.un.org/ilc/texts/instruments/english/commentaries/8_1_8_2_1956.pdf> access 21 December 2023; Myron H. Nordquist ed., *United Nations Convention on the Law of the Sea, A Commentary* (Martinus Nijhoff Publishers, 1985), Volume I, 182.

on the Law of the Sea.[16] The term 'and' in Article 20 of the final text of UNCLOS also indicates that 'other underwater vehicles' cannot be equated with 'submarines'. As seen, UUVs are not 'submarines' within the meaning of Article 20.

Second, are UUVs, which are currently widely used for civil and military purposes, the 'other underwater vehicles' referred to by the negotiators of the Third Conference on the Law of the Sea? Two questions need to be addressed before interpreting 'other underwater vehicles' broadly: (1) If UUVs are to be considered 'other underwater vehicles' under Article 20, they should 'navigate on the surface' and 'show their flag' when passing through the territorial sea of another State. How such a provision would apply to UUVs that are unmanned and remotely controlled is a question that needs to be addressed. (2) Second, at the Third Conference on the Law of the Sea, the reference to 'other submersibles' was first added to the proposal of eight states, including Cyprus, to the Seabed Committee, and Fiji's proposal categorized 'submarines and other underwater vehicles' as 'ships with special characteristics'. The State parties' proposals are primarily directed at the possible impact on the coastal State of the innocent passage through the territorial sea and transit passage through archipelagic waters of the abovementioned underwater installations.[17] The development of UUVs began in the 1960s for civilian use. Navies have been investing in the development of military UUVs since the 1990s.[18] It can be assumed that the constitutors of UNCLOS anticipated the emergence of other forms of submersibles or submarines for commercial use in view of the impact of the application of science and technology to the oceans on UNCLOS.[19]

In sum, analyzed from the perspective of treaty interpretation, UUVs are not 'submarines' within the meaning of Article 20 of UNCLOS; however, from the point of view of the 'ordinary meaning' of the treaty, the plural use of the words 'other' and 'vehicles' for 'other underwater vehicles' in Article 20 allows for the application of UUVs, which opens up the possibility of pluralistic characterization of legal status and incorporation by state parties into domestic law.

2.2 *The 'Ship's Apparel' or 'Vessel's Theory' in the Context of Maritime Law*

The biggest flaw in the 'warship theory' is the lack of justification for treating a UUV as a warship independent of the mother ship (warship or submarine) that

16 ibid 182.

17 ibid 180–185.

18 Xu Yihang (n 4) 11.

19 Zhang Guobin, 'Research on the Legal System of Innocent Passage' (Ph.D. dissertation, East China University of Political Science and Law, 2015) 154.

carries it. The relatively flexible legal regulations for 'ship's apparels' or 'vessels' in the context of maritime law also provide another feasible way of thinking about the legal status of UUVs. 'Ship's apparels' means fixed and movable equipment, facilities, articles, etc., on board a ship. The presence of a UUV in the mother ship's apparel is an important legal basis for determining the liability of the mother ship. According to Anglo-American case law, there are three criteria for assessing ship apparels: (1) Position criteria. The object must be on board; (2) Ownership criteria. The owner of the object must be the owner of the ship. (3) Necessity criteria. The item must be equipped with the ship for the current voyage. The necessity criterion is playing an increasingly important and decisive role in determining ship apparels in comparison with the other two criteria.[20] There are few cases dealing with the legal status of UUVs in practice, and the one that can be referred to is the case of Anderson v. United States in 2003. In this case, warplanes taking off from the aircraft carrier USS John F. Kennedy fired two shells that missed the target ship but accidentally injured Mr. Anderson, who was operating at sea. The district court found that the warplanes were apparels of the aircraft carrier and that they formed part of the ship even if the apparels left the mother ship.[21] This judgment was upheld by the appellate court. Among the scholars who support the 'ship's apparels theory', Rob McLaughlin argues that UUVs should be considered part of the ship on which they are carried. He believes that the international law of the sea (including the domestic law of the United States) is sufficient to provide a legal basis for the regulation of UUVs.[22] Song Shuhua asserts that ship-based remotely operated UUVs are deployed for the purpose of carrying out in-water operations by mother ships or warships. Such UUVs do not have an independent legal status as vessels but are important instruments attached to ships. It constitutes an apparel of its mother ship or warship.[23] In light of the jurisprudence and the practice of maritime law, the 'ship's apparels theory' can explain the relationship between ship-based remotely operated UUVs and the mother ship.

If ship-based remotely operated UUVs are difficult to characterize as vessels and are more appropriately characterized as ship apparels, then how are fully autonomous, programmable, shore-based remotely operated and weaponized

---

20 Song Shuhua, 'Legal criteria for defining the ship's attributes' in *Research on Marine Law* (2nd series), edited by Xue Guifang (Shanghai Jiao Tong University Press, 2018) 18–36.

21 See Gary L. Anderson v. United States, 317 F.3d 1235, 2003 AMC 94 (11th Cir.2003), <https://law.justia.com/cases/federal/appellate-courts/F3/317/1235/484420/> accessed November 23, 2023.

22 See Rob McLaughlin (n 10) 108–109.

23 Song Shuhua (n 20) 18–19.

UUVs characterized, and can they be characterized as vessels? Supporters of vessel theory, such as James Kraska and Raul Pedrozo, who have backgrounds in the U.S. military, and scholars such as Rob McLaughlin and Julian Ku,[24] have also endorsed the view that UUVs are 'vessels' that 'enjoy sovereign immunity'.[25] Since UNCLOS does not provide a clear definition of 'vessels', the elements of 'vessels' are to be found in other conventions or legal documents. Article 1 of the Convention for the Suppression of Unlawful Acts against the Safety of Maritime Navigation in 1988 defines a 'ship' as 'a vessel of any type whatsoever not permanently attached to the sea-bed, including dynamically supported craft, submersibles, or any other floating craft'. Because the Convention excludes ships that are 'military' or 'owned or operated by a State when using as a naval auxiliary or for customs or police purposes',[26] civilian UAVs may be applicable, while military UAVs are excluded from the scope of application of the Convention. The 'Vessel' in the International Maritime Organization (IMO)'s Convention on the Regulations for Preventing Collisions at Sea (COLREGS) includes every description of watercraft, including nondisplacement crafts and seaplanes, used or capable of being used as a means of transportation on water, i.e., 'nondisplacement rafts, ground effect vessels and seaplanes'.[27] Other conventions of IMO, such as the 1962 Amendments to the 1954 Convention for Prevention of Pollution of the Sea by Oil in 1954,[28] MARPOL 73/78,[29] and the Ship Registration Convention[30] (not yet in force), define 'ship' in a way that emphasizes its attributes of 'carriage on water'. What is the judicial practice in determining the attributes of a UUV in relation to the 'transport function' of a ship, as emphasized in these legal documents? The Anglo-American case law

24 See Rob McLaughlin (n 10) 110; James Kraska and Raul Pedrozo, 'China's Capture of U.S. Underwater Drone Violates Law of the Sea' (December 16, 2016) <https://www.lawfareblog.com/chinas-capture-us-underwater-drone-violates-law-sea> accessed 2 Feburary 2024; Julian Ku, 'The Nonexistent Legal Basis for China's Seizure of the U.S. Navy's Drone in the South China Sea' (16 December 2016) <https://www.lawfareblog.com/nonexistent-legal-basis-chinas -seizure-us-navys-drone-south-china-sea> accessed 2 Feburary 2024.

25 See Sam LaGrone, 'Chinese Seize U.S. Navy Unmanned Vehicle' (December 16, 2016, USNI News) <https://news.usni.org/2016/12/16/breaking-chinese-seize-u-s-navy-unmanned-vehicle> accessed 2 Feburary 2024.

26 Convention for the Suppression of Unlawful Acts against the Safety of Maritime Navigation art 2(1).

27 International Regulations for Preventing Collisions at Sea art 3(1).

28 1962 Amendments to the 1954 Convention for Prevention of Pollution of the Sea by Oil, 11 April 1962, Annex art 1(1).

29 International Convention for Prevention of Pollution from Ships, 1973, as modified by the Protocol of 1978 relating thereto (MARPOL 73/78), Feb. 17, 1978, art 1, Annex I.

30 Ship Registration Convention art 2(4).

provides two criteria for determining 'ships': (1) Navigation criteria. Whether the device was seaworthy; (2) Functional criteria. The transportation function or operational function of the device is also important. The courts have been more stringent on the first navigational criterion and less stringent on the second criterion, 'transport function'.[31] This provides greater scope for national legislation and practice to incorporate UUVs into 'vessels'.

With regard to the definition of 'vessels', the Law of the Sea Committee of the American Branch of the International Law Association in 2003, on the basis of the Consolidated Technical Terminology Report of the International Hydrographic Organization, argued for a broad interpretation of the term 'ship' as 'a man-made device capable of traversing the seas and oceans, including submarines'.[32] United States maritime law used to define a 'ship' as 'a vessel or other artificial facility used as a means of transportation on water'.[33]

The 2007 edition of the Commander's Handbook on the Law of Naval Operations treats UUVs as 'other naval vessels' and enjoys immunity in the same way as official government vessels.[34] In light of the controversy over the legal status of UUVs, several United States scholars have also offered pragmatic advice on the legal problems encountered by UUVs in practice: (1) When the United States military applies UUVs for military use, it should ensure that they comply with COLREGS to be exempted;[35] (2) In fact, there is a discrepancy between the official caliber of the United States and the military documents, and UUVs should be included in the list of 'ships' in the future revision of the 2007 edition of the Commander's Handbook on the Law of Naval Operations.[36] In sum, the vague and uniform official characterization of military UUVs in the U.S. as 'ships' (the connection between the refined characterization of military UUVs by U.S. academics and sovereign immunity will be discussed in detail in chapter 3 has the disadvantage of being unconvincing because of the general characterization without distinguishing between the types of operations they are capable of performing.

---

31 Song Shuhua and Zhao Jinsong, (n 2) 22.

32 See George K. Walker, "Defining Terms in the 1982 Law of the Sea Convention III: The International Hydrographic Organization ECDIS Glossary," (2004) 34 CWILJ211 238.

33 See 1 U.S.C. § 3 (2000); 16 U.S.C. § 916(e) (2000); 33 U.S.C. §§ 1471(5), 1502(19) (2000); 47 U.S.C. § 153(39) (2000).

34 See U.S Office of the Chief of Naval Operations, U.S. Marine Corps, U.S. Coast Guard, 'The Commander's Handbook on the Law of Naval Operations' (July 2007) arts 2.3 & 2.3.6, <https://permanent.access.gpo.gov/gpo56195/1-14M_(Jul_2007)_(NWP).pdf> accessed 23 November 2023.

35 Jane G. Dalton, Future Navies—Present Issues' (2006) 59 UWCR17 305.

36 See Michael N. Schmitt and David S. Goddard (n 6) 578.

Taking into account international treaties and common law jurisprudence, this author believes that ship-based remotely operated UUVs constitute the apparels of their mother ships or warships. For the three types of UUVs, fully autonomous, programmable, and shore-based remotely operated, when they are used as independent devices to carry out surface or underwater tasks, they have the legal status of independent ships; even when these three types of UUVs occasionally navigate on the surface of the water, they also meet the criteria of 'navigation' and can be recognized as ships.[37]

2.3 *Weaponized UUVs—'Autonomous Weapon Systems' in the Context of IHL*

At present, the international community not only does not have a unified definition of 'autonomous weapon systems' (AWS) but also has not yet formed a convention or regulated it by other forms of legislation.

The International Committee of the Red Cross (ICRC)'s codification of AWS issues in the field of international humanitarian law is relatively informative for the characterization of weapon-based UUVs. In 2011, at the 31st International Red Cross and Red Crescent Conference, the ICRC expressed its concerns about autonomous weapons. Two key points of the AWS definition were summarized in a presentation by Catherine Lavande, Head of the ICRC Weapons Division, at the Fully Autonomous Weapons Systems Symposium in Switzerland in 2013. First, an AWS is a weapon that is capable of learning or adjusting its functioning at any time according to its own environment; second, an AWS is capable of operating without intervention or manipulation, without any human intervention or manipulation. search, identify, and attack targets, including humans, with lethal force without intervention or manipulation.[38] In 2017, according to a report submitted by Neil Davidson, Legal Advisor for Science and Technology at the ICRC, AWS were defined as "weapons with critical autonomous functions, i.e., systems that are free from human interference and capable of selecting (finding, locating, tracking, or selecting) and attacking (using force, force, etc.). Davidson's report to the United Nations defines AWS as "weapons systems with critical autonomous functions, i.e., weapons systems that are immune to human interference and are capable of selecting (finding, locating, tracking, or choosing) and attacking (using force,

37 Song Shuhua and Zhao Jinsong, (n 2) 23–25.

38 ICRC, 'Fully autonomous weapons' (21 December 2018) <https://www.icrc.org/zh/doc/resources/documents/statement/2013/09-03-autonomous-weapons.htm.> accessed 2 February 2024.

counteracting, damaging, or destroying) targets".[39] In the above definitions, AWS often requires basic elements such as "autonomy of attack" and "freedom from human interference or manipulation".

Strictly speaking, 'fully autonomous weapons' include anti-rocket systems; anti-missile systems such as the SAD system; anti-artillery and mortar systems; and air defense systems such as the S-400. Unmanned aerial vehicles, unmanned vehicles and UUVs, which can fly, travel or navigate but do not automatically select and attack their targets, would seem to be difficult to qualify as AWSs.[40] However, weaponized UUV technology has evolved rapidly in recent years, and their ability to make autonomous decisions about attacks has been greatly enhanced. The Russian Navy's Poseidon nuclear-powered unmanned underwater vehicle, which was tested in July 2018, is the most advanced and representative. Poseidon UUVs can be launched from two different classes of nuclear submarines, either to launch conventional torpedoes or equipped with nuclear warheads for nuclear strikes; additionally, Poseidon UUVs are capable of automatic intercontinental submergence after locking on to a target, and the depth of the torpedoes they use and the speed of their voyage are both greater than those of similar weapons.[41] The technological development of weapon-type UUVs and their improved ability to select and strike targets have provided them with the essential elements of AWS.

In summary, the type and weight of UUVs have no impact on their legal status; the mode of operation affects their legal status. It is difficult to characterize UUVs as 'warships' in the context of the 'crewed' element of the definition of 'warship' in UNCLOS. From the point of view of UNCLOS and maritime law, and depending on the mode of operation, UUVs have a threefold legal status—ships/ships' apparels or submarines. With the exception of ship-based remotely operated UUVs, which do not have the legal status of independent ships and are more appropriately characterized as appurtenances to a mother ship or warship, i.e., 'ship's apparels', fully autonomous, programmable, and shore-based remotely piloted UUVs can be recognized as 'ships'. A State may also legislate the regulation of various types of UUVs by defining them in general terms as 'submarines'. In addition, from the perspective of international humanitarian law, UUVs carrying weapons against military targets could be considered 'AWS'.

39 Neil Davison, *A legal perspective: Autonomous weapon systems under international humanitarian law*, UNODA Occasional Papers, No. 30 (New York: United Nations, 2017) 5.

40 Ajey Lele, *A Military Perspective on Lethal Autonomous Weapon Systems*, UNODA Occasional Papers, No. 30 (New York: United Nations, 2017) 59.

41 Fang Xiaozhi and Lin (n 3).

3 Legal Challenges Invoked by the Marine Application of UUVs

3.1 *Challenges to the Maritime Jurisdiction of Coastal States under the Law of the Sea Posed by Military UUVs*

UNCLOS provides for the rights and obligations of ships in relation to navigation in different areas of the sea in the form of "zonal approach" management.[42] Accordingly, the navigational rights of UUVs (including the mother ships) in different maritime areas within and beyond the jurisdiction of the coastal State and the limitations thereof are specified below:

First, the issue of the 'innocent passage' of military UUVs in the territorial sea.

Part II of the UNCLOS, titled 'The Territorial Sea,'[43] provides for the innocent passage of all ships (including foreign warships, submarines or other submersibles) but also establishes corresponding restrictions, including refraining from engaging in 'noninnocent activities', complying with the laws and regulations of the coastal State relating to innocent passage,[44] and complying with the provisions of the domestic law of the coastal State when the coastal State has expressly declared that prior authorization or prior notification is required for the passage of warships through its territorial sea. The multiple statuses of military UUVs (ships/ships' apparels, submarines) challenge the 'innocent passage' provision of UNCLOS in the territorial sea: first, in the territorial sea, the launching, landing, or carrying on board a foreign ship of any military device, or its research and surveying activities,[45] are considered by UNCLOS to be 'nonharmless'. Can the activities of pre-programmed UUVs in the territorial sea be included in the category of 'nonharmless passage', given that the deployment of such UUVs from outside the territorial sea to carry out their mission often does not require 'launching, landing or picking up from a vessel'? Second, Article 20 of UNCLOS requires submarines or 'other submarines' to 'on the surface and show their flag' in the territorial sea of another State. However, not only does the practice of States vary as to whether the rule of innocent passage of submarines is strictly observed,[46] but there is also a doctrinal dispute as

---

42 Yoshifumi Tanaka, *The International Law of the Sea* (Singapore: Cambridge University Press, 2012) 4–5.

43 UNCLOS (n 7) art 17.

44 UNCLOS (n 7) art 19(2).

45 UNCLOS (n 7) art 19(2)(f)(j).

46 For example, in October 1981, a submarine from the former Soviet Union ran aground near a Swedish port. The submarine neither notified Sweden before entering its territorial waters, nor received the consent of the Government of Sweden, nor surfaced and navigated and displayed a flag while passing through its territorial waters. In contrast, in June

to whether or not it is 'innocent' when a submarine violates the requirement that 'submarines shall navigate on the surface of the sea and shall display their flags.'[47] Therefore, even if the rule in Article 20 is applicable to UUVs, the details of whether the passage of UUVs in the territorial sea of another State in violation of the 'on the surface and show their flag' rule is an innocent passage and what the legal consequences are in the event of a violation of the rule have yet to be tested in the domestic legislation of the contracting States and in the practice of the States concerned.

Second, passage of military UUVs in international straits/archipelagic waters.

While Article 38 of the UNCLOS provides for the right to transit through international straits for 'ships of all States,'[48] it also emphasizes restrictions on warships. Neither threatens the sovereignty, territorial integrity or political independence of the states bordering the straits nor engages in any activity other than those incidental to the 'normal mode' of their continued uninterrupted and expeditious transit.[49] Articles 52, 53 and 54 apply the regimes of innocent passage and transit passage to archipelagic waters and archipelagic sea lanes, respectively.[50] Article 53, while providing for the 'right of passage through archipelagic sea lanes'[51] in archipelagic sea lanes and airways for 'all ships and aircraft', also emphasizes that such passage is for the 'purpose of continued uninterrupted, expeditious and unobstructed transit' and for

---

2016, a Chinese nuclear submarine surfaced and raised its flag while crossing the Strait of Malacca. A spokesman for the Indonesian navy said that 'the Chinese naval escort operation did not violate the rules and there was no need for an investigation.' See M. Jacobsen, Sweden and the Law of the Sea, in *The Law of the Sea: the European Union and its Member States,* eds. Laura Pineschi and Tullio Treves (Brill/Nijhoff, 1996) 495–500.

47 Huang Zhongcheng, a Chinese scholar based in Taiwan, maintains that submarines are stealthy and that passing through submerged beneath the surface of the water is the usual way of submarines, and does not fall into the category of harmful acts against the coastal State as stipulated in the Convention on the Law of the Sea. Li Hongyun, a mainland scholar, argues that the Convention singles out submarines for the purpose of excluding their underwater navigation from 'nonharmless' acts. Only when a submarine carries out acts in the territorial sea of another State that are not detrimental to the 'peace, good order or security of the coastal State' under article 19, paragraph 2, of the Convention does its submerged conduct fall into the category of 'nonharmless' acts. See LI Hongyun, 'Rights and obligations of the coastal State in the regime of innocent passage through the territorial sea' in *Chinese Yearbook of International Law* (Beijing: Law Press, 1996) 175–176.

48 UNCLOS (n 7) art 38(1).

49 UNCLOS (n 7) art 39(1)(b)(c).

50 Ren Xiaofeng and Cheng Xizhong, 'A Chinese Perspective' (2005) 29 MP 143.

51 UNCLOS (n 7) art 53(1).

the 'exercise of the rights of navigation and overflight in the usual manner'.[52] Unlike ships navigating the surface of the water, submarines (including submersibles) will face the real problem of how to pass through straits or archipelagic sea lanes 'in the `usual manner' of continuing uninterrupted and rapid transit'. On the one hand, the state to which the submarine belongs would interpret the 'usual manner' as underwater rather than surface navigation; on the other hand, the states bordering the strait would argue that the submerged navigation of a submarine in its territorial waters is a threat to its security.[53]

Third, military surveying activities by military UUVs in EEZ of other States.

The United States Navy has a strong 'civilian-military' presence, with overseas military surveying activities generally carried out by warships or naval auxiliaries carrying out surveying activities, including oceanographic, marine geological, geophysical, chemical, biological and acoustic data.[54] The USS Bowditch, the United States survey vessel involved in the 'China–United States unmanned underwater vehicle incident', is a military vessel in civilian 'clothing' used by the United States Naval Meteorology and Oceanography Command and operated by the Military Sealift Command, which employs civilian or contracted crew members in conjunction with scientific researchers from the Naval Oceanographic Service.[55] In the context of the Sino-US UUV Incident and the doctrinal controversy described above, challenges to the jurisdiction of coastal states in the EEZ arising from military surveying activities carried out by UUVs include the following:

1. UNCLOS does not distinguish between 'marine scientific research', 'hydrographic surveys' and 'military surveys'. It is not easy to identify whether marine data collected by UUVs in the EEZs of other states are useful for marine scientific research or military surveys. The use of new technology allows mother ships outside the EEZ to collect data by presetting their data collection programs and then releasing UUVs into the EEZ for data collection. From a military perspective, oceanographic data collected from UUVs are important for the effective operation of submarines in the East and South China Seas, for antisubmarine warfare, for mine warfare, and for antimine warfare; moreover, such classified data

52 UNCLOS (n 7) art 53(3).

53 Donald R. Rothwell and Tim Stephens, *The International Law of the Sea* (Hart Publishing, 2010) 240.

54 J.A. Roach and R.W. Smith, *United States Response to Excessive Maritime Claims* (The Hague: Nijhoff, 1996) 427.

55 Liu Dan (n 5).

are not made public by the military. However, distinguishing between marine scientific research and military measurements on the basis of the use of these data alone is difficult. Many of the technologies used for marine scientific research or military measurements are essentially the same, such as precision navigation systems, multibeam sonars, current meters, and seafloor sampling devices. Currently, there are new technologies, such as UUVs and submarine landers, that are widely used to collect ocean data for both military and civilian purposes.[56] By emphasizing the jurisdiction of the coastal State over marine scientific research, it has been suggested that, in addition to the motivation for the collection of marine data, the economic and applied value of such data to the coastal State is a criterion for distinguishing between marine scientific research or military measurements.[57] Notably, 'criteria', such as the motivation for collecting marine data and the economic value of the data itself, are subjective, making it difficult to distinguish between marine scientific research and military surveying activities carried out by UUVs in the EEZs of other states.

2. There is a difference in State practice as to whether military surveying activities in the EEZ of other States should be subject to the consent or jurisdiction of the coastal State, and military surveying activities carried out by UUVs will tend to complicate that difference. Should military surveying or reconnaissance activities be subsumed under Article 246 of UNCLOS, 'Marine scientific research', to be regulated by the consent regime of the coastal State? Or should it be subsumed under Article 87, 'Navigation-related activities', thus incorporating 'other lawful uses of the sea'?[58] With the exception of the United States and the United Kingdom, which have not legislated on the regulation and jurisdiction of marine scientific research activities, China,[59] India, Australia and other coun-

56 Funnell C and Barton B, *Jane's Survey Vessels*, 3rd ed., 2002–2003 (Coulsdon, Jane's Information Group, 2002) 12.

57 Sam Bateman, "Hydrographic Surveying in the EEZ: Differences and Overlaps with Marine Scientific Research" (2005) 29 MP 166–172.

58 Qu Guangqing and Qu Bo, *The Law of the Sea* (Renmin University Press, 2017) 217.

59 Article 8 of the Surveying and Mapping Law of the People's Republic of China (amended for the second time in 2007) provides that 'foreign organizations or individuals engaging in surveying and mapping activities in the territory of the People's Republic of China and in other maritime areas under the jurisdiction of the People's Republic of China shall be subject to the approval of the competent department for surveying, mapping and geoinformation under the State Council, in conjunction with the surveying and mapping department of the armed forces, and shall comply with the provisions of the relevant laws and administrative regulations of the People's Republic of China'.

> tries prohibit, in principle, military activities of other countries in their EEZ and apply a system of prior consent from the coastal State.[60] In addition to the 'UUV incident' in the South China Sea in 2016, incidents such as the 'Bowditch' in the Yellow Sea in 2001 and the 'Immaculate' in the South China Sea in 2009 confirmed the different positions of China and the U.S. in terms of military surveying activities in the EEZ. First, the United States argues that military surveying activities do not fall within the scope of 'marine scientific research' under Part 13 of UNCLOS and that Article 56 grants a coastal State jurisdiction over '(scientific) research' rather than 'surveying' in its EEZ; therefore, a coastal State does not have jurisdiction over military intelligence-gathering or surveying activities in its EEZ;[61] second, military surveying activities fall within the 'freedom of the seas' in article 58, paragraph 1, as 'other internationally lawful uses of the seas and oceans' within the meaning of Article 87, and may be carried out freely within the EEZ of the coastal State without the authorization of that State;[62] third, the Convention restricts the activities of warships only in the provisions relating to the territorial sea and other waters, while there is no explicit restriction in Part 5, and military reconnaissance or surveying activities in the EZZ should be lawful in accordance with the principle of international law of 'Nullum crimen sine lege'. as stated in the 'Lotus' case.[63]

In contrast, China maintains that, first, the rules on marine scientific research in Part 13 of UNCLOS apply not only to waters under national jurisdiction, such as the territorial sea and EEZ but also to the high seas beyond the limits of national jurisdiction. The rules in Part 13 therefore apply to all marine scientific research activities, including military surveying and reconnaissance activities, irrespective of the type of waters;[64] second, the 'freedom of navigation and overflight' and 'other internationally lawful uses of the seas and oceans' of the EEZ referred to in Article 58 do not include military surveying activities in the

60 Jin Yongming, 'Military activities in the exclusive economic zone and the State practice' (2008) 2 LS 121.

61 Raul P. Pedrozo, "Preserving Navigational Rights and Freedoms: The Right to Conduct Military Activities in China's Exclusive Economic Zone" (2010) 9*CJIL* para. 4.

62 J.A. Roach and R.W. Smith (n 54) 448–449.

63 See Raul P. Pedrozo (n 61) para.4; Yoshifumi Tanaka (n 42) 344.

64 Ren Xiaofeng and Cheng Xizhong (n 50) 141–142; Jin Yongming, Modern System of the Law of the Sea and China' s Practice (2018) 6CRIL 122; Haiwen Zhang, 'Maritime Hegemony of the United States? Comments on Raul (Pete) Pedrozo's Article on Military Activities in the EEZ' (2010) 9 CJIL 12.

EEZs of other States;[65] third, the obligation of a State to exercise 'due regard' in its activities in EEZ of another State,[66] Whether a foreign military activity in EZZ of a coastal State is carried out with due regard for the coastal State shall be judged by whether the activity jeopardizes the security interests, sovereign rights, jurisdiction and other rights of the coastal State under general international law and UNCLOS;[67] fourth, Article 58 and 246 of UNCLOS provide, by way of reference to Article 88 and 240, respectively, that marine scientific research in EEZ shall be conducted 'exclusively for peaceful purposes'.[68] These provisions may be invoked by the coastal State to exercise jurisdiction over activities, including military surveying and reconnaissance, which it considers to be nonpeaceful uses.

As the control of the ocean by military powers such as the United States shifts from the surface to the underwater space, the 'underwater war' and 'legal war' triggered by UUVs will cause disputes in the waters surrounding coastal states in the future,[69] complicating the differences among countries on the issue of military surveys in the EEZ.

3.2 *Challenges to the Traditional Doctrine of Sovereign Immunity Posed by Military UUVs*

On the question of whether military UUVs can enjoy immunity, before the United States–China UUV Incident in 2016, some scholars were skeptical of the US Commander's Handbook on the Law of Naval Operations, which states that "UUVs used exclusively by the government and engaged in non-commercial service enjoy sovereign immunity and that their status" does not depend on the platform from which they are launched". This would seem to suggest that governmental UUVs deployed by or under the control of commercial vessels that do not enjoy immunity would not lose their immunity;[70] but in reality, such UUVs have a subordinate status to the mother ships and do not even enjoy sovereign immunity. However, 'skeptics' are not the majority in the United States. In the aftermath of the incident, the United States Department of State and Pentagon spokespersons both claimed that the UUV identified by the Chinese was a 'vessel' that 'enjoys sovereign

65 Yoshifumi Tanaka (n 42) 345.
66 UNCLOS (n 7) art 58(3).
67 Zou Ligang, 'On the right of the State to regulate foreign military activities in peacetime in the exclusive economic zone' (2012) 6 CLS 53.
68 Ren Xiaofeng and Cheng Xizhong (n 50) 142.
69 Hu Bo, 'The Transformation of US Military Maritime Strategy: From 'From Land to Sea' to 'Return to Sea Control' (2018) 5 JISSS 83–84.
70 Rob McLaughlin (n 10) 110.

immunity' and went on to accuse the 'Chinese side of violating international law in its salvage actions'.[71] Several United States scholars have even argued that the UUVs deployed by the Bowditch were carrying out military activities, while the United States has consistently insisted that military activities outside territorial waters should be exempted from the jurisdiction of the coastal State. The legal basis for military UUV immunity is Articles 29, 32, 95–96, etc., of UNCLOS.[72] The military UUVs do pose a proactive challenge to the traditional doctrine of immunity under international law, and the United States official characterization of military UUVs in general terms as 'ships' rather than 'warships' still has difficulty concealing the dilemma of military UUV positioning for the following reasons:

First, the United States has transplanted the concept of a 'government ship' from UNCLOS and replaced it with the concept of a 'public vessel' in the domestic law of the United States, thus claiming that military UUVs are entitled to treatment beyond that of 'government ships'. The studies by Jimmie Kraska and Raul Pedrozo, as well as Commander's Handbook on the Law of Naval Operations, point to military UUVs as 'government vessels' that are 'used exclusively for government noncommercial services.'[73] The concepts of 'public vessel' under United States domestic law and 'governmental vessel' under UNCLOS are the most similar. The United States Code defines a 'public vessel' as a vessel engaged in 'noncommercial service' and 'owned or bareboat chartered and operated by the Government of the United States or a foreign government.'[74] These include hydrofoils, hovercraft, submersibles, floating rafts with or without power, and fixed or floating platforms;[75] this definition could even include warships, naval auxiliaries, and marine police vessels in the category of public vessels.[76] In 1812, in the landmark case of the Schooner Exchange v. McFaddon,

71 See Sam LaGrone, 'Chinese Seize U.S. Navy Unmanned Vehicle' (December 16, 2016) <https://news.usni.org/2016/12/16/breaking-chinese-seize-u-s-navy-unmanned-vehicle> accessed 23 November 2023; 'China Agrees to Give Back US Underwater Drone Seized in South China Sea' (17 December 2016) <https://abcnews.go.com/International/china-agrees-give-back-us-underwater-drone-seized/story?id=44257232> accessed 23 November 2023.

72 See James Kraska and Raul Pedrozo (n 24); Michael N. Schmitt and David S. Goddard (n 6) 580.

73 See U.S. Office of the Chief of Naval Operations, U.S. Marine Corps, U.S. Coast Guard, *The Commander's Handbook on the Law of Naval Operations* (July 2007) Article 2.3.6; James Kraska and Raul Pedrozo (n 24).

74 See "Public Vessel", 46 U.S. Code § 2101. General definitions.

75 See Article 2, 33 U.S. Code § 2502—Definitions.

76 Zhao Weidong and Peng Yin,'The U.S. Coast Guard Cutters and Boats—Warship or Government Ships?' (2016) 2JCMPA 46–48; Kim Kiel, 'The Dauntless Incident: Should a United

the U.S. Supreme Court affirmed that because warships are instruments in the political and military service of the state, the domestic courts of the U.S. do not have jurisdiction over the military vessels of a sovereign state.[77] UNCLOS juxtaposes warships, naval auxiliaries and government ships and treats them differently from merchant ships. The associations between military UUVs and these three ship types are as follows: (1) Warships. As noted in Chapter II, military UUVs cannot be characterized as warships because they do not meet the key elements of Article 29, 'Warships', and the U.S. has never made such a claim. (2) Naval auxiliary ships. Article 236 of UNCLOS refers to naval auxiliary[78] without defining it, and the 2007 edition of Commander's Handbook on the Law of Naval Operations defines it as 'a ship, other than a warship, owned by and under the absolute control of the armed forces of a nation,'[79] with a number of U.S. Navy ships, U.S. Coast Guard ships, including those that are not combat ships, such as the Immaculate and the Bowditch. A number of U.S. Coast Guard ships, including those that are not combatants, such as the USS Immaculate and the USS Bowditch,[80] are categorized as naval auxiliaries. (3) The Convention distinguishes between 'government ships' and warships and naval auxiliaries and further divides them into two categories of government ships, 'for commercial purposes' and 'for noncommercial purposes'. The latter may enjoy corresponding immunity under the convention. Therefore, despite the similarity of concepts, the scope of vessels covered by 'service vessels' under the domestic law of the U.S. is obviously much broader than that of 'government vessels' under the UNCLOS. On the surface, the U.S. side characterizes military UUVs as 'government ships' under UNCLOS, but in fact, it intends to confuse the boundaries between 'government ships' and warships and naval auxiliary vessels and asserts that they enjoy the rights of 'service ships' under the context of U.S. domestic law. It claims that it enjoys the treatment of an 'official vessel' over a 'government vessel' in the context of the domestic law of the U.S.

Second, even if military UUVs enjoy immunity because of their status as 'government ships' that are 'independent of the mother ship' and 'owned or operated by the State and used exclusively for government noncommercial

States Public Vessel Be Declared a Floating Piece of United States Territory for Citizenship Purposes' (1989) 21UMIALR 136.

77 The Schooner Exch. v. McFaddon (1812) 11 U.S. (7 Cranch) 116, 3 L. Ed. 287.

78 UNCLOS (n 7) art 232.

79 U.S Office of the Chief of Naval Operations, U.S. Marine Corps, U.S. Coast Guard, *The Commander's Handbook on the Law of Naval Operations* (July 2007) Article 2.3.1.

80 See James Kraska, 'Convention on the Law of the Sea-warship immunity-scope of applicability of Convention-provisional measures-definition of warship-arbitral jurisdiction' (2013) 2AJIL 409–410.

services,'[81] the U.S. claims that they enjoy 'absolute immunity' without any maritime boundaries or limitations, which is inconsistent with UNCLOS. The U.S. assertion that it enjoys 'absolute immunity' regardless of maritime zone and without restrictions is also inconsistent with UNCLOS. 'In the 'UUV Incident', the United States side claimed that (1) the unmanned aerial vehicle deployed by the Bowditch was engaged in military activities, and the United States has consistently maintained that military activities in 'international waters' outside the territorial sea are exempt from the provisions of the United Nations Convention on the Law of the Sea. The United States has consistently maintained that military activities in 'international waters' outside the territorial sea are exempt from the jurisdiction of the coastal State. (2) The United States has interpreted the immunity of military UAVs as 'a privilege granted by one State to the government of another State on the basis of comity', i.e., 'absolute immunity' from arrest, seizure, interference, and other measures of enforcement from the coastal State.[82]

However, the U.S. claim is inconsistent with the relevant regulation of UNCLOS for the following reasons:

First, the U.S. treats maritime areas beyond the territorial sea as 'international waters' primarily for reasons of naval operational convenience rather than international law.[83] The 'subregional management' regime of UNCLOS divides the global maritime area into a territorial sea, a contiguous zone, the EEZ and high seas.[84] Types of ships, such as government ships, enjoy different immunities in different sea areas: (1) Article 32 of the Convention excludes from immunity the cases listed in subsection A (rules of innocent passage, etc.), article 30 (noncompliance with the laws and regulations of the coastal State), and article 31 (loss or damage suffered by the coastal State) of the regime of the territorial sea; (2) Article 58 (1) and (2), while introducing freedom of navigation and overflight on the high seas into the EEZ, attach a number of prerequisites, such as 'not inconsistent with this Part', 'with respect to the rights and obligations of the coastal State', 'subject to the laws and regulations made by the coastal State', etc.; (3) Article 95 and 96 "complete immunity" granted to warships and government ships is also limited to the high seas; and (4) the immunity granted by Article 236 to warships, naval auxiliaries, government ships or aircraft refers specifically to the fact that the provisions of the Convention 'relating to the protection and preservation of the marine environment' do not

---

81 See James Kraska and Raul Pedrozo (n 24); Michael N. Schmitt and David S. Goddard (n 6) 580.

82 Ibid.

83 Bao Yinan, 'The US 'Excessive Maritime Claims': A Critical Analysis' (2017) 5 IS 113.

84 Yoshifumi Tanaka (n 42) 4–5.

apply to these subjects. The exemptions granted by Article 236 to warships, naval auxiliaries, government ships or aircraft are also limited to the high seas.

Second, the content of the immunity of government ships under general international law is not the 'absolute immunity' from control that the United States side advocates. State immunity in international law is the right of a State not to be subject to the jurisdiction of its domestic courts in another State, also known as jurisdictional immunity of the State; it is one of the various forms of jurisdictional immunity in international law, also known as 'sovereign immunity' or 'sovereign immunity of the State'. 'sovereign immunity of the State'.[85] Articles 32 and 96 of UNCLOS do not specify what immunities are enjoyed by government ships, but the 'answer' can be found in the following treaties or rules of general international law: (1) The Protocol of 1934 to the Convention for the Unification of Certain Rules relating to the Immunity of State-owned Ships (1926) provides for immunity for government ships from 'any form of detention or arrest' in judicial proceedings [Articles 3, 5 and 7, The Protocol of 1934 additional to the 1926 International Convention for the Protection of the Marine Environment]. The 1934 Protocol to the Convention for the Unification of Certain Rules relating to the Immunity of State-owned Ships (1926) states that government ships enjoy immunity from 'any form of detention or arrest' in judicial proceedings.[86] (2) The 1994 UN International Law Commission Draft Articles on Jurisdictional Immunities of States and Their Property[87] states that 'ships owned or operated by States' are immune from the jurisdiction of States other than the flag State with respect to such matters as collisions of ships, common sea losses, repairs, contracts relating to the ship and the consequences of pollution of the marine environment.[88] It can be seen that 'sovereign immunity' does not exempt foreign warships or government ships from liability for violating the law, nor does it exempt the coastal State from taking certain measures in accordance with the law, such as removal, surveillance, verification and identification.[89]

85 Bai Guimei and Meng Xianweieds., *Peking University Encyclopedia of Law Public International Law—Private International Law* (Peking University Press, 2016) 271–272.

86 Article 3, 5 and 7, The Protocol of 1934 additional to the 1926 International Convention for the Unification of Certain Rules Relating to the Immunity of State-owned Vessels.

87 The International Law Commission's Draft Articles on Jurisdictional Immunities of States and Their Property were adopted by the General Assembly of the United Nations on 2 December 2004 as the Convention on Jurisdictional Immunities of States and Their Property, open for signature by States parties. See Bai Guimei and Meng Xianwei eds. (n 85) 271–272.

88 Draft Articles on Jurisdictional Immunities of States and Their Property, art 16(3).

89 Guo Zhonguan and Zou Ligang, 'Analysis on the Incident of Unmanned Underwater Vehicle in the South China Sea From the Angle of International Law' (2017) 4 JHU(HSC) 18.

3.3 *Challenges to International Humanitarian Law Posed by Weapon-type UUVs*

With the development of artificial intelligence and information technology, technology has basically ceased to be the bottleneck restricting the development of military unmanned systems, and various unmanned technologies, including unmanned aircraft and UUVs, have been widely used in the military field and have achieved effective results.[90] Not all military UUVs can be categorized as autonomous weapons; however, given their multifunctional characteristics and the advantages of carrying out multiple missions, weapon-type UUVs such as Russia's Poseidon can carry fish or even nuclear warheads to carry out military strikes; thus, such UUVs are undoubtedly autonomous weapon systems. This raises the question of the legality of and responsibility for the use of weapon-type unmanned underwater vehicles under the existing international law governing 'autonomous weapon systems'.

The use of drones, weapon-type unmanned underwater vehicles and battlefield robots; intelligent unmanned combat weapon arms control; 'autonomous weapon systems'; and the 'Lethal Autonomous Weapons System' (LAWS) has received close attention from the international community. In November 2012, Human Rights Watch, a human rights organization, and the International Human Rights Clinic at Harvard University jointly released a report titled Losing Humanity: The Case Against Murderous Robots, which called on governments to prohibit the development, manufacture and use of fully autonomous weapons systems by signing binding international agreements and enacting domestic laws.[91] Currently, there are two types of platforms for international discussions on autonomous weapon systems, namely, specialized discussions within the framework of the United Nations in the Human Rights Council, the First Committee of the General Assembly of the United Nations (the Disarmament and International Security Committee) and the Convention on Certain Conventional Weapons (CCW), and ongoing discussions of ICRC on the topic of 'autonomous weapons'.[92] The CCW negotiating mechanism has now become the central platform for arms control on autonomous weapons.

90 Chen Huibin and Zeng Yangzhi, 'Legitimacy, and future challenges of military unmanned systems' (2018) 6 MD 49.

91 Human Rights Watch and The International Human Rights Clinic (IHRC), 'Losing Humanity, the Case Against Killer Robots' (19 November 2012) 5 <http://hrp.law.harvard.edu/staff/the-case-against-killer-robots-an-international-human-rights-clinic-and-human-rights-watch-report/> accessed 23 November 2023.

92 MA Xinmin, 'International Humanitarian Law in Flux: Development and New Agendas—Commemoration of the 40th Anniversary of the 1977 Additional Protocols to the Geneva

From 2013–2018, a total of 85 countries publicly stated their position on AWS in multilateral settings, and as of April 2018, 26 countries, including Argentina, Austria, Mexico, Chile, Brazil, and Palestine, have called for a ban on LAWs, but there are still many disagreements among these countries on restricting AWS.[93] On the one hand, the U.S., U.K., and Russia tend to view LAWs as future weapon systems and reject bans or restrictions on LAWs.[94] On the other hand, autonomous weapon systems have a high technological threshold and high financial investment, and groups of developing countries, such as the Group of African States and the Organization of the Non-Aligned Movement, have either emphasized the need to prohibit fully autonomous weapons not under the control of mankind or called for the elaboration of a binding convention to prohibit or restrict fully autonomous weapons.[95]

One of the major reasons for the disagreement among States on the control of AWS is that the future development of AWS in the direction of autonomy into lethal autonomous weapons will seriously challenge the constraints of modern warfare under general international law and ethics, particularly international humanitarian law, as reflected in the following aspects:

First, AWS challenges the definition of the 'subject of war' in existing international law.

International humanitarian law, represented by the Geneva Conventions of 1949 and the two Additional Protocols of 1977, solidifies the concept of 'combatant' as 'a person authorized to take a direct part in hostilities'.[96] With the growing anthropomorphic trend of autonomous weapon systems such as UUVs, drones, and battlefield robots, the Italian scholar Ugo Pagallo has proposed applying the criterion of the combatant to autonomous weapon systems and thus judging the legitimacy of AWS when using force.[97] Although this view is not mainstream, the trend of 'dehumanization' and 'dehumanization of

---

Conventions' (2017) 4CRIL 17; LIU Yangyue, 'Arms Control of Autonomous Weapons in the Context of Global Security Governance' (2018) 2 JISS 54.

93 See Campaign to Stop Killer Robots, 'Country Views on Killer Robots' (April 13, 2018) 1 <https://www.stopkillerrobots.org/wp-ontent/uploads/2018/04/KRC_CountryViews_13Apr2018.pdf> accessed 23 November 2018.

94 See Elsa Kania, 'China's Strategic Ambiguity and Shifting Approach to Lethal Autonomous Weapons Systems', (17 April 2018) <https://www.lawfareblog.com/chinas-strategic-ambiguity-and-shifting-approach-lethal-autonomous-weapons-systems> accessed 23 November 2023.

95 Campaign to Stop Killer Robots, 'Country Views on Killer Robots' (13 April 2018) 2.

96 Protocol Additional to the Fourth Geneva Convention of 12 August 1949, and relating to the Protection of Victims of International Armed Conflicts, art 43(2).

97 Ugo Pagallo, 'Robots of Just War: A Legal Perspective' (2011) 24 PT 313–314.

control'[98] in the use of AWS in future wars will not only impact the inherent notion that 'human beings are the only subjects of war' but also raise the issue of responsibility for violations of international humanitarian law. By granting 'subject status' to 'machines', the causal chain of reasonable attribution based on the responsibility of the commander would be broken.[99]

Second, AWS will challenge the fundamental principles of IHL, such as the principles of distinction, proportionality, and the precautionary principle.

First, the ability of autonomous weapon systems to comply with the principle of distinction is severely limited by the complex operational environment. There is a 'gray area' in the target identification criteria of the principle of distinction, and the risk of violation is not reduced by the fact that vague criteria are preprogrammed into the artificial intelligence programs of AWS to differentiate between combatants and civilians or between civilian objects and military targets.[100]

Second, the principle of proportionality requires that 'the loss of civilian life and property or injury to civilians must not be excessive in relation to the concrete and direct military advantage anticipated'. While the sensors of autonomous weapons allow for the quantitative processing of battlefield information, situational awareness and capabilities are lacking, making it difficult to make qualitative judgments about the target of attack. According to the ICRC, when assessing the programming aspects of fully autonomous weapons, adhering to the principle of proportionality requires a unique level of human judgment that current programming technology does not yet allow artificial intelligence to achieve.[101]

Again, the precautionary principle requires that constant care be taken in the conduct of military operations to spare civilians and civilian objects and that all possible precautions be taken to avoid civilian deaths, minimize incidental loss of civilian life or damage to civilian objects, whatever the circumstances.[102] Due to the complexity of the battlefield environment and the emergence of dual-use installations, the assessment, selection and application

98 Dong Qingling, 'The New Ethics of War: Supervise and Constrain the Lethal Autonomous Weapons Systems (LAWS)' (2018) 4 IR 51.

99 He Bei, 'Nature and Path: International Regulation of Autonomous Weapon System' (2016) 4 JXPIP 98.

100 ibid 99–100.

101 International Committee of the Red Cross, 'Fully autonomous weapons' (21 December 2018) <https://www.icrc.org/zh/doc/resources/documents/statement/2013/09-03-autonomous-weapons.htm.> accessed 23 November 2023.

102 See 'Rule 15. Precautions in Attack, <https://ihl-databases.icrc.org/customary-ihl/eng/docs/v1_rul_rule15> accessed 23 November 2023.

of the precautionary principle required in an attack to minimize civilian casualties is not a matter of retrofitting an autonomous weapon with an 'enemy identification device.'[103]

Third, the issue of AWS attribution was also a difficult issue before IHL. With the further improvement of intelligence and learning capabilities, AWS will evolve toward less human intervention, more independent decision-making, and more unpredictable operational consequences. If a highly autonomous weapon system mistakenly injures (kills) civilians or makes a mistake that violates the principles of international humanitarian law due to unpredictable reasons such as incomplete information, miscalculations, and hardware and software failures, how to attribute responsibility becomes a difficult question.[104] These dilemmas include the following: who is responsible for the violations of international humanitarian law committed by AWS? Who will be held accountable for the decisions made by AWS, the programmers, the manufacturer, or the commanders who deployed the weapon system? It is difficult to deny that neither the manufacturer or programmers of the AWS, the commanders carrying out the military mission, nor the AWS itself can be the subject of responsibility for the killings.[105]

Due to their special characteristics, underwater battlefields have high requirements for the autonomous operation of UUVs. Existing technologies can embed automatic target recognition devices in UUV platforms to enable them to detect, classify, localize, and recognize targets autonomously. However, the underwater environment is characterized by complexity, ambiguity and uncertainty, and the sea state will have a significant impact on the performance of UUV platforms, especially sensors, in shallow waters.[106] The development of future UUVs toward full autonomy is a goal pursued by all navies. Attack UAVs themselves do not violate the existing IHL, but as an autonomous weapon system, they, like other AWSs, may be used by human beings in a way that violates IHL; therefore, the IHL and ethical issues of war that may accompany them should not be ignored.

103 See Ronald C. Arkin, *Governing Lethal Behavior in Autonomous Robots* (2010, CRE Press) 127–153.

104 Liu Yangyue, (n 92) 57.

105 See Robert Sparrow, "Robotic Weapons and the Future of War," in Paolo Tripodi and Jessica Wolfendale, eds.*New Wars and New Soldiers: Military Ethics in the Contemporary World* (Ashgate Publishing Limited, 2011) 121–126.

106 Qian Dong, Zhao Jiang and Yang Dong, 'A Review of U.S. Military Unmanned System Development Plan' (2017) 2 JUUS 107–147.

4 China's Response to the Application of UUV in the Ocean

With the strategic transformation of long-term planning for underwater warfare[107] in the U.S., the struggle for sea control will shift from the surface of the water to the underwater space in the future. The deployment of military unmanned submarine vehicles by the United States and its alliance in the East China Sea, the South China Sea and other waters to achieve military goals and political objectives will complicate the maritime situation in the jurisdiction zones of China. In addition to the technological research and development of its own UUVs, China should comprehensively respond to the following legal aspects:

4.1 *To Legislate, Amend and Consolidate Laws Corresponding to the Activities of UUVs and Their Mother Ships in Other Countries in Maritime Areas under China's Jurisdiction*

Regarding the legal regulation of unmanned submarine vehicles and their mother ships in other countries in maritime areas under our jurisdiction, in addition to amending the Maritime Traffic Safety Law, China should also sort out and consolidate other relevant maritime-related laws and regulations.

First, the draft Basic Law on the Oceans, which is being prepared by the legislative and maritime affairs departments, should categorize UAVs as 'ships' and implement differentiated controls according to maritime areas. In refining the draft Basic Law of the Oceans, attention should be given to the connection between the application of unmanned technology in the oceans and China's maritime rights and interests, in addition to clearly categorizing unmanned submarine vehicles as 'vessels' and implementing differentiated control according to maritime areas in the 'Definition of Terms' or 'Supplementary Provisions' sections. In addition to clearly categorizing UAVs as 'ships' in the 'Definition of Terms' or 'Supplementary Provisions' section and including civil and military UAVs in the regulation, differentiated control should be carried out on UAVs in different sea areas, such as territorial waters and exclusive economic zones; in the 'Comprehensive Management of the Oceans and Seas' chapter, differentiated control should be carried out on UAVs and their mother ships entering different types of sea areas in China. In the chapter titled 'Comprehensive management of the oceans', an authorization system should be adopted for the entry of unmanned underwater vehicles and their mother ships into different types of maritime areas.[108]

107 Hu Bo (n 69) 81–84.
108 Wang Shumin and Tang Xiaocong (n 13) 3–7.

Second, the flaws in article 53 of the Exposure Draft of the Maritime Traffic Safety Law regarding 'submersibles' should be amended. Since the concept and mode of management of the Maritime Traffic Safety Law lag behind the needs of the national strategy of 'building a strong maritime nation', scholars in China have long called for attention to be given to the problem of illegal intrusion by foreign vessels (including submersibles) and corresponding amendments to be made.[109] In February 2017, 33 years after the adoption of the Safety of Maritime Traffic Law, Article 53 of the Ministry of Transportation's Safety of Maritime Traffic Law (Draft Revision for Public Opinion) stipulated that 'a submersible of foreign nationality passing through China's territorial sea shall navigate on the surface of the sea, fly the flag of the flag state, and report to the maritime administration agency.' The separate article on 'submersibles of foreign nationality'[110] in the Exposure Draft not only absorbs and draws on Article 20 of UNCLOS and Article 7 of China's 1992 Law on the Territorial Sea and Contiguous Zone on submersibles 'navigating on the surface of the sea and displaying its flag' but is also a response of China's legislation to the 'Sino-US UUV incident' at the end of 2016.

Again, laws and regulations related to marine scientific research should also be revised. Since UUVs can be launched from shore-based and surface ships and submarines[111] and the boundaries between the military missions carried out by UUVs and surveying or scientific research are not sufficiently clear, the revision of laws and regulations relating to marine scientific research should also be put on the agenda. China implements an endorsement system for marine scientific research in the exclusive economic zone and continental shelf by international organizations, foreign organizations or individuals, and the Exclusive Economic Zone and Continental Shelf Law not only stipulates that China exercises jurisdiction over marine scientific research in the exclusive economic zone and continental shelf[112] but also stipulates that such marine scientific research shall comply with Chinese laws and regulations.[113] Such a provision is also embodied in article 8 of the Law on

109 Li Zhiwen and Fan Tianjiao, 'On the amendment to Maritime Traffic Safety Law from the perspective of national marine interests' (2014) 2CJML 3–8; Li Jian, 'China intends to amend the Maritime Traffic Safety Law—safeguarding maritime rights and interests and polishing the maritime 'traffic light'' (China Defense News, February 24, 2017) 10.

110 Exposure Draft of the Maritime Transportation Safety, art 130.

111 Qian Dong, Zhao Jiang and Yang Dong (n 106) 137.

112 Law on the Exclusive Economic Zone and the Continental Shelf of the People's Republic of China (PRC) art 3(2), 4(2).

113 ibid, art 9.

Surveying and Mapping.[114] However, the lack of supporting regulations or bylaws in the abovementioned laws has led to practical problems in marine law enforcement regarding what constitutes marine scientific research activities[115] as well as determining the scope of activities and the types of activities, which need to be refined in future amendments to the law. In addition, the 1996 Regulations on the Administration of Marine Scientific Research Involving Foreign Countries point to the scope of application of foreign parties, either alone or in cooperation with the Chinese side, to 'use ships or other means of delivery or facilities' to conduct marine scientific research in China's 'inland sea, territorial sea, and other sea areas under China's jurisdiction'.[116] This provision is not included in its scope of application of marine scientific research activities carried out by unmanned underwater vehicles, which should be fully taken into account in future revisions.

4.2 *Participation in International Conventions on the Creation of Autonomous Weapon Systems and the Enhancement of China's Voice in this Field*

For many years, China has appeared in the area of the law of the sea as a participant and a follower. With the changes in the international situation and in the maritime situation around China, in the process of constructing and reshaping the order and rules of the oceans, China is transforming itself from a passive to an active formulator of the rules of the oceans and from a bearer to a provider of the rules of the oceans.[117] The adoption of the Code for Unplanned Encounters at Sea, which China pushed through at the annual meeting of the Western Pacific Naval Forum held in China in 2014, or the Code of Conduct in the South China Sea, which is being negotiated between China and ASEAN countries,[118] are strong evidence of China's creation of, or participation in, international rule-making.

114 Law of the People's Republic of China on Surveying and Mapping, adopted at the 29th meeting of the Standing Committee of the 7th National People's Congress on December 28, 1992, and amended for the 2nd time at the 27th meeting of the Standing Committee of the 12th National People's Congress on April 27, 2017.

115 Jin Yongming (n 64) 125.

116 Article 2 of the Provisions on the Administration of Foreign-Related Marine Scientific Research (PRC) (June 18, 1996).

117 Jin Yongming (n 64) 45.

118 State Council Information Office, "China's Asia-Pacific Security Cooperation Policy," (11 January 2017) <http://www.gov.cn/zhengce/2017-01/11/content_5158864.htm> accessed 23 November 2023.

The current attention of the international legal community to the international law and ethical and moral challenges posed by military unmanned technologies, including UUVs, is reflected in the discussion and development of international rules on autonomous weapons, but the relevant legislation is still in its infancy. While unmanned systems and smart weapons can keep commanders and fighters off the battlefield and out of harm, they also reduce the political risks and moral pressures of waging war.[119] IHL has a limited role in constraining armed conflict; it does not prohibit the use of force, nor does it prevent the application of new scientific and technological breakthroughs to armed conflict.[120] The fact that the international community has not yet concluded a specific treaty banning or restricting autonomous weapon systems does not mean that autonomous weapon systems are not subject to relevant treaties or customary international law in the field of international humanitarian law.[121] In the international arena of the CCW Talks, the two position papers issued by China to date represent the evolution of China's strategic considerations of AWS and its corresponding diplomatic stance. The position paper submitted by China at the Fifth Review Conference of the CCW in 2016, while stating that 'Defining the concept and scope of LAWs is a prerequisite for exploring other aspects', also endorsed the idea of developing countries 'promoting the formulation of a binding agreement to regulate LAWs'.[122] In April 2018, the representative of China emphasized that the ban on LAWs is an 'ban on their use.'[123] China's position paper released in the same month identified five characteristics of LAWs: (1) lethality; (2) autonomy, i.e., they do not require human intervention and control throughout the execution of the mission; (3) inability to terminate, i.e., once activated, there is no way to end the device's mission; (4) indiscriminate effect, i.e., the ability to carry out lethal and maiming missions no matter what the conditions, scenarios, and targets are; and (5) evolution, i.e., they can learn autonomously through interaction with its environment and expand its functions and capabilities in ways that exceed

119 Hu Bo (n 69) 95–96.

120 Sheng Hongsheng, 'The Use of Force: Evolving Norms since World War II' (2016) 2 JISS 110.

121 He Bei (n 99) 98–99.

122 See 'The position paper submitted by the Chinese delegation to CCW 5th Review Conference' <https://www.unog.ch/80256EDD006B8954/(httpAssets)/DD1551E60648CEBBC125808A005954FA/$file/China's+Position+Paper.pdf> accessed 23 November 2023.

123 See Campaign to Stop Killer Robots, 'Country Views on Killer Robots' (13 April 2018) <https://www.stopkillerrobots.org/wp-ontent/uploads/2018/04/KRC_CountryViews_13Apr2018.pdf> accessed 23 November 2023.

human expectations.[124] 'Scholars at the Center for a New American Security have commented on two Chinese position papers: first, China's 'strategic ambiguity' on LAWs and its desire to preserve options; and second, the '2018 Position Paper' on LAWs.' The narrow interpretation of LAWs implies that China will in the future take a legitimizing position on the development of semi-automated or even fully autonomous weapon systems.[125] In fact, there is no excuse for China's position adjustment; AWS itself is not a prohibited weapon but rather whether and where it is deployed still depends on human beings; therefore, even though AWS is still in the experimental stage and its ability to make distinctions and proportionality judgments is limited, its technological risks can still be circumvented through appropriate deployment.[126] The international law regulation of AWS must start from the discussion of its technical characteristics, on the basis of which further consideration will be given to issues such as AWS and artificial intelligence, AWS and arms control, and the application of IHL to AWS.[127]

With the development of artificial intelligence technology, unmanned submarine vehicles could be developed into fully autonomous weapon systems, and attack-type unmanned submarine vehicles could be included in the scope of discussions on CCW talks, thus impacting the 'underwater warfare' of technologically developed countries and the struggle for sea control in our neighboring waters. Instead of focusing only on the technology of military unmanned systems, China should take the initiative to participate in discussions and rule-making on international platforms for autonomous weapon systems and explore the norms for the research, development, deployment and use of military unmanned systems that are appropriate for China's national conditions, thereby enhancing China's right to speak in the field of military unmanned technology at the international level.[128]

5 Conclusion

In the marine sector, the law tends to lag behind the development of science and technology, while the former can provide finer and more subtle

124 See 'Position Paper of China' CCW/GGE.1/2018/WP.7 (11 April 2018) <https://www.unog.ch/80256EDD006B8954/(httpAssets)/E42AE83BDB3525D0C125826C0040B262/$file/CCW_GGE.1_2018_WP.7.pdf> accessed 23 November 2023.

125 See Elsa Kania (n 94).

126 Shao Di, *Study on the legality of autonomous weapons systems from the perspective of international humanitarian law* (2017) 2 LV133, 133–134.

127 'Position Paper of China' (n 124).

128 Chen Huibin &Zeng Yangzhi (n 90) 53.

management and regulation of technological innovation.[129] UUVs can be used for both military and civilian purposes, and current study on their legal status has focused on three doctrines: the 'warship and submarine theory', the 'ship's apparels theory and the vessel's theory', and the 'autonomous weapons system theory'. This paper argues that, from the point of view of the operation mode, UAVs have a threefold legal status: ships (including ship's apparels), submarines and autonomous weapon systems.

To meet the requirement of 'zero casualties' in future wars, intelligent and unmanned weapons have become important trends, and as described by Rob Mycock, 'sinking an UUV is relatively less harmful than sinking a more expensive, manned submersible.'[130] The application of UUVs by technologically advanced countries for the control of the sea, especially for 'underwater warfare', is and will continue to be a challenge to many areas of international law, such as the law of the sea and the law of international humanitarian law. China should make early preparations in terms of technological research and development of UUVs, domestic legislative amendments and international rule-making to provide better technical and legal protection and support for maritime security in the context of the strategy as a future maritime State.

Acknowledgements

This work was supported by National Social Science Foundation of China (Grant Number: 23BGJC80).

References

Ajey Lele, *A Military Perspective on Lethal Autonomous Weapon Systems*, UNODA Occasional Papers, No. 30 (New York: United Nations, 2017) 59

Bai Guimei and Meng Xianweieds., *Peking University Encyclopedia of Law Public International Law—Private International Law* (Peking University Press, 2016) 271–272

Bao Yinan, 'The US 'Excessive Maritime Claims': A Critical Analysis' (2017) 5 IS

Campaign to Stop Killer Robots, 'Country Views on Killer Robots' (April 13, 2018) <https://www.stopkillerrobots.org/wp-ontent/uploads/2018/04/KRC_Country Views _13Apr2018.pdf> accessed 23 November 2023

129 Rob McLaughlin (n 10) 102.

130 ibid 174.

Chen Huibin and Zeng Yangzhi, 'Legitimacy, and future challenges of military unmanned systems' (2018) 6 MD

'China Agrees to Give Back US Underwater Drone Seized in South China Sea' (17 December 2016) <https://abcnews.go.com/International/china-agrees-give-back-us-underwater-drone-seized/story?id=44257232> accessed 23 November 2023

Code for Unplanned Encounters at Sea (version 1.0) (China, 22 April 2014) at the 2014 Western Pacific Navy Symposium

Convention for the Suppression of Unlawful Acts against the Safety of Maritime Navigation.

Donald R. Rothwell and Tim Stephens, *The International Law of the Sea* (Hart Publishing, 2010)

Dong Qingling, 'The New Ethics of War: Supervise and Constrain the Lethal Autonomous Weapons Systems (LAWS)' (2018) 4IR

Elsa Kania, "China's Strategic Ambiguity and Shifting Approach to Lethal Autonomous Weapons Systems," (17 April 2018) <https://www.lawfareblog.com/chinas-strategic-ambiguity-and-shifting-approach-lethal-autonomous-weapons-systems> accessed 23 November 2023

Fang Xiaozhi and Lin Weimin, 'Russian Poseidon unmanned underwater vehicle' (2018) 15WV

Funnell C and Barton B, *Jane's Survey Vessels*, 3rd ed., 2002–2003 (Coulsdon, Jane's Information Group, 2002)

Gary L. Anderson v. United States, 317 F.3d 1235, 2003 AMC 94 (11th Cir.2003), <https://law.justia.com/cases/federal/appellate-courts/F3/317/1235/484420/> accessed 23 November 2023

George K. Walker, "Defining Terms in the 1982 Law of the Sea Convention III: The International Hydrographic Organization ECDIS Glossary," (2004) 34 CWILJ211 238

Guo Zhonguan and Zou Ligang, 'Analysis on the Incident of Unmanned Underwater Vehicle in the South China Sea From the Angle of International Law' (2017) 4 JHU(HSC)

Haiwen Zhang, 'Maritime Hegemony of the United States? Comments on Raul (Pete) Pedrozo's Article on Military Activities in the EEZ' (2010) 9 CJIL

He Bei, 'Nature and Path: International Regulation of Autonomous Weapon System' (2016) 4 JXPIP

Hu Bo, 'The Transformation of US Military Maritime Strategy: From 'From Land to Sea' to 'Return to Sea Control' (2018) 5 JISSS

Human Rights Watch and The International Human Rights Clinic (IHRC), 'Losing Humanity, the Case Against Killer Robots' (19 November 2012) 5 <http://hrp.law.harvard.edu/staff/the-case-against-killer-robots-an-international-human-rights-clinic-and-human-rights-watch-report/> accessed 23 November 2023

International Committee of the Red Cross, 'Fully autonomous weapons' (December 21, 2018) <https://www.icrc.org/zh/doc/resources/documents/statement/2013/09-03-autonomous-weapons.htm.> accessed 23 November 2023

J.A. Roach and R.W. Smith, *United States Response to Excessive Maritime Claims* (Nijhoff, 1996)

James Kraska and Raul Pedrozo, 'China's Capture of U.S. Underwater Drone Violates Law of the Sea' (16 December 2016) <https://www.lawfareblog.com/chinas-capture-us-underwater-drone-violates-law-sea> accessed 2 February 2024

James Kraska, 'Convention on the Law of the Sea-warship immunity-scope of applicability of Convention-provisional measures-definition of warship-arbitral jurisdiction' (2013) 2 AJIL 409–410

Jane Dalton, "Future Navies-Present Issues," (2006) 59UNWR17

Jin Yongming, 'Military activities in the exclusive economic zone and the State practice' (2008) 2 LS

Jin Yongming, 'Modern System of the Law of the Sea and China' s Practice' (2018) 6CRIL

Julian Ku, 'The Nonexistent Legal Basis for China's Seizure of the U.S. Navy's Drone in the South China Sea' (16 December 2016) <https://www.lawfareblog.com/nonexistent-legal-basis-chinas-seizure-us-navys-drone-south-china-sea> accessed 2 February 2024

Kim Kiel, 'The Dauntless Incident: Should a United States Public Vessel Be Declared a Floating Piece of United States Territory for Citizenship Purposes' (1989) 21 UMIALR

LI Hongyun, 'Rights and obligations of the coastal State in the regime of innocent passage through the territorial sea' in *Chinese Yearbook of International Law* (Beijing: Law Press, 1996)

Li Jian, 'China intends to amend the Maritime Traffic Safety Law—safeguarding maritime rights and interests and polishing the maritime 'traffic light'' (China Defense News, 24 February 2017)

Li Zhiwen and Fan Tianjiao, 'On the amendment to Maritime Traffic Safety Law from the perspective of national marine interests' (2014) 2 CJML

Liu Dan 'The Chinese Navy captured a U.S. Unmanned Underwater Vehicle, who has the upper hand in international law in this matter?' (*Pengpai News,* December 22, 2016) <https://www.thepaper.cn/newsDetail_forward_1585150> accessed 2 February 2024

Liu Yangyue, 'Arms Control of Autonomous Weapons in the Context of Global Security Governance' (2018) 2 JISS

M. Jacobsen, Sweden and the Law of the Sea, in *The Law of the Sea: the European Union and its Member States,* eds. Laura Pineschi and Tullio Treves (Brill/Nijhoff, 1996)

Ma Xinmin, 'International Humanitarian Law in Flux: Development and New Agendas—Commemoration of the 40th Anniversary of the 1977 Additional Protocols to the Geneva Conventions' (2017) 4 CRIL

Michael N. Schmitt and David S. Goddard, "International law and the military use of unmanned maritime systems," (2016) 98I RRC

Myron H. Nordquist ed., *United Nations Convention on the Law of the Sea, A Commentary* (Martinus Nijhoff Publishers, 1985), Volume I

Neil Davison, *A legal perspective: Autonomous weapon systems under international humanitarian law*, UNODA Occasional Papers, No. 30 (United Nations) (2017)

'Position Paper of China' CCW/GGE.1/2018/WP.7 (11 APRIL, 2018) <https://www.unog.ch/80256EDD006B8954/(httpAssets)/E42AE83BDB3525D0C125826C0040B262/$file/CCW_GGE.1_2018_WP.7.pdf> accessed 23 November 2023

Qian Dong, Zhao Jiang and Yang Dong, 'A Review of U.S. Military Unmanned System Development Plan' (2017) 2 JUUS

Qu Guangqing and Qu Bo, *The Law of the Sea* (Renmin University Press, 2017)

Raul P. Pedrozo, "Preserving Navigational Rights and Freedoms: The Right to Conduct Military Activities in China's Exclusive Economic Zone" (2010) 9 CJIL para. 4

Ren Xiaofeng and Cheng Xizhong, 'A Chinese Perspective' (2005) 29 MP

Rob McLaughlin, 'Unmanned Naval Vehicles at Sea: USVs, UUVs, and the Adequacy of the Law' (2011) 21 JLIS100

Robert Sparrow, "Robotic Weapons and the Future of War," in Paolo Tripodi and Jessica Wolfendale, eds. *New Wars and New Soldiers: Military Ethics in the Contemporary World* (Ashgate Publishing Limited, 2011)

Ronald C. Arkin, *Governing Lethal Behavior in Autonomous Robots* (2010, CRE Press)

'Rule 15. Precautions in Attack' <https://ihl-databases.icrc.org/customary-ihl/eng/docs/v1_rul_rule15> accessed 23 November 2023

Sam Bateman, "Hydrographic Surveying in the EEZ: Differences and Overlaps with Marine Scientific Research" (2005) 29 MP

Sam LaGrone, 'Chinese Seize U.S. Navy Unmanned Vehicle' (December 16, 2016) <https://news.usni.org/2016/12/16/breaking-chinese-seize-u-s-navy-unmanned-vehicle> accessed 23 November 2023

Shao Di, *Study on the legality of autonomous weapons systems from the perspective of international humanitarian law* (2017) 2 LV 133

Sheng Hongsheng, 'The Use of Force: Evolving Norms since World War II' (2016) 2 JISS

Song Shuhua and Zhao Jinsong, 'The legal status of UUV' (2017) NX

Song Shuhua, 'Legal criteria for defining the ship's attributes' in *Research on Marine Law* (2nd series), edited by Xue Guifang (Shanghai Jiao Tong University Press, 2018)

Surveying and Mapping Law of the People's Republic of China (amended for the second time in 2007).

'The International Law Commission (ILC), Articles concerning the Law of the Sea with commentaries' In ILC, Yearbook of the International Law Commission, (1956) vol. II., 273 <http://legal.un.org/ilc/texts/instruments/english/commentaries/8_1_8_2_1956.pdf> accessed 21 December 2023

'The position paper submitted by the Chinese delegation to CCW 5th Review Conference' <https://www.unog.ch/80256EDD006B8954/(httpAssets)/DD1551E60648CEBBC125808A005954FA/$file/China's+Position+Paper.pdf> accessed 23 November 2023

U.S Office of the Chief of Naval Operations, U.S. Marine Corps, U.S. Coast Guard, *The Commander's Handbook on the Law of Naval Operations* (July 2007)

U.S. Dep't of Navy, 'The Navy Unmanned Undersea Vehicle (UUV) Master Plan' (November 9, 2004)4 <https://www.navy.mil/navydata/technology/uuvmp.pdf> accessed 2 February 2024

Ugo Pagallo, 'Robots of Just War: A Legal Perspective' (2011) 24 PT

Wang Shumin and Tang Xiaocong, 'Research on Legal Status of Unmanned Undersea Vehicles in International Law—Reflections on the Unmanned Undersea Vehicles Event between China and America' (2017) 4 PLS

Xu Yihang, 'How Underwater Spy Unmanned Underwater Vehicles Threaten Our National Security' *China Youth News*, 16 February 2017

Yoshifumi Tanaka, *The International Law of the Sea* (Cambridge University Press, 2012)

Zhang Guobin, 'Research on the Legal System of Innocent Passage' (Ph.D. dissertation, East China University of Political Science and Law, 2015)

Zhao Weidong and Peng Yin, 'The U.S. Coast Guard Cutters and Boats—Warship or Government Ships?' (2016) 2 JCMPA

Zou Ligang, 'On the right of the State to regulate foreign military activities in peacetime in the exclusive economic zone' (2012) 6 CLS

CHAPTER 7

Challenges Raised by Unmanned Ships and Flag State's Possible Jurisdiction Cooperations with Other Stakeholders

*Haibo Chen**

1 Introduction

The Review of Maritime Transport 2023 presented by the United Nations Conference on Trade and Development (UNCTAD) notes that '[i]ncreased levels of automation are gradually being achieved by commercial vessels of all sizes.'[1] Technological innovation is leading to swift advancements that will witness the increased utilization of unmanned ships in the international shipping industry in the future.[2]

Due to the numerous differences between unmanned ships and conventional vessels,[3] scholars and practitioners are keenly focused on this emerging technology and the potential impacts it may have on the traditional maritime industry and the existing legal framework,[4] especially compliance issues of unmanned ships with current legal rules when they possess a high degree autonomy.[5]

---

* Associate Professor at Ningbo University Law School.

1 UNCTAD, Review of Maritime Transport 2023, https://unctad.org/system/files/official-document/rmt2023_en.pdf.

2 Ziaul Haque Munim, 'Autonomous ships: a review, innovative applications and future maritime business models'(2019) 20SCFIL4 266–279.

3 Johan Schelin, 'Manning of Unmanned Ships, in Henrik Ringbom' Erik Røsæg, and Trond Solvang (eds.), *Autonomous Ships and the Law* (Routledge 2021); Tingting Yang, 'Intelligent Ships' in Proshanto K. Mukherjee, Maximo Q. Mejia, Jr., and Jingjing Xu (eds.), *Maritime Law in Motion* (Springer 2020).

4 Paul W. Pritchett, 'Ghost Ships: Why the Law Should Embrace Unmanned Vessel Technology' (2015) 40TMLJ 197; Henrik Ringbom, 'Regulating Autonomous Ships—Concepts, Challenges and Precedents' (2019) 50ODIL 141–169.

5 Robert Veala, Michael Tsimplisb, and Andrew Serdyc, 'The Legal Status and Operation of Unmanned Maritime Vehicles' (2019) 50ODIL 23–48.

 | DOI:10.1163/9789004706279_009

In terms of international regulations, ongoing discussions are addressing potential amendments to relevant legal frameworks,[6] including the International Convention on Salvage 1989[7] and international conventions regulating the carriage of goods[8] from the private law perspective, and the SUA Conventions[9] and others from the public law perspective. For International Maritime Organization (IMO) instruments, the IMO has decided to organize a regulatory scoping exercise to ensure that these instruments can keep pace with the rapid technological advancements of unmanned shipping.[10] Barbara Stępien suggests adopting a specialized convention or code as a much quicker and easier approach to adapt the 'manning' characteristics of the unmanned ship.[11] Regarding the nature of new rules, professor Anna Petrig suggests a soft approach, emphasizing the prevention and suppression of crimes at sea through informal laws.[12] More focus is on the legal status of unmanned ships

---

6 Måns Jacobsson, 'What Challenges Lie Ahead for Maritime Law?' In Proshanto K. Mukherjee, Maximo Q. Mejia, Jr., and Jingjing Xu (eds.), *Maritime Law in Motion* (Springer 2020).

7 International Convention on Salvage, (1989) adopted on 28 April 1989, entered into force on 14 July 1996, UNTS, Vol. 1953.

8 Mayank Suri, Maritime Autonomous Surface Ships (MASS) and the Salvage Convention 1989, NUS Center for Maritime Law Working Paper 22/05, NUS Law Working Paper No 2022/016; Professor Simon Baughen, 'Unmanned Vessels and International Conventions for the Carriage of Goods by Sea' in Barış Soyer and Andrew Tettenborn (eds.), *Artificial Intelligence and Autonomous Shipping: Developing the International Legal Framework* (Hart 2021); Richard Williams, 'Unmanned ships—a challenge to the current international regime regulating the carriage of goods?' In Barış Soyer and Andrew Tettenborn (eds.), *Ship Operations: New Risks, Liabilities and Technologies in the Maritime Sector*, (Informa 2021).

9 Convention for the Suppression of Unlawful Acts Against the Safety of Maritime Navigation, (10 March 1988) 1678 UNTS 221. [hereinafter '1988 SUA Convention']. 2005 Protocol to the 1988 Convention for the Suppression of Unlawful Acts Against the Safety of Maritime Navigation, (14 October 2005) IMO Doc. LEG/CONF.15/21. [hereinafter '2005 SUA Convention']. Protocol to the Convention of 10 March 1988 for the Suppression of Unlawful Acts Against the Safety of Fixed Platforms Located on the Continental Shelf (10 March 1988, entered into force on 1 March 1992, 1678 UNTS 201. [hereinafter '1988 Fixed Platforms Protocol']. Protocol of 2005 to the Protocol for the Suppression of Unlawful Acts Against the Safety of Fixed Platforms Located on the Continental Shelf, (14 October 2005) entered into force on 28 July 2010, IMO Doc. LEG/CONF.15/22. [hereinafter '2005 Fixed Platforms Protocol'].

10 See IMO website <https://www.imo.org/en/MediaCentre/HotTopics/Pages/Autonomous-shipping.aspx.> accessed 24 February 2024.

11 Barbara Stępien, 'Can a ship be its own captain? Safe manning of autonomous and uncrewed vessels' (2023) 148MP 105451.

12 Anna Petrig, 'Maritime Security in the Age of Autonomous Ships', in Tafsir Johansson, Jonatan Echebarria Fernandez, Dimitrios Dalaklis, Aspasia Pastra and Jon Skinner (eds),

under United Nations Convention on the Law of the Sea (UNCLOS)[13] and how UNCLOS can effectively adapt to new changes.[14]

Meanwhile, scholars are continually observing the exclusive flag state jurisdiction under UNCLOS from various perspectives.[15] Frank Smeele has proposed that flag states of the unmanned ships could 'switch off' its regulatory requirements to facilitate the trials and tests of unmanned shipping technology. Chris Whomersley contends that, given the prevalence of open registries and multiple challenges in the maritime sphere, it is not 'tenable to slavishly follow' this principle. Instead, other mechanisms, especially port State control, should be taken into consideration.[16] The challenges mentioned by Chris Whomersley include maritime safety, the popularity of cruise holidays, the promotion of human rights for those working at sea, and the need to combat illegal, unreported and unregulated fishing (IUU fishing).[17]

Nevertheless, unmanned shipping poses a novel and intricate challenge to flag state jurisdiction. Professor Eric Van Hooydonk raises doubts, suggesting

---

Autonomous Vessel in Maritime Affairs: Law & Governance Implications (Palgrave Macmillan, 2023).

13 United Nations Convention on the Law of the Sea (10 December 1982) entered into force on 16 November 1994, UNTS, Vol. 1833. [hereinafter 'UNCLOS'].

14 Include but not limited to: Sabrina Hasan, 'Analysing the definition of "ship" to facilitate Marine Autonomous Surface Ships as ship under the law of the sea' (2023) 15AJMOA 268–283; Henrik Ringbom and Felix Collin, 'Terminology and Concepts' in Henrik Ringbom, Erik Røsæg, and Trond Solvang (eds.), *Autonomous Ships and the Law* (Routledge 2021); Youri Van Logchem, 'International Law of the Sea and Autonomous Cargo 'Vessels" in Barış Soyer and Andrew Tettenborn (eds.), *Artificial Intelligence and Autonomous Shipping: Developing the International Legal Framework* (Hart 2021); Tomas Heidar, How Does the Law of the Sea Adapt to New Knowledge and Changing Circumstances?' In Tomas Heidar (ed.), New Knowledge and *Changing Circumstances in the Law of the Sea* (Brill 2020); Kara Chadwick, 'Unmanned maritime systems will shape the future of naval operations: is international law ready?' In Malcolm D. Evans and Sofia Galani (eds.), *Maritime Security and the Law of the Sea: Help or Hindrance?* (Edward Elgar Publishing 2020); Anna Petrig, 'The commission of maritime crimes with unmanned systems: an interpretive challenge for the United Nations Convention on the Law of the Sea' In Malcolm D. Evans and Sofia Galani (eds.), *Maritime Security and the Law of the Sea: Help or Hindrance?* (Edward Elgar Publishing 2020).

15 Emmanuel Kofi Mbiah, 'Coastal, Flag and Port State Jurisdiction: Powers and Other Considerations Under UNCLOS', in Proshanto K. Mukherjee, Maximo Q. Mejia, Jr., and Jingjing Xu (eds.), *Maritime Law in Motion* (Springer 2020); Reshmi Mukherjee, 'Ship Nationality, Flag States and the Eradication of Substandard Ships: A Critical Analysis' in Proshanto K. Mukherjee, Maximo Q. Mejia, Jr., and Jingjing Xu (eds.), *Maritime Law in Motion* (Springer 2020).

16 Chris Whomersley, 'The Principle of Exclusive Flag State Jurisdiction: Is It Fit for Purpose in the Twenty-First Century?' (2020) 5 APJOLP 330–47.

17 Ibid.

that the concept of a 'genuine link' between an unmanned ship and its flag state might be 'entirely illusionary' in the context of unmanned shipping, and therefore needs a 'thorough overhaul'.[18] Difficulties might also arise for the flag state in exercising flag state jurisdiction on its unmanned ships in accordance with UNCLOS.[19]

In view of these development and discussions, this study seeks to identify and clarify the challenges posed by unmanned ships to the 'exclusive flag state jurisdiction' principle, and accordingly propose possible solutions to safeguard maritime safety and security, and protect marine environment in the upcoming era of unmanned shipping.

In terms of organization, this paper will outline, in section 2, the characteristics of possible unmanned ships operations compared to conventional ships. In section 3, by sketching a historical background will be provided, the rationale and objective of the exclusive flag state jurisdiction, the requirement of a 'genuine link', and fulfillment problems will be discussed. In section 4, potential negative effects of unmanned ships operation on the exercise of flag state jurisdiction will be analyzed. It could be anticipated that the flag state jurisdiction will be indirect and unclear, and there could be some jurisdiction vacuum and/or conflict between the flag state and other states. The rationale and objective of the exclusive flag state jurisdiction will be obscured. Subsequently, in Section 5, three potential solutions will be proposed. Strengthening the exercise of flag state jurisdiction within the IMO framework and enhancing the role of delegated classification societies are deemed highly practical. Simultaneously, establishing and/or fortifying jurisdictional collaborations between the flag state and the port state, the states of shore-based operators and the remote operation center, and the state of the ship operator are considered essential. The conclusion is in Section 6.

2 New Changes of the Unmanned Ship and Its Operation Party

2.1 *Existing Rules as Basis of Conventional Ships and Its On-board Operation*

As Mansell summarizes, 'shipping is the oldest truly global industry and continues to play a vital role in the carriage of cargo and people in support of the

18 Eric Van Hooydonk, 'The law of unmanned merchant shipping—an exploration' (2014) 20 JIML 403, 410.

19 Youri Van Logchem (n 14).

world economy.'[20] For centuries, the master and the crew on board are vital to the navigation for a ship at sea.[21]

Through extensive global operations, numerous legal principles regarding the status and responsibilities of both the ship's master and the crew have been established in the legal framework and mechanism of maritime law. Significantly, these principles have positioned the ship, the master, and the crew on equal footing.

In March 2017, Committee Maritime International (CMI) Working Group on Unmanned Ships distributed a questionnaire among the Member Associations of the CMI (MLAs).[22] One of the inquiries asked 'could other remote-controllers constitute the 'crew' for the purposes of your national merchant shipping laws?' Among 19 MLAs of the CMI who submitted their responses, ten stated that their national laws included a definition of 'crew' or 'seamen'. Nine explicitly required physical presence on board as part of the definition.[23] Additionally, eight of them concluded that their definition did not encompass shore-based individuals.[24]

International conventions, such as UNCLOS and International Convention for the Safety of Life at Sea (SOLAS),[25] also commonly emphasize 'on board presence'. For instance, professor Anna Petrig concludes that the gaining of direct, physical control over a ship and individuals on board fell within the ambit of Article 101(a) of UNCLOS.[26] However, it is important to note that this 'constitution for the oceans'[27] did not include unmanned ships when drafted.[28] Additionally, Chapter V Rule 13 of SOLAS mandates that contracting governments ensure their national ships are adequately and effectively manned.

20 John N. K. Mansell, Flag State Responsibility: Historical Development and Contemporary Issues (Springer 2009) 1.

21 See Lokesh Kumar Mavilla, 'The Conflict between Maritime Law & Unmanned Shipping: Manning the Unmanned Ghost Ships?' (2019) 10 SA 142–52.

22 See Summary of Responses to the CMI Questionnaire on Unmanned Ships, ANNEX 1 to the CMI IWG Submission to MSC 99th Session, 1.

23 ibid 3.

24 Ibid.

25 International Convention for the Safety of Life at Sea, (1 November 1974) entered into force on 25 May 1980, UNTS, Vol. 1184. [hereinafter 'SOLAS'].

26 See Anna Petrig, 'The Commission of Maritime Crimes with Unmanned Systems: An Interpretive Challenge for the United Nations Convention on the Law of the Sea' in Evans, D. Malcolm; Galani, Sofia (eds), *Maritime Security and the Law of the Sea* (Edward Elgar Publishing, 2020) 124.

27 See CMI International Working Group Position Paper on Unmanned Ships and the International Regulatory Framework 3.

28 ibid 20.

Accordingly, with the emergence of the concepts of unmanned ships and unmanned shipping within the industry, a primary and pivotal question arising is whether vessels without a crew on board should be classified as 'ships' or 'vessels' within the framework of the existing conventions like UNCLOS and SOLAS.[29] The answer is straightforward. There is no compelling reason why unmanned ships should not be classified as 'ships' or 'vessels', and why the existing international rules which have been designed to address risks at sea could not be used to regulate both manned and unmanned ships 'doing similar tasks involving similar dangers'. Moreover, the existing international regulations crafted to mitigate risks at sea can feasibly govern both manned and unmanned ships 'doing similar tasks involving similar dangers'.[30]

2.2 *Characteristics and Classifications of Unmanned Ships*

It is evident that existing international rules and domestic regulations, tailored for traditional manned maritime activities, cannot be directly transplanted to unmanned operations. Unmanned activities are diversified. Therefore, a more thorough examination of the current regulatory framework becomes imperative. Through the examination, the international community can evaluate the relevance of the framework to unmanned ships, and ascertain the required extent of amendments and clarifications.

International Maritime Organization (IMO) has concluded a regulatory scoping exercise aimed at evaluating the potential application of existing IMO instruments to unmanned ships (Maritime Autonomous Surface Ships, MASS).[31] Subsequently, IMO has established the Joint MSC-LEG-FAL Working Group on Maritime Autonomous Surface Ships (MASS-JWG) to identify any regulatory voids or gaps and propose future actions for developing a legal framework adaptable to unmanned shipping.[32]

Various segments of the shipping industry can devise distinct identifications pertaining to unmanned shipping issues. For instance, the China Classification Society (CCS) Rules for Intelligent Ships 2022 introduced class notations such as i-Ship (Ai, Ri, Nx, Hx, Mx, Ex, Cx, I) from a technical standpoint.[33] Mean-

29 ibid 3.

30 ibid 3, 20.

31 See Outcome of the Regulatory Scoping Exercise for the Use of Maritime Autonomous Surface Ships (MASS) (3rd June 2021) MSC. 1/Circ. 1638.

32 See Joint MSC-LEG-FAL Working Group on Maritime Autonomous Surface Ships (MASS) <https://www.imo.org/en/MediaCentre/MeetingSummaries/Pages/Joint-MSC-LEG-FAL-Working-Group-on-Maritime-Autonomous-Surface-Ships-(MASS)-.aspx.> accessed 24 February 2024.

33 China Classification Society, 'Rules for Intelligent Ships' (2020) 1.4 Class notation for intelligent ships.

while, Maritime UK, while using the IMO MASS identifications, has proposed classifying Maritime Autonomous Surface Ships into five categories based on the length and speed of the ships.[34]

IMO identified four degrees of autonomy for the scoping exercise concerning unmanned ships for commercial purposes as follows:[35]

> Degree one: Ship with automated processes and decision support. Seafarers are on board to operate and control shipboard systems and functions. Some operations may be automated and at times be unsupervised but with seafarers on board ready to take control.
>
> Degree two: Remotely controlled ship with seafarers on board. The ship is controlled and operated from another location. Seafarers are available on board to take control and to operate the shipboard systems and functions.
>
> Degree three: Remotely controlled ship without seafarers on board: The ship is controlled and operated from another location. There are no seafarers on board.
>
> Degree four: Fully autonomous ship: The operating system of the ship is able to make decisions and determine actions by itself.

Smaller ships are often confined to domestic or port waters due to their size and operational limitations.[36] However, our discussion focuses on larger vessels engaged in international transportation. IMO's identification brings autonomy into consideration, which is essential for risks and legal responsibility analysis. Hence, IMO's four-degree classification is adopted as the foundation for our discussion.

2.3 *Possible Types of Future Operation Party of the Unmanned Ships*

It is predicted that the evolving MASS technologies could present numerous advantages. These advancements are expected to enhance navigation safety and security, protect the marine environment, facilitate international trade

34 Maritime UK, 'Maritime Autonomous Ship Systems (MASS) UK Industry Conduct Principles and Code of Practice, A Voluntary Code Version' (6 November 2022) 2.1.

35 Annex of the Outcome of the Regulatory Scoping Exercise for the Use of Maritime Autonomous Surface Ships (MASS), MSC. 1/Circ. 1638 (3rd June 2021) 3–4.

36 The second paragraph of Article 94 of UNCLOS stipulates that, every State shall maintain a register of ships containing the names and particulars of ships flying its flag, except those which are excluded from generally accepted international regulations on account of their small size.

and shipping, reduce industry expenses, and aid personnel both on board and ashore.

Nevertheless, there remain persistent concerns that the heightened risks associated with ships controlled by shore-based operators or under complete autonomous control outweigh the afore-mentioned conveniences. In addition, distinct differences exist between the working and living conditions of shore-based operators and onboard crew. Hence, it is imperative to assess the need for fixed personnel, a combination of operators, and operational platforms for ships, as well as the strategies or successive order of ship operations.

The clarifications reached by the IMO MASS-JWG during its second session in April 2023 can be viewed as a response to these concerns. The MASS-JWG aims to tackle safety, legal, and facilitation issues which are of high priorities for MASS. As per MASS-JWG, the characteristics of the master, the Remote Operations Center (ROC), and the remote operator of a MASS could be outlined as follows:[37]

Frist, there should be a human master responsible for a MASS, regardless of mode of operation or degree or level of autonomy of the ship. The master may not be required to be physically present on board but should possess the means to intervene when necessary. Under certain conditions, a single master could be accountable for multiple MASS simultaneously, or alternatively, multiple masters may oversee a single MASS during a single voyage.

Second, a Remote Operations Center (ROC) is a distant location from the MASS capable of controlling some or all aspects of the functions of the MASS. In specific circumstances, it may be feasible for one or more ROCs to oversee a MASS during a single voyage. However, only one ROC should bear responsibility for a MASS at any given time.

Third, a remote operator is a qualified individual employed or engaged to operate some or all functions of a MASS from a ROC. In specific scenarios, an individual at a ROC may supervise multiple MASS simultaneously. This individual could serve as the master for that MASS or multiple MASS.

From these clarifications and for prospective considerations, it can be concluded that it is possible for the master and the crew (if any), the ROC, and the remote operator(s) to be physically situated outside the vessel. This contrasts

37 IMO (n 32). According to the 2nd Session summary, the Committee(s) were invited to further consider that those certain conditions are. The role of the master and the roles of the crew of MASS will be discussed at future sessions of the Working Group. The technology used on the MASS and the human presence on board a MASS will determine the identification of the master of a MASS. The Maritime Safety Committee (MSC) need to further discuss the requirements for a ROC as well as the requirements relating to a remote operator when developing the MASS Code.

with a conventional ship where the captain and crew reside and operate on board throughout a single voyage. This presents a new challenge to the notions of 'genuine link' and 'exclusive flag State jurisdiction'.

3 Exclusive Flag State Jurisdiction and the 'Genuine Link'

3.1 *Principle of Freedom and the Purpose of Flag State Jurisdiction*

3.1.1 Principle of Freedom of the Seas

Historically, various maritime powers asserted control or division over the oceans during different periods. Examples include the kingdoms of Sweden and Denmark, the city-states of Venice, Genoa, and Pisa, and the United Kingdom, designating extensive sea areas under their sovereign authority.[38] Through the Treaty of Tordesillas, Spain and Portugal demarcated ocean territories,[39] restricting navigation rights of other states on their claimed oceans.[40] These states pursued their political and economic interests by levying tolls on foreign ships for passage through their claimed waters.

Against this historical background, Grotius wrote against the Portuguese monopoly of navigation and commerce in the East Indies to defend Dutch policies of supporting freedom of navigation and fishing.[41] This principle of freedom of the seas was supported by British, French, and US later on in the 19th century. The concept of the high seas, considered as a distinct maritime zone legally separate from national waters and immune to appropriation by any state, was established.[42]

De Vattel made a clear distinction between the sea under territorial sovereignty and the high seas.[43] This dualism in maritime zones was affirmed at the international level in the Bering Sea Fur-Seals arbitration case between

---

38 Philipp Wendel, State Responsibility for Interferences with the Freedom of Navigation in Public International Law (Springer 2007) 7.

39 John N. K. Mansell, Flag State Responsibility: Historical Development and Contemporary Issues (Springer 2009) 17.

40 Philipp Wendel, State Responsibility for Interferences with the Freedom of Navigation in Public International Law (Springer 2007) 7.

41 James Crawford, *Brownlie's Principles of Public International Law,* 9th edn (Oxford University Press 2019) 281–82. M.C.W. Pinto, Chapter 3 'Hugo Grotius and the Law of the Sea' in Lilian del Castillo (ed), *Law of the Sea, From Grotius to the International Tribunal for the Law of the Sea* (Brill Nijhoff 2015) 18–47.

42 Robin Churchill, Vaughan Lowe and Amy Sander, The Law of the Sea, 4th edition (Manchester University Press 2022) 433.

43 Yoshifumi Tanaka, *The International Law of the Sea 4th Edition,* (Cambridge University Press 2023) 25–26.

Great Britain and the United States of America in 1893.[44] Afterward, this long-standing dispute between the closed sea and open sea doctrines seemed to be conclusively resolved. The coastal state was granted sovereignty over a belt of territorial waters, with the acknowledgment of the general right of innocent passage. Meanwhile, the high seas beyond the belt the maritime belt were designated as res communis, with international freedoms enjoyed by the flags of all nations.[45]

On basis of these two principles, namely the principle of sovereignty and the principle of freedom, the ocean is categorized into two maritime zones: the territorial sea and the high seas. UNCLOS introduces a third principle of common heritage of mankind,[46] seeking for the protection of the collective interest of humanity.[47] UNCLOS governs a multitude of maritime zones, encompassing the territorial sea, contiguous zone, straits used for international navigation, archipelagic maritime zone, exclusive economic zone, continental shelf, the high seas, and the Area.

3.1.2 Right of Navigation

Derived from the principle of freedom of the seas, also known as the freedom of the high seas, no state possesses the authority to obstruct other states from utilizing the high seas for any 'lawful purpose'. This customary freedom is codified in Article 2 of the Convention on the High Seas 1958 (HSC),[48] which stipulates that '[t]he high seas being open to all nations, no State may validly purport to subject any part of them to its sovereignty.' Additionally, Article 87 of UNCLOS declares, '[t]he high seas are open to all States, whether coastal or land-locked.'

Both the HSC and UNCLOS accord the freedom of seas to all states. For this purpose, both conventions stipulate that every state, whether coastal or land-locked, possesses the 'right of navigation' to sail ships flying its flag on the high seas.[49] A ship without a flag or not flying its flag will be deprived of many benefits and rights outlined by the law of the sea. According to Article 110 of UNCLOS, such ships subject to be boarded by a warship. Article 6 of the HSC and Article 92 of UNCLOS also stipulate that ships shall sail under the flag of only one state. If a ship sails under the flags of two or more states, it may be deemed as a stateless vessel.

---

44 ibid 27.

45 R. Jennings, A Changing International Law of the Sea, (1972) 31 CLJ 32.

46 Yoshifumi Tanaka (n 43) 201.

47 See UNCLOS, art 140.

48 Convention on the High Seas (29 April 1958) entered in force on 30 September 1962, UNTS, Vol. 450. [hereinafter 'HSC'].

49 See HSC, art 4; UNCLOS, art 90.

3.1.3 Flag State Jurisdiction

With the development of technology and global exchanges, the volume of ships navigating on seas have significantly increased. This includes commercial ships, fishing boats, government vessels, and military ships. It is anticipated that the sovereign state, benefiting from the freedom of the seas, should put its ships into the legal order for the seas and oceans. 'The absence of any authority over ships sailing the high seas would lead to chaos.'[50] The order maintenance of the legal order on the high seas relies on the foundational concept of the nationality of the ship.[51]

Therefore, flag state jurisdiction represents a special arrangement which encapsulates not only the freedom of navigation enjoyed by all States,[52] but also the understanding that the flag state serves as a custodian to exercise jurisdiction in order to maintain the public order of the oceans, to facilitate international communication, and to promote the peaceful use of the seas and oceans.[53] The International Law Commission (ILC) clarified that a fundamental aspect of the principle of the freedom of the seas is that a ship must fly the flag of a single state and be subject to the jurisdiction of that state.[54] Both the HSC and UNCLOS mandate ships to be subject to their flag states' exclusive jurisdiction on the high seas.[55] In the M/V 'Norstar' Case adjudicated by the International Tribunal for the Law of the Sea (ITLOS),[56] the tribunal affirmed that 'the notions of the invalidity of claims of sovereignty over the high seas and of exclusive flag State jurisdiction on the high seas are inherent in the legal status of the high seas being open and free'.[57]

Flag state jurisdiction is not only a right but also an obligation and responsibility, serving as a reasonable restriction on the flag state's exercise of freedom of navigation. It encompasses a broad range of duties. Article 94 of UNCLOS outlines the 'duties of the flag State', emphasizing the effective exercise of

50 See the commentary of Article 30 by the International Law Commission (ILC), in Articles Concerning the Law of the Sea with Commentaries adopted by the ILC at its eighth session in 1956.

51 Malcolm N. Shaw, *International Law*, 8th edition, (Cambridge University Press 2017) 455.

52 See UNCLOS, arts 87, 90.

53 See UNCLOS, preamble.

54 See the commentary of Article 30 by the International Law Commission (ILC), in Articles Concerning the Law of the Sea with Commentaries adopted by the ILC at its eighth session in 1956.

55 See HSC, art 6(1); UNCLOS, art 92(1).

56 The International Tribunal for the Law of the Sea is an independent judicial body established by the UNCLOS to adjudicate disputes arising out of the interpretation or application of UNCLOS. [hereinafter 'ITLOS'].

57 See M/V 'Norstar' Case (*Panama v. Italy*), Judgment, ITLOS Reports (2019) para. 218.

jurisdiction and control over ships in administrative, technical, and social matters.[58]

Flag state jurisdiction covers ships, crew members and properties on board. For example, Articles 94(3) and 94(4) of UNCLOS stipulate that the flag state shall take necessary measures to ensure maritime safety, including relevant measures for ships, master, officers and crew members of the ship, and properties on board. In ITLOS cases, the tribunal clarified that the ship, the captain, the crew, the cargo and their owners and interested parties constitute a unit, on which the flag state exercises flag state jurisdiction.[59] Besides, flag state jurisdiction is not a diplomatic protection and is not on condition of exhaustion of local remedies.[60]

3.2 *Nationality of Ships and the 'Genuine Link' Requirement*

3.2.1 Nationality of Ships

As previously mentioned, the conferral of nationality to ships arises from the freedom of the high seas. To ensure the order of the high seas and the safety of navigation, it is imperative to subject the ship to a certain regulatory mechanism.[61] Restricting sea usage only to ships that can prove their nationality can prevent potential abuse of the freedom of the seas. Therefore, even when the flag state enjoys the freedom of navigation, there is a limit to it. Preserving the peaceful use of the ocean is an obligation of the flag state, who should exercise its jurisdiction over ships as a custodian of the international community.[62]

The flag state shall establish a rigorous system and require the ship flying its flag to adhere to it. Moreover, the flag state shall determine the conditions for the grant of its nationality to ships, for the registration of ships in its territory, and for the right to fly its flag. It shall enforce its municipal legal rules and the international legal rules.

3.2.2 'Genuine Link' under the HSC and UNCLOS

Both the HSC and UNCLOS mandate the existing of a genuine link between the (flag) state and the ship.[63] However, neither convention provides a specific

58 See UNCLOS, art 94(1).

59 See M/V 'Saiga' (No. 2) Case (St. Vincent and the Grenadines v. Guinea), Judgment, ITLOS Reports (1999) and M/V 'Virginia G' Case (Panama/Guinea-Bissau) Judgment, ITLOS Reports (2014).

60 ibid.

61 Boleslaw Adam Boczek, *Flags of Convenience: An International Legal Study* (Harvard University Press, 1962) 259.

62 R. Jennings (n 45) 47.

63 See the HSC, art 5; UNCLOS, art 91.

definition for the term 'genuine link'. The meaning of the 'genuine link' requirement in relation to the flag state jurisdiction is complicated.

Article 5(1) of the HSC stipulates that '[t]here must exist a genuine link between the State and the ship; in particular, the State must effectively exercise its jurisdiction and control in administrative, technical and social matters over ships flying its flag.' However, what is required to constitute a real or 'genuine' link remain unclear.[64] Besides, neither convention specifies the consequences (if any) that will arise when there is no genuine link in accordance with their context or their object and purpose.[65] These two questions have been extensively discussed in the literature, yet no consensus has been reached.[66] Churchill summarizes that 'opinions on these two questions are so diverse that it cannot even be said that a predominant view emerges.'[67]

Based on Churchill's study, Article 5 of the HSC lacks a universally accepted requirement for establishing a genuine link.[68] The flag state has its own choice on this issue by adopting domestic legislations and/or requirements. Since the legal order of the high seas needs to be fulfilled by the flag state's jurisdiction, an effective exercise of flag state jurisdiction could constitute an essential element of the genuine link.[69] Yet, from an international law perspective, there is no clearly defined criterion for the effective exercise of jurisdiction. Moreover, since the HSC does not mention the consequences of the absence of a genuine link, one possible interpretation is that no consequences are intended to follow in such cases.[70]

Article 91 of UNCLOS simply stipulates that '[t]here must exist a genuine link between the State and the ship', without further requirements. However, the first paragraph of Article 94 named 'Duties of the flag State' writes, 'in particular, the State must effectively exercise its jurisdiction and control in administrative, technical and social matters over ships flying its flag'.[71] It is followed closely by the second paragraph stipulating that '(i)n particular every State shall: (a) maintain a register of ships containing the names and

64 Robin R. Churchill, *The Meaning of the 'Genuine Link' Requirement in Relation to the Nationality of Ships* (A Study prepared for the International Transport Workers' Federation, 2000) ISBN: 0901969508 15.

65 ibid 4, 15.

66 ibid 33, 37.

67 ibid 37.

68 ibid 38.

69 ibid 39.

70 ibid.

71 Article 94(1) of UNCLOS provides that: Every State shall effectively exercise its jurisdiction and control in administrative, technical and social matters over ships flying its flag.

particulars of ships flying its flag, except those which are excluded from generally accepted international regulations on account of their small size; and (b) assume jurisdiction under its internal law over each ship flying its flag and its master, officers and crew in respect of administrative, technical and social matters concerning the ship.'

3.2.3 Meaning of the 'Genuine Link'

The M/V Saiga (No. 2) Case (St. Vincent and the Grenadines v. Guinea) addressed by ITLOS delved into the interpretation of Article 91 of UNCLOS. In determining the existence of a genuine link between the Saiga and Saint Vincent and the Grenadines during the incident, the tribunal concluded that the purpose of requiring a genuine link in this article is to ensure the effective fulfillment of flag State duties, rather than to establish criteria by reference to which the validity of the registration of ships in a flag State can be challenged by other States.[72]

The tribunal in the M/V 'Virginia G' Case, following the interpretation of the tribunal in the M/V Saiga (No. 2) Case, held that once a ship is registered, the flag state is obligated, as per Article 94 of UNCLOS, to exert effective jurisdiction and control over the ship to ensure its compliance with generally accepted international regulations, procedures, and practices.[73] According to the tribunal, this constitutes the essence of 'genuine link'.[74] In other words, there is no 'genuine link' requirement as a pre-condition of the ship registration by the flag state, which would demand a real and close connection between the ship and the state. Essentially, the 'genuine link' does not mandate ownership or operation of the vessel by a national of the flag State.[75]

The tribunal in the M/V 'Virginia G' Case was tasked with resolving another matter related to the 'genuine link', namely, whether the lack of a genuine link between a flag State and a ship gives another State the right to reject the recognition of the ship's nationality.[76]

The tribunal concludes that the absence of a genuine link between a ship and the flag state does not grant other states the right to refuse recognition of the ship's nationality.[77] The tribunal seems to take the view that the party in

72 St. Vincent and the Grenadines v. Guinea (n 59) para 83.

73 Panama/Guinea-Bissau (n 59) para. 113.

74 ibid.

75 Alexander Proelss (ed.), United Nations Convention on the Law of the Sea: A Commentary (Hart 2017) 498.

76 St. Vincent and the Grenadines v. Guinea (n 59) paras. 83–88.

77 ibid, paras. 72–74.

dispute who claims that the flag state is absence of a genuine link, bears the burden of proving such absence.[78]

3.3 *Problems of the Exercise of the Flag State Jurisdiction*

In practice, challenges arise in the effective implementation of flag state obligations, particularly when addressing issues of compliance with IMO conventions, maritime safety and security, marine environmental protection, illegal, unreported, and unregulated (IUU) fishing and maritime human rights protection.

In 2006, IMO convened an Ad Hoc Consultative Meeting involving senior representatives from international organizations to discuss the role of the 'genuine link' and the potential consequences of non-compliance with duties and obligations of flag States outlined in relevant international instruments.[79] Participating organizations included the Division for Ocean Affairs and the Law of the Sea of the Office of Legal Affairs of the United Nations (DOALOS), the Food and Agriculture Organization of the United Nations (FAO), the International Labour Organization (ILO), and the United Nations Conference on Trade and Development (UNCTAD).

The role of the 'genuine link' under UNCLOS, considered as a different question, is directly and inseparably linked to effective exercise of flag State obligations.[80] The examination and clarification of the role of the 'genuine link' should serve as a basis for strengthening the fulfillment of duties and obligations imposed by UNCLOS and other international instruments upon flag states. The effective exercise of flag State responsibilities, as part of state jurisdiction, seems to rely on a robust link between the flag State and the ships flying its flag.[81]

However, due to a lack of clear and applicable criterion for the 'genuine link' and no requirements for the flag state to prove its genuine link with the ship, the burden of proof regarding the absence of the 'genuine link' falls on the counter party, who cannot refuse to recognize the nationality of the ship on basis of the absence. Since there are no restrictions on the shipowner's forum shopping for the registration place, if the original flag state imposes sanctions

78 ibid, paras. 83–88.

79 See the Note by the Secretary-General: Item 69 (a) of the provisional agenda, Oceans and the law of the sea, UN General Assembly 61 session (17 July 2006) A/61/160.

80 See the report of the Ad Hoc Consultative Meeting of senior representatives of international organizations, convened by IMO, on the subject of the 'genuine link', p. 11, which was an annex to the Note by the Secretary-General: Item 69 (a) of the provisional agenda, Oceans and the law of the sea, UN General Assembly 61 session (17 July 2006) A/61/160.

81 See the Annex of the Note (n 79) para. 11.

consisting of suspension of registration and the use of the flag, these sanctions could be counterproductive and lead to the unwanted consequences of re-registration with the states that do not properly adhere to the 'genuine link' requirements stipulated by UNCLOS.[82] The flag state is given an absolute discretion for the fulfillment of its jurisdiction. As Churchill comments, 'some kind of consequence must nevertheless surely follow, otherwise the genuine link requirement serves no purpose'.[83] This concern will be more obvious for unmanned ships.

4 Challenges to Flag State Jurisdiction Arising from the Unmanned Operation of Ships

4.1 *Article 94 of UNCLOS*

Article 94(1) of UNCLOS stipulates that the flag state shall effectively exercise its jurisdiction and control in administrative, technical and social matters over ships flying its flag. Subsequently, Article 94(2) makes a specification: (1) to maintain a register containing the names and particulars of ships flying its flag;[84] and (2) to assume jurisdiction under its internal law over each ship flying its flag and its master, officers and crew in respect of administrative, technical and social matters concerning the ship.

With the core objectives of maintaining maritime safety and security, and protecting the marine environment, IMO has formulated a number of international conventions and standards to urge member states, particularly those holding flag state status, to fulfill their obligations in administrative, technical and social matters over ships. These conventions and standards cover issues of not only the ship itself, but also master and crew members, and ships' maintenance, inspection and operation details as well. Flag states are required to ensure that onboard masters and crew members comply with relevant technical and qualification requirements.

However, the use and operation of unmanned ships will challenge and weaken the flag state jurisdiction.

82 See the Note (n 79).

83 Robin R. Churchill (n 64) 72.

84 This requirement has an exception. For ships in small size, the flag state could except itself from maintaining the ship register containing these ships' names and particulars if these ships are excluded from generally accepted international regulations on account of their small size. See Article 94(2) of UNCLOS.

4.2 *A Further Weakening of the Substantial Connection with the Flag State*

For unmanned ships, numerous ship operation and external liaison works are handled by shore-based operators or preset software. Therefore, associated risks of navigation and operation will be under the control of these remote operators and/or remote operation center and/or preset software.

Based on current discussion within IMO's MASS-JWG, remote operators, remote operation centers, and designers of preset software are not required to work on board, nor are they required to hold the nationality of the flag state or be established and/or having business place within the flag state.[85] They could even be located everywhere in the world.

In this new scenario, remote operators and operation centers, unlike traditional onboard master and crews, will not be physically present on unmanned ships. Consequently, the flag state faces challenges in establishing a substantial connection and exerting effective control over remote operators, remote operation centers, or software designers located outside its territory and off the ship.

4.3 *Challenges to the Foundation of Flag State Jurisdiction*

A single shore-based operator may control multiple ships. The remote operation center can supervise multiple ships simultaneously. Their geographical locations differ from the ships'. Consequently, the risks encountered by shore-based operators and remote operation centers may not be synchronized with those faced by a specific ship.

Subjective and emotional elements may be brought into ship operations by shore-based operators, influenced by factors such as their onshore work and lifestyle, communication patterns, and interactions with remote operation centers. This may give rise to new types of human risks and accidents.

Additionally, the applicability and stability of networks necessary for remote operations might be out of sync with specific risks in ship navigation and operation, which will also induce new risks or accidents.

However, due to the afore-mentioned lack of the physical connection or 'on board' nexus, especially when the shore-based operators and/or remote operation center locate in a different country, the flag state will face difficulties in exercising effective jurisdiction. Without such distinctive connection during the ship's navigation and operation, the flag state therefore cannot sustain its

85 See IMO (n 32).

role as the custodian of the ship. Consequently, the foundation for 'exclusive flag state jurisdiction' will be questionable or even unacceptable.

4.4 *Jurisdiction Vacuum*

Disregarding the registration relationship between the unmanned ship and its flag state, and that the ship is the subject matter of the unmanned operations, most of the social matters, including the labour rights of the shore-based operators and the duties and responsibilities of the remote operation center, will be more closely linked to the countries where these entities are located, hold nationality, or have business registration than the flag state of the unmanned ship.

The Maritime Labour Convention 2006 (MLC)[86] is a crucial international instrument addressing the social matters of seafarers in maritime perspective. The MLC aims to secure decent employment right of all seafarers.[87] According to Article 2(1)(f) of the MLC, a seafarer is defined as any person employed, engaged, or working in any capacity on a ship. However, as mentioned above, shore-based operators of the unmanned ship and the remote operation center undertake their operation on land. Therefore, they do not qualify as seafarers as defined and protected by the MLC. Accordingly, their social matters are not safeguarded by Articles 4(5),[88] 5(1),[89] 5(2),[90] and 5(3)[91] of the MLC, even though the effects of their ship operation are equivalent to the work of seafarers on conventional ships.

---

86 The Maritime Labour Convention 2006 (23 February 2006) entered in force on 20 August 2013, UNTS, Vol. 2952. [hereinafter 'MLC'].

87 Article 1(1) of the MLC stipulates that: 'Each Member which ratifies this Convention undertakes to give complete effect to its provisions in the manner set out in Article VI in order to secure the right of all seafarers to decent employment.'

88 Article 4(5) of the MLC stipulates that: 'Each Member shall ensure, within the limits of its jurisdiction, that the seafarers' employment and social rights set out in the preceding paragraphs of this Article are fully implemented in accordance with the requirements of this Convention.'

89 Article 5(1) of the MLC stipulates that: 'Each Member shall implement and enforce laws or regulations or other measures that it has adopted to fulfil its commitments under this Convention with respect to ships and seafarers under its jurisdiction.'

90 Article 5(2) of the MLC stipulates that: 'Each Member shall effectively exercise its jurisdiction and control over ships that fly its flag by establishing a system for ensuring compliance with the requirements of this Convention, including regular inspections, reporting, monitoring and legal proceedings under the applicable laws.'

91 Article 5(3) of the MLC stipulates that: 'Each Member shall ensure that ships that fly its flag carry a maritime labour certificate and a declaration of maritime labour compliance as required by this Convention.'

4.4.1 Jurisdiction Vacuum

Even if the shore-based operators or the remote operation center could be deemed as seafarers of the unmanned ship, the flag state will still face the problem of whether they fall within the jurisdiction of the flag state or not. Both Articles 4(5) and 5(1) of MLC require each member state to fulfil its obligations concerning seafarers 'within the limits of its jurisdiction' or 'under its jurisdiction'. If the shore-based operators or the remote operation center are deemed to be beyond the flag state's jurisdiction, the flag state will not be obligated with Articles 4(5) and 5(1) of MLC.

According to Article 5(5) of MLC,[92] only when the seafarer recruitment and placement services are established in the territory of one member state of MLC, that member state is required to effectively exercise its jurisdiction and control over the seafarer recruitment and placement services of the shore-based operators and the remote operation center. In other words, ship-operation related social matters, other than the seafarer recruitment and placement services, is beyond the jurisdiction of both the flag state and the state where the shore-based operators of the unmanned ship and the remote operation center are located. This jurisdiction vacuum needs to be resolved in international legal framework.

The concerns of the Tribunal in M/V 'SAIGA' (No. 2) Case can be relevant here. Given the potential multinational composition of a shore-based operation group and/or remote operation center for unmanned ships, expecting individuals to seek protection from their respective states or for each state where each operator/operation center locates to exert territorial jurisdiction over ship operation issues would result in 'undue hardship'.[93]

4.4.2 Possible Vacuum or Conflict in the Exercise of Jurisdiction

If the shore-based operators and the remote operation center are deemed to be within the flag state's jurisdiction, there might still be a possible vacuum or conflict in the exercise of jurisdiction.

It is generally assumed that seafarers and cargoes are all on board the same ship. The Tribunal of the M/V 'Virginia G' Case refers to the finding in the M/V 'SAIGA' (No. 2) Case[94] that, under UNCLOS, the ship is to be treated as a unit 'as

---

92 Article 5(5) of the MLC stipulates that: 'Each Member shall effectively exercise its jurisdiction and control over seafarer recruitment and placement services, if these are established in its territory.'

93 The Tribunal in the M/V 'SAIGA' (No. 2) Case stated that, '[a]ny of these ships could have a crew comprising persons of several nationalities. If each person sustaining damage were obliged to look for protection from the State of which such person is a national, undue hardship would ensue.' See St. Vincent and the Grenadines v. Guinea (n 59).

94 St. Vincent and the Grenadines v. Guinea (n 59) para. 106.

regards the obligations of the flag State with respect to the ship and the right of a flag State to seek reparation for loss or damage caused to the ship by acts of other States'.[95] Therefore, the Tribunal determines that the M/V 'Virginia G' is to be considered as a unit, encompassing the ship itself, its crew and cargo on board as well as its owner and every person involved or interested in its operations, which should be treated as a whole entity linked to the flag State.[96]

Article 92(1) of UNCLOS mandates the flag state's exclusive jurisdiction over ship-related matters. Additionally, Article 94(6)[97] of the convention further stipulates that, the flag state, upon receiving the report by some other state that the flag state's jurisdiction and control with respect to its registered ship has not been properly exercised, shall investigate this matter and take necessary actions to remedy the situation.

However, if the shore-based operators and the remote operation center are located in other countries' territory, the unique nature of the flag state jurisdiction on them will be compromised,[98] and shall be superseded by the territorial jurisdiction of the specific country(s) where they actually locate.

In such a scenario, the concerns expressed by the Tribunal in the M/V 'SAIGA' (No. 2) Case[99] may also arise. If each shore-based operator and/or members of the remote operation center sustaining damage were obliged to seek protection from the state of which they are nationals, or if the state where the operators or operation center locate were to exercise its jurisdiction on the unmanned operation issues, undue hardship would ensue.

The legal basis and content of the national jurisdiction, territorial jurisdiction, and the flag state jurisdiction are different from each other. For example,

95 Panama/Guinea-Bissau (n 59) para. 126.

96 Ibid, para. 127.

97 Article 94(6) of UNCLOS stipulates that: 'A State which has clear grounds to believe that proper jurisdiction and control with respect to a ship have not been exercised may report the facts to the flag State. Upon receiving such a report, the flag State shall investigate the matter and, if appropriate, take any action necessary to remedy the situation.'

98 According to Sondre Torp Helmersen, the sui generis nature of flag State jurisdiction is supported by the possibility to exercise diplomatic protection on behalf of foreign citizens located on a State's flagged ships. See Sondre Torp Helmersen, 'The Sui Generis Nature of Flag State Jurisdiction' (2015) 58JYIL 319–335. To be noted, the Tribunal in the M/V 'Virginia G' Case observes that, in accordance with international law, the exercise of diplomatic protection by a state in respect of its nationals is to be distinguished from claims made by a flag State for damage in respect of natural and juridical persons involved in the operation of a ship who are not nationals of that State. See Panama/Guinea-Bissau (n 59) para. 128.

99 The Tribunal in the M/V 'SAIGA' (No. 2) Case stated that, '[a]ny of these ships could have a crew comprising persons of several nationalities. If each person sustaining damage were obliged to look for protection from the State of which such person is a national, undue hardship would ensue.' See St. Vincent and the Grenadines v. Guinea (n 59) para. 107.

under Article 94 of UNCLOS, countries exercising national or territorial jurisdiction do not assume the obligations and responsibilities of a flag state. Therefore, they cannot exert jurisdiction over the manning of the unmanned ship. Besides, if the flag state lacks jurisdiction over the human resources of shore-based operators and the remote operation center, there could be a potential vacuum of jurisdiction on certain operators and their operation of the unmanned ship.

As for the flag state's investigation, even if the shore-based operators and the center fall within the flag state's jurisdiction and the flag state could therefore investigate under Article 94(6) of UNCLOS, the flag state might encounter practical challenges if the individuals and/or subjects under investigation are situated in other countries.

5 Solving Flag State Jurisdiction Issues through Cooperations

5.1 *To Strengthen the Flag State's Jurisdiction Exercises within IMO Framework*

The continuous development of unmanned shipping technology underscores the enduring importance of flag state jurisdiction under UNCLOS, particularly as outlined in Article 94.

According to the IMO assembly, flag states bear the primary responsibility for establishing an adequate and effective system to exert control over their ships, ensuring their compliance with international rules and regulations pertaining to maritime safety, security, and environmental protection.[100] For conventional ships, IMO and other international organizations are concerned about potential issues arising from the flag State's failure to fulfil its obligations.[101] Tanaka highlights that even though non-compliance with relevant international rules is by no means peculiar to flag of convenience states, there is a valid concern that they may not fully commit themselves to enforcing relevant rules and standards for vessels flying their flag, pertaining to safety of navigation, labour conditions of the crew, the regulation of fisheries and marine pollution.[102]

The same concern holds true for unmanned ships. Accordingly, endeavors within IMO framework on flag state jurisdiction exercising will still be one practical solution for unmanned ships.

---

100 IMO Assembly Resolution A. 1157(32) (15 December 2021).

101 See the Note (n 79) para. 12.

102 Yoshifumi Tanaka (n 43) 213.

International regulatory regimes should be reinforced by a sound framework offering incentives to shipowners and operators, coupled with an effective enforcement and compliance strategy in order to ensure effective flag State jurisdiction and control over ships.[103] Initiatives by the IMO, including the IMO Member State Audit Scheme (IMSAS)[104] and the IMO Instruments Implementation Code (III Code), form part of the framework.[105] Under this framework, the anonymous consolidated audit summary reports (CASR) prepared by the IMO Secretariat, like the 2021 Non-exhaustive list of obligations under instruments relevant to the IMO Instruments Implementation Code (III Code), could assist member states in addressing specific issues of flag state jurisdiction, identifying the root causes, proposing corrective actions and best practices. Based on these insights, flag states can enhance implementation and enforcement of mandatory IMO instruments,[106] and strengthen their jurisdiction over unmanned ships flying their flag.

5.2 *Cooperations between the Flag State and the Classification Society*

In practice, flag states commonly delegate activities entailed by their obligations to private classification societies to effectively exercise jurisdiction and control in 'administrative, technical and social matters' as required by Article 94(1) of UNCLOS.[107] These classification societies are mandated to carry out the inspection of ships and to issue certificates on behalf of the flag States.[108]

---

103 See the Note (n 79) para. 13.

104 The IMO Member State Audit Scheme (IMSAS) commenced as a voluntary Scheme in 2006 and became a treaty obligation in January 2016. It aims to promote the consistent and effective implementation of applicable IMO instruments and to assist Member States to improve their capabilities, whilst contributing to the enhancement of global and individual Member State's overall performance in compliance with the requirements of the instruments to which it is a Party. See IMO website 'Member State Audit Scheme' <https://www.imo.org/en/OurWork/MSAS/Pages/default.aspx.> accessed 2 February 24, 2024. See also the Note (n 79) para. 30.

105 IMO Instruments Implementation Code (III CODE), IMO Resolution A.1070(28), Adopted on 4 December 2013 (Agenda item 10). The IMO Member State Audit Scheme (IMSAS) uses the IMO Instruments Implementation Code (III Code) as the audit standard for a comprehensive and objective assessment of how effectively it administers and implements those mandatory IMO instruments which are covered by the Scheme. See IMO (n 104).

106 2021 Non-exhaustive list of obligations under instruments relevant to the IMO Instruments Implementation Code (III Code), annex of the IMO Assembly Resolution A. 1157(32) (15 December 2021).

107 Alexander Proelss (ed.), United Nations Convention on the Law of the Sea: A Commentary (Hart 2017) 1484.

108 Ibid.

In the M/V 'Virginia G' Case, Panama as the flag state of M/V 'Virginia G' asserted a compliance with Article 94(3) of UNCLOS by delegating the control and issuance of technical certification for the M/V 'Virginia G' to recognized organizations, and a pursuance of Article 94(4) of UNCLOS by monitoring the M/V Virginia G through an annual safety inspection.[109] The Tribunal acknowledged these points,[110] stating that Panama exercised its authority to delegate the annual safety inspection and the issuance of technical certificates to Panama Shipping Registry Inc., one of its recognized organizations.[111] According to the Tribunal, in light of these and other matters,[112] a genuine link existed between Panama and the M/V Virginia G.[113]

Amid the rapid progress of unmanned shipping technology, many crucial classification societies[114] are also contributing to this endeavor by actively discussing the technical classifications and standards for unmanned ships and publishing relevant guidelines.

An essential objective of exercising flag state jurisdiction is to ensure the unmanned ship maintains a sound technical status, and is environmentally friendly. Therefore, the flag state can oversee and control these critical aspects of unmanned ships through delegated classification societies.

Before adopting specific legal rules and pertinent technical standards for unmanned ships, the practices of these delegated classification societies, such as the publishing of relevant guidelines, could be considered, to a certain extent, as indicative of the flag state's stance toward the design, construction, building, operation of unmanned ships, and the evolution of unmanned ship technologies.

---

109 Panama/Guinea-Bissau (n 59) para. 106.

110 ibid, paras. 114–16.

111 ibid, para. 116.

112 The Tribunal observed that Panama's legislation sets out the conditions for granting Panamanian nationality to ships, for the registration of ships in its territory, and for the right to fly its flag. Under Panamanian law, ship-owners are required to take specific actions, to carry out certain activities and to submit substantial information and documentation to fulfil all these requirements, in line with Panama's international obligations. The Tribunal in this regard noted that the M/V Virginia G obtained the required documents and technical certificates. It further noted that Panama imposed on owners of vessels specific conditions such as the requirement of a continuous synopsis record, in accordance with the International Convention for the Safety of Life at Sea, 1974 (SOLAS 1974). See Panama/Guinea-Bissau (n 59) para. 115.

113 Panama/Guinea-Bissau (n 59) para. 118.

114 These classification societies include ABS, China Classification Society, and Bureau Veritas Marine & Offshore, etc.

Besides, for unmanned ships in autonomy degree 4, as identified in IMO for its Regulatory Scoping Exercise for the Use of Maritime Autonomous Surface Ships (MASS),[115] the design, compilation and maintenance of unmanned operation software are currently not part of ship registration content. Similarly, for unmanned ships in autonomy degree 3, the working place and hosting state of the shore-based operator and the remote operation center are not registration information, either. While neither UNCLOS nor IMO conventions require consistency between these two aspects of information and the flag state's ship registration requirements, the two aspects are crucial to the effective jurisdiction of the flag state.

Therefore, in the future, it is advisable for classification societies to formulate and implement technical standards for these two aspects, through which the flag state of the unmanned ship could effectively implement flag state jurisdiction so as to align with the objectives of UNCLOS and the international conventions and instruments within the IMO framework.

5.3 *Flag State's Jurisdiction Cooperation with Other States*

5.3.1 Flag State's Jurisdiction Cooperation with Port State

Cooperation between port states and flag states is essential. Article 5(4) of MLC states that, in accordance with international law, a ship can be inspected by a member state of MLC other than the flag State when the ship is in one of its ports, to assess compliance with the convention.

Port state control mechanism is a jurisdiction cooperation between the port state and the flag state, operating within the IMO framework, aiming to reinforce flag state jurisdiction and encourage active jurisdictional exercise. This mechanism provides additional channels for the flag state to gather information about its unmanned ship with the assistance of the port state investigation and evidence collection. It also facilitates the flag state in taking necessary measures to enforce its flag state jurisdiction, so as to enhance the technical condition, management practices, and operational status of the ship. For unmanned ships, port state supervision should be intensified.

5.3.2 Flag State's Jurisdiction Cooperation with the States of Shore-Based Operators and the Remote Operation Center

Flag state jurisdiction should not undermine the jurisdiction of the states of shore-based operators and the remote operation center. The Tribunal in the M/V 'Virginia G' Case clarifies that the right of the State of nationality of the

115 See Outcome of the Regulatory Scoping Exercise for the Use of Maritime Autonomous Surface Ships (MASS) (3rd June 2021) MSC.1/Circ. 1638.

crew members to exercise diplomatic protection is not affected by the right of the State of nationality of a ship to seek redress on behalf of those crew members, irrespective of their nationality.[116]

On the contrary, Article 1(2) of MLC stipulates that member states of the convention shall cooperate with each other to ensure effective implementation and enforcement of the convention. While the applicability of the MLC to unmanned ships may be questionable, the cooperative spirit outlined in this convention among states should be taken into consideration.

5.3.3 Flag State's Jurisdiction Cooperation with the States of the Ship Operator

According to the Tribunal in the M/V 'Virginia G' Case, the ship operator could also be deemed as part of the whole ship 'unit'. However, in many ITLOS cases, including the M/V 'Virginia G' Case, the state to which the ship operator belongs rarely participated; instead, representation was typically by the flag state. This exposes certain limitations of the flag state jurisdiction.

This situation should be changed. As for unmanned ships, the ship operator is more involved in administrative, technical and social matters of the ship. Therefore, the flag state needs to establish a cooperation agreement with the state to which the ship operator belongs to strengthen the jurisdiction of the flag state. It will be more helpful if all ship operators involved in the ship operation could be registered. In addition, the examination and certification of the ship operators' qualifications should be carefully considered for maritime safety and security, as well as the marine environment protection.

6 Conclusion

According to UNCLOS, each state shall fix the conditions for the grant of nationality to ships, for the registration of those ships, and for the right of those ships to fly its flag.[117] Ships meeting the conditions outlined in the flag state's domestic legal framework are considered to have the nationality of that flag state. Consequently, these ships are entitled to exercise the right of navigation granted by international law, including UNCLOS.[118]

---

116 Panama/Guinea-Bissau (n 59) 121.

117 See UNCLOS, art 91.

118 See UNCLOS, art 90. Article 104 of UNCLOS also stipulates that the retention or loss of nationality is determined by the law of the State from which such nationality was derived.

Since conventional ships often operate in distant waters far from the flag state, flag States are not always in the best position to ensure their ships' compliance with UNLOS, IMO conventions, and other international requirements.[119] In the future, with the constant development of unmanned shipping technology, flag state jurisdiction will face more challenges. The whole international community might be called upon to resolve the jurisdiction vacuum or conflict issues.

It's also important to recognize that while UNCLOS establishes exclusive flag state jurisdiction, in many fields, it does not regard the flag state as the only subject of international law exercising jurisdiction and undertaking supervision and monitoring obligations. This is especially true for activities off the ship. For example, Article 109(3) of UNCLOS designates multiple states with jurisdiction over 'unauthorized broadcasting', including the flag state, the registration state of the installation, the state of which the alleged person is a national, any state where the transmissions can be received, any state where authorized radio communication is suffering interference.

In practice, there are some jurisdictional cooperation arrangements based on common goals. Examples of such arrangements include the Agreement on Strengthening Implementation of the Niue Treaty on Cooperation in Fisheries Surveillance and Law Enforcement in the South Pacific Region (NTSA)[120] and the Agreement on Port State Measures to Prevent, Deter and Eliminate Illegal, Unreported and Unregulated Fishing (PSMA).[121] NTSA permits one party to

119 Zoe Scanlon, 'Addressing the Pitfalls of Exclusive Flag State Jurisdiction: Improving the Legal Regime for the Protection of Submarine Cables' (2017) 48 JMLC 295–340.

120 Agreement on Strengthening Implementation of the Niue Treaty on Cooperation in Fisheries Surveillance and Law Enforcement in the South Pacific Region. [hereinafter 'NTSA']. NTSA is an agreement on cooperation between Forum Fishery Agency (FFA) members about monitoring, control and surveillance of fishing. It includes provisions on exchange of fisheries data and information, as well as procedures for cooperation in monitoring, prosecuting and penalizing operators of IUU fishing vessels. See <https://sdgs.un.org/partnerships/implementation-niue-treaty-subsidiary-agreement-ntsa-monitoring-control-and#:~:text=The%20Niue%20Treaty%20Subsidiary%20Agreement%20%28NTSA%29%20is%20an,prosecuting%20and%20penalising%20operators%20of%20IUU%20fishing%20vessels> accessed 24 February 2024.

121 The Agreement on Port State Measures to Prevent, Deter and Eliminate Illegal, Unreported and Unregulated Fishing was approved by the FAO Conference during 18–23 November 2009, and entered into force on 5 June 2016. [hereinafter 'PSMA']. This agreement seeks to prevent, deter and eliminate illegal, unreported and unregulated fishing through the adoption and implementation of effective port State measures as a means of ensuring the long-term conservation and sustainable use of living marine resources. See <https://www.fao.org/port-state-measures/resources/detail/en/c/1111616/> accessed 24 February 2024.

take extensive enforcement actions against a ship on behalf of another party (with the consent of the latter).[122] It could be a very useful mechanism when the flag state lacks sufficient resources or cannot carry out law enforcement actions.[123]

Therefore, with the evolving unmanned shipping technology and increasing prevalence of unmanned ships, flag state jurisdiction can be just one type of jurisdictions rather than an exclusive one. Relevant states can opt to exercise sole jurisdiction or engage in cooperative jurisdiction in specific situations to collaboratively address the challenges posed by the future development of unmanned shipping.

This paper suggests that the flag states of unmanned ships should bolster their flag state jurisdiction within the IMO framework. This can be achieved through collaborative efforts between flag states and their delegated classification societies, as well as through jurisdiction cooperations between flag states and port states, states of shore-based operators and the remote operation center, and states of the ship operator.

Acknowledgements

This research is supported by Southern Marine Science and Engineering Guangdong Laboratory (Zhuhai) (No. SML2020SP005).

References

Books and Chapters

Alexander Proelss (ed.), United Nations Convention on the Law of the Sea: A Commentary, Hart 2017.

Anna Petrig, Maritime Security in the Age of Autonomous Ships. In: Tafsir Johansson, Jonatan Echebarria Fernandez, Dimitrios Dalaklis, Aspasia Pastra and Jon Skinner (eds), Autonomous Vessel in Maritime Affairs: Law & Governance Implications, Palgrave Macmillan, 2023.

Anna Petrig, The commission of maritime crimes with unmanned systems: an interpretive challenge for the United Nations Convention on the Law of the Sea. In: Malcolm D. Evans and Sofia Galani (eds.), Maritime Security and the Law of the Sea: Help or Hindrance? Edward Elgar Publishing 2020.

122 See NTSA, art 8 ('Cooperative surveillance and enforcement activities').

123 Zoe Scanlon (n 119) 309.

Boleslaw Adam Boczek, Flags of Convenience: An International Legal Study, Harvard University Press 1962.

Emmanuel Kofi Mbiah, Coastal, Flag and Port State Jurisdiction: Powers and Other Considerations Under UNCLOS. In: Proshanto K. Mukherjee, Maximo Q. Mejia, Jr., and Jingjing Xu (eds.), Maritime Law in Motion, Springer 2020.

Henrik Ringbom and Felix Collin, Terminology and Concepts. In: Henrik Ringbom, Erik Røsæg, and Trond Solvang (eds.), Autonomous Ships and the Law, Routledge 2021.

James Crawford, Brownlie's Principles of Public International Law, 9th edition, Oxford University Press 2019.

Johan Schelin, Manning of Unmanned Ships. In: in Henrik Ringbom, Erik Røsæg, and Trond Solvang (eds.), Autonomous Ships and the Law, Routledge 2021.

John N. K. Mansell, Flag State Responsibility: Historical Development and Contemporary Issues, Springer 2009.

Kara Chadwick, Unmanned maritime systems will shape the future of naval operations: is international law ready? In: Malcolm D. Evans and Sofia Galani (eds.), Maritime Security and the Law of the Sea: Help or Hindrance? Edward Elgar Publishing 2020.

M.C.W. Pinto, Chapter 3 Hugo Grotius and the Law of the Sea. In: Lilian del Castillo (ed), Law of the Sea, From Grotius to the International Tribunal for the Law of the Sea, Brill Nijhoff 2015.

Malcolm N. Shaw, International Law, 8th edition, Cambridge University Press 2017.

Måns Jacobsson, What Challenges Lie Ahead for Maritime Law? In: Proshanto K. Mukherjee, Maximo Q. Mejia, Jr., and Jingjing Xu (eds.), Maritime Law in Motion, Springer 2020.

Philipp Wendel, State Responsibility for Interferences with the Freedom of Navigation in Public International Law, Springer 2007.

Reshmi Mukherjee, Ship Nationality, Flag States and the Eradication of Substandard Ships: A Critical Analysis. In: Proshanto K. Mukherjee, Maximo Q. Mejia, Jr., and Jingjing Xu (eds.), Maritime Law in Motion, Springer 2020.

Richard Williams, Unmanned ships—a challenge to the current international regime regulating the carriage of goods? In: Barış Soyer and Andrew Tettenborn (eds.), Ship Operations: New Risks, Liabilities and Technologies in the Maritime Sector, Informa 2021.

Robin Churchill, Vaughan Lowe and Amy Sander, The Law of the Sea, 4th edition, Manchester University Press 2022.

Simon Baughen, Unmanned Vessels and International Conventions for the Carriage of Goods by Sea. In: Barış Soyer and Andrew Tettenborn (eds.), Artificial Intelligence and Autonomous Shipping: Developing the International Legal Framework, Hart 2021.

Tingting Yang, Intelligent Ships. In: Proshanto K. Mukherjee, Maximo Q. Mejia, Jr., and Jingjing Xu (eds.), Maritime Law in Motion, Springer 2020.

Tomas Heidar, How Does the Law of the Sea Adapt to New Knowledge and Changing Circumstances? In: Tomas Heidar (ed.), New Knowledge and Changing Circumstances in the Law of the Sea, Brill 2020.

Yoshifumi Tanaka, The International Law of the Sea 4th Edition, Cambridge University Press 2023.

Youri Van Logchem, International Law of the Sea and Autonomous Cargo 'Vessels'. In: Barış Soyer and Andrew Tettenborn (eds.), Artificial Intelligence and Autonomous Shipping: Developing the International Legal Framework, Hart 2021.

Articles

Barbara Stępien, Can a ship be its own captain? Safe manning of autonomous and uncrewed vessels, Marine Policy 148 (2023) 105451.

Chris Whomersley, The Principle of Exclusive Flag State Jurisdiction: Is It Fit for Purpose in the Twenty-First Century? Asia-Pacific Journal of Ocean Law and Policy, 5 (2020) 330.

Eric Van Hooydonk, The law of unmanned merchant shipping—an exploration, Journal of International Maritime Law, 20 (2014) 403.

Henrik Ringbom, Regulating Autonomous Ships—Concepts, Challenges and Precedents, Ocean Development & International Law, 50 (2019), 141.

Lokesh Kumar Mavilla, The Conflict between Maritime Law & Unmanned Shipping: Manning the Unmanned Ghost Ships? 10 Supremo Amicus (2019) 142–152.

Paul W. Pritchett, Ghost Ships: Why the Law Should Embrace Unmanned Vessel Technology, Tulane Maritime Law Journal, 40 (2015) 197.

R. Jennings, A Changing International Law of the Sea, Cambridge Law Journal, 31 (1972) 32–49.

Robert Veala, Michael Tsimplisb, and Andrew Serdyc, The Legal Status and Operation of Unmanned Maritime Vehicles, Ocean Development & International Law, 50 (2019) 23–48.

Sabrina Hasan, Analysing the definition of "ship" to facilitate Marine Autonomous Surface Ships as ship under the law of the sea, Australian Journal of Maritime & Ocean Affairs, 15 (2023) 268–283.

Sondre Torp Helmersen, The Sui Generis Nature of Flag State Jurisdiction, Japanese Yearbook of International Law, (58) 2015 319–335.

Ziaul Haque Munim, Autonomous ships: a review, innovative applications and future maritime business models, Supply Chain Forum: An International Journal, 20 (2019) 266–279.

Zoe Scanlon, Addressing the Pitfalls of Exclusive Flag State Jurisdiction: Improving the Legal Regime for the Protection of Submarine Cables, Journal of Maritime Law and Commerce, 48 (2017) 295–340.

Conventions

1988 Fixed Platforms Protocol, Protocol to the Convention of 10 March 1988 for the Suppression of Unlawful Acts Against the Safety of Fixed Platforms Located on the Continental Shelf, adopted on 10 March 1988, entered into force on 1 March 1992.

2005 Fixed Platforms Protocol, Protocol of 2005 to the Protocol for the Suppression of Unlawful Acts Against the Safety of Fixed Platforms Located on the Continental Shelf, adopted on 14 October 2005, entered into force on 28 July 2010. IMO Doc. LEG/CONF.15/22.

2005 SUA Convention, 2005 Protocol to the 1988 Convention for the Suppression of Unlawful Acts Against the Safety of Maritime Navigation, adopted on 14 October 2005, IMO Doc. LEG/CONF.15/21.

HSC, Convention on the High Seas, adopted on 29 April 1958, entered in force on 30 September 1962, UNTS, Vol. 450.

International Convention on Salvage 1989, adopted on 28 April 1989, entered into force on 14 July 1996, UNTS, Vol. 1953.

MLC, Maritime Labour Convention 2006, adopted on 23 February 2006, entered in force on 20 August 2013, UNTS, Vol. 2952.

Niue Treaty Subsidiary Agreement (NTSA), Agreement on Strengthening Implementation of the Niue Treaty on Cooperation in Fisheries Surveillance and Law Enforcement in the South Pacific Region, adopted on 2 November 2012, entered into force on 30 July 2014.

SOLAS, International Convention for the Safety of Life at Sea, adopted on 1 November 1974, entered into force on 25 May 1980, UNTS, Vol. 1184.

SUA, Convention for the Suppression of Unlawful Acts Against the Safety of Maritime Navigation, adopted on 10 March 1988, 1678 UNTS 221.

UNCLOS, United Nations Convention on the Law of the Sea, adopted on 10 December 1982, entered into force on 16 November 1994, UNTS, Vol. 1833.

Cases

M/V 'Norstar' Case (Panama v. Italy), Judgment, ITLOS Reports 2019.

M/V Saiga (No. 2) Case (St. Vincent and the Grenadines v. Guinea), Judgment, ITLOS Reports 1999.

M/V 'Virginia G' Case (Panama/Guinea-Bissau) Judgment, ITLOS Reports 2014.

Reports and Documents

(CCS) China Classification Society Rules for Intelligent Ships 2020.

(CMI) International Working Group Position Paper on Unmanned Ships and the International Regulatory Framework.

(CMI) Summary of Responses to the CMI Questionnaire on Unmanned Ships, ANNEX 1 to the CMI IWG Submission to MSC 99th Session.

(FAO) The Agreement on Port State Measures to Prevent, Deter and Eliminate Illegal, Unreported and Unregulated Fishing.

(ILC) International Law Commission, Articles Concerning the Law of the Sea with Commentaries, 1956.

(IMO) IMO Instruments Implementation Code (III CODE), IMO Resolution A.1070(28), Adopted on 4 December 2013 (Agenda item 10).

(IMO) Annex of the Outcome of the Regulatory Scoping Exercise for the Use of Maritime Autonomous Surface Ships (MASS), MSC. 1/Circ. 1638, 3rd June 2021.

(IMO) Outcome of the Regulatory Scoping Exercise for the Use of Maritime Autonomous Surface Ships (MASS), MSC. 1/Circ. 1638, 3rd June 2021.

(IMO) IMO Assembly Resolution A. 1157(32), adopted on 15 December 2021.

(IMO) 2021 Non-exhaustive list of obligations under instruments relevant to the IMO Instruments Implementation Code (III Code), annex of the IMO Assembly Resolution A. 1157(32), adopted on 15 December 2021.

(Maritime UK) Maritime Autonomous Ship Systems (MASS) UK Industry Conduct Principles and Code of Practice, A Voluntary Code Version 6, November 2022.

Mayank Suri, Maritime Autonomous Surface Ships (MASS) and the Salvage Convention 1989, NUS Center for Maritime Law Working Paper 22/05, NUS Law Working Paper No 2022/016.

Robin R. Churchill, The Meaning of the 'Genuine Link' Requirement in Relation to the Nationality of Ships, A Study prepared for the International Transport Workers' Federation, 2000, ISBN: 0901969508.

(UN) Annex of the Note by the Secretary-General: Item 69 (a) of the provisional agenda, Oceans and the law of the sea, UN General Assembly 61 session, 17 July 2006, A/61/160.

(UN) Note by the Secretary-General: Item 69 (a) of the provisional agenda, Oceans and the law of the sea, UN General Assembly 61 session, 17 July 2006, A/61/160.

(UN) Report of the Ad Hoc Consultative Meeting of senior representatives of international organizations, convened by IMO, an annex to the Note by the Secretary-General: Item 69 (a) of the provisional agenda, Oceans and the law of the sea, UN General Assembly 61 session, 17 July 2006, A/61/160.

(UNCTAD) Review of Maritime Transport 2023, https://unctad.org/system/files/official-document/rmt2023_en.pdf.

CHAPTER 8

IMO Legal Regulation of Maritime Autonomous Surface Ships: Progress, Trends and China's Response

Xue Yuan and Bo Yu***

1 Introduction

Unmanned ships have great application value and broad development prospects, and the international community is very concerned about the technological development and commercial operation of unmanned ships, but they pose a challenge to the traditional legal framework. Currently, the conceptual terms related to unmanned ships have not yet been clearly defined, among which, Maritime Autonomous Surface Ship (MASS) is the International Maritime Organization's (IMO) generic term for this category of ships that can operate, to varying degrees, independent of human interaction. In recent years academia and industry have been focusing on the development of MASS and its potential benefits in terms of reduced operating costs and environmental protection. Several countries have continued to follow the MASS research and development process: in 2020, the Nippon Kaiji Kyokai (ClassNK) issued Approval in Principle (AIP) to a framework for manned autonomous ships developed under a fully autonomous action plan and execution system codenamed APEXS-auto; in 2020, the Korean government launched the Korea Autonomous Surface Ship (KASS) project with several companies within the shipping sector, universities and related organizations in the shipping sector. Korea's Samsung Heavy Industries and Hyundai Heavy Industries each completed sea trials of their respective built MASS in 2021 and announced that they would proceed with the commercialization of MASS in 2022; on 28 June 2021, Lloyd's Register awarded the first milestone Unmanned Marine System (UMS) certificate to SEA-KIT International; in March 2022, ClassNK and Bureau Veritas approved the framework principles for fully autonomous ships under

* School of Humanities and Social Sciences Harbin Engineering University, Harbin, China, yuanx8088@163.com.

** School of Humanities and Social Sciences Harbin Engineering University, Harbin, China, yb1212330@163.com.

 | DOI:10.1163/9789004706279_010

APExS-auto.[1] In April 2022, the American Bureau of Shipping and the Maritime and Port Authority of Singapore awarded the first autonomous and remotely controlled navigation mark for the first autonomous vessel 'Maju 510' tugboat developed by Keppel Offshore & Marine Singapore.[2] With the development of MASS technology and the achievement of certification comes the era of its commercialization, influencing the future direction of the shipping industry. Although the IMO started the topic of autonomous ships and their regulation relatively late, it has experienced exponential growth since the beginning of 2017 to date, making the development of international law norms for MASS an important issue in international shipping today.

The initial discussion in the academic community focused on the legal status of MASS. Two general views have emerged among scholars as to whether the legal status of MASS should be clarified: one view is that the legal status of unmanned ships is mainly regulated by UNCLOS and that the 1969 Vienna Convention on the Law of Treaties can also be applied to guide the application of UNCLOS to unmanned ships;[3] on the other hand, some scholars believe that commercial unmanned ships can obtain the legal status of 'ship' legal status, but they still need to overcome the gap between them and traditional ships in terms of ship registration and ship seaworthiness.[4] Secondly, scholars have discussed the legal issues and liability of MASS, including the legal status of MASS crew and shore-based manning personnel,[5] the collision liability of MASS, the salvage liability of MASS, the need for intelligent ship distress relief in the allocation of liability, the liability of AI navigation systems, the applicability of the innocent passage regime to MASS in territorial waters, and the discussion on the construction of MASS rules.[6] The legal issues related to MASS

---

1 Nippon Kaiji Kyokai, 'Class NK issues AiP for Fully Autonomous Ship Framework Developed by NYK, MTI and Japan Marine Science', (*Nippon Kaiji Kyokai*, 2022) <https://www.classnk.or.jp/hp/en/hp_news.aspx?id=7482&type=press_release&layout=1> accessed 27 January 2024.

2 Heli Harri, 'ABB and Keppel O&M verify next level of vessel autonomy with collision avoidance trials', (*Asea Brown Boveri*, 22 August 2022) <https://new.abb.com/news/detail/94104/abb-and-keppel-om-verify-next-level-of-vessel-autonomy-with-collision-avoidance-trials> accessed 27 January 2024.

3 Craig H. Allen, 'Determining the Legal Status of Unmanned Maritime Vehicles: Formalism vs Functionalism', (2018) 49 JMLC 477, 498–500.

4 Robert Veal, Michael Tsimplis, Andrew Serdy, The Legal Status and Operation of Unmanned Maritime Vehicles, (2019) 50 ODIL 23, 41.

5 Anastasiya Golovina, 'On the issue of the legal status of persons exercising control of a maritime autonomous surface vessel', (2022) 134 SHS Web Conf 1; Junghwan Choi, Sangil Lee, 'Legal Status of the Remote Operator in Maritime Autonomous Surface Ships (MASS) Under Maritime Law', (2021) 52 ODIL 445, 445.

6 Brendan Gogarty, Meredith Hagger, 'The Laws of Man over Vehicles Unmanned: The Legal Response to Robotic Revolution on Sea, Land and Air', (2008) 19 JLIS 73, 74; Rob McLaughlin,

have gradually been discussed. The discussion of legal issues related to MASS is gradually developing. The joint interest of academics and practitioners in MASS has driven the process of IMO legislation to regulate MASS. Although IMO started the topic of autonomous ships and their regulation relatively late, it has experienced exponential growth since 2017, and the development of international law regulation for MASS has become an important issue in international maritime transport nowadays.

2 Phased Development of MASS Legislation within the IMO Framework

IMO has played a leading role in the formulation of MASS legal norms. In 2017, IMO released the 2018–2023 Strategic Plan, which proposed to incorporate advanced technologies into the scope of the regulatory framework, providing a normative development path for ship autonomous technologies. IMO and its Maritime Safety Committee (MSC) and Legal Committee (LEG) will discuss MASS regulations in stages in their follow-up meetings. The MASS rule-making study within the IMO framework has started the first phase of work. In 2017, MSC 98 proposed to regard regulatory scoping exercise (RSE) as the starting point for the development of MASS regulation, focusing on legal issues including civil liability in the event of an accident in MASS. In 2018, MSC 99 and 2019 LEG 106 announced the approval of the RSE working framework of the conventions within their framework based on the preliminary definition of MASS and the 4 autonomous levels, respectively, and in 2019, the Interim Guidelines for Autonomous Ship Trials were approved. This document requires taking measures to identify the MASS crew, and risk for trial and to reduce the risk to a reasonable and acceptable minimum level.[7]

In May 2021, the MASS rulemaking study reached the start of the rulemaking phase with the announcement that MSC 103 had completed the current phase of RSE analysis within its framework. Two key documents emerged from this phase, the MSC and the LEG's respective RSE analysis, with key areas of legal vulnerability such as MASS terminology and definitions, the function of

'Unmanned Naval Vehicles at Sea: USVs, UUVs, and the Adequacy of the Law', (2011) 21 Journal of Law, Information and Science 100, 114; Jennifer Parker, 'The Challenges Posed by the Advent of Maritime Autonomous Surface Ships for International Maritime Law', (2021) 35 AMZMLJ 31, 41–42; Craig H. Allen, 'Why the COLREGS Will Need to be Amended to Accommodate Unmanned Vessels' (2021) SSRN <https://ssrn.com/abstract=3854220> accessed 27 January 2024.

7 IMO, International Maritime Organization, Maritime Safety Committee, *Interim guidelines for MASS trials*, MSC.1/Circ.1604 (2019) paras. 1–3.

remote control stations, and the legal status of remote operators receiving key attention. The development of a target-based MASS Code with corresponding provisions for functional requirements is the ultimate solution to the legal aspects of MASS application. In this phase, IMO sees the review of the Convention as a basis for understanding whether the new body of law, MASS, applies to the conventions within the IMO framework and, if so, how the provisions of the existing conventions need to be adapted. However, the review of the conventions on an article-by-article basis was seen as time-consuming and labor-intensive, implying that the review of the conventions was of little use.[8] While the effectiveness of the IMO Convention review exercise has been questioned, the high-priority issues common to both RSE outcome analysis papers that need to be addressed set the overall direction for the MASS legislation. It is also an important basis for initiating MASS rulemaking.

With the release of MSC's Draft Roadmap for maritime autonomous surface ships (hereinafter referred to as the Draft Roadmap) on 10 January 2022, the formulation of the MASS Code has entered a substantive negotiation stage. The Draft Roadmap lists MSC's work plan for the content of the instrument, the formulation process, and the legislative model in the next few years, and it is announced that the legislative work will be completed in 2025. The MSC 105 meeting reviewed and finalized the Draft Roadmap and agreed to set up a joint MSC-LEG-FAL working group to set the ultimate goal of striving for the implementation of the mandatory MASS Code in January 2028. LEG 109 has also announced that it will develop its draft roadmap, approving the establishment of a joint working group on a cross-cutting mechanism on MASS to reach a consensus on the legislative steps that the MSC will take. The work of IMO is still going on at this stage. In the future, IMO will also introduce the Marine Environment Protection Committee (MEPC) into the formulation process of the MASS Code. The MASS Working Group submitted a report on the work of its second meeting, in which it presented the status of the development of the MASS Code and issued a draft of the MASS Code on 8 November 2023.

The work of IMO at this stage is continuing. In future work, in addition to the common application issues sorted out in the review of MSC, LEG and other conventions, IMO will continue to discuss the content of pre-requisite clauses such as MASS autonomy level and MASS rule application subject.

8 See Danish Maritime Authority, *Analysis of regulatory barriers to autonomous ships*, (December 2017), available online: <https://dma.dk/Media/637745499808186153/Analysis%20of%20Regulatory%20Barriers%20to%20the%20Use%20of%20Autonomous%20Ships.pdf> accessed 27 January 2024.

3 The Construction of a System of MASS Code Guidelines for National Classification Societies

3.1 *Core of the System: MASS Classification Society Rules*

The act of inspection and certification of ships by classification societies by The International Safety Management (ISM) Code has a special irreplaceable and important role to play in promoting the safety of human life, ships and other property at sea. The rapid development of MASS technology has prompted the classification societies of various countries to successively issue normative documents for the design, construction, operation and classification of MASS, mainly including MASS classification society rules and MASS classification rules, to protect the marine operation of MASS Safety, safety of life, property and the environment.

China Classification Society (CCS) released the world's first Intelligent Ship Rules (2015) and underwent two updates in 2020 and 2022; Lloyd's Register (LR) also released the Unmanned Marine Systems Code in 2017. CCS takes smart ships as the main body, and according to the IMO issue process and practical experience, the intelligent navigation of remotely controlled ships and autonomously operated ships are functionally subdivided and described in detail within the specification, to adapt to the development needs of adaptive smart ships. Unmanned Marine Systems Code, on the other hand, takes unmanned ships and unmanned submersibles as the main body of unmanned systems, follows the traditional ship code system and addresses unmanned systems from an unmanned perspective on four levels: scope of application, purpose, functional objectives and performance requirements. Russian Register of Shipping (RS), Det Norske Veritas (DNV) and Bureau Veritas (BV) have successively confirmed the MASS classification rules in two ways: separate release and document revision. In June 2020, RS published the Regulations for Classification of Maritime Autonomous and Remotely Controlled Surface Ships (MASS), which incorporate MASS situational awareness systems, data communications, autonomous navigation systems, and MASS regulatory mid-track markers and remote control centers into the classification rules.[9] In October 2021, BV published the latest version of its Additional Service Feature SMART, which also covers smart functions related to data collection, transmission, analysis and visualization in remote monitoring, onshore maintenance or remote operation of systems, completing its specification framework for smart

9 See Russian Maritime Register of Shipping, *Regulations for Classification of Maritime Autonomous and Remotely Controlled Surface Ships*, ND No. 2–030101-037-E (27 September 2022), accessed 27 January 2024.

systems.[10] In October 2020, Det Norske Veritas (DNV) added the classification criteria for smart ships in Section 24 of Equipment and Design Features, Chapter 5, Equipment and Design Features, Part 6 of the Ship Classification Rules.[11]

3.2 *Main Content: MASS Guidelines Issued by Classification Societies*

Although inferior to the MASS Code and Classification Rules in terms of effectiveness, MASS Guidelines have two major advantages over the normative documents issued by classification societies. Firstly, horizontally, MASS Guides are more specific in the standards they cover, as they are mostly based on the functions of the relevant systems. Secondly, from a vertical perspective, some MASS guidelines have been introduced to supplement specific provisions of the classification society codes and to promote the continuous progress of the classification society code guidance system. This is shown in Table 8.1.

TABLE 8.1 MASS Guidelines for classification societies

Classification society	Guidelines
CCS	Guide for Autonomous Cargo Ships (2018) Guide for Intelligent Energy Efficiency Management for Ships Guide for Ship Smart Cabin Inspection
ClassNK	Guidelines for Automated/Autonomous Operation on Ships Guidelines for Digital Smart Ships
DNV	CLASS GUIDELINE: Autonomous and remotely operated ships CLASS GUIDELINE: Smart vessel
KR	Guidelines for Smart System Application Interim Guidelines for Smart Ship Infrastructure
ABS	Guide for Autonomous and Remote Control Functions Guide for Smart Functions for Marine Vessels and Offshore Units
RS	Guidelines on Cyber Safety

10 See Bureau Veritas, *Additional Service Feature SMART, SECTION 1 ADDITIONAL SERVICE FEATURE SMART*, NR675 (January 2024), available online: <https://erules.veristar.com/dy/data/bv/pdf/675-NR_2024-01.pdf> accessed 27 January 2024.

11 See Margrethe Andersen, 'New DNV GL rules drive smart ship operation and management' (*Det Norske Veritas*, 2 November 2020) <https://www.dnv.com/news/new-dnv-gl-rules-drive-smart-ship-operation-and-management-188497> accessed 27 January 2024.

The first editions of the Classification Societies' MASS guidelines were issued during the first phase of the IMO Code development. During this period, the number of classification societies issuing MASS guidelines increased as the topic became more widely discussed by the maritime community. The MASS guidelines have been updated on a trajectory of practical experience gained by classification societies. The main body of the guide also includes MASS system functions such as intelligent energy efficiency and ship data security, demonstrating a level of detail that is different from the MASS Code. Similar to many unmanned units, MASS navigation is powered primarily by batteries and axle-belt generators, and more advanced fuel-saving technologies are used to maintain cruise time. It is worth noting that *the Guide for Autonomous Cargo Ships (2018)* published by the CCS requires that the overall safety and environmental protection levels are not lower than those of existing international conventions; the recognition of smart support for energy efficiency and green operations and the concept of whole life management of MASS, as set out in DNV's *Smart Ship Guidelines* published in 2018 and updated in 2022, is in line with the IMO Marine Environmental Protection Committee (MPEC)'s initial strategic objectives for greenhouse gas emissions reduction from ships adopted at MEPC 72. These key elements illustrate the important role of MASS in the development of green shipping.

4 National Responses to MASS Code Developments

4.1 *Proposing MASS Rulemaking as an IMO Member*

4.1.1 National Perspectives in MSC Meetings

In the MSC meetings, countries' opinion papers on the MASS rulemaking mainly focused on the meetings within the second phase after the MSC RSE work, using both the RSE results analysis and the Draft Roadmap as the basis for their opinion outputs. Before the IMO published the MASS Code, the scope of the MASS terminology, definitions, operations and other fundamental elements discussed in the national proposals were broadly defined. This is shown in Table 8.2.

The legal meaning and structure of SOLAS became an important basis for the elaboration of the content of the national MASS Code. According to the current technical development of MASS, the co-sponsor of MSC 105/7/2 raised the question of whether the MASS Code should be based on SOLAS as the main part of the content; MSC 105/7/3, on the other hand, referred to the structure of SOLAS with preamble as the first part, objectives and definitions as the introduction of rules, and general rules, ship structure, subdivision and stability as the main content for rule construction; the autonomous class of

TABLE 8.2 Representative views of various countries at the MSC meeting

File number	Abstract
MSC 105/7/2	Developing non-mandatory instruments as an intermediate step; focusing on an outline of the draft MASS operating rules related to SOLAS requirements; proposing the structure of the draft MASS specification.
MSC 105/7/3	The status of the regulatory instruments, the types of regulatory instruments, and the purpose and objectives of the instruments are considered in the formulation of the MASS Code; a draft of the MASS Code is proposed in the document.
MSC 105/INF.2	Suggestions on the development of terms, definitions, minimum safe manning and remote operation of MASS; MASS autonomy levels within the IMO framework need to be reclassified with special consideration of human factors; all levels of automation require different degrees of human attention.
MSC 105/7/6	The purpose and objectives of the MASS instrument, the definition and terminology of MASS, and the scope of application of the MASS Code instrument; due to the characteristics of the current MASS technology development stage, the MASS rules should be based on the second-level autonomy of MASS, and should focus on navigation-related issues. and should focus on the systematic regulation of navigation-related issues.
MSC 105/7/7	Develop a non-mandatory MASS instrument for industry and administration to establish an experience accumulation phase; propose key principles for MASS rulemaking, with general requirements, functional requirements, communication and data requirements, operational requirements, and risk assessment and control requirements as content structures; Figures suggest further adjustments accordingly.

MSC 105/INF.2 focuses on this feature and advocates the reclassification of the autonomous class of MASS set by IMO, which should be improved as a prerequisite for the formulation of MASS Code.

In addition, some member states suggested that the status of the regulatory instrument, the objectives of the instrument, etc. should be described as the preamble, and the formulation of a non-mandatory instrument should be a necessary first step. IMO's legislative instruments can be broadly divided into two categories: formal mandatory instruments and non-mandatory instruments, the former including treaties and the latter including recommendations. The only instruments that the IMO itself can issue are Recommendations.[12] However, many resolutions may even have an effect close to a mandatory norm,[13] depending on whether IMO has an authoritative position in the discussion of the proposed topic, whether international and non-international organizations are actively involved in the legislative process, and whether the resolutions as general rules reflect the broad consensus among member states. As the first step of MASS legislation, the non-mandatory instrument is in line with IMO's legislative logic.

4.1.2 *National Perspectives in LEG Meetings*

LEG 109 closed on 25 March 2022 and the Committee agreed that the MASS Code rules should operate within the UNCLOS legal framework, with a focus on the human factor. MASS technology has not yet reached a fully autonomous level of development and humans are present throughout the life cycle of MASS. While much of the current research has focused on the interface between MASS technology and law, the classical human factor issues also require attention due to the dynamics of technological development, as shown in Table 8.3.

Based on the analysis of the LEG RSE results and the Draft Roadmap, in addition to the fundamental issues of MASS terminology, definitions and operation, the commercialization of MASS for the carriage of cargo and passengers, as mentioned in LEG 108/7/1; the liability and indemnity system and compulsory insurance system of MASS, as advocated in LEG 109/13/2; the concerns of LEG 109/13/1 on the impact of MASS on the marine environment; and the maritime administrative jurisdiction of port states, which is a common concern of LEG 109/13/1 and LEG 109/13/2, have been the subject of proposals by member states. 109/13/1 concerned about the impact of MASS on the marine environment; LEG 109/13/1 and LEG 109/13/2 involve the maritime administrative jurisdiction of the port state, which should be noticed in the future. In other words, these countries have set high expectations for the MASS Code to be constructed in the future. The 'extension' referred to here is not content that is irrelevant to the development of the MASS Code, but compared to the current autonomous technology as the core of the MASS Code discussion. This

12 See Cleopatra Elmira Henry, *The Carriage of Dangerous Goods by Sea: The Role of the International Maritime Organization in International Legislation* (St. Martin's Press 1985) 58.

13 Frederic L Kirgis, Specialized Law-Making Processes, in Oscar Schachter, Christopher C Joyner (eds), *United Nations Legal Order, Volume 1* (Cambridge University Press 1995) 157.

TABLE 8.3 Representative views of various countries at the LEG meeting

File number	Abstract
LEG 108/7/1	Development of a document on the key details of the laws and regulations governing the operation of MASS, including the definition of MASS, the regulations for remote operators, the liability for damage that may be caused by MASS, and the legal aspects of MASS for the transport of goods and passengers.
LEG 109/13/1	Explanation of IMO's future goals; introduction of relevant guidance for MASS; noting the adverse impact of MASS on maritime safety, and marine environment; lack of current MASS standards; handling legal instruments within the LEG's remit for the past two years so that MASS is applicable to existing Regulatory Framework; Accompanying Checklist for Identifying Administrative Requirements.
LEG 109/13/2	Discuss the establishment of a liability and indemnity system that provides a clear framework for payment and indemnity amounts for identifying parties responsible for specific types of maritime loss or damage; consider the issue of introducing a compulsory insurance system; attach a Checklist for Identifying Administrative Requirements.
LEG 109/13/5	It is recommended that a comprehensive roadmap be developed as part of the joint working group's draft terms of reference on MASS, addressing common issues identified by the three committees, with recommendations to the committees after each meeting.

part of the content has a lower priority to solve, and the discussion of some issues also needs to be based on. The finalization of the core content is the premise. It can be said that the extension content is a continuation of the core content, and it can be said that discussing the extension content is the pursuit of the improvement of the MASS rule system.

4.2 *Representative National and Regional Regulatory Responses to the Development of the MASS Code*

The construction of MASS international rules is still going on. In addition to the suggestions and opinions expressed by member states within the IMO framework on the gradual incorporation of MASS into the regulatory system, the responses of many countries and regions are reflected in the adjustment dynamics oriented by the application of relevant domestic laws to MASS. The promulgation of regulatory policies and the update of the classification society's MASS specification guide system reflect the different attitudes of different entities toward MASS regulations.

From the perspective of the UK's domestic legal framework and the new movement of industry guidelines, both the UK legal and practical communities are very positive in their expectations for the development of MASS within the regulatory framework. To keep pace with the development of MASS, the UK domestic proposed that the existing regulations such as the *Merchant Shipping Act 1995* and *the Workboat Regulations V2* should be sorted out to enable MASS to be applied by removing, amending or updating the existing regulations, breaking the legal barriers to the application of autonomous innovative technologies and providing a good regulatory environment for MASS.[14] In September 2021, the UK Department for Transport highlighted the need for the Merchant Shipping Act to identify key definitions of MASS operations, to ensure MCA regulation of all MASS, and to give the MCA new powers to develop regulations relating to remote control stations, among other areas, to prepare the domestic legal framework for future changes in international law. The call for community-level views on future regulation in the areas of ports, unmanned underwater vehicles, marine equipment, maritime safety, industry insurance and MASS-designated test areas is also being recycled in November 2021.[15] The UK Maritime Autonomous System Regulatory Working Group (MASRWG) released the first Code of Practice in November 2017, which was well received by the global industry. As of November 2023, the Code has been updated to the 7th edition. Version 7 adds updated guidance on a variety of topics including Inland Waterways and Operator Standards. The Code of Practice provides the ideal focus to enable industry to develop ahead of the anticipated international and national regulatory frameworks.[16] In terms of the UK's

---

14 See Maritime & Coastguard Agency, *Maritime Autonomy Regulation Lab (MARLab) Report* (11 November 2020), available online: <https://www.gov.uk/government/publications/maritime-autonomy-regulation-lab-marlab-report/maritime-autonomy-regulation-lab-marlab-report> accessed 27 January 2024.

15 See Department for Transport, *Future of transport regulatory review consultation: Maritime autonomy and remote operations* (September 2021), available online: <https://assets.publishing.service.gov.uk/government/uploads/system/uploads/attachment_data/file/1020986/future-of-transport-regulatory-review-maritime-autonomy-and-remote-operations-print-version.pdf> accessed 27 January 2024.

16 See Maritime UK, 'Maritime UK launches Version 7 of the Industry Code of Practice for Maritime Autonomous Ship Systems.' (*Maritime UK*, 29 November 2023) <https://www.maritimeuk.org/media-centre/news/news-maritime-uk-launches-version-7-industry-code-practice-maritime-autonomous-ship-systems/> accessed 27 January 2024.

response to the current stage of domestic law changes, the UK has accepted the content of the MASS Code as currently discussed by the IMO, but based on its consideration of ports and unmanned underwater vehicles as subjects of law for consultation, the changes to the UK's domestic law and rules are notable for ensuring the administrative powers of its executive authorities in the context of the MASS impact on the traditional maritime industry.

Judging from expressions such as '2021 is the Year of Science and Technology in Russia, and November is named the Month of Artificial Intelligence',[17] the Russian state attaches great importance to the development of autonomous AI technology. The emergence of MASS marks the organic integration of artificial intelligence and traditional shipping. On 5 December 2020, the Government of the Russian Federation adopted a draft federal law and a government decree on autonomous ships, allowing shipping companies to equip their Russian-flagged ships with a-Navigation systems and operate under a state test order after the tests are completed.[18] In 2021, the Ministry of Industry and Trade of the Russian Federation amended the Merchant Shipping Law of the Russian Federation and some regulatory documents of the Russian Federation in accordance with the legal relationship arising from the operation of MASS.[19] The relevant Russian ministries and commissions reviewed the draft federal law on MASS, and with the participation of the practical community, considering the documents submitted by IMO members and observers to advance the work of RSE within the framework of LEG and MSC, it was openly discussed in the Russian shipping community. However, the content of the draft contradicts other regulations, and the proposed amendments cannot fully ensure the safety of navigation under the MASS operational framework. Therefore, the question of legislative integration, classification of MASS, and the establishment of the legal status of manipulators at the level of state legislation of the Russian Federation remains unresolved.[20]

17 See Anna Nadibaidze, 'Russian Perceptions of Military AI, Automation, and Autonomy' (*Foreign Policy Research Institute*, 27 January 2022) <https://issuu.com/foreignpolicyresearchinstitute/docs /012622_russia_ai_/4> accessed 27 January 2024.

18 See PortNews, 'Эксперимент по опытной эксплуатации автономных судов под флагом РФ пройдёт с 2020 по 2025 годы', (*Port News*, 8 December 2020) <https://portnews.ru/news/ 305932/> accessed 27 January 2024.

19 IMO, International Maritime Organization, *Comments on documents LEG 107/8 and LEG 107/8/17 in respect of legal regulation of MASS trials in the Russian Federation*, LEG 108/7/1 (2021), para. 4.

20 Anastasiya Golovina (n 5) 2, 3.

Based on the goal of promoting the commercialization of MASS, Pacifi's domestic regulatory response to the MASS Code mainly revolves around the formulation of MASS standards and the approval of MASS. As one of the countries leading the commercialization of MASS, Norway has been working on the establishment of MASS standards since the initial stages of MASS development. Since the DNV report *The Future of Shipping* was published in 2014. DNV published two classification society guidelines in 2018 and in October 2020, DNV updated its classification society entry specifications to enable MASS to move into the shipping industry in a safe and orderly manner. Regulation of MASS in Norway exists not only in the classification society guidelines issued by DNV and the updated classification society entry norms, but also in the Norwegian Maritime Authority's Guidance related to the construction or installation of automated functions intended to perform unmanned or partially unmanned operations, issued on 27 August 2020, which guides administrative authorities in assessing and approving autonomous, fully or partially remotely operated ships to ensure that the safety level of their domestic MASS is in line with conventional ships.[21]

The EU has also demonstrated its concern about the imbalance between MASS development and regulation. Compared to the UK and Russia, the EU currently still focuses on the normative aspects of the MASS test phase and is also at odds with the two-pronged regulatory path of domestic standards and regulation in Norway and Australia. The EU published the first edition of the EU Operational Guidelines for Safe, Secure and Sustainable Trials of MASS (hereafter referred to as the Operational Guidelines) in October 2020, based on the Interim Guidelines for Autonomous Vessels published by the IMO. On 30 November of the same year, on the occasion of the 2nd International Ship Autonomy and Sustainability Summit, the members of the EU MASS Expert Group agreed on the key principles for the use of the Operational Guidelines to guide the safe and sustainable development of autonomous shipping and that, for the safe management, monitoring, communication and control of MASS and its navigation, consideration should be given to the integration of MASS with the Union Maritime Information and Exchange System (SafeSeaNet) as a

21 See Norwegian Maritime Authority, Guidance in connection with the construction or installation of automated functionality aimed at performing unmanned or partially unmanned operations, RSV 12–2020 (27 August 2020), available online: <https://www.sdir.no/en/shipping/legislation/directives/guidance-in-connection-with-the-construction-or-installation-of-automated-functionality-aimed-at-performing-unmanned-or-partially-unmanned-operations/> accessed 27 January 2024.

maritime data sharing platform. To achieve safe management, monitoring, communication and control of MASS and its navigation, consideration should be given to the in-depth interaction between MASS and SafeSeaNet[22] as a maritime data-sharing platform and its further development.[23]

5 An Exploration of MASS Code Trends

5.1 *The MASS Autonomous Level Division Needs to be Improved Urgently*

5.1.1 Blurred Standards: Defects in the Division of MASS Autonomy Levels within the IMO Framework

Several MASS autonomy classes have been proposed by IMO and classification societies:

- IMO: Degree one: Ship with automated processes and decision support: Seafarers are on board to operate and control the ship; Degree two: Remotely controlled ship with seafarers on board; Degree three: Remotely controlled ship without seafarers on board; Degree four: Fully autonomous ship;
- CCS: R1, Remote control boat with crew on board; R2, Remote control boat without crew on board; A1, Anchorage to anchorage, someone diverts water; A2, Anchorage to anchorage, remote control water diversion; A3, berth to berth;
- LR: AL 0 Manual; AL 1 On-board Decision Support; AL 2 On & Off-board Decision Support; AL 3 'Active' Human in the loop; AL 4 Human on the loop, Operator/ Supervisory; AL 5 Fully autonomous (Rarely supervised operation where decisions are entirely made and actioned by the system); AL 6 Fully autonomous (Unsupervised operation where decisions are entirely made and actioned by the system during the mission).
- ABS: Manual; Smart; Semi-Autonomy; Full Autonomy.

The level of autonomy is also widely used as a criterion for the classification of automation systems in many different fields, the higher the autonomy level, the higher the level of machine decision-making and the less reliance on humans. Although IMO and the major classification societies vary in their classification of ship autonomy, they generally consider the three dimensions of

22 Commission Directive 2014/100/EU of 28 October 2014 amending Directive 2002/59/EC of the European Parliament and of the Council establishing a Community vessel traffic monitoring and information system Text with EEA relevance [2014] OJ L 308/82.

23 European Commission, 'Maritime Autonomous Ships and Shipping' (European Commission website) <https://transport.ec.europa.eu/transport-modes/maritime/maritime-autonomous-ships-and-shipping_en> accessed 27 January 2024.

autonomous system functionality, operational complexity and human involvement in the classification of MASS autonomy. Although the degree of detail of the MASS autonomy classes introduced by different entities varies, a consensus has been formed on the future development direction and technical route of MASS.

Therefore, three main factors affect the classification of MASS autonomy levels: operational complexity, automation level, and human participation in its operation.[24] The complexity of the operation determines how complex the operation is and what features are required to support the operation. This will also define limits on the complexity of automated functions, and the extent to which specific actions can be done autonomously. The level of automation determines the ratio between the functions implemented in the autonomous system and the functions assigned to human operators. Human presence will determine the minimum level of automation required. Human involvement defines the role and location of the human operator, i.e., where the outcome of a control function can be directly observed or perceived, be it below deck on another vessel nearby, or at a remote control station. Compared with complex operations and different levels of automation, the uncertainty of human participation may not fully grasp the actions of autonomous systems, lack of awareness of autonomous system patterns, and over-reliance on autonomous systems.[25] Therefore, it is necessary to consider whether someone is responsible for the overall safety of the ship, which is the content of the liability section in the laws and regulations. The responsibility assumed by humans has become a potential factor affecting the MASS autonomous classification.

Under the premise of ensuring navigational safety and environmental protection, the legal requirements for the number of personnel on board should be moderated accordingly, and the legal status of shore-based operators should be re-examined from a new perspective, or even given the status of the crew to a certain extent. Although current research has identified an unmanned, highly autonomous ship as the ultimate target, MASS needs to be developed gradually to achieve a high degree of autonomy. Onboard manning also needs to be reduced in stages: some of the MASS remotely controlled by ROC still need to have a certain crew on board; the other part of the highly autonomous MASS remotely controlled by ROC does not need to be manned, but the technology is now fully mature in both. At this stage, humans will still play an

---

24 IMO, International Maritime Organization, Maritime Safety Committee, *Proposal for a classification scheme for degrees of autonomy*, MSC 100/5/1 (2018) para. 3.

25 Mehdi Poornikoo, Kjell Ivar Øvergård, 'Levels of automation in maritime autonomous surface ships (MASS): a fuzzy logic approach', (2022) 24 MEL 278, 280.

important role. Issues such as fatigue, information overload and other issues of the crew's rights and interests need to be paid attention to.[26] Although the draft of MASS Code was released, how the autonomy levels will be classified is still undetermined at this time. The classification of MASS autonomy levels will still be left to the MSC.[27]

5.1.2 The Human Element: the Path to Refinement of the MASS Autonomy Hierarchy

According to the IMO definition of MASS, MASS is capable of operating with varying degrees of independence from humans, and the definition is formulated more generally in terms of autonomous navigation functions. The definition of MASS has a different conceptual standard to that of autonomy,[28] as the IMO's proposed classification of MASS autonomy levels indicates that they are to some extent linked to the level of manning on board. As the MASS autonomy class is to some extent linked to the manning level on board, its autonomy class depends to a large extent on the stage of the ship's voyage.[29] Existing classifications of autonomy classes use a class-based taxonomy, with higher classes implying that more work is done by the autonomous system, while lower classes have more of the navigational tasks performed by humans. This results in a flow between levels of autonomy at different stages of navigation when faced with different situations. This flux is not possible to accurately define the MASS that lies between the two levels of autonomy, and there is no standard for determining the smaller variations within each level of autonomy. As MASS technology advances and commercialization accelerates, the investment in MASS in the maritime industry is bound to grow, but this trend will also bring risks to the safety of maritime navigation, the safety of life at sea and the marine environment. The flow of classes will have a negative impact on the allocation of legal liability, and therefore the legal aspects of MASS may require a more precise classification of autonomous classes. Accordingly, the level of automation and manning of the ship and the level of human

26 Thomas Porathe, 'Autonomous Ships: A Research Strategy for Human Factors Research in Autonomous Shipping', (International Conference on Applied Human Factors and Ergonomics: Advances in Human Aspects of Transportation; Springer International Publishing, July 2021), 480.

27 IMO, International Maritime Organization, Maritime Safety Committee, *Report of the Maritime Safety Committee on Its 107th Session*, MSC 107/20 (26 June 2023) para. 5.22.25.

28 Mehdi Poornikoo, Kjell Ivar Øvergård (n 25) 18.

29 Marilia Abilio Ramos, Ingrid Bouwer Utne, Ali Mosleh, 'Collision Avoidance on Maritime Autonomous Surface Ships: Operators' Tasks and Human Failure Events' (2019) 116 SS 33, 34–35.

involvement should be the main factors to be considered in the classification of the autonomy class. The attitude of MSC 105 in considering the revision of the MASS autonomy levels and the respective definitions to be submitted to the Joint Working Group for negotiation indicates that IMO also has doubts about the compatibility of its initial classification of autonomy levels with the subsequent MASS Code.

In MSC 105/INF.2 Finland proposes to frontload the classification of levels of autonomy based on the different levels of observation, operation and reflection of the operator to reduce the occurrence of potential legal liability issues arising from the confusion of levels of autonomy in the future.[30] Although this classification of levels of autonomy cannot be directly translated into regulations, its existence can clarify the different levels of human involvement and interaction with automated systems. This definition can be referred to for the classification of MASS levels of autonomy.

5.2 *The Content and Structure of the MASS Code Is Becoming Clearer*

The core content of the MASS Code is clear. In the RSE results analysis document of MSC and LEG, the two committees stated that they had sorted out the common problems applicable to their respective conventions after reviewing the navigation safety rules, navigation control rules, operation control rules and cyber security rules clauses involved in the convention one by one. In the MSC RSE result analysis document, MSC clarified 11 common issues for MASS to apply the conventions within its framework with the main purpose of ensuring the safety of ship navigation.[31] LEG has sorted out five major problems faced by MASS in applying the conventions within its framework: the definition of the terms of master and crew; clarifying the responsibilities of remote control personnel; reviewing the existing definitions and general terms of the liability and compensation system, taking into account the current exemption clauses and regulations on transportation liability and whether the provisions on subrogation are adequately applicable; whether MASS or its manufacturers or programmers fall within the scope of 'managers and operators' or other subjects; without prejudice to the operation of MASS within the framework of the LEG's existing conventions below, some specific legal terms need to be considered in

30 IMO, International Maritime Organization, Maritime Safety Committee, *Terminology, definitions, and levels of automation for Maritime Autonomous Surface Ships* (MASS), MSC 105/INF.2 (2022) para. 9.

31 IMO, International Maritime Organization, Maritime Safety Committee, *Outcome of the regulatory Scoping Exercise for the use of Maritime Autonomous Surface Ships* (MASS), MSC.1/Circ.1638 (2021) para. 5.2.

TABLE 8.4 Circulation of MASS autonomous levels within the IMO framework

Degrees of autonomy	Role of the operator
Degree one: Ship with automated processes and decision support	Seafarers operate and control shipboard systems and functions on board. Some operations may be automated, for example, the bridge may sometimes be unattended, with a crew on call in preparation for taking over and taking on the navigational watch.
Degree two: Remotely controlled ship with seafarers on board	Controlled and operated by a shore-based remote control station or other vessel, onboard seafarers with training in navigational watchkeeping and ship handling will be on board. In this case, the autonomous level transitions to Degree one.
Degree three: Remotely controlled ship without seafarers on board	Operated by a shore-based remote control station or other vessel control, with no crew on board.
Degree four: Fully autonomous ship	Ship operating systems can calculate risks and be able to make their own decisions and actions. If the system fails or prompts manual intervention, the operator ashore is only involved in the decision, in which case the autonomy level switches to Degree two or Degree three, depending on whether there is a crew on board.

terms of damage caused by autonomous technology, such as concepts such as 'fault', 'negligence' and 'intent'.[32] Although the responsibilities of MSC and LEG are different, both list the legal status and responsibilities of MASS captains and telehandlers as a common issue to be addressed with high priority. Any discussion of the different new subject responsibilities introduced through MASS-related technologies relies on a clear definition, legal status and responsibilities. The relevant terminology needs to be revisited and agreed upon. Many of the terms that need to be clarified overlap between the committees, but there are specific legal terms that need to be considered in the context of damage caused by autonomous technology. As noted, there is a convergence

32 IMO, International Maritime Organization, Legal Committee, *Outcome of the Regulatory Scoping Exercise and Gap Analysis of Conventions emanating from the Legal Committee with respect to Maritime Autonomous Surface Ships* (MASS), LEG.1/Circ.11 (2021) paras. 5.5, 5.6.

of clarity on the meaning of terms such as master, crew or person in charge, remote control centers and remote operators designated as crew members, which are core elements of the MASS Code.

In addition to the core content of the MASS rule described above, the extension content of MASS is also mentioned. In particular, the objectives related to maritime safety and environmental protection are being achieved in the context of compulsory insurance becoming a standard provision of maritime conventions in many areas involving liability to third parties. Therefore, it should also be discussed whether MASS navigation is necessary to introduce a compulsory insurance system. Furthermore, in the *Checklist for Identifying Administrative Requirements* issued by some Member States and the IMO Committee, 'administrative requirements' are defined as obligations to provide, and retain information or data arising from mandatory IMO instruments. Similar to the responsibilities of traditional ships in port states, maritime administrative legal issues such as the jurisdiction of coastal states over Mass in the framework of IMO, which need to be faced by MASS entering and leaving port states, have also received attention.[33]

6 China's Response in the Context of the Development of the MASS Code

6.1 *Analysis of the Necessity of Constructing MASS Regulation in China*

Globally, MASS is now beginning to be integrated into the maritime industry, with MASS participating in shipping alongside traditional vessels. MASS is breaking away from the traditional maritime model and moving from the initial pilot stage to the commercial stage. The UK, the US, Japan, Korea and other countries have also continued to follow up on research and development. The MASS industry is driven by its value, its certified operation and its regulation as a sustainable path for development, forming a driving model with a positive interaction between technological progress, classification society certified operation and regulatory needs. Similar to traditional ships, MASS is mainly responsible for the carriage of goods and passengers by sea, and it is an indispensable prerequisite to obtaining the legal status of traditional ships. MASS

33 IMO, International Maritime Organization, Legal Committee, *Introduction of Maritime Autonomous Surface Ships (MASS) operations in IMO instruments*, LEG 109/13/1 (2022), Annex.; IMO, International Maritime Organization, Legal Committee, *Proposal for a new output to develop a consistent legal framework for the regulation of Maritime Autonomous Surface Ships (MASS) across IMO instruments*, LEG 109/13/2 (2022) Annex.

requires clear construction standards, classification criteria, and legal oversight of its design, construction, and operation. Similar to traditional ships, MASS is mainly responsible for cargo and passenger transportation when it enters the maritime industry. However, it is an indispensable prerequisite to clarify its legal status first. MASS requires clear construction standards, classification criteria, and legal oversight of its design, construction, and operation.

The Smart Ship Development Action Plan (2019–2021), released by China in 2018, integrates the development of smart ships into the strategic goal of accelerating the building of manufacturing and maritime power. It is suggested that China should grasp the development opportunity of intelligent ships and complete the establishment of the standard system of intelligent ship rules. In May 2019, the Ministry of Transport of the People's Republic of China jointly issued *the Guidance on the Development of Smart Shipping*, and in April 2020, the Ministry of Industry and Information Technology of the People's Republic of China issued a new edition of *the Guide to the Construction of Autonomous Ship Standard System (consultation draft)*. These two documents set out phased plans for the full-cycle development of smart ships, which require intelligent ship design, intelligent ship testing and verification standards and other basic technologies of intelligent ships to achieve breakthroughs, at the same time, it is required to perfect the supporting standards of shore-based service and operation management in the course of intelligent ship navigation. Driven by the policy, construction of the *Zhi Fei*, China's first self-propelled container ship, began on 18 December 2019, and the 2021 successfully carried out sea trials on 14 September 2019, completing its maiden voyage to Qingdao Port on 22 April 2022. On 18 May 2022, China's first intelligent unmanned system mothership that meets intelligent ship specifications and has remote control and open water autonomous navigation functions was successfully launched. As a major shipping country, China has steadily acquired experience in the whole process of MASS from design, and construction to operation, and has further stepped out of the status quo of concentrating on MASS development with an eye on the construction of platforms such as intelligent unmanned system motherships to build a complete unmanned system. Therefore, China should promote the formulation of MASS-related domestic laws and regulations through the discussion process of international issues combined with the practical experience of MASS.

6.2 *China's Perspectives at the IMO Conferences*

As mentioned above, although a non-mandatory instrument has not yet been issued, the MASS Code has already taken shape in terms of content and framework. China has submitted several documents on its views during the meetings held by the IMO to discuss the development of the MASS Code, mainly focusing on the following aspects. First, a comprehensive framework for the development of MASS instruments should be considered holistically. At present, most of the existing conventions cannot be directly applied to MASS. Compared with the establishment of a comprehensive management framework including the revision of relevant conventions, mandatory rules, supporting technical guidelines and implementation arrangements, the establishment of mandatory rules alone has little effect. Therefore, it is essential to have a mandatory instrument with a comprehensive framework.

Second, due to the limitations of the current state of technical development of MASS, a non-mandatory instrument that is not regarded as an interim document should be developed at the moment, providing a basic framework structure for a future mandatory instrument for reference and mandatory implementation in due course.

Third, as a new subject, MASS has joined the international maritime field, not replacing traditional ships. So, it should not be seen as an additional instrument to existing conventions within the IMO framework, and the resulting MASS Code should cover key factors affecting the safe operation of ships, including seafarers and remote operators.

Fourth, regarding the development route of the MASS Code, if it is agreed to formulate non-mandatory instruments at this stage, priority should be given to drafting rather than amending the existing conventions. To emphasize the legislative process, it is suggested that the development route of the MASS Code should be divided into the stage of reviewing the common issues and framework of regulatory instruments, the stage of formulating various regulations, and the stage of reviewing existing conventions to ensure the efficiency of the legislative process.[34]

6.3 *Controversies and Responses to the Application of the Maritime Law to MASS*

Although the above-mentioned point of view is put forward by China in response to MASS legislation at the international level, however, China's domestic legislation and revision work can also be based on timely consideration of whether the IMO's work experience in regulating MASS applies to the domestic law revision process, to carry out the review of domestic laws on the formulation of objectives, procedures and contents. At the end of this work,

---

34 IMO, International Maritime Organization, Maritime Safety Committee, *Comments on key principles and common understanding of a MASS instrument and the draft road map*, MSC 105/7/7 (2022) paras. 4–13.

the legislative content, framework and direction can be adjusted according to the IMO conference process and MASS practice. Among them, MASS should be applied to *the Maritime Law of the People's Republic of China* (hereinafter referred to as Maritime Law) to conduct content review.

As for whether MASS applies to the Maritime Law, the legal status of MASS should first be resolved. The legal definition of a ship has not yet formed a unified view, and the definition of a ship in the domestic law of different countries varies, but when describing the concept of a ship, the expressions mostly appear as a combination of 'purpose' and 'mobile device'.[35] The definition of the ship is met. However, the key to defining the legal status of a MASS is to determine whether it satisfies the three legal characteristics of a ship: (1) the personalization of the ship. The ship acquires nationality after legal registration and has a specific name, and the law endows the ship with characteristics similar to natural persons or legal persons; (2) the ship is a special movable property, and its legal nature is based on meeting the 'movable' entity requirements; and (3) a ship is a composite object. The composition of a ship is not single, and various kinds of equipment make up a ship, including hull, hull, deck, cabin and other structures. Therefore, in theory, MASS can be defined as a 'ship'. However, the *Maritime Law of the People's Republic of China (Revised Draft for Examination)* (hereinafter referred to as Revised Draft for Examination) submitted by the Ministry of Transport to the State Council on 7 January 2020 does not address the issue of how to confirm the legal status of MASS. As mentioned above, the prevailing academic view is positive toward the recognition of MASS as a ship; and it is easy to see from the various classification societies' rules and guidelines that the attitude of the practical community is more positive than that of the academic community. The author believes that there is no dispute that MASS has obtained the legal status of 'ship' today.

The identification of MASS masters and crew members is also a major issue that should be addressed to ensure the healthy and sustainable development of MASS in the future. Revised Draft for Examination also does not change the 'on board' position restriction that defines the crew concept as 'all persons serving on board'. At present, there are still some MASS with low autonomy levels that still retain onboard manning, and high autonomy level MASS does not require ship manning, but transfers traditional ship manning to shore or mother ships. With the development of autonomous technology, remote operators with varying degrees of responsibility will take over the role of master and crew for the safe navigation of the MASS. Therefore, an attempt could be made in the

35 U.S.C. 2011 Title 1 CHAPTER 1 § 3, U.S. C. Title 33 CHAPTER 29 § 1502; Canada Shipping Act 2001 Definitions 2; Marine Safety (Domestic Commercial Vessel) National Law Act 2012 Part 1 Preliminary Section 8 Definition of vessel.

current revision of the Maritime Law to create some legal interfaces between the remote operator and the crew. On this basis, the issue of attribution of liability for MASS should also be taken into consideration, such as the choice of the principles of attribution and the allocation of liability between multiple entities, to reasonably avoid the operational risks of MASS. This is also the key to the fact that the proportion of MASS in the future shipping industry can be coordinated with the development needs of the times.

At the time of the publication of the Review Draft, the RSE work led by MSC and LEG had not yet been completed and the IMO's work schedule to regulate MASS was still fragmented, therefore, the Revised Draft for Examination did not mention MASS and its legal status. The application of the Maritime Law to MASS is an inevitable development in the future. It needs to be fully considered when further breakthroughs are made in the real ship operation of MASS in the industry field and the MASS Code under IMO are gradually mature. China, as a category A member of the IMO Council, should continue to follow up on the regulation of MASS in the various committee meetings. It is foreseeable from China's current attitude toward MASS that if the MASS Code is successfully introduced in 2028 and is compatible with China's MASS development needs and legislative objectives, there is a high probability that China will become a contracting party to the MASS Code. Under this assumption, the MASS and its legal relationship stipulated in the future Maritime Law must be consistent with the MASS Code. However, we still need to be cautious about whether to introduce relevant regulations in the current legislative revision and how to regulate MASS.

6.4 *The Path to Constructing China's Domestic Rule System before the Promulgation of the MASS Code*

Due to the current lack of experience in operating MASS on actual ships, it is still ahead of time to structure MASS regulation by amending domestic laws. The author believes that before the introduction of the MASS Code in the future, the thinking of MASS regulation can be changed to build a domestic MASS rule system with classification societies and administrative departments as the main body in China.

6.4.1 Classification Societies Improve the Content of the Rule-and-Guide System

The subjects of navigational safety rules, navigation control rules, operational control rules and cyber security rules are the general conceptual direction for the construction of the content of the current MASS Code. The core legal issues such as the meaning of terms like captain, crew or officer in charge, remote control stations and shore-based operators are the basis for the construction.

IMO aims to formulate a non-mandatory MASS Code as a phased goal and plans to make it mandatory in 2028. According to the development route of MASS rules, the construction of the domestic MASS rule system should start with the improvement of the MASS code guide system by classification societies. Although the rules and guidelines of classification societies are not mandatory, there are slight rank differences between them. As the official text of the classification society, the rules indicate that the classification society has sufficient experience support. Most of the guidelines are supplementary trial documents for the norm, which indicates that the classification society does not have enough experience to support it as a norm. Since the main business of classification societies is the inspection and review of ships and their equipment for classification and maintenance, they play an irreplaceable role in the MASS access process. Therefore, if the non-mandatory MASS rules are constructed in China, the author believes that it is feasible to use the rules and guidelines of domestic classification societies as the main body.

6.4.2 Government Departments Issue Administrative Regulations for MASS Supervision

When formulating international conventions, the combination of artificial intelligence technology and the maritime industry was not foreseen by the framers, resulting in the congenital defects of MASS. Although establishing a regulatory system for MASS has become an important topic for IMO in the next five years, the author believes that China should fully consider the development of MASS when formulating domestic MASS laws and regulations. If the domestic MASS development conditions allow entering the legislative stage, in the case of a long period of revision of the new law, the relevant provisions in the existing laws and regulations should be supplemented first. The working methods of RSE, such as formulating legal interpretations and amending existing laws, can be selected to change the application basis of MASS.

With the advancement of MASS technology and the accumulation of practical experience, it is necessary to further seek MASS regulatory measures. Therefore, it is a long-term solution to intensify discussions to introduce a MASS regulatory system with overall awareness and consistent rules. According to the current situation of MASS operation, MASS should be encouraged to apply the existing general principles and adopt a gradualist approach to deal with the legal challenges brought by MASS. It is reasonable to formulate a detailed management system after more MASS has gained practical experience.[36] *The Guidelines on the Development of Intelligent Shipping* released

36 Rob McLaughlin, Unmanned Naval Vehicles at Sea: USVs, UUVs, and the Adequacy of the Law, 115.

in 2019 clarified the direction of China's smart ship development. According to *the Interim Guidelines for Trials of Maritime Autonomous Surface Ships* (*MASS*) issued by the 101st session of the IMO MSC in 2019, China submitted *the Report on MASS trials* to the 104th session of the IMO MSC on 30 July 2021[37] (IMO, 2021). In the report, China shared the details and experience of using the autonomous cargo ship *Jindouyun 0 Hao* for multiple sea trials by Interim Guidelines for Trials of MASS. At the same time, in combination with the development status of domestic autonomous ship technology and the need for testing, China has also begun to formulate the requirements for ship autonomous navigation test technology and inspection. On 3 April 2023, the Maritime Bureau of the Ministry of Transport of China issued *the Interim Guidelines for Technical and Inspection of MASS Trials, which came into force on 1 May 2023 formally.* The Interim Guidelines take full account of China's domestic policies and the current status of the development of autonomous navigation-related technologies, focus on safeguarding the safety of ship navigation tests and fill the gaps in domestic technical regulations in the field of autonomous ship navigation. This approach is to localize the IMO work results for the development of domestic MASS rules to express China's recognition of the phased achievements in the construction of MASS international rules, and it is also an indispensable first step in building China's MASS legal system. It is believed that the MASS Code will progress by leaps and bounds in the coming years, driven by the goal of completing the introduction of the MASS Code by 2025. In this process, China should also give full play to the subjective initiative, under the goal driven by the coordination with the MASS Code, seize the opportunity, take the lead in the world, and construct the MASS rule system in line with our national conditions.

7 Conclusion

The shipping industry's acceptance of MASS will increase when it is perceived as safer, more cost-effective and more environmentally friendly. Constructing an appropriate MASS regulatory regime that minimizes any potential adverse effects on MASS operations is necessary to keep pace with technological developments, which will be integral to future progress in the international law of the sea. According to the process of building the MASS Code, China should also follow the international footsteps immediately and contribute Chinese wisdom, while establishing legal regulations for the standardized development of

37 See IMO, International Maritime Organization, Maritime Safety Committee, *Report on MASS trials* (*China*), MSC 104-INF.14 (2021) 1–4.

MASS in China based on the law of MASS development and the current situation of MASS development in China. In the era of artificial intelligence where opportunities and challenges coexist, a good legal environment should be created for the steady expansion of China's shipping industry.

Acknowledgements

This work was supported by National Social Science Foundation (No. 23BFX198); Southern Marine Science and Engineering Guangdong Laboratory (Zhuhai) (No. SML2020SP005); Heilongjiang Province Philosophy and Social Science Research Planning Project (No. 22GJB13).

References

Aldo Chircop, 'Maritime Autonomous Surface Ships in International Law: New Challenges for the Regulation of International Navigation and Shipping', in Myron H. Nordquist, John Norton Moore, Ronán Long (eds.), *Cooperation and Engagement in the Asia-Pacific Region* (Brill Nijhoff, 2019).

American Bureau of Shipping, *Requirements for Autonomous and Remote Control Functions* (August 2022).

Aybüke Naz Durmuş, 'The Intersection Between Law and Technology in Maritime Law', in Kyriaki Noussia and Matthew Channon (eds.), *The Regulation of Automated and Autonomous Transport* (Springer International Publishing, 2023).

Brendan Gogarty, Meredith C. Hagger, 'The Laws of Man Over Vehicles Unmanned: The Legal Response to Robotic Revolution on Sea, Land and Air', (2008) 19 JLIS 73.

Bureau Veritas, *Guidelines for Autonomous Shipping*, NI641 R01 (October 2019).

Bureau Veritas, *Unmanned Surface Vessels (USV)*, NR681 (July 2022).

China Classification Society, *Guidelines for Autonomous Cargo Ships 2018*, GD20-2018 (30 August 2018).

China Classification Society, *Rules for Intelligent Ships 2022 Amendments* (1 April 2022).

Craig H. Allen, 'Determining the Legal Status of Unmanned Maritime Vehicles: Formalism vs functionalism', (2018) 49 JMLC 4 477.

Det Norske Veritas, *Smart vessel*, DNV-CG-0508 (August 2021).

Det Norske Veritas, *Certification scheme for remote control center operator*, DNV-RP-0323 (August 2021).

Det Norske Veritas, *Autonomous and remotely operated ships*, DNV-CG-0264 (September 2021).

Det Norske Veritas, *Competence of remote control center operators*, DNV-ST-0324 (October 2022).

Dong Xiaoming (ed), *Haishang wuren zhuangbei tixi gailan* [*Introduction to Maritime Unmanned Systems*] (in Chinese) (Harbin Engineering University Press 2020).

Hadi Ghaderi, 'Wider implications of autonomous vessels for the maritime industry: Mapping the unprecedented challenges', in Dimitris Milakis, Nikolas Thomopoulos, and Bert van Wee (eds.), *Advances in Transport Policy and Planning* (Academic Press, 2020).

He Tiantian, Lianheguo haiyangfa gongyue 40nian: lichen tiaozhan he zhongguo juese [The United Nations Convention on the Law of the Sea at 40: Course Challenges and China's Role] (in Chinese) (2022) 30 PJ 9.

Henrik Ringbom, 'Regulating Autonomous Ships—Concepts, Challenges and Precedents', (2019) 50 ODIL 2–3 141.

Henrik Tunfors, 'Evolution of IMO's MASS: Through the Prism of the Chair', in Tafsir Matin Johansson, et al. (eds.), *Autonomous Vessels in Maritime Affairs: Law and Governance Implications* (Springer International Publishing, 2023).

Hu Zhengliang, Shan Hongjun, 'Chuanjishe de xingwei zhunze he falüzeren [Code of Conduct and Legal Liability of Classification Societies]' (in Chinese), (1998) 9 ACML 1.

IMO, International Maritime Organization <https://www.imo.org/en/MediaCentre/HotTopics/Pages/Autonomous-shipping.aspx> accessed 27 January 2024.

IMO, International Maritime Organization, 'Autonomous ships: regulatory scoping exercise completed' (25 May 2021) <https://www.imo.org/en/MediaCentre/PressBriefings/pages/MASSRSE2021.aspx> accessed 27 January 2024.

IMO, International Maritime Organization, Maritime Safety Committee, *Report of the MSC-LEG-FAL Joint Working Group on Maritime Autonomous Surface Ships* (*MASS*) *on its second session*, MSC 107/5/1 (2 May 2023).

IMO, International Maritime Organization, Maritime Safety Committee, *Report of the Maritime Safety Committee on Its 107th Session*, MSC 107/20 (26 June 2023).

IMO, International Maritime Organization, Maritime Safety Committee, *Report of the Intersessional MASS Working Group*, MSC 108/4/1 (8 November 2023).

Jennifer Parker, 'The challenges posed by the advent of maritime autonomous surface ships for international maritime law', (2021) 35 ANZMLJ 1 31.

Levent Bahadır, 'The Legal Status Issue of Unmanned Maritime Vehicles (UMVs) Used for Military Purposes', (2023) 5 JATSS 4 39.

Li Xiaohui Zhou Nan, Wang Bing, Haishang zizhu hangxing chuanbo dui IMO sanda gongyue de yingxiang ji woguo yingdui celüe [The lnfluence of MASS on the Three Key Conventions of IMO and Associated Countermeasures of China] (in Chinese), (Oct. 2020) China Maritime Safety 67.

Marilia Abilio Ramos, Ingrid Bouwer Utne, and Ali Mosleh, 'Collision avoidance on maritime autonomous surface ships: Operators' tasks and human failure events', (2019) 116 Safety Science 33.

Nippon Kaiji Kyokai, *Rules for Automatic and Remote Control Systems*, (30 June 2023).

Rob McLaughlin, 'Unmanned naval vehicles at sea: USVs, UUVs, and the adequacy of the law', (2011) 21 JLIS 2 100.

Russian Maritime Register of Shipping, *Regulations for Classification of Maritime Autonomous and Remotely Controlled Surface Ships* (*MASS*), ND No. 2–030101-037-E (27 September 2022).

Si Yuzhuo (ed), *Haishang Fa* [*Maritime Law*] (in Chinese) (Law Press China 2023).

CHAPTER 9

From Experimentation to Legislation: Understanding Russia's Approach to Autonomous Vessels

*Valentin Koshkin**

1 Introduction

Presently, autonomous vessels are emerging as a prevailing global trend, sparking a competition for leadership in autonomous navigation. This competition involves governments and major technological companies from leading maritime nations such as Rolls-Royce (UK), Kongsberg Gruppe (Norway), ABB (Sweden), Sea Machines Robotics, and IBM (USA). The expectation is that accident rates will see a substantial decrease of 70–80%, primarily attributed to the reduction of the human factor in ship management. Unmanned navigation is reshaping perspectives on the organization of water transportation, influencing advancements in ship equipment, port infrastructure configuration, cargo handling technologies, and the skillsets of professionals in these fields. However, the existing regulatory frameworks in many countries, along with standardization and technical regulation bases, shipbuilding technologies, and educational programs, fall short of adequately addressing the global challenges posed by unmanned navigation.[1]

Numerous states are actively developing legal regulations at the national level for the operation of autonomous vessels or Maritime Autonomous Surface Ships (MASS). Given that current legislation operates within the paradigm of crewed ships, a new legal foundation for autonomous vessels is a necessity. Establishing this legal framework for autonomous vessels will have a profound transformative effect on the industry, permitting autonomous navigation in major commercial ports and along high-traffic sea routes. Autonomous vessel navigation represents a highly promising avenue for maritime and inland waterway transport development, with widespread adoption expected in the near future.

* PhD, Lecturer at the Jilin University School of Law, China; koshkin24@jlu.edu.cn.

1 'Strategic project No. 3 Electronic navigation and unmanned (autonomous) navigation' (2021) <https://www.miit.ru/page/178854> accessed 24 January 2024.

 | DOI:10.1163/9789004706279_011

Russia has emerged as one of the pioneers in the development of autonomous vessels. The first route where autonomous vessels operate in Russia is the line from the 'Ust-Luga Seaport' to the 'Kaliningrad Seaport'. The semi-autonomous ferries, 'Marshal Rokossovsky' and 'General Chernyakhovsky', which operate on this route under 'Rosmorport' Federal State Unitary Enterprise (hereafter referred to as Rosmorport), received the first maritime autonomous and MASS certificates in Russia at the end of September 2023. These documents, issued by the Russian Maritime Register of Shipping, authorize remote control of the vessels with the ability to switch to manual control during sea navigation. Assigning the autonomy class to the ferries 'Marshal Rokossovsky' and 'General Chernyakhovsky' by the Russian Maritime Register of Shipping marks a significant milestone in the development of domestic autonomous navigation technology. This step will enable the accumulation of practical experience in autonomous navigation, paving the way for the widespread adoption of autonomous navigation technologies in Russia.[2]

Since 2022, Rosmorport, in collaboration with Sitronics KT, a leading Russian developer of maritime intelligent solutions, has been implementing autonomous navigation systems on ferries as part of the federal project 'Autonomous Navigation'. As of today, ferries are equipped with autonomous navigation technology, comprising a navigation system, an optical system for analyzing the surrounding environment and the ship's condition, a traffic and maneuvering control system, as well as a monitoring and observation system for ship systems. To enable remote control of the vessels, the Remote Control Center of Rosmorport has been established in Saint Petersburg. This center facilitates the monitoring of surrounding navigation conditions, control of key parameters of ferry movement, and remote operation of vessels situated in open waters. Equipped with necessary tools, including a remote control console, the Remote Control Center serves as the operational workspace for the autonomous vessel operator.

Manual control is employed during narrow passages and port entry in conjunction with decision support systems. As per the plan, the ferry 'General Chernyakhovsky' is expected to autonomously cover approximately 500 nautical miles. Throughout this distance, the vehicle's navigation will be monitored by personnel at the Remote Control Center. Consequently, the onboard ship crew will not directly manage navigation during the voyage; everything will be executed remotely. With advanced technologies in place, it is

2 'Rosmorport ferries have received the first certificates of marine autonomous and remotely operated surface vessels in Russia' (2023) <https://www.cnews.ru/news/line/2023-10-03_paromy_rosmorporta_poluchili> accessed 24 January 2024.

anticipated that the captain can oversee not just one ship but potentially dozens simultaneously.[3]

The autonomous navigation systems being experimentally implemented on the two ferries between Kaliningrad and Saint Petersburg may potentially find application in navigating the waters of the Northern Sea Route (referred to as the NSR) in the future.[4]

In 2020, the Russian President tasked the Government and the Marinet Industry Center, a non-profit organization supporting high-tech development in the marine industry, with creating proposals to encourage the production and utilization of unmanned navigation equipment on Russian-flagged ships. Consequently, the Government approved the 'Marinet' action plan or 'roadmap' for establishing an intelligent management system for maritime transport and ocean exploration technologies. This action plan proposes projects to further research and development in digital navigation, ocean resource development technologies, and innovative shipbuilding. As part of the 'Marinet' action plan, the Autonomous and Remote Navigation Trial Project, involving the Ministry of Transport of Russia and the Russian Maritime Register of Shipping, is being implemented. Vessels from PJSC 'Sovcomflot', LLC 'Paula Rise', and Rosmorport are participating in the Project. According to the 'Marinet' action plan, strategic goals in terms of refining the regulatory framework include the development and implementation of standards and regulatory acts to facilitate the rapid introduction of new technologies into Russia's marine industry.

In 2023, Russia made substantial updates to its existing legislation by incorporating provisions specifically related to autonomous vessels. The development of Russian legislation in the field of autonomous navigation involves several stages. At the initial stage, in 2020, the Government endorsed the Regulation for conducting the experiment on the trial operation of autonomous vessels flying the Russian State flag (hereafter referred to as the Regulation for conducting the experiment). The Regulation for conducting the experiment established the legal foundation in Russia for conducting experiments related to the introduction of autonomous navigation technologies until 2025. The author provides a brief assessment of the temporary experimental legal regime established for the testing period of autonomous vessels in the second part of the article.

3 'The first autonomous sea ferry has been put into operation in Russia: it has been developed for many years' (2023) <https://trashbox.ru/link/2023-12-20-ego-razrabatyvali-mnogo-let> accessed 24 January 2024.

4 'The first unmanned passenger ships may appear in Russia in 2024' (2023) <https://tass.ru/ekonomika/18781457> accessed 24 January 2024.

In the subsequent stage, the Ministry of Industry and Trade of Russia, in collaboration with relevant specialist departments, initiated the development of legal norms for the use of autonomous vessels. In July 2023, the Federal Law 'On Amendments to Certain Legislative Acts of the Russian Federation' (hereafter referred to as the Federal Law) was passed. The Federal Law establishes a legal framework enabling the operation of autonomous vessels and will come into effect on March 1, 2024. The Federal Law provides for amendments to the Merchant Shipping Code of Russia, the Code of Inland Water Transport of Russia, the Federal Law 'On Seaports in Russia and on Amendments to Certain Legislative Acts of Russia', and the Federal Law 'On Transport Security'. In the third part of the article, the author will scrutinize the Federal Law, aiming to identify its key features and shortcomings. Some Russian experts think that adopting such a law at this time is too premature.[5] However, the author disagrees with this stance and will present counterarguments.

The article will specifically focus on the provisions of the Federal Law that impact the navigation of foreign autonomous vessels. These provisions may apply to both foreign autonomous vessels entering Russian ports and foreign autonomous vessels passing through the NSR. Russia is actively developing plans to encourage the navigation of autonomous vessels along the NSR. However, alongside the new norms introduced by the Federal Law, it is likely that the current rules applied by Russia to foreign crewed vessels navigating the NSR will also apply to foreign autonomous vessels. Currently, Russia enforces its internal regulation on this route in compliance with Article 234 of the 1982 United Nations Convention on the Law of the Sea (hereafter referred to as UNCLOS). In the fourth part, the author will discuss the legitimacy of Russia's right to enforce its domestic regulations on foreign autonomous vessels passing through the NSR.

The article unfolds in several intricately interconnected sections, sequentially addressing the experimental legal regime on the trial operation of autonomous vessels introduced in 2020, subsequent amendments through the Federal Law and the specific regulatory landscape governing the NSR and autonomous vessels. This study may be of interest to countries that are also developing legislation to regulate the navigation of autonomous vessels.

5 2020 Expert opinion on the draft federal law 'On Amendments to the Code of Merchant Shipping of the Russian Federation and Certain Legislative Acts of the Russian Federation in Terms of Legal Relations arising from the use of autonomous Vessels (Экспертное заключение по проекту федерального закона "о внесении изменений в кодекс торгового мореплавания российской федерациии отдельные законодательные акты российской федерациив части правоотношений, возникающих при использовании автономных судов) (RUS).

2 The Experimental Legal Regime

The experimental legal regime, as enacted by the Federal Law 'On Experimental Legal Regimes in the Field of Digital Innovations in Russia', facilitates the testing of autonomous vessels on sea routes and in ports. Adopted in 2020, this law provides opportunities for experimenting with innovative digital technologies. Some of these technologies, due to one reason or another, are currently prohibited by existing legislation. The creation of special regulatory 'sandboxes' or 'digital sandboxes' allows for exceptions to these restrictions. This experimental legal regime introduces special regulation applicable to a specific group of persons or entities within a defined territory for a limited period of time. This includes the total or partial exemption from mandatory requirements. As a result, various companies gain more flexibility, allowing businesses to demonstrate the efficiency of innovative products and services to the state. If these initiatives prove successful, the temporary regulation may become a standard regulation across the entire territory of Russia. The experimental legal regime can be in place for a maximum of three years. However, the Russian Government reserves the right to extend this period by an additional 12 months given a justifiable request from a participant.

The Government's approval of the Regulation for conducting the experiment marked the first effective regulatory act in Russia regarding the legal regulation of autonomous vessel activities. The Regulation for conducting the experiment, adopted based on the Interim Guidelines for Maritime Autonomous Surface Ships approved by the Maritime Safety Committee in June 2019, established the legal framework in Russia for experiments related to the implementation of autonomous navigation technologies while the Federal Law was still in the development stage. The experiment is planned to run from 10 December 2020 to 31 December 2025, in designated sea waters areas.

The regulation permits any shipping company to participate in these experiments, equip their vessels with autonomous navigation systems, and utilize them in commercial operations. The document lays down the conditions and procedure for conducting experiments on the pilot operation of autonomous vessels, registered by the captains of seaports located in various regions across Russia, including the Krasnodar Territory, Primorsky Territory, Khabarovsk Territory, Astrakhan Region, Kaliningrad Region, Leningrad Region, Magadan Region, Murmansk Region, Rostov Region, Sakhalin Region, and Saint Petersburg.[6]

6 'The Regulation for conducting the experiment on the trial operation of autonomous ships flying the Russian State flag' (2020) <http://government.ru/docs/all/131362/> point 1 accessed 24 January 2024.

The Regulation for conducting the experiment introduces concepts such as 'autonomous vessel', 'autonomous navigation system' into legal circulation for the first time in national legislation. An essential feature of the Regulation for conducting the experiment was the introduction of the term 'autonomous navigation system', which encompasses all technical means for automatic and remote control of a vessel.

The experiment's participants include the Ministry of Industry and Trade; the Ministry of Transport of Russia; the Federal Agency for Sea and River Transport; and autonomous vessel shipowners. To join the experiment, a shipowner must send an application to the Federal Agency for Maritime and River Transport at least 20 working days before the start of the autonomous vessel's trial operation. This application should include all necessary information, such as the designated area, the anticipated duration of the trial operation, details regarding the installation of an autonomous navigation system, and the appointment of an official from the shipowner responsible for the safety of the autonomous vessel's trial operation. In addition, the shipowner should provide the contact details and email address for receiving the Federal Agency for Maritime and River Transport's approval or denial decision.[7]

The application should also be accompanied by the autonomous vessel's trial operation program, which includes:

- rules for the interaction between the shipowner's officials responsible for conducting and ensuring the safety of the autonomous vessel's trial operation, its crew members, and coastal services;
- operational communication methods with the autonomous vessel, the shipowner's personnel responsible for the trial operation of the autonomous vessel, and coastal services;
- risks related to navigation safety and environmental protection, due to the trial operation of the autonomous vessel, and measures developed to mitigate such risks.[8]

Within 10 days from the date of receipt of the application, the Federal Agency for Sea and River Transport will assess the safety of the autonomous vessel's trial operation and approve it if the following conditions are met:

- the applicant is the shipowner of an autonomous vessel;
- the autonomous vessel has a valid certificate to sail under the Russian State flag;
- the autonomous vessel holds a valid classification certificate;

7 ibid, point 8.
8 ibid, point 9.

– the autonomous vessel's authorized navigation area aligns with the designated area;
– the trial operation of the autonomous vessel in the designated area does not pose risks to the vessel itself, other vessels operating in this area, or the environment;
– the vessel has an autonomous navigation system installed.[9]

If an application is denied, the autonomous vessel's shipowner may reapply once the reasons for the denial have been addressed.

During the trial operation of the autonomous vessel, the shipowner must:

a. carry out the operation within the agreed designated areas and timeframes;
b. identify and implement measures to mitigate risks to navigation safety and environmental protection before the trial operation begins;
c. continuously monitor the operation's safety and halt operation in the event of threats to the navigation safety of the autonomous vessel or other vessels in the designated area until such threats are resolved;
d. comply with the requirements of international treaties and Russian legislation regarding navigation safety and environmental protection;
e. consider the human factor as a key element in the autonomous vessel's automatic and remote control systems, instruct the crew and outside management specialists about the specifics and risks associated with the operation;
f. take measures to ensure the cybersecurity and fault tolerance of the vessel's automatic and remote control systems;
g. notify cargo owners whose cargo is being transported on the autonomous vessel, insurers, seaport captains, and ship traffic control system operators in the areas where the autonomous vessel is navigating about the trial operation at least three days before its commencement;
h. inform the Federal Agency for Maritime and River Transport about the results of the trial operation no later than three months from its completion date.[10]

To facilitate the execution of the experiment and the development of autonomous vessels, the Russian Maritime Register of Shipping has approved a set of technical solutions for automatic and remote navigation. This approval enables the use of autonomous navigation on ships regulated by the Russian Maritime Register of Shipping, most of which are registered under the Russian flag.

9 ibid, point 10.
10 ibid, point 13.

In 2020, the Russian Maritime Register of Shipping published the Guidelines on the Classification of Maritime Autonomous Surface Ships (autonomous vessels). These guidelines regulate the technical supervision aspects related to the design and construction of autonomous vessels, the conversion of existing vessels into autonomous vessels, and the manufacturing of materials and products for autonomous vessels. The Guidelines on the Classification apply to several facilities and systems, such as situational awareness systems, means of radio communication and data exchange, navigation and maneuvering systems, and the ship's power plant. Detailed conditions for marking facilities and the remote control center are also included. The Guidelines on the Classification provide in-depth risk assessment criteria for the design, manufacturing, testing, and operation of autonomous vessels and their infrastructure. The provisions consider a broad spectrum of autonomous vessel, factoring in varying degrees of human involvement in the management of the vessel, its systems, and technical means. Depending on the modes of movement in the open sea and in limited water areas, such as narrow areas, ports, and docking sites, different categories of vessels have been introduced. The document also contains detailed conditions for the marking tools and the remote control center, both of which are vital for ensuring safe navigation and monitoring of autonomous vessels movement.[11]

The establishment of an experimental legal regime has significantly propelled the development of autonomous navigation in Russia. Under this experimental legal framework, autonomous navigation technology underwent operational testing on vessels for several years. In 2021 alone, 28 voyages were conducted, during which the technology was tested and demonstrated its practical applicability.[12] In May 2021, during the trials of the dry cargo ship 'Pola Anfisa' equipped with autonomous navigation from Sitronics KT, it successfully operated in remote control and autonomous motion modes. After an hour of testing in the Azov Sea, control was returned to the ship's onboard personnel.[13] In 2021, the research vessel 'Pioneer-M' was launched. It is the first fully autonomous vessel in Russia where unmanned navigation technologies are being tested. Over the past few years, within the framework of the

11 В. Устинов *v. Ustinov* (2021) TBR2 148–149.

12 'Sitronics KT to equip ferries connecting Kaliningrad and Leningrad regions with autonomous navigation technologies' (2022) < https://www.akm.ru/press/sitronics_kt_osnastit_tekhnologiyami_avtonomnogo_sudovozhdeniya_paromy_soedinyayushchie_kaliningrads/> accessed 24 January 2024.

13 'Sitronics creates a platform for driving ships without a crew on its own software' (2021) <https://www.cnews.ru/news/top/2021-07-08_sitroniks_sozdaet_platformu> accessed 24 January 2024.

experimental legal regime, the vessel has been actively involved in various research expeditions.

Furthermore, in Russia, the development of a unified technological platform for unmanned control of maritime vessels of various purposes in the commercial fleet has been completed. The Ministry of Industry and Trade entrusted Sitronics KT with the development of an unmanned ship control system.[14] A platform for the development of unmanned navigation technology through computer modeling has been created. The solution is designed to provide ships with an autonomous driving system, virtual testing, and training for maritime vessel operators. The system allows loading a mathematical model of an autonomous vessel and testing its functionality on the platform. For example, one can set a route and observe its movement virtually, or modify weather conditions, add oncoming vessels, and repeat the tests. In the future, the developed platform will be complemented with autonomous control simulators and become a kind of virtual environment for machine learning for other unmanned systems.[15]

3 The Federal Law 'On Amendments to Certain Legislative Acts of the Russian Federation'

The Federal Law introduces a series of concepts related to autonomous and unmanned navigation, including terms such as 'autonomous vessel', 'semi-autonomous vessel', 'fully autonomous vessel', 'external crew', and 'organization competent in the field of autonomous navigation'. Changes are also proposed to the legislative acts of Russia, taking into account the unique operation of autonomous vessels. This includes the complete or partial absence of crew on board (depending on the degree of automation of ship control).

An autonomous vessel is defined as a self-propelled vessel whose control processes are partially (a semi-autonomous vessel) or completely (fully autonomous vessel) carried out automatically without the participation of the ship's crew members. The definition of an autonomous vessel in the Federal Law suggests that autonomous vessels can be categorized into two

14 'A government system for managing unmanned ships has been established in Russia' (2023) <https://www.cnews.ru/news/top/2023-02-28_v_rossii_sozdana_gossistema> accessed 24 January 2024.

15 'Sitronics creates a platform for driving ships without a crew on its own software' (2021) <https://www.cnews.ru/news/top/2021-07-08_sitroniks_sozdaet_platformu> accessed 24 January 2024.

types: semi-autonomous and fully autonomous vessels. A semi-autonomous vessel is defined as one whose degree of automation allows for the discontinuation of constant monitoring of the ship's machinery, mechanisms, and devices (keeping a running watch), as well as forgoing constant control of the vessel's movement by the crew who, instead, conduct general surveillance of the vessel and control it and its machines and mechanisms when necessary.[16] The definition of a semi-autonomous vessel in the Federal Law, however, might seem confusing at first glance because modern vessels already incorporate a certain level of automation. In this setup, crew members oversee the operation of automation and restore it in the event of a malfunction. Therefore, almost any marine vessel today could, to varying degrees, be classified as 'semi-autonomous'. The regulation proposed by the Federal Law for the semi-autonomous vessels primarily involves the possibility of reducing the crew and consolidating various functions among crew members.

Some Russian experts argue that if an alternative classification is established at the international level, relevant amendments will be necessary in the corresponding legislative regulations. Possible discrepancies between Russian national regulations and international acts may arise, posing organizational and economic challenges for parties involved in merchant shipping. Therefore, the enactment of the Federal Law in this regard may appear premature.[17] Nonetheless, the author posits that the definition used in the Federal Law generally aligns with the position of the International Maritime Organization (hereafter referred to as the IMO), which focuses on two levels of autonomy (autonomous vessels with a crew and without a crew on board). The IMO proposes to categorize vessels based on the degree of automation into four types:

1. Degree one: Ship with automated processes and decision support—seafarers are on board to operate and control shipboard systems and functions. Some operations may be automated, and at times be unsupervised, but with seafarers on board ready to take control.
2. Degree two: Remotely controlled ship with seafarers on board—the ship is controlled and operated from another location, but seafarers are available on board to take control and operate the shipboard systems and functions.

16 'The Federal Law 'On Amendments to Certain Legislative Acts of the Russian Federation' (2023) art 2 <https://rg.ru/documents/2023/07/17/document-o-vnesenii-izmenenij-v-otdelnye-zakonodatelnye-akty-rossijskoj-federacii.html> accessed 24 January 2024.

17 Expert opinion (n 5) 3.

3. Degree three: Remotely controlled ship without seafarers on board—the ship is controlled and operated from another location with no seafarers on board.
4. Degree four: Fully autonomous vessel—the operating system of the ship can make decisions and determine actions by itself.[18]

According to the Federal Law, an autonomous vessel is assigned a unique identifier, in addition to its name, which enables the determination of the nationality of the autonomous vessel and its owner. The format of the unique identifier for an autonomous vessel, the process of its assignment, and the requirements for its application will be established by the Ministry of Transport.[19] The identification process for autonomous vessels is simplified due to the new provisions in the Federal Law regarding the vessel documents. The ship's log, engine log, radio log, and sanitary log are electronically maintained by the shipowner of a fully autonomous vessel, following the procedure set by the Ministry of Transport of Russia. These logs, along with other ship documents outlined in the the Merchant Shipping Code, need not be physically present on board an autonomous vessel. The shipowner presents them in electronic form during state port control and other designated instances.[20]

During the development stage, the Federal Law faced criticism for not including a mechanism to identify shipowners and specialists operating foreign autonomous vessels. It also did not address the recognition of qualification requirements for foreign specialists. Experts opined that these deficiencies may pose security risks to Russian seaport infrastructure.[21]As a result, the Federal Law was supplemented with an important provision concerning the identification of foreign autonomous vessels. According to the Federal Law, when a foreign autonomous vessel enters a Russian seaport, the documents of such a vessel, including those related to the crew, external crew, or other specialists managing the autonomous vessel, are recognized. Additionally, documents confirming the technical properties of the autonomous vessel, issued by a foreign state or an organization authorized for the classification and inspection of vessels and recognized by a foreign state, are also acknowledged.[22] The Federal Law still lacks a detailed mechanism for identifying qualifications of

18 International Maritime Organization, 'Autonomous shipping' <https://www.imo.org/en/MediaCentre/HotTopics/Pages/Autonomous-shipping.aspx≥ accessed 24 January 2024.

19 The Federal Law 'On Amendments to Certain Legislative Acts of the Russian Federation 2023 (RUS) art 2 <https://www.imo.org/en/MediaCentre/HotTopics/Pages/Autonomous-shipping.aspx> accessed 24 January 2024.

20 ibid, art 3.

21 Expert opinion (n 5) 6.

22 The Federal Law (n 19).

shipowners and specialists operating foreign autonomous vessels, deferring the regulation of this matter to the Ministry of Transport. Most likely, in the future, nations will employ electronic systems and databases to facilitate the exchange of information regarding the qualifications. Such systems and databases are already being used today to exchange information on the qualifications of crews of crewed vessels. Examples include International Maritime Shipping Database, CrewInspector, Ship Inspection Report Exchange, and others.

The Federal Law governs the navigation of autonomous foreign warships and other autonomous state vessels operated for non-commercial purposes in the internal sea waters and territorial sea of Russia. Navigation of these vessels is permitted only with the authorization of the Ministry of Defense, under the supervision and in accordance with the instructions of the commander of the Russian warship.[23] Consequently, the navigation of foreign non-commercial autonomous vessels along the NSR will become significantly more complex, given that certain segments of this sea route traverse the territorial sea of Russia. These stipulations, however, do not apply to commercial autonomous vessels navigating the NSR; they will remain subject to the regulations outlined in Russian legislation concerning navigation on the NSR. Further details on these requirements will be addressed in the fourth part of this article.

The Federal Law has clarified regulations concerning vessel crews. A semi-autonomous vessel has a crew of a semi-autonomous vessel and an external crew of a semi-autonomous vessel. The external captain of a semi-autonomous vessel is responsible for coordinating the activities of the external crew of a semi-autonomous vessel. The captain of a semi-autonomous vessel, when it comes to the management of the vessel, follows the guidance provided by the external captain or a member of the external crew of a semi-autonomous vessel. However, ultimate decisions regarding the management of a semi-autonomous vessel rest with the captain of the semi-autonomous vessel.[24]

A fully autonomous vessel is staffed solely by an external crew. The external crew of an autonomous vessel includes an external captain of an autonomous vessel and specialists who meet the requirements for the number and qualifications specified for members of external crews of autonomous vessels, as established by the Ministry of Transport. Members of the external crew of an autonomous vessel are required to have professional experience as a captain or senior assistant to the captain of a maritime vessel with a capacity of at least 3,000 tons. Additionally, they must have completed an advanced training

23 ibid, art 1.
24 ibid, art 2.

program in autonomous vessel management or hold a higher technical education and have undergone training in the professional retraining program for autonomous vessel management. In relation to a fully autonomous vessel, the Federal Law provides for the issuance of a certificate on the minimum composition of the external crew of an autonomous vessel ensuring safety. The certificate of the minimum composition of the external crew of an autonomous vessel is issued by the captain of the seaport in accordance with the regulations approved by the Ministry of Transport.[25]

The Federal Law outlines the fundamental responsibilities of the captain and owner of an autonomous vessel. These include ensuring compliance with safety navigation requirements, safeguarding the marine environment from pollution, and overseeing the management of the autonomous vessel, including navigation and measures to ensure its supervision.

The Federal Law has established a category known as 'special personnel', encompassing individuals on board the vessel who are neither passengers nor crew members. Special personnel includes:

1. Officials, in connection with the performance of their official duties within their official powers in the fields of border, customs, sanitary, port, transport, and other state control or supervision.
2. Individuals engaged in the search, exploration, and extraction of minerals, maintenance of artificial islands, installations, and structures not requiring permanent personnel presence, as well as in construction, track, hydrotechnical, underwater-technical, and similar works. This category also includes those involved in rescue operations, measures to protect water bodies, retrieval of sunken property, investigation of transport accidents, scientific research, pilotage, and icebreaking operations.
3. Individuals transported to other vessels for crew changes or work, and those transported to autonomous vessels for work, including maintenance and management. This encompasses personnel involved in changing crews on other vessels or performing tasks on these vessels, as well as those engaged in work on autonomous vessels.

The Federal Law regulates the procedures for transporting special personnel, outlining the duties and rights of the shipowner facilitating the transportation of special personnel on their vessels. Such transportation is permitted on vessels with either a certificate for transporting special personnel or a passenger certificate. It is worth noting that this certificate can be issued by an authorized

25 ibid.

Russian organization or a foreign classification society. The Federal Law specifies that fully autonomous vessels are not allowed to carry passengers.[26]

The Federal Law introduces new amendments regarding the utilization of electronic contracts for the sea carriage of goods and electronic bills of lading. These provisions are applicable to both crewed and non-crewed vessels. Consequently, a contract for the sea carriage of goods can now be created in the format of an electronic document (an electronic contract for the carriage of goods by sea). Both the electronic contract for the carriage of goods by sea and the electronic bill of lading are required to be submitted to a dedicated state information system for electronic transportation documents.[27]

The Federal Law does not clarify how cargo is loaded and unloaded onto the autonomous vessels, who issues a bill of lading and how, what are the mechanisms for financial support of liability for damage potentially caused by autonomous vessels. It is highly probable that the legislator, with the aim of standardizing the regulations applicable to vessels with crew and autonomous vessels, deemed the existing provisions in Russian legislation adequate to address these matters.

A key concern of operating uncrewed vehicles is the high level of cyber threats. These include malfunctions caused by software and equipment failures, as well as intentional or careless interference with automated devices and software by third parties. However, these issues have not been addressed in the Federal Law. It does not differentiate the main types of cyber threats in the field of navigation, which could include:

– Encryption of critical system data with subsequent ransom demands for restoration
– Cyber espionage with the intent of stealing confidential information
– Installation of malware to disrupt vehicle computer systems
– Phishing attacks aimed at obtaining confidential information
– Unauthorized access to passenger lists.[28]

The Federal Law lacks provisions regulating the rights to software enabling vessel operation. It would be advisable to stipulate that the shipowner is the rights holder to information technologies and software controlling cargo ships' operation. Requirements for such technologies and software, methods for evaluating software security, and sanctions for non-compliance with technical and legal requirements related to software and information technology usage should be

26 ibid.

27 ibid.

28 Igor Yurin, Gregory Lebedev, Ilya Livshitz, 'Application prospects for unmanned transport ships in the seas of the Russian Arctic Basin' (2021) STJITMO 79.

specified. These requirements should be a prerequisite for permitting vessels to operate. Furthermore, the Federal Law does not address the software developer's responsibility for damage caused due to software deficiencies, and how this responsibility correlates with the liability of others involved in the operation of autonomous and semi-autonomous vessels.[29]

According to the Federal Law, if hostilities occur in the port of departure or port of destination of an uncrewed vessel, or in any area the vessel must traverse, or in other instances of military danger, the shipowner of an autonomous vessel is obliged to take all measures to prevent the destruction, damage, and seizure of the vessel, people, documents, cargo, and other property, and to keep the vessel in seaworthy condition. This provision of the Federal Law merely gives a general description of this obligation ('to take all measures'), fails to define specific actions to be taken by the shipowner, and does not propose any sanctions or enforcement mechanism. Additionally, the Federal Law does not contain provisions regulating the duties of an autonomous vessel's shipowner in relation to other significant maritime hazards that could increase with the remote operation of the vessel, such as piracy and terrorist acts.[30]

While developing the Federal Law, the stipulations of the International Safety Management (ISM) Code were not considered. Article 1.2 of the Code mandates each shipowner to devise a safety management system for each vessel. This system outlines the actions of each crew member and other employees of the shipowner during regular and emergency situations. It also lays down communication protocols between ship crew members and on-shore personnel, the procedure for emergency message transmission, emergency preparedness, and the process for compliance verification with the developed requirements. The Federal Law overlooks the development and implementation of a safety management system, specifically the coordination among various individuals involved in vessel management.

During the development stage, the Federal Law faced criticism for its failure to regulate certain duties of the captain, command staff, and crew members, such as collision prevention duties under the 1972 International Regulations for Preventing Collisions at Sea (hereafter referred to as the COLREGS) and responsibilities related to towing and rescue.[31] However, this opinion is not entirely justified. The Regulation for conducting the experiment requires the Federal Agency for Maritime and River Transport to develop recommendations for the adherence of autonomous vessels to the COLREGS. These

29 Expert opinion (n 5) 5.
30 ibid 6.
31 ibid 3.

recommendations were issued by the agency in January 2021 and are utilized in Russia to facilitate the automatic divergence of autonomous vessels from other ships.

The Federal Law provides clarification on the rules governing the pilotage of vessels as they pertain to autonomous vessels. The owner of an autonomous vessel is required to guarantee safe conditions for the boarding and disembarking of the pilot on the autonomous vessel, along with ensuring the pilot's access to the vessel's controls. In cases where the pilotage duration of an autonomous vessel exceeds four hours, the vessel must provide a separate room for the pilot, along with offering free meals to both the pilot and their trainee, if applicable.

The Federal Law does not provide regulations for the crew and remote operators of autonomous vessels engaged in salvage at sea. This is a complex issue, and it seems the Russian legislator has chosen to await international-level regulations. The absence of a captain and crew does not automatically exempt autonomous vessels from providing necessary maritime rescue services. For instance, autonomous vessels can serve as rescue platforms to evacuate people in distress from danger, assist them ashore, or offer precise positioning to determine the exact location of a distressed ship. The existing international legal framework does not fully cover the specific roles and responsibilities of external captains or remote operators in maritime search and rescue operations. According to Article 6, paragraph 2, of the 1989 International Convention on Salvage (hereafter referred to as the Salvage Convention), the master is authorized to enter salvage operation contracts on behalf of the vessel owner. Similarly, the master or the vessel owner has the authority to enter such contracts on behalf of the owner of the property on board.[32] However, the Salvage Convention lacks regulations concerning the legal status of external captains or remote operators, and their ability to sign salvage operation contracts and seek salvage remuneration remains unclear. Traditional salvage remuneration assessment standards heavily rely on human-centered factors, and determining remuneration in cases of salvage by autonomous vessels will be influenced by the absence of on-board crew members and the significant reliance on technical capabilities. Therefore, a less discretionary approach should be taken in determining salvage remuneration, favoring a more standardized formula.[33]

Pilotage of a semi-autonomous vessel follows the provisions outlined in Chapter VI of the Merchant Shipping Code, which is already applicable

32 1989 International Convention on Salvage, art 6, paragraph 2.

33 Mayank Suri & Krzysztof Wróbel, 'Identifying Factors Affecting Salvage Rewards of Crewless Vessels: Lessons from a Case Study', (2021) 21 WMU Journal of Maritime Affairs 229, 230.

to crewed vessels. In the case of a fully autonomous vessel, the pilot boards accompanied by a representative of the vessel's owner possessing the requisite qualifications for vessel operation. The pilot presents his certificate to the owner's representative and may not leave the vessel without the consent of the external captain until anchoring, mooring, setting sail, or being replaced by another pilot. The presence of a pilot on a fully autonomous vessel does not absolve the external captain of responsibility. If there are valid concerns about the pilot's recommendations, the external captain can refuse their services to ensure navigation safety. When pilotage is compulsory, the external captain must request a pilot replacement.[34]

The provisions of the Federal Law regarding autonomous vessels technically conflict with several international conventions to which Russia is a signatory. These international conventions include UNCLOS, the 1974 International Convention for the Safety of Life at Sea (hereafter referred to as SOLAS), and the ISM Code. For instance, UNCLOS necessitates each state to take measures for the recruitment and training of ship crews. Specifically, the flag state is obliged to ensure that each vessel is captained by suitably qualified officers, and that the crew's qualifications and numbers correspond to the vessel's type, size, mechanisms, and equipment. Article 217 of UNCLOS bans vessels that do not comply with international norms and standards, particularly manning, from setting sail. SOLAS mandates permanent watchkeeping by a responsible crew member, along with training standards and requirements for seafarers' diplomas and watchkeeping certification. According to Article 6 of ISM Code, the company (shipowner) should ensure each ship is manned with qualified, certified, and medically fit seafarers in line with national and international requirements. As of now, these international agreements have not been amended. The IMO plays a significant role in developing international standards for the operation of autonomous vessels. Recently, the IMO completed a regulatory scoping exercise on autonomous vessels, aiming to assess the applicability of existing IMO instruments to ships with varying degrees of automation. The safety treaties' regulatory scoping exercise was finalized at the 103rd Session of the Maritime Safety Committee (MSC) in 2021. Documents regulating the broader issues of autonomous vessels are still in development and have not yet been published. IMO's Legal and Facilitation Committees are currently also in the process of conducting regulatory scoping exercises on conventions under their purview. Further progress on the development of a goal-based instrument regulating the operation of autonomous vessels was made at the MSC's

34 The Federal Law (n 19) art 2.

106th session in November 2022. This followed the completion of the regulatory scoping exercise. The MSC noted that the best way forward to address autonomous vessels in the IMO regulatory framework could, preferably, be in a holistic manner through the development of a goal-based autonomous vessels instrument. Such an instrument could take the form of the MASS Code, with goal(s), functional requirements and corresponding regulations, suitable for all four degrees of autonomy, and addressing the various gaps and themes identified by the regulatory scoping exercise.[35] The MASS Code is expected to be enforced from 1 January 2028.[36] Hence, the adoption of the Federal Law at this time, when the legal regulation of autonomous vessel operation is still under discussion at the international level, may seem premature. However, this is not an issue, as in the event of a discrepancy with the MASS Code, Russia is likely to make necessary adjustments to its domestic maritime legislation. For instance, Russia has previously aligned its maritime legislation with the Polar Code. From both a legal and technical standpoint, the MASS Code, similar to the Polar Code, will incorporate additional chapters and sections into existing agreements like SOLAS, MARPOL, etc.

4 Regulations for the Northern Sea Route and Autonomous Vessels

In the Arctic context, shipping remains restricted due to icy conditions, inadequate mapping, and the scarcity of ports that can accommodate existing container ships. Despite gradual investments in both ice-capable and digitally connected ships with shore-based bridges, the Arctic region is optimal for the deployment of autonomous vessels. The construction of ship's hulls can proceed without consideration for crew quarters, and powerful ice breakers would lead unmanned cargo ships across the Northern Sea Route. Future shipping of autonomous vessels in the Arctic region could prove more cost-effective and safer.[37]

The All-Russian Scientific Research Institute of Experimental Physics, in collaboration with the Krylov State Research Center and the Shirshov Institute of Oceanology of the Russian Academy of Sciences, is participating in a joint project to develop an autonomous vessel for the Arctic. As part of this

35 IMO (n 18).

36 ibid.

37 Thomas Nilsen, 'Russia to develop unmanned ships for the Arctic' (2018) *The Barents Oberver* <https://thebarentsobserver.com/en/arctic/2018/04/russia-develop-unmanned-ships-arctic> accessed 24 January 2024.

project, a digital model of an autonomous vessel is being created, with simulations accounting for the influence of hydrometeorological conditions and geographical features on the vessel and its processes. The aim of this project is to increase the efficiency of maritime transportation in the Arctic. A subsequent step in the study is the development of digital models and simulations of such autonomous cargo ships. Cargo can be optimally placed in the bow, and the vessels' dimensions will be further optimized, making the voyage more effective in Arctic waters.[38] Similar studies of autonomous shipping are being conducted in Norway and other European countries. In southern Norway, the industrial company Yara plans to open a route for shipping by fully electric, autonomous container ships between the fertilizer plant at Herøya and the port of Brevik. Experts suggest that autonomous vessels in the Arctic region will be safer than those operated by onboard crew members, given that 60–80% of all ship incidents are caused by human errors, either in navigation or for other reasons.[39]

Despite this, icebreakers will sail first, clearing the ice for a convoy of autonomous vessels either en route to or from a domestic Arctic port, or in transit between Asia and Europe. However, it is evident that autonomous vessels can only function with reliable and accurate determination of the vessel's current coordinates, implying the need for a stable operation of the satellite navigation system. Likely, Russia will need to establish a network of coastal points to monitor the internal condition of ships and control their movement along the NSR remotely. A network of coastal maintenance and repair complexes in the Arctic region may also need to be created. Moreover, a necessary condition for the navigation of autonomous vessels is a reliable hydrographic study of the area, implying the need for dependable navigation maps with regularly confirmed depth measurements.

With the advancement of autonomous vessel navigation, regulations governing Russian and foreign vessels along the NSR are expected to change and expand. Russia applies its domestic regulation to this route within the boundaries of its exclusive economic zone, in line with Article 234 of UNCLOS. Such regulation includes the Rules of Navigation in the Waters of the NSR, approved by the Government of Russia in 2020, and the Rules of Icebreaking Pilotage of Vessels in the Waters of the NSR, approved by the Russian Ministry of Transport. The Rules of Navigation on the NSR incorporate provisions concerning the organization of vessel navigation in NSR waters and introduce a permit

38 Igor Yulin (n 28) 82.

39 'Rosatom creates a digital model of an unmanned vessel for the Arctic' (2018) <https://ria.ru/20180405/1517956613.html> accessed 24 January 2024.

procedure for vessel navigation along this sea route. Vessels cannot enter the NSR waters without obtaining a permit.

The Administration of the NSR, established in 2013 to organize ship navigation, ensure navigation safety, and protect the marine environment from ship pollution in the NSR waters, issues these permits. Both Russian and foreign vessels sailing on the NSR must comply with special ice requirements, have insurance, and inform the Administration 72 hours in advance about their approach to the borders of the NSR water area. In addition, they must provide daily updates on the vessel's movement, its condition, and the actual time of crossing the water area borders. As per the Rules, sailing in the NSR waters is carried out with mandatory pilotage (icebreaking, ice pilotage) of vessels. The NSR Administration issues such permits and certificates for the right of icebreaking pilotage in the NSR waters after considering applications. Guided by the Rules of Navigation in the NSR waters, the NSR Administration may, in some cases, permit a vessel to pass without icebreaking pilotage if the vessel's ice reinforcement category corresponds to the type of ice conditions during the passage.

Article 234 of UNCLOS stipulates that coastal States have the right to adopt and enforce non-discriminatory laws and regulations for the prevention, reduction, and control of marine pollution from vessels in ice-covered areas within the limits of the exclusive economic zone. This right is particularly relevant where severe climatic conditions and the presence of ice covering such areas for most of the year pose obstructions or exceptional hazards to navigation, and pollution of the marine environment could cause significant harm to or irreversible disturbance of the ecological balance. In academic discourse, there is a view that the consistent reduction of the Arctic ice cover could significantly impact the further application of Article 234. This leads to the question of whether Russia can apply the above regulations to autonomous vessels based on Article 234, considering the decreased ice cover in the Arctic Ocean.

In the wording of Article 234 of UNCLOS, the states involved in its development used the term 'vessels', which encompasses both crewed and autonomous vessels. The primary intent of Article 234's creators was to establish rules that apply exclusively to the protection of the Arctic region's marine environment, irrespective of the type of vessels. This is supported by the fact that Article 234 is the only article in Section 8, Part XII 'Protection and Preservation of the Marine Environment' of UNCLOS.[40]

---

40 Vyacheslav Gavrilov, 'Roman Dremlyuga, Alexandra Kripakova, "Interpretation and Application of Article 234 of the United Nations Convention on the Law of the Sea of 1982 in Light of the Shrinking Ice Cover in the Arctic' (2017) 12 JRL 156.

The typical interpretation, in light of the intentions that guided the states, is that the term 'ice-covered areas' is synonymous with the Arctic sea spaces as a whole. It is apparent that Canada and Russia, as the primary beneficiaries of Article 234, intended to use it to legitimize their national navigation rules internationally, which were adopted to reduce the threat of marine pollution from foreign vessels transiting through their Arctic waters.[41] These intentions were supported by other states (including the United States) during the drafting and adoption of UNCLOS.

Some experts argue that if sea areas are ice-free for more than six months a year, they should not be subject to Article 234 of UNCLOS, and a different legal regime should be applied. However, this view is derived from a literal interpretation of Article 234.[42] Solely relying on a literal interpretation is not entirely accurate, as the Vienna Convention on the Law of Treaties of 1969 prescribes in Article 31, paragraph 1, that a treaty should be interpreted in good faith according to the ordinary meaning of its terms. The main purpose of Article 234 is to preserve the delicate marine environment of the Arctic Ocean. The melting of Arctic ice does not negate this purpose but instead makes it more urgent since, according to scientific research, this process only increases the Arctic region's vulnerability.[43] The threats of Arctic environmental pollution due to oil spills, an increase in waste, sources of artificial lighting, and other negative consequences of intensified human activity in the region are escalating every year. Low temperatures, persistent strong winds, snowstorms, reduced visibility in foggy conditions, and long polar nights continue to pose challenges to Arctic shipping. Risks associated with the region's remoteness from navigation support points and the provision of other services remain relevant.[44] The use of autonomous vessels does not eliminate these problems. The goals and objectives set by states during the development of Article 234, and the practice of its application, indicate that the provisions of UNCLOS are valid in the exclusive economic zones of the Arctic coastal states, regardless of the state and size of the Arctic Ocean's ice cover.[45] The Arctic's natural environment today is more vulnerable and faces more threats than when UNCLOS was developed. Thus, the internal Russian acts that have been or will be adopted based on Article 234 also extend their effect to the navigation of autonomous vessels.

---

41 S.P. Fields, 'Article 234 of the United Nations Convention on the Law of the Sea: The Overlooked Linchpin for Achieving Safety and Security in the U. S. Arctic' (2016) 7 HNSJ 1 75.

42 ibid 159.

43 J Ho, 'The Implications of Arctic Sea Ice Decline on Shipping' (2010) 34 MP 3 713, 715.

44 Aldo Chircop 'Climate Change and the Prospects of Increased Navigation in the Canadian Arctic' (2007) 6 WJMA 2 195, 196.

45 Vyacheslav Gavrilov, Roman Dremlyuga, Alexandra Kripakova (n 40) 159.

5 Conclusion

While the IMO is actively working to align its regulatory framework for MASS with rapidly advancing technologies, states are confronted with a decision between two courses of action. The first involves patiently awaiting the completion of IMO's work and subsequently reforming domestic legislation in harmony with its recommendations. The second option entails crafting independent legislation without delay, bypassing the need to wait for IMO's finalization. Russia has opted for the latter approach, but it is structuring its legislation while taking into account the preliminary developments available from IMO.

Looking ahead, should conflicts arise between national norms and international standards, Russia is likely to introduce amendments to its legislation. The crucial aspect is that the rapid progress of autonomous shipping in Russia now rests on a solid legal foundation and framework. Opting for the second course raises inquiries about the feasibility of operating autonomous vessels beyond Russian jurisdiction. Consequently, the initial route for autonomous or unmanned navigation in Russia currently links internal Russian ports, specifically Kaliningrad and Ust-Luga.

The new Federal Law introduces a comprehensive legal framework for the testing and operation of autonomous vessels. The legislation defines key concepts such as 'autonomous vessel', 'semi-autonomous vessel' and 'fully autonomous vessel', categorizing them based on the degree of automation. The Federal Law introduces a unique identifier for autonomous vessels, streamlining the identification process through electronic maintenance of ship documents. However, challenges persist in identifying qualifications for foreign shipowners and specialists. The Federal Law deals with the navigation of foreign autonomous warships and other non-commercial autonomous vessels in Russian waters. While the Federal Law clarifies regulations for vessel crews, safety management, and special personnel, it lacks detailed mechanisms for certain crucial aspects, such as handling cyber threats in the field of navigation and addressing software rights. The Federal Law does not differentiate between the main types of cyber threats, nor does it not provide clarity on responsibilities during military or maritime hazards. Notably, the Federal Law introduces amendments facilitating the use of electronic contracts and bills of lading, but gaps remain in addressing cargo handling procedures and liability mechanisms. The absence of provisions considering the ISM Code and cyber threats reveals areas where future regulatory developments may be needed. The Federal Law emphasizes the obligations of autonomous vessel owners during hostilities, but lacks specificity in defining actions and proposing sanctions. In terms of pilotage, the Federal Law provides clarity on safe conditions for boarding and disembarking.

The Federal Law appears to clash with international conventions such as UNCLOS, SOLAS, and ISM. These agreements outline requirements for crew qualifications, training, and vessel operation standards. The IMO is actively addressing the regulation of autonomous vessels, with the proposed the MASS Code set to be enforced from January 1, 2028. As international discussions continue, some experts consider the adoption of the Federal Law at this time to be premature. However, if conflicts arise with the MASS Code, Russia is likely to adjust its domestic legislation, a practice observed with the Polar Code in the past.

The internal Russian regulations governing navigation along the NSR, based on Article 234 of UNCLOS, also extend their influence to the operation of autonomous vessels. Despite the potential for increased safety in the future shipping of autonomous vessels in the Arctic region, Russia is expected to persist in applying its current and forthcoming domestic legislation to autonomous vessels navigating the NSR. In this context, even with a consistent reduction in Arctic ice cover, it is unlikely to impact the continued application of Article 234 of UNCLOS.

References

1989 International Convention on Salvage.

2020 Expert opinion on the draft federal law 'On Amendments to the Code of Merchant Shipping of the Russian Federation and Certain Legislative Acts of the Russian Federation in Terms of Legal Relations arising from the use of autonomous Vessels (Экспертное заключение по проекту федерального закона «о внесении изменений в кодекс торгового мореплавания российской федерациии отдельные законодательные акты российской федерациив части правоотношений, возникающих при использовании автономных судов) (RUS).

'A government system for managing unmanned ships has been established in Russia' (2023) <https://www.cnews.ru/news/top/2023-02-28_v_rossii_sozdana_gossistema> accessed 24 January 2024.

Aldo Chircop 'Climate Change and the Prospects of Increased Navigation in the Canadian Arctic' (2007) 6 WJMA 2 195. International Maritime Organization. 'Autonomous shipping' <https://www.imo.org/en/MediaCentre/HotTopics/Pages/Autonomous-shipping.aspx> accessed 24 January 2024.

B. Устинов v. Ustinov (2021) TBR 2.

Igor Yurin, Gregory Lebedev, Ilya Livshitz, 'Application prospects for unmanned transport ships in the seas of the Russian Arctic Basin' (2021) STJITMO 79.

J Ho, 'The Implications of Arctic Sea Ice Decline on Shipping' (2010) 34 MP 3 713.

Mayank Suri & Krzysztof Wróbel, 'Identifying Factors Affecting Salvage Rewards of Crewless Vessels: Lessons from a Case Study; (2021) 21 WMU Journal of Maritime Affairs 229.

'Rosatom creates a digital model of an unmanned vessel for the Arctic' (2018) <https://ria.ru/20180405/1517956613.html> accessed 24 January 2024.

'Rosmorport ferries have received the first certificates of marine autonomous and remotely operated surface vessels in Russia' (2023) <https://www.cnews.ru/news/line/2023-10-03_paromy_rosmorporta_poluchili> accessed 24 January 2024.

S.P. Fields, 'Article 234 of the United Nations Convention on the Law of the Sea: The Overlooked Linchpin for Achieving Safety and Security in the U. S. Arctic' (2016) 7HNSJ 1.

'Sitronics creates a platform for driving ships without a crew on its own software' (2021) <https://www.cnews.ru/news/top/2021-07-08_sitroniks_sozdaet_platformu> accessed 24 January 2024.

'Strategic project No. 3 Electronic navigation and unmanned (autonomous) navigation' (2021) <https://www.miit.ru/page/178854> accessed 24 January 2024.

'Sitronics KT to equip ferries connecting Kaliningrad and Leningrad regions with autonomous navigation technologies' (2022) <https://www.akm.ru/press/sitronics_kt_osnastit_tekhnologiyami_avtonomnogo_sudovozhdeniya_paromy_soedinyayushchie_kaliningrads/> accessed 24 January 2024.

The Federal Law 'On Amendments to Certain Legislative Acts of the Russian Federation 2023 (RUS) Article 2 <https://rg.ru/documents/2023/07/17/document-o-vnesenii -izmenenij-v-otdelnye-zakonodatelnye-akty-rossijskoj-federacii.html> accessed 24 January 2024.

'The first autonomous sea ferry has been put into operation in Russia: it has been developed for many years' (2023) <https://trashbox.ru/link/2023-12-20-ego-razrabatyvali-mnogo-let> accessed 24 January 2024.

'The first unmanned passenger ships may appear in Russia in 2024' (2023) <https://tass.ru/ekonomika/18781457> accessed 24 January 2024.

'The Regulation for conducting the experiment on the trial operation of autonomous ships flying the Russian State flag' (2020) <http://government.ru/docs/all/131362/> point 1 accessed 24 January 2024.

Thomas Nilsen, 'Russia to develop unmanned ships for the Arctic' (2018) The Barents Oberver<https://thebarentsobserver.com/en/arctic/2018/04/russia-develop-unmanned-ships-arctic> accessed 24 January 2024.

Vyacheslav Gavrilov, 'Roman Dremlyuga, Alexandra Kripakova, "Interpretation and Application of Article 234 of the United Nations Convention on the Law of the Sea of 1982 in Light of the Shrinking Ice Cover in the Arctic' (2017) 12 JRL 156.

CHAPTER 10

Status Quo, Problems of Shipping Administration and the Counter-Measures on Uncrewed Vessels—From the Perspective of the Guangdong-Hong Kong-Macao Greater Bay Area

*Ping Guo**

1 Forwarding

The research and practice of uncrewed vessels (UVs) in the world has a solid foundation on the application of artificial intelligent technologies to the shipping industry. Although UVs have been employed in commercial operations in several countries such as Japan, Norway, China, and South Korea, it could not be denied that the research and practice promotion of UVs is still at its early stage in the general sense. No comprehensive legal system is capable of regulation most maritime activities of UVs has emerged in the world until now. With the aim of coping with possible impacts of the evolving science and technology on the use of uncrewed vessels in the shipping industry as well as the aim of ensuring the marine transportation safety, it is necessary to discuss the issues arising from applying existing laws and regulations to uncrewed ships. This paper focuses on the conflicts between existing legislation involving shipping administrative management within the Guangdong-Hong Kong-Macao Greater Bay Area (hereinafter GBA), and further puts forward some feasible suggestions based on the policy of mechanism innovation in the GBA for the purpose of tackling the challenges brought about by technology revolutions to the administration of UVs.

* Research Fellow of Southern Marine Science and Engineering Guangdong Laboratory (Zhuhai), Professor in Maritime Law and Ocean Environmental Law, School of law, SUN Yat-sen University, Executive Director, Research Center for International Maritime and Ocean Law (Sun Yat-sen University) of The Supreme People's Court Fourth Civil Judicial Division, China. E-mail: guop26@mail.sysu.edu.cn.

 | DOI:10.1163/9789004706279_012

2 Determination of Legal Nature: Whether an UV Is a Ship

2.1 *Descriptions of UV Vary in Different Respects*

One precondition for UVs to be regulated by current laws on shipping administration is that they meet the requirements of those laws, for instance, those concerning ship construction, inspection, testing and operation. Unfortunately, that precondition has not been achieved, as the descriptions of UVs in various countries and in the international maritime organizations are different. These are some examples of the terms often used: unmanned ship (US), unmanned vessel (UV), intelligent ship (IS), autonomous surface vehicle (ASV), autonomous surface cargo ship (ASCS), maritime autonomous surface ships (MASS), and unmanned underwater vehicle (or unmanned undersea vehicle) (UUV).

2.1.1 From the Perspective of International Organizations

The Comité Maritime International (CMI) prefers to use the term 'unmanned vessel' (UV) in its legal documents. According to the CMI International Working Group Position Paper on Unmanned Vessels and the International Regulatory Framework, UVs are those which are capable of controlled movement on the water in absence of any onboard crew.[1] By comparison, the International Maritime Organization (IMO)—one intergovernmental organization within the United Nations system, which has greater influence to that of the CMI on the maritime industries, prefers using the term MASS. For the purposes of the Regulatory Scoping Exercise, one MASS is defined as a ship which, to varying degrees of autonomy, can operate independently of human interaction.[2] The four levels of autonomy with respect to MASS are as follow: (a) At the first level are the ships with automated processes and decision support. Seafarers are on board to operate and control shipboard systems and functions. Some operations may be automated. (b) At the second level are the remotely controlled ships with seafarers on board. The ships are controlled and operated from another location, but seafarers are on board. (c) At the third level are the remotely controlled ships without seafarers on board. A ship at this level is controlled and operated from another location. There are no seafarers on board. (d) At the fourth level are the fully autonomous ships. The operating system of such fully autonomous ship is capable of decisions-making and actions-determining by itself. Obviously, the scope of MASS as is indicated by

1 'CMI International Working Group Position Paper on Unmanned Vessels and the International Regulatory Framework' <https://comitemaritime.org/work/mass/> accessed 5 May 2020.

2 'IMO takes first steps to address autonomous ships' <http://www.imo.org/en/MediaCentre/PressBriefings/Pages/08-MSC-99-MASS-scoping.aspxv> accessed 5 May 2020.

the IMO is wider than that of UV defined by the CMI, because only the ships at the third and fourth levels of autonomy as are described by the IMO may be considered equivalents for the UV defined by the CMI, which have no seafarers on board.

2.1.2 From the Perspective of the Shipbuilding Industry

The term 'intelligent ship' (IS) is used commonly by the shipbuilding industry. Despite the wide application of the artificial intelligent technology in the shipbuilding industry, the major shipbuilders have defined IS in their own ways.[3]

The China Classification Society (CCS) published the Rules for Intelligent Ships in 2015, which were amended in 2020 and 2022. Art 1.1.3 of the Rules for Intelligent Ships (2020) provides that,

> 'Intelligent Ships' refer to the ships or vessels which use of sensors, communications, internet of things, internet and other technical means to automatically perceive and obtain information and data on the ship itself, marine environment, logistics, ports, etc., to process and analyze technology based on computer technology, automatic control technology and big data, to achieve intelligent operation of the ship in the navigation, management, maintenance, cargo transportation and other aspects, so as to make the ship safer, environment more friend, shipping operation more economical and more efficient.

With different degrees of autonomy, the IS, according to the CCS, include the ships that carry either the function of auxiliary decision-making or that of complete autonomy. The various autonomous systems of an IS cover partial application or whole applications on ability from auxiliary decision-making to complete autonomy according to different autonomous degree. The function of IS include, generally, intelligent navigation, intelligent hull, intelligent engine room, intelligent energy efficiency management, intelligent cargo management, intelligent integration platform, remote control and autonomous operation.[4] The CCS further points out that an IS differs from an Unmanned Surface Vehicle (USV), in that the latter, the length of which is generally between 5 and 20 meters, can be navigated, maneuvered and operated directly by autonomous navigation or remote control. The description of IS under the Rules for Intelligent Ships (2020) excludes the USVs, because the USVs, having no crew member on board, refer to the small boats within the length limits.

---

3 Liu Wei and Shang Jiafa, 'Research on the Development Status of Intelligent Ships and its Development Strategy in China' (2017) 11 SST 189, 193.

4 See art. 1.14 of Rules for Intelligent Ships (2020) CCS.

However, the USVs defined by the CCS shall be considered as one kind of UVs in this paper, because the USVs can also carry out various mission loads including platforms, communication systems and control systems,[5] in order to perform designated tasks widely in the field of shipping, especially in ocean economic activities other than commercial transportation.

In coping with the development of artificial intelligent technology in the shipbuilding, the CCS also published the Guide on Automatic Identification System (AIS) Inspection in 2003, the Intelligent Ships on the Tanker Cargo Management in 2018, the Intelligent Engineering Room in 2017, the Intelligent Energy Efficiency Management in 2018, and the Specification for Unmanned Cargo Transport Ships in 2017.[6]

In the context where smart functions (SF), which provide the crew and support personnel with key information for decision-making, have become increasingly common onboard marine vessels and offshore units, the American Bureau of Shipping (ABS) published the Guide for Smart Functions for Marine Vessels and Offshore Units in 2018, which was amended in July 2020, October 2021,June 2022 and December 2023 accordingly.[7] The Guide defines SF as systems installed and service deployed to collect, transmit, manage, and analyse continuously, as well as to report data for enhanced health and condition awareness, operational assistance, operational optimization, and decision-making support. The ABS categorizes SF into the following levels: manual, smart, semi-autonomy, and full autonomy (as is shown in Table 10.1)—the standards of which appear similar to those developed by the IMO for MASS.

(Table 10.1 is drawn from the Guide for Smart Functions for Marine Vessels and Offshore Units of 2022.)

In addition, the ABS published the Requirements for Autonomous and Remote Control Functions in July 2022 as well as August 2022.[8] Article 7 in Section 1 of those Requirements provides that, 'The autonomous and remote

5 See art 1.1.1.1 and art 1.1.2.1 of Unmanned Surface Boat Inspection Guide published in 2018 by the CCS.

6 See Art. 1.1.3 of the *Specification for Unmanned Cargo Transport Ships* (2017), Unmanned cargo transport ship refers to a cargo transport ship that is not manned on board during situations such as berthing, unberthing, navigation, anchoring, etc.

7 American Bureau of Shipping (ABS), 'Guide for Smart Functions for Marine Vessels and Offshore Units' (December 2023) <https://ww2.eagle.org/content/dam/eagle/rules-and-guides/current/other/307-guide-for-smart-functions-for-marine-vessels-and-offshore-units-2023/307-smart-guide-dec23.pdf> accessed 27 February 2024.

8 ABS, 'Requirements for Autonomous and Remote Control Functions' (August 2022) <https://ww2.eagle.org/content/dam/eagle/rules-and-guides/current/other/323_gn_autonomous_2022/323-autonomous-reqts-aug22.pdf> accessed 27 February 2024.

LE 10.1 Smart-to-autonomy levels

vel	Features	Data handling	Decision making	Execution of action
nual	No system augmentation	System and Human	Human	Human
art	System augmentation of human functions	System and Human	Human with System support	Human
ii-Autonomy	Human augmentation of system functions	System	System with Human supervision	System with Human supervision
Autonomy	No human augmentation	System	System	System

control functions described in this document do not imply unmanned vessels. The vessel manning level is determined with consideration of all onboard activities, system maintenance, incidence handling, and regulation requirements ...'. It seems that the ABS prefer using the terms 'smart' and 'autonomous' to 'unmanned'.

The United Kingdom (UK) Maritime Autonomous Systems Working Group drafted the Maritime Autonomous Surface Ships (MASS) UK Industry Conduct Principles and Code of Practice (hereinafter 'the UK Code'), which was reviewed by the UK Maritime and Coast Guard (MCA) and was published in November 2019 by the British Maritime Association through the Maritime Industry Association. Although the term 'MASS' in the UK Code does not exclude the ships less than 24 meters, it is clarified therein that the MASS less than 24 meters differ from the Maritime Autonomous Systems (MAS) which, generally, cover the systems such as Autonomous Underwater Vehicles (AUV), Remotely Operated Vehicles (ROV) and Unmanned Air Systems (UAS).[9] The UK Code regulates only the MAS that are movable on surface, and excludes those under water or in the air. It should be noted that the Lloyd's Register in the UK published the LR Code for Unmanned Marine Systems (hereinafter

9 UK Maritime, 'Being a Responsible Industry: Maritime Autonomous Surface Ships (MASS) UK Industry Conduct Principles and Code of Practice' <https://safety4sea.com/wp-content/uploads/2019/11/UK-Maritime-Maritime-Autonomous-surface-ships-UK-Code-of-Practice-2019_11.pdf> accessed 8 February 2023.

'the LR Code') in February 2017, in which the term 'Unmanned Marine Systems' (UMS) is used. The LR Code defines UMS as a surface or submersible system that can be operated without personnel on board.[10] UMS in the LR Code also include autonomous vehicles and remote-control vehicles operated on or below the surface. The autonomy levels (AL) therein are divided between AL 0 (manual) and AL 6 (fully autonomous),[11] which are adapted from those in the Lloyd's Register Cyber Enabled Ships.

Obviously, the different descriptions of Intelligent Ship (IS), Smart Function (SF), Maritime Autonomous Systems (MAS), Unmanned Marine Systems (UMS) are used in various national classification or shipping association, and there is no unified term recognized widely for UVs in the world shipping industry.

2.1.3 From the Perspective of Academicians

Some scholars prefer to use the term of Unmanned Underwater Vehicle (UUV) and insist on that UUV is a small submersible vehicle capable of non-manned operation by preset programs or remote control, which carries a lethal or non-lethal payload underwater navigation power device.[12] An UUV may fall into one of the following types: (a) a Fully Autonomous UUV, which has the ability to plan the route, navigate and perceive by its autonomous system independently; (b) a Remote Control UUV, which does control, sail and perform tasks by the built-in procedures and which may be controlled remotely by a shore-based or a ship-based personnel; and (c) a Weapon UUV, which is deployed for attacking, combating and killing enemies and is widely used in military surveying, military defence, marine exploration and other fields.

Some believe that Underwater Vehicles (also called Underwater Robots: UR) include Human Occupied Vehicles (HOVs) and UUVs, and that the UUVs can be further divided into Remotely Operated Vehicles (ROVs), Autonomous Underwater Vehicles (AUVs) and Autonomous and Remotely Operated Vehicles (ARVs). ROV is widely used in marine scientific research, marine survey, marine observation, marine rescue, water conservancy, archaeology, military, and offshore oil and gas development—with its comprehensive advantages

10 See LR Code for Unmanned Marine Systems, art 4.1.27 <https://www.lr.orgenunmanned-code> accessed 8 February 2023.

11 See ibid, art 4.1.2.

12 Song Shuhua and Zhao Jinsong, 'Legal Status of Unmanned Underwater Vehicles (2017) 3 JSCSS 21, 27.

of economy, high efficiency, large operation depth, unlimited operation time, strong adaptation to extreme environment, and no personnel safety risks.[13]

As is revealed above, the descriptions of UVs vary at the domestic and international level, and the scopes of different terms vary in many respects. In this paper, it is argued that all of these autonomous marine systems that can be described as UVs have common characteristics in essence, no matter whether they are on or below the surface of seawater, whether they can be controlled by shore based personnel or be operated autonomously, whichever their length or tonnage are, and whether they are used for commercial transportation, military, scientific research, marine rescue, exploration and development of marine resources, or any other marine activities.

The common characteristics of UVs are these: First, they possess the 'ability to perceive', which is a precondition for the realization of intelligence by collecting data through sensing the characteristics and changes of the external environment. Second, they have the 'ability to sort out and discern data, further to summarize, analyse and compare the stored information' through the application of information technology to provide a data basis for decision-making. Third, they are capable to take actions autonomously based on decision-making and banish the intervention from human beings completely. The last but not least, no crew are on board the vessels, no matter whether they operate autonomously or are controlled remotely by land-based personnel.

In this paper, the term 'Uncrewed Vessels' (UVs) is preferred to others, because there are more and more females working on board as crew member in shipping practice now. The express of explicit words of Uncrewed Vessels are much more objective, neutral without any sexual discriminations. Based on the consideration that, regardless of the level of autonomy, if there are personnel working on board, there would be no substantive difference between UVs and the traditional merchant ships in the light of ship administrative management. Only those with no crew on board may face the challenges from ship administration. For purpose of discussion in this paper, the terms 'Uncrewed Vessels', 'Unmanned Vessels', 'Uncrewed Ships' and 'Unmanned Ships' bear the same meaning.

13 Huang Mingquan, Xu Jingping and Shi Linwei, 'Application and prospect of ROV in offshore oil and gas field development' (2021) 2 MGF 77, 84; Wang Yongding , Wang Peng and Sun Pengfei , 'A Review of Research on Autonomous Underwater Robot Control Technology' the World Science and Technology Research and Development Network <https://doi.org/10.16507/j.issn.1006-6055.2021.01.004> accessed 8 July 2021.

2.2 *Definitions of Ship in International Conventions and Nation Laws*

The IMO and other international organizations have promulgated a couple of international conventions in past decades, which concern safety, prevention of collision, training of seafarers, marine search, rescue at sea etc., such as the International Convention on the Safety of Life at Sea (SOLAS),[14] the Convention on the International Regulations for the Prevention Collisions at Sea (COLREGS),[15] the International Convention on Load Lines (Load Lines),[16] the International Convention on Standards of Training, Certification and Watchkeeping for Seafarers (STCW),[17] the International Convention on Maritime Search and Rescue (SAR),[18] the International Convention on Tonnage Measurement of Ships (Tonnage Convention),[19] and the International Convention for the Prevention of Pollution from Ships (MARPOL 73/78).[20] None of those conventions set forth 'crew onboard' as a precondition for a vessel to be treated as a ship covered thereby.

According to Article 1 of the 1986 United Nations Convention on Conditions of Registration of Ships, 'ship' means any self-propelled sea-going vessel used in international seaborne trade for the transport of goods, passengers, with exception of those less than 500 gross registered tons. That definition makes no reference to personnel either.[21]

Ships have been defined in divergent ways in national laws as well in some occasions, including those under construction, and in some others, as transport means. Nonetheless, in the law of most countries, crew or personnel are not mentioned as a necessary element of a ship.[22] It should be noted that the CMI circulated a questionnaire on the attributes of vessels to all its member states in 2017, with a view to examining the possible obstacles for applying international rules to UVs. The feedback report of 2018 shows that under domestic laws of most CMI members (including China), a transport means operating autonomously and without a crew onboard can be recognized as a ship.[23]

14 See the definition of ship in regulation 2 of part A provided in chapter one of annex of SOLAS 1974.
15 See the definition of vessel in part A Rule 3 (a) of COLREG 1972.
16 See the definition of ship in art 2 of Load Line 1966.
17 See art 3 of STCW 1978.
18 See annex chapter 1 of SAR 1979.
19 See art 2 of Tonnage Convention 1969.
20 See art 2 (4) of MARPOL 73/782.
21 1986 United Nations Convention on Conditions of Registration of Ship, art II, para. 1.
22 Sun Yuqing, 'Defining the Legal Status of Commercial Unmanned Ships'(2019) 3 WUILR 125, 128.
23 See CMI, 'Summary of Responses to the CMI Questionnaire on Unmanned Ships' <https://comitemaritime.org/work/mass/> accessed 30 January 2021.

The discussions above reveal that, current shipping industry practices in the world sustain the major view that UVs have the legal characteristics of ships and fall within the scope of existing rules or guidelines related to ships or shipping operation. Most international conventions and domestic legislation define a ship as transport means in the light of the loading/discharging or transportation functions. Whether it is manned or not does not prevent UVs to be identified as ships in the law.

By virtue of literature interpretation, UVs satisfy the characteristics of a ship as transportation means and meets the concept of a ship stipulated by national laws as well as the relevant international conventions concerning ships. As commented, UVs should be within the scope of the ship in the law,[24] and can be considered as one kind of ships. Therefore, an UV should comply with the regulations and rules on ship administration.

3 Development of Research and Practice Concerning UVs in China

3.1 *Development in Mainland China*

In June 2017, the Conference and First Council of the Development Alliance on Unmanned Vessels for Cargo Transportation (hereinafter 'Development Alliance on Unmanned Vessels') initiated by Hainan Airlines Science and Technology Group was held in Shanghai. The event launched the prelude to upgrading technology of intelligent ships for cargo transportation in China officially. The Development Alliance on Unmanned Vessels is the first of this kind union in China, being also the organizer and leader of shipping development as well as the founder and promoter of the rules and regulations on technical products. It integrates advanced technologies domestically and abroad to develop unmanned cargo carriers to realize the combination of the technologies of independent decision-making, independent navigation, environmental awareness, remote control, and green safety. The Alliance gains the support from the CCS in establishing ship standards, promoting regulatory revision, and providing assessment, verification, and inspection services to UVs.[25]

On 1 December 2018, the Wanshan Unmanned Ship Offshore Test Site—the first uncrewed ship offshore test site in Asia and the largest in the world at that

24 Ma Jinxing, 'Artificial Intelligence Ships Lead the Reform of the International Maritime Rules System' in China Ocean News (8 October 2019) (2nd edn).

25 Shi Xiufen, 'The Autonomous Vessel Development Alliance is Established' (7 July 2017) <http://info.chineseshipping.com.cn/cninfo/News/201707/t20170707_1291688.shtml> accessed 30 January 2021.

time—was officially launched in Zhuhai, China.[26] The test site is certified by the CCS for providing uncrewed ship test service. The first autonomous cargo ship in China, the *JinDouyun* 0 completed successfully its first autonomous journey for carriage near the area of Dong'ao Island in Zhuhai, China on 15 December 2019.[27]

In May 2020, the construction of the first self-navigating container merchant ship 'Zhi Fei' began in Qingdao, China. Being the first in China and the world's largest autonomous navigation container experimental ship, it was completed in Qingdao Shipyard, and the navigation trial test thereof was completed in June 2021 in the sea water near Qingdao Blue Valley, China's first IS test site.[28]

In September 2020, a comprehensive search and rescue exercise was held in the Yangtze River around Taicang, China. Lots of uncrewed boats, uncrewed drones, and surface life-saving robots controlled remotely were displayed in the exercise, together with some intelligent equipment such as life jackets with the location tracking function through the BeiDou satellites in emergency. The comprehensive search and rescue exercise greatly expand the application of new scientific and technological means such as the BeiDou navigation system and other artificial intelligence technologies to the field of water search and rescue.[29]

From 17 December 2021 to 17 January 2022, three UVs with tonnage of 3, 7 and 40, respectively, conducted sea trials in the water of Yazhou Bay, China.[30] The first intelligent uncrewed system mothership in the world, the Zhuhai Cloud, was put into use in Guangzhou on 18 May 2022. The ship, being owned by the Southern Marine Science and Engineering Guangdong Laboratory (Zhuhai), is the world's first research vessel with remote control and autonomous navigation functions in open water. It is reported that the Zhuhai Cloud, having been

26 'The first unmanned ship offshore test site in Asia is launched in Zhuhai, making it the largest in the world' (6 December 2018) <https://news.sina.com.cn/o/2018-12-06/doc-ihmutuec6566567.shtml> accessed 30 January 2021.

27 'Unmanned vessel 'Cloud Somersault No. 0' details fully revealed' (9 January 2020) <https://www.eworldship.com/html/2020/OperatingShip_0109/156008.html> accessed 30 January 2021.

28 'Autonomous Ships Win with 'Intelligence', from the website of China Water Transport Network' (19 January 2022) <http://www.zgsyb.com/news.html?aid=614492> accessed 27 March 2022.

29 'Jiangsu Province Holds Comprehensive Exercise on Water Search and Rescue to Improve Integrated Emergency Rescue Capacity in the Yangtze River Delta' (China Maritime Search and Rescue Center) <http://www. mot.gov.cn> accessed 16 March 2022.

30 'Notice on Conducting Unmanned Boat Maritime Tests in the Waters of Yazhou Bay' (Maritime Safety Administration of the People's Republic of China) <http://www.msa.gov.cn> accessed 16 March 2022.

equipped with an advanced artificial intelligence operating system which can automatically control dozens of uncrewed vessels, underwater vehicles and uncrewed aircrafts carried on the deck and other cabin areas, can conduct 3D observations in specific marine areas. That research vessel is greatly helpful with the collection of marine scientific research data in the future to enhance the ability of marine scientific research in China.[31]

Therefore, the era of UVs is moving from a stage of researching and developing, testing, and construction to that of commercial transportation and other wide use in maritime activities in mainland China.

3.2 *Development in Hong Kong SAR and Macao SAR*

There are few media reports officially on the research and practice promotion of UVs from the Hong Kong SAR and the Macao SAR. The Hong Kong Water Supplies Department purchased five fully automated sampling and monitoring UVs in 2016 from one ship builder company engaged business activities in the GBA. Those five UVs have been devoted into the governmental service for regular automatic water-quality-monitoring-and-sampling analysis in Chuan Wan Freshwater Lake, the second largest reservoir in Hong Kong. The UVs can also be used extensively to detect water quality and to conduct sample analysis in other reservoirs in Hong Kong. Therefore, the administrative ability of local government to monitor reservoir water quality and deal with emergency water quality accidents has been strengthened greatly.[32]

4 Legislation on Administration of UVs in China

At present, there are no special administrative regulations on UVs in China. As discussed above, an UV is of the legal nature of a ship. Therefore, the legal norms and the relevant international maritime treaties concerned with ship administration to which China is a party may apply to UVs.

4.1 *Administrative Policies concerning UVs in China*

The National Development and Reform Commission, the Ministry of Science and Technology, the Ministry of Industry and Information Technology, and the Central Cyberspace Administration of China issued jointly the 'Internet +'

31 Southern Marine Science and Engineering Guangdong Laboratory (Zhuhai) official website <https://www.sml-zhuhai.cn/info/1403.html> accessed 9 September 2022.

32 Website of Hong Kong Water Supplies Department. <http:// www. wsd.gov.hk> accessed 15 March 2022.

Three-Year Action Implementation Plan for Artificial Intelligence in May 2016. The fifth part of that Plan clearly proposes the application project of intelligent uncrewed systems to promote the integration and application of artificial intelligence technology in the field of uncrewed systems, as well as to develop uncrewed drones, uncrewed vessels and other forms of uncrewed equipment. It also aims to improve the management of the airworthiness or seaworthiness, safety and operation mechanisms of all uncrewed systems.

The State Council issued the Notice on the Development Plan of a New Generation of Artificial Intelligence in July 2017, which clearly proposes to cultivate a high-level and efficient intelligent economy, to vigorously develop emerging artificial intelligence industries (especially to develop the professional service system on test identification, testing, competition of uncrewed drones and UVs which are used for the consumption and commercial purposes), and to improve the management measures. The Notice further strengthens the approach and regulation of uncrewed ships in the progress of research and testing.

The Ministry of Industry and Information Technology, the Ministry of Transport, and the State Administration of Science, Technology and Industry for National Defence issued jointly the Notice of the Action Plan for the Development of Intelligent Ships (2019–2021) in 2018, which requires a deep integration of artificial intelligence technology and shipping to create a new format for shipping industry. It further suggests that relevant laws and regulations be sorted out systematically in order to improve technical research based thereon.

The State Council issued the Notice of the 14th Five-Year Plan for the National Emergency Response System in January 2021, emphasizing to develop the technology of UVs to improve their roles in water search and rescue.

All the policies mentioned above have underscored the importance of the development of UVs, have provided powerful supports to the development of autonomous system industries, and will contribute to a rapid development of UVs in China in the future.

4.2 *Industrial Rules and Recommendations concerning UVs in China*

In order to promote the development of IS, the CCS published the Rules for Intelligent Ships in 2015. The Rules divide IS into four categories, namely (a) those with perception ability; (b) those with auxiliary manual decision-making ability; (c) those capable of partial autonomous navigation under remote control; and (d) those capable of complete uncrewed autonomous navigation.

The Rules for Intelligent Ships was amended and took effect on 1 April 2020, becoming more suitable for the development of IS in China. The revised rules are made especially for the purposes of applying new intelligent technologies, implementing new environmental protection requirements, and improving the advantages, accuracy and operability of ISs from time to time. The main changes of the Rules for Intelligent Ships 2020 focus on the following: (1) to create a new mark in order to perform the inspection requirements and to further verify the effectiveness of the implementation of the intelligent solution on board; (2) to revise the network security requirements for IS; (3) to modify the security requirements for remote control or autonomous operation of ships; (4) to add requirements for intelligent system operation manuals on board; (5) to add requirement for autonomous ships having the function of multi-perception data fusion in open water; and (6) to require additionally that autonomous ships should determine the requirements of suitable fail-safe modes through analysis and evaluation, and clarify the main factors that need to be considered in the analysis of fail-safe modes etc.[33]

In order to meet the needs of intelligent ship development, intelligent new technology application, and implementation of new environmental protection requirements, the CCS continues to improve the progressiveness, accuracy and operability of intelligent ship specification standards. The CCS launched the latest regulatory revision on 6 March 2023, the Rules for Intelligent Ships 2023, which shall take effect from 1 April 2023.[34]

There are no specific rules or recommendations concerning UVs in Hong Kong or Macao. However, a few regulations on uncrewed equipment other than ships have emerged in Hong Kong, such as the Small Unmanned Aircraft Order (Cap. 448G).[35]

5 Problems with Applying Current Administrative Legislation to UVs

5.1 *In Mainland China*

The ship registration system mainly deals with the issues of ship nationality and ownership, which in turn influence the related matters such as the taxation on, and inspection of ships. The current legal provisions on ship registration are provided in the Regulations of the People's Republic of China on Ship Registration (as amended in 2014). It is contended in this paper that most

33 'Revision Circular for the Rules for Intelligent Ships 2022' (CCS) <http://ccs.org.cn> accessed 22 March 2022.

34 2023 Rules for Intelligent Ships 2023 (CCS) <https://www.ccs.org.cn/ccswz/specialDetail?id =202303061016018608> accessed 22 March 2023.

35 See Hong Kong Regulations <https://www.hklii.hk/eng/hk/legis/reg/448G/empowering-20210716.html> accessed 22 March 2023.

existing provisions may apply to UVs with few exceptions, such as the provision on the detailed information recorded in ship's register may not apply to UVs completely. Due to the virtue of UVs and the difference between UVs and traditional merchant ships, more detailed information on the function of UVs as well as how to recognize relevant responsible persons should be necessary required. However, these much more important information is not provided for ship registration by existing law. For example, the information of research & design personnel of one UV, whether there are shore-to-ship remote control personnel, whether one UV is operated autonomously without any human being interruption etc. are material information in the operation of UVs. In fact, the identification of responsible person is a key issue for safe operation of UVs. As there is no crew on board UVs, the identification of contact persons by the rescue and other relevant authorities is a major concern where an accident occurred in the navigation or where failures of operation were detected. Therefore, the required information to be registered for UVs should be more detailed than that for traditional ships and be clarified in the future from the view of administration of ship registration.

As for ship manning, although Article 3 of the Chinese Maritime Code (CMC), which contains a definition of ship, does not require crew on board. Chapter 3 of the CMC, which is entitled 'Crew', provides for the qualification of crew and functions of the master. The Regulation of Crew as promulgated by the Ministry of Transport in 2007,[36] which is the core legislative regulation for administrative management of crew. The Regulation of Crew provides relative issues concerned with crew which are made on the reference to Maritime Labor Convention 2006 (MLC) ratified by the Central People's Government of the PRC in 2011.[37] The Regulation applies to those activities, such as crew registration, employ appointment, training, job security, and crew services providing within the territory of the PRC.[38]

The Minimum Safe Manning Rules was promulgated by the Ministry of Transport in 2004,[39] which contain the main legal norms and the minimum requirements for ship manning. If the numbers of crew members working on

36 The ordinance of crew had been revised separately on 18 July 2003, 7 December 2003, 29 July 2014, 1 March 2017, 2 March 2019 and 27 March 2020.

37 MLC is effective for China on 12 November 2016.

38 See Article 2 of the Regulation of Crew (2020). The Regulation of Crew was promulgated in 2007, amended in July 2013, July 2014, March 2017, March 2019 and March 2020 separately.

39 The Minimum Safe Manning Rules had been amended on 5 September 2014 and 28 November 2018.

board do not meet the minimum requirements, the ship will be prohibited by the authority to leave the port.[40]

Although UVs do not satisfy the manning requirements, the fact that no one works on board does not mean that no person is responsible for the ship. If one UV may operate by its own autonomous decision-making system or even under the monitor by remote shore-based personnel, it is quite common that there are no human factors involvement in most cases during the navigation. However, if it is necessary in case UVs may bear the risks of out of control by itself, UVs still need remote shore-based personnel to monitor and intervene in the navigation and the operation of ship. Therefore, all the manning requirements in the current Chinese legislation should be appropriately converted into those for remote shore-based personnel who may monitor and control UVs, although the number of shore-based personnel can be greatly reduced compared with traditional manning of the ship. It can not be denied that the duties requirements and the professional skills for those remote shore-based personnel shall be as same as all crew and captain provided in existing law, or even higher, because those remote shore-based personnel need much more intelligent knowledge and technical skills on the monitoring, operating and controlling of one UV than those crew members work on traditional merchant ship. However, if one UV is an autonomous decision-making ship, the ability of decision-making itself should also satisfy the manning requirement by existing law as if there were crew work on board. Therefore, it is foreseeable that in the future, the qualification requirements for shore-based operators or UVs designers shall be clarified in the legislation, addressing the requirements for both nautical technical professionals and artificial intelligence technical talents.

With respect to administrative legislation on ship operation, the State Council issued the International Maritime Transport Regulations on 11 December 2001[41] and the Ministry of Transport released the Detailed Rules for the Implementation of the International Maritime Transport Regulations on 20 January 2003.[42] Both documents are formulated to regulate international maritime transport activities, to protect fair competition, to maintain the order of the international maritime transport market, and to safeguard the lawful rights and interests of all parties involved in international maritime transport

---

40 See The Minimum Safe Manning Rules, art 23.

41 The International Maritime Transport Regulations has been amended separately on 6 February 2016 and 2 March 2019.

42 Detailed Rules for the Implementation of the International Maritime Transport Regulations has been revised on 29 August 2013, 21 June 2019 and 28 November 2019 separately.

and auxiliary business activities related to international maritime transport for entering and leaving the ports of China.[43] As the provisions in these documents do not exclude explicitly the application to UVs, it seems that UVs engaged in the operation of international maritime transport should follow them theoretically. However, there are other rules or regulations providing the requirements for business qualification or operation certificates in international maritime transport, especially those concerning ship seaworthiness and transportation for carriage of dangerous goods. Some administrative authorities undertake to perform regular or irregular inspections for purpose of supervising the enforcement of those regulations. Since UVs should also satisfy all those requirements in the law, the practicability of, and the approach to, the inspections should be the subject of regulation.

Discussed as above, being one kind of ships, UVs shall follow those legal administrative legislations concerning to ship registration, traffic safety, manning of ships, the operation of international maritime transport etc. And some of these legislations may not apply to UVs completely. Therefore, it should be clarified in future in mainland China whether the legislation on the administrative supervision of ships may apply to UVs, or in which degree it shall apply to UVs or which provisions shall be amended accordingly.

5.2 *In Hong Kong SAR and Macao SAR*

When China resumed the exercise of sovereignty over Hong Kong in 1997 and over Macao in 1999, the country established SARs in the two places in accordance with Article 31 of the Constitution of the PRC. Articles 16 and 62 of the Basic Law of the Hong Kong SAR as well as Articles 16 and 64 of the Basic Law of the Macao SAR stipulate explicitly that the governments of Hong Kong and Macao shall have administrative power within the two SARs respectively, to handle administrative affairs in accordance with the law. All departments in the Central People's Government PRC and the governments of all provinces, autonomous regions and municipalities directly under the Central People's Government may not interfere with the affairs administered by the governments of Hong Kong and Macao. Therefore, maritime affairs fall within the scope of administrative power of the governments of Hong Kong and Macao.

There are several ordinances or regulations concerning the management of ships, ports and seafarers in the Hong Kong SAR. For example, the Merchant

---

43 See International Maritime Transport Regulations, arts 1, 2.

Shipping Ordinance (Cap. 281, amended on 9 June 2012), the Merchant Shipping (Safety) Ordinance (Cap. 369, amended on 24 February 2022), the Merchant Shipping (Seafarers) Ordinance (Cap. 478, amended on 2 January 2021), the Ship and Port Control Regulation (Cap. 313A, amended on 24 June 2021), the Merchant Ships (Safety) (Construction and Inspection of Cargo Ships, Built on or after 1 September 1984), Regulation and Merchant Ships (Safety) (Construction and Inspection of Passenger Ships, Built on or after 1 September 1984), the Dangerous Goods (Shipping) Regulation, the Merchant Ships (Safety) (Inspection of Safety Equipment on Cargo Ships) Regulations, and other relevant subsidiary legislation and technical standards.[44]

Similarly, there are several maritime administrative regulations in Macao which concern the registration and operation activities of ships. They are the Decree on Maritime Activities (No. 90/99, as amended in 2020), the Ship Commercial Registration Act 2019, the Regulations on Yacht Navigation, Legal System for Approving Commercial Matters at Sea, the Rules on Pilotage, the Regulations on Navigation and Safety on the Sea and Ports of the Macao SAR (No. 1/98 of the Port Authority), the Notice of Instruction on Compliance with the Ship Traffic Management Center in Macao (No. 1/2007 of the Port Authority), General Guidelines for the Inspection of Local Navigation Vessels 2020, Safe Manning on Board Ordinance 1997, Minimum Safe Manning Guidelines for Local Navigation Motor Vessels, in addition to other administrative orders and policies promulgated by the Governor of Macao SAR.[45]

Scrutinizing on the maritime affairs legislation of Hong Kong SAR and Macao SAR, similar those in mainland China, none of the ordinances and decrees concerning crew or manning of ships can apply to UVs, and it should be clarified whether the legal requirements for crew in Hong Kong and Macao may apply for remote shore-based personnel of UVs. The similar situations shall be faced that those ordinances or regulations on the administrative management or supervision of ship, shipping business or relative shipping operation activities do not exclude the application of UVs in Hong Kong and Macao literally, but those ordinances or regulations were made without consideration of nature of the UVs, therefore these legislation in Hong Kong and Macao shall

44 See the official website of HK SAR <https://www.doj.gov.hk/tc/our_legal_system/index.html> accessed 27 March 2022.

45 See the official website of Marine and Water Bureau Macao (SAR) <https://www.marine.gov.mo/subpage.aspx?a_id=1431335356> accessed 27 March 2022.

be clarified whether apply to UVs completely or needs some amendments for the application of UVs in the future.

6 The Counter-Measures on Coping with Potential Conflicts within the GBA

In fact, the *status quo* of 'One Country, Two Political Systems, Three Legal Jurisdictions' will continue in the GBA. According to Article 31 of the Constitution of the PRC, the State may, when necessary, establish SARs. The systems to be implemented in SAR shall be prescribed by law by the National People's Congress in accordance with the specific circumstances. According to article 2 of the Basic Law of the Hong Kong SAR, the National People's Congress authorizes the Hong Kong SAR to exercise a high degree of autonomy in accordance with the provisions of this Basic Law and to enjoy executive, legislative, independent judicial and final adjudication powers. Almost the exact same provision is made under the article 2 of the Basic Law of the Macao SAR. Therefore, the governments of Guangdong Province, the Hong Kong SAR and the Macao SAR have also formulated corresponding local regulations and other normative documents within their own legal jurisdiction to implement the laws of mainland China, Hong Kong SAR and Macao SAR separately. It is estimated that the conflicts of legislation in the GBA will further aggravate, especially in respect to detailed legal provisions on administrative supervision of ships, crew, shipping operation etc.[46]

According to the Constitution of the PRC, the Basic Law of the Hong Kong SAR and the Basic Law of the Macao SAR, there is no unified shipping administrative law applied in GBA widely and commonly. Therefore, the conclusion of cooperation agreement on administration affairs and establishment of cooperation regimes among the GBA shall be the good choice in the future, which has the support basis from both the practice activities and the policy steer.

In fact, there have been successful cooperation practices in the GBA for the past decades. For instance, after Hong Kong's return to China, the Guangdong-Hong Kong Cooperation Joint Conference Mechanism was established in Guangzhou on 30 March 1998, upon the approval of the State Council.[47] After

46 Chen Jian, 'State-led Integration of Public Governance in the Guangdong-Hong Kong-Macao Greater Bay Area: Condition Guarantee, Practical Dilemma and Path Analysis' (2021) 1 GSS 18, 24.

47 Leap Forward, 'Guangdong and Hong Kong Join Hands to Create a New Era' (1998) 5 HKME 1.

Macao's return to the motherland, upon the approval of the State Council in 2001, the Macao SAR Government and the Guangdong Provincial Government established a co-operation mechanism for high-level intergovernmental meetings. Furthermore, the governments of Guangdong Province and the Macao SAR established the Guangdong-Macao Cooperation Joint Conference Mechanism with reference to the mechanism of the Guangdong-Hong Kong Co-operation Joint Conference in 2003.[48]

On 30 September 2003, in order to promoting economic and trade cooperation between the Mainland and Hong Kong, the Ministry of Commerce and the Government of the Hong Kong SAR signed the Mainland and Hong Kong Closer Economic Partnership Arrangement (CEPA), which was expanded by ten Supplementary Agreements concluded between October 2004 and August 2013.[49]

On 27 October 2005, in order to promote economic and trade cooperation between the Mainland and Macao, the Ministry of Commerce and the Government of the Macao SAR signed CEPA between the Mainland and Macao, which was followed by ten Supplementary Agreements concluded between October 2005 and August 2013.[50]

With respect to policy support, the National Development and Reform Commission formulated the Outline of the Reform and Development Plan for the Pearl River Delta Region (2008–2020) in December 2008 (hereinafter 'Outline Plan'), which was approved by the State Council in principle.[51] The Outline Plan aims to keep the Mainland cooperating closely with the Hong Kong SAR and the Macao SAR, to innovate cooperation methods, to encourage the Mainland to reach the formulation of regional cooperation plans with Hong Kong and Macao on the premise of consensus, and to enhance the practical effectiveness of the Joint Conference in promoting cooperation.

In order to implement the Outline Plan, the CEPA concluded between the Ministry of Commerce and the governments of Hong Kong and the CEPA concluded between the Ministry of Commerce and the governments of Macao, the government of Guangdong Province signed the Framework Agreement on Guangdong-Hong Kong Cooperation with the government of the Hong Kong SAR on 7 April 2010, and the Framework Agreement on Guangdong-Macao

48 Yang Aiping, 'Experience and Enlightenment of Guangdong-Macao Government Cooperation since the Handover' (2015) 4 HKMS 15, 23.

49 See the official website of the Ministry of Commerce of China <http://tga.mofcom.gov.cn/article/zt_cepanew/> accessed 1 April 2022.

50 Ibid.

51 See the Reply of the State Council on the Outline of the Reform and Development Plan for the Pearl River Delta Region (2008–2020) Guo Han [2008] No. 129.

Co-operation with the government of the Macao SAR on 6 March 2011. Both Framework Agreements stipulate specific contents of trade facilitation, business environment reform, industrial coordination and cooperation, and public service co-operation between Guangdong and Hong Kong as well as between Guangdong and Macao. All Framework Agreements specify that one regional cooperation plan should be formulated in the Guangdong-Hong Kong area and the Guangdong-Macao area, address to promote the mechanism and arrangements for high-level meetings, joint meetings, working bodies and advisory bodies existed in GBA shall play a positive role in improving and establishing the cooperation between the governments of Guangdong and Hong Kong as same as the government of Guangdong and Macao.

On 18 February 2019, the Central Committee of the Communist Party of China and the State Council issued the Outline Development Plan for the Guangdong-Hong Kong-Macao Greater Bay Area, which is a programmatic document guiding the cooperation and development of the GBA.

On 2 June 2020, the Ministry of Transport promulgated the Opinions of the Ministry of Transport on Promoting the Development of Maritime Services in the Guangdong-Hong Kong-Macao Greater Bay Area (Jiao Hai Fa [2020] No. 57) (hereinafter 'Opinions for Maritime Services'). These Opinions clearly propose to deepen the maritime coordination and cooperation mechanism in the GBA. They include, but are not limited to, establishing and improving a maritime cooperation mechanism which should rely on the high-level dialog mechanism between the governments of Guangdong, Hong Kong and Macao to coordinate maritime administration affairs comprehensively in the GBA.[52] The Opinions for Maritime Services also address to share Guangdong-Hong Kong-Macao maritime administration information in accordance with the law,[53] to promote the coordinated and mutual recognition of maritime management and technical standards in Guangdong, Hong Kong and Macao,[54] to strengthen cooperation and communications between the maritime safety administration authorities of Guangdong, Hong Kong and Macao. Because several international maritime Conventions promulgated by IMO on the field of ship administrative management have been approved by the Central People's Government PRC, which apply to the mainland China, Hong Kong and Macao as well. Therefore, the discretionary degree of administrative authorities

52 See Opinions of the Ministry of Transport on Promoting the Development of Maritime Services in the Guangdong-Hong Kong-Macao Greater Bay Area, subpart 4.

53 ibid, subpart 6.

54 ibid, subpart 7.

in the GBA on enforcement of these international conventions shall be uniformed. The cooperation in the implementation of these Conventions shall be strengthened to enhance the maritime compliance capacity in the GBA.

Furthermore, the Opinions for Maritime Services address to help the GBA to motivate the shipping industry, to support the innovation of shipping technology such as IS and seaplanes, to promote the development of intelligent shipping etc.[55] Obviously, the Opinions for Maritime Services have provided powerful policy support for the scientific research and development of UVs in the GBA in the future.

The Maritime Safety Administration of the People's Republic of China (MSA), the Marine Department of the Hong Kong SAR and the Marine and Water Department of the Macao SAR signed jointly the Guangdong-Hong Kong-Macao Greater Bay Area Maritime Cooperation Agreement (hereinafter 'Maritime Cooperation Agreement 2020') on 20 August 2020, which is the detailed and implementing document for the Opinion of Maritime Services.

The overall objective of the Maritime Cooperation Agreement (2020) is to establish a trilateral maritime cooperation mechanism to facilitate the implementation of maritime cooperation projects and activities in the GBA and to provide jointly excellent maritime services and guarantees for the development of the shipping economy in the region.

Article 2.5 of the Maritime Cooperation Agreement (2020) entitled 'Deepening Maritime Coordination and Cooperation' stipulates that the exchange of marine traffic safety legislation and regulations in the GBA shall be strengthened, and the coordinated mutual recognition of maritime technical standards shall be promoted. The third part entitled 'Cooperation Mechanism' under the Maritime Cooperation Agreement (2020) also stipulates to establish a Mainland-Hong Kong-Macao Maritime Cooperation Conference, a GBA Maritime Work Coordination Conference, and other specific cooperation mechanisms.

To summarize, the existing cooperation practice and mechanisms in the GBA mentioned above as well as the Maritime Cooperation Agreement 2020 may play a positive and core rule in promoting administrative maritime management coordinated much more, the maritime technical standards recognized more mutually in the GBA, and in promoting the convergence of marine traffic management systems more safety. The paper estimates that, based on the consensus on UVs management standards and management mechanisms,

55 ibid, subpart 18.

the policies and the high-level cooperation mechanisms will be helpful to resolve legal obstacles discussed above in section 5 on the administrative management of UVs in the GBA.

Although there are policy supports from the Central People's Government PRC and provincial governments for the intelligent transportation industry in mainland China, the conflicts between existing laws on the administrative management of UVs in the GBA can not be avoided either. The paper proposes that the following measures be taken to promote the research and industrial development of intelligent transportation equipment including UVs:

a. The maritime affair cooperation regime between the administrative authorities in the GBA should be deepened and strengthened.
b. The unified supervision requirements for UVs traffic safety in the GBA should be provided with some exemptions for test and trial operation of UVs, in order to promote the application of autonomous intelligent technology into shipping industry.
c. Insurance or mutual insurance mechanisms for the test and trial operation of UVs as well as the commercial operation of UVs in the future shall be established to distribute the risks born by the potential responsible body.
d. Since the technology and research of intelligent transportation equipment are on their way, the purpose of comprehensive supervision of UVs in the GBA should be clarified to balance the intelligent industrial interests, operators and administrators of UVs in the future.

7 Conclusions

It is foreseeable that the different legislation systems, legal obstacles and law conflicts between three judicial jurisdictions in GBA will last for long time in the future, however, which shall not frustrate the process of technology development and intelligent application in the ships as well as shipping. The current legislation concerning the administrative management of ships and shipping will co-exist variously in the GBA. All those effective laws or regulations should apply to UVs with some amendments in the light of the development of intelligent technology. The maritime affair cooperation regime between the administrative authorities in the GBA shall still be one of the best choices to implement the innovative development concept based on the thought of socialism with Chinese characteristics in the new era, ensuring a full play of Guangdong Province in the process of economic reform in China.

Acknowledgements

The paper is based on the speech delivered on the International Symposium on 'Ocean Governance in the New Ear: Current Challenges and the Law of the Sea' held on 10–11 November 2022. It is the stage achievement of Project supported by Southern Marine Science and Engineering Guangdong Laboratory (Zhuhai) (No. SML2020SP005). The author would like to thank associate professor Lijuan Xing for valuable suggestions on the grammars and words of this paper.

References

Articles

Chen Jian, 'State-led Integration of Public Governance in the Guangdong-Hong Kong-Macao Greater Bay Area: Condition Guarantee, Practical Dilemma and Path Analysis' (2021) 1 GSS 18.

Huang Mingquan, Xu Jingping and Shi Linwei, 'Application and prospect of ROV in offshore oil and gas field development' (2021) 2 MGF 77.

Leap Forward, 'Guangdong and Hong Kong Join Hands to Create a New Era' (1998) 5 HKME 1.

Liu Wei and Shang Jiafa, 'Research on the Development Status of Intelligent Ships and its Development Strategy in China' (2017) 11 SST 189.

Ma Jinxing, 'Artificial Intelligence Ships Lead the Reform of the International Maritime Rules System' China Ocean News (8 October 2019) (2nd edn).

Song Shuhua and Zhao Jinsong, 'Legal Status of Unmanned Underwater Vehicles (2017) 3 JSCSS 21.

Sun Yuqing, 'Defining the Legal Status of Commercial Unmanned Ships'(2019) 3WUILR 125.

Wang Yongding, Wang Peng and Sun Pengfei, 'A Review of Research on Autonomous Underwater Robot Control Technology' the World Science and Technology Research and Development Network <https://doi.org/10.16507/j.issn.1006-6055.2021.01.004> accessed 8 July 2021.

Yang Aiping, 'Experience and Enlightenment of Guangdong-Macao Government Cooperation since the Handover' (2015) 4 HKMS 15.

Electronic Materials

American Bureau of Shipping (ABS), 'Guide for Smart Functions for Marine Vessels and Offshore Units' (December 2023) <https://ww2.eagle.org/content/dam/eagle/rules-and-guides/current/other/307-guide-for-smart-functions-for-marine

-vessels-and-offshore-units-2023/307-smart-guide-dec23.pdf> accessed 27 February 2024.

American Bureau of Shipping ABS, 'Requirements for Autonomous and Remote Control Functions' (August 2022) <https://ww2.eagle.org/content/dam/eagle/rules-and-guides/current/other/323_gn_autonomous_2022/323-autonomous-reqts-aug22.pdf> accessed 27 February 2024.

'Autonomous Ships Win with 'Intelligence', from the website of China Water Transport Network' (19 January 2022) <http://www.zgsyb.com/news.html?aid=614492> accessed 27 March 2022.

'CMI International Working Group Position Paper on Unmanned Vessels and the International Regulatory Framework' <https://comitemaritime.org/work/mass/> accessed 5 May 2020.

CMI, 'Summary of Responses to the CMI Questionnaire on Unmanned Ships' <https://comitemaritime.org/work/mass/> accessed 30 January 2021.

Hong Kong Regulations <https://www.hklii.hk/eng/hk/legis/reg/448G/empowering-20210716.html> accessed 22 March 2023.

'IMO takes first steps to address autonomous ships' <http://www.imo.org/en/MediaCentre/PressBriefings/Pages/08-MSC-99-MASS-scoping.aspxv> accessed 5 May 2020.

'Jiangsu Province Holds Comprehensive Exercise on Water Search and Rescue to Improve Integrated Emergency Rescue Capacity in the Yangtze River Delta' (China Maritime Search and Rescue Center) <http://www. mot.gov.cn> accessed 16 March 2022.

'Notice on Conducting Unmanned Boat Maritime Tests in the Waters of Yazhou Bay' (Maritime Safety Administration of the People's Republic of China) <http://www.msa.gov.cn> accessed 16 March 2022.

Shi Xiufen, 'The Autonomous Vessel Development Alliance is Established' (7 July 2017) <http://info.chineseshipping.com.cn/cninfo/News/201707/t20170707_1291688.shtml> accessed 30 January 2021.

Southern Marine Science and Engineering Guangdong Laboratory (Zhuhai) official website <https://www.sml-zhuhai.cn/info/1403.html> accessed 9 September 2022.

'The first unmanned ship offshore test site in Asia is launched in Zhuhai, making it the largest in the world' (6 December 2018) <https://news.sina.com.cn/o/2018-12-06/doc-ihmutuec6566567.shtml> accessed 30 January 2021.

The official website of HK SAR <https://www.doj.gov.hk/tc/our_legal_system/index.html> accessed 27 March 2022.

The official website of Marine and Water Bureau Macao (SAR) <https://www.marine.gov.mo/subpage.aspx?a_id=1431335356> accessed 27 March 2022.

The official website of the Ministry of Commerce of China <http://tga.mofcom.gov.cn/article/zt_cepanew/> accessed 1 April 2022.

UK Maritime, 'Being a Responsible Industry: Maritime Autonomous Surface Ships (MASS) UK Industry Conduct Principles and Code of Practice' <https://safety4sea.com/wp-content/uploads/2019/11/UK-Maritime-Maritime-Autonomous-surface-ships-UK-Code-of-Practice-2019_11.pdf> accessed 8 February 2023.

'Unmanned vessel 'Cloud Somersault No. 0' details fully revealed' (9 January 2020) <https://www.eworldship.com/html/2020/OperatingShip_0109/156008.html> accessed 30 January 2021.

Website of Hong Kong Water Supplies Department <http://www.wsd.gov.hk> accessed 15 March 2022.

Index

Printed in the United States
by Baker & Taylor Publisher Services